About the Author

Professionally a soil scientist, Dr. Singh spent his post-retirement years researching on European colonialism. He concentrated on machinations behind acquisition of colonies and travails of destitute natives of colonies which deserved more space in books on colonialism.

Dr. Singh earned his Ph.D. from University of California, Davis. He held research and teaching positions at the Punjab Agricultural University before moving out to join administration positions in the government of India as director of two research institutes. Besides authorship of scores of research papers, he co-authored a book "Plant Resources of Andaman and Nicobar Islands" and authored another book "Irrigation and Soil Salinity in the Indian Subcontinent Past and Present", published by the Lehigh University Press.

European Supremacism and the Colonial World

Nirmal Tej Singh

European Supremacism and the Colonial World

Additional Editing and Notes by
J.C. Dagar

Olympia Publishers
London

www.olympiapublishers.com
OLYMPIA PAPERBACK EDITION

A CIP catalogue record for this title is
available from the British Library.

ISBN: 978-1-78830-872-4

This book is a historical narrative. The author does not bear witness to events,
people, and places, which are taken from published works.

First Published in 2021

Olympia Publishers
Tallis House
2 Tallis Street
London
EC4Y 0AB

Printed in Great Britain

Dedication

To the natives of those lands who became victims of European supremacism

Acknowledgements

This book is a labour of love as it accomplishes my cherished desire of writing about the experiences of natives who one day found themselves alien in their own land, hunted and maimed. The first task was to uncover how Europeans annihilated them. That involved researching books, journals, newspapers, and other documents to cull what I wanted. I am deeply indebted to authors of the matter which is incorporated in the book. Authors of many of these works may not be alive today, but they, too, deserve my gratitude.

Home is the best retreat for a retiree. My wife, Charanjit endured my absence as I spent days on end bent over my desk, reading and taking notes. I thank her for this forbearance. My daughter, Ravi, has spent endless hours by the computer, shaping the manuscript into proper form. My granddaughter, Samreen, helped me in preparing the index. My grandson, Jesper, finalized the book cover. They all deserve my loving gratitude. Finally, I am thankful to Olympia Publishers for undertaking the project, especially Kristina Smith for her cooperation at various stages of the publication process.

Nirmal Tej Singh
Sacramento, California

Contents

Portugal's pre-eminence in maritime trade; Discovery of sea route to India and the East Indies; Portugal's trading monopoly in India and East Indies breached by the Dutch, British and French trading companies; Exploits of Dutch ruffians and explorers.

Battle of Plassey a disgraceful act of Robert Clive; arrogance the hallmark of British rule in India; Heavy tax burden on poor farmers; Sepoy revolt and coldblooded British retribution; End of the East India Company rule heralds direct British rule in India; Britain captures Malay states of the Peninsula; Dutch establish rule over the Indonesian archipelago.

Psyche of pioneer European voyagers; Voyages of Christopher Columbus; Papal bulls in favour of Portugal and Spain; Expeditions of Hernan Cortes (1519–1521) and Francisco Pizarro (1531–1532); Plunder and destruction of magnificent Aztec and Inca Kingdoms during the expeditions; Senseless murder of the natives; European diseases take heavy toll of native lives.

Spanish and French colonising efforts precede those of the British; English shipping companies chartered to colonise North America; Arrival of Pilgrims on the Virginia Coast; Establishment of European colonies; American Revolution; Exit of Britain from America. Subsequent acquisitions turn colonies into the United States of America. Natives lose their lands; their brutalization and confinement into reserves.

Chapter 3. Australasian Natives, the Innocent Victims

The 1769 exploratory voyage of James Cook to Tahiti, New Zealand, and Australia; Choice of Botany Bay in Australia as a penal settlement for the British convicts; Arthur Phillip steers first fleet of convict ships; Establishment of a penal settlement on the Australian soil to the anguish of the natives; Native resistance and punitive expeditions against them; Australian High Court affirms native land rights; Private British company brings settlers to New Zealand; the Treaty of Waitangi; Native Maoris rise against private purchase of Maori lands; Anglo-Maori wars; the French establish control over Tahiti amid British efforts to exert their hegemony.

Chapter 4. Europe's Trespass to Plunder China

China's reluctance for free trade with other countries; Opium wars and sanctions against China; Chinese public aggrieved with overbearing behaviour of foreign nations; Boxer rebellion; European powers, Russia, and Japan forge alliance against China; China suffers defeat and accepts humiliating terms to buy peace; Europeans get free access to all Chinese ports and usurp slices of the Chinese territory; Once dejected China rises to be a World's powerful nation.

Chapter 5. Pan-European Slicing of Africa

The Dutch as first colonists of the Cape in 1652; British take control of the Cape colony, Great Trek of the Boers; Discovery of gold and diamond mines in the Boer colonies tempt the British to seize their republics; Anglo-Boer wars; Berlin Conference of Europeans to slice Africa into areas of influence; British South Africa Company of Cecil Rhodes; Rhode's penchant for Cape-Cairo link and his wicked exploits; Inhuman treatment of African natives by white settlers; Pass laws; French colonisation of Africa; Razzia expeditions to evict Arabs from their lands; German calamitous rule in Africa; Genocide of the native Herero and Nama; Portuguese exploitive rule: Travails of natives in the Belgian Congo where atrocities of the Belgian King attract world attention.

Chapter 6. Perfidious Treaties That Helped Colonisation

Europeans deceive native chiefs and rulers into signing deals/treaties leading to loss of their territories; Implicit role of Christian missionaries in these transactions; Matabele Chief Lobengula defrauded in to signing the Rudd concession; A saga of lies behind Lochner concession awarded by Lozi King Lewanika; Land fraud of Luderitz against Bethany chief Joseph Fredrick; Robert Clive and the East India Company trick Amin Chand into helping against the Nawab of Bengal that led the company to ultimately establish her rule over India.

Chapter 7. Natives Lose Their Lands in the Americas, Africa and Australia

Iberian Church-owned estates; Indian Removal Act of 1830 in North America; Cherokee suffer in the *Trail of Tears* exodus; Dawes Act of 1887 renders 90,000 natives landless; Eviction of natives from their ancestral abodes in different colonies, native resentment invites harsh retribution; Boer-Xhosa wars in the Cape Colony; Southern Rhodesia's 1913 Law restricts 84 percent native population to 13 percent land area; Confiscation of Masai lands in Kenya; Germans grab Herero and Nama lands; France confiscates Kabayle lands in Algeria; All lands in Congo declared State property; Land grab in Australia, Van Diemans Land Company in Australia allotted 250,000 acres land of Australian natives after killing or pushing them out.

Chapter 8. Slavery and Colonisation: The Connection

Arab slave trade; Portuguese start ferrying African slaves in to the colonies; Elmina Fort the famous Portuguese slaving centre on the West Coast of Africa changes hands; Europe exploits American, Caribbean and Australian colonies using slave labour; European companies ply lucrative transatlantic slave trade; Plight of slaves and their role in the success of European colonies.

Chapter 9. Instruments of Stranglehold: A Muzzled Press

East India Company wants English and Vernacular press to toe official line; Imposition of fines and banishment of non-conforming editors; Introduction of press censorship; Harsh measures like Press Act of 1878 against the Vernacular press; Confiscation of sureties and press machinery; India Press Act of 1910; Press restrictions in Sierra Leone; Ordinance No. 21 of 1934 in the Gold Coast.

Chapter 10. Instruments of Stranglehold: Despotic Laws and Flawed Justice

Natives of colonies at the receiving end of the European justice system; East India Company wanted her all-pervading bribery under wraps; It manages death penalty against the whistle blower Nand Kumar; First and Second Law Commission in India; Ilbert Bill; European's up in arms in opposition; Thomas O'Hara case; Indictment of Horace Lyall; Interventions of Lord Curzon on behalf of victims offer no solace to them.

Laws of colonial Africa fashioned on the Indian Penal Code of 1860; Native (Urban areas) Act 1923; Case of Galbraith Cole; Case against Nathanial Low in New South Wales, Australia; French Laws in Africa; Germans administer rough justice in African colonies; Shooting death of Jan Christian and its aftermath.

Chapter 11. They Embodied Terror to the Natives

Governor Edward Eyre earned infamy with the Jamaican massacre; Field Marshal Thomas Robert Bugeaud's Razzia expeditions against Arab tribal people of Algeria; Raymond Pierre Paul-Westerling's mass killings in South Sulawesi, Indonesia; General Adrian Dietrich Lothar von Trotha's genocide of Herero and Nama tribes of Southwest Africa; Horatio Herbert Kitchener's barbarous military campaign against the Mahdi sect of Sudan; Acting Brigadier General Reginald Dyer's atrocities against innocent civilians of Amritsar in India.

Chapter 12. From Company Clerks to Society "Nabobs"

Poor educational and social background of lower-rung employees of merchant companies; Unethical methods of their amassing wealth through pillage of the host country; Earning of the title of "nabob", a synonym for Moghul Nawab, by flaunting their wealth, purchasing magnificent real estates and membership of the British parliament.

Unethical exploits of individual "nabobs".

Chapter 13. Colonies as Population Outlets

Europeans migrate to the American colonies; Ireland contributes large number of immigrants; The British settled its convicts first in North America and later in Australia; British colonial governments encourage immigrants in to African colonies; Irish Poor Act 1838 for assisted immigration; European immigrants in South America; French settlers in Algeria; Portuguese settlers in the African colonies.

Chapter 14. Europeans, Tyrannical Supremacists or Crafty Freebooters

Shabby treatment of non-Christian non-white natives in the European colonies; Shedding of innocent blood by Iberian conquistadors and other Europeans in quest of colonisation; Racial prejudice against natives of the colonies, depriving them of equal justice; Exploitation of native populations after appropriating their means of sustenance; Extraction of mineral and agricultural wealth of the colonies for the home country; Defrauding poor peasants; Tyranny of colonists; Institution of railways, extension of roads, banking, postal, telegraphic facilities primarily for smooth functioning of colonial administration; admirable British legacy recounted.

Notes

Preface

Europeans descended upon the unfamiliar outside world with an air of supremacy reinforced by the authority of the church. As a teenager, I witnessed the dread of foreign rulers. Common village folks would address even a lowly white official as 'Lord' or 'Laat Sahib' because they behaved as such. Once an official visiting my village ordered the beating of those villagers who failed to stand up and salute him as he passed by on horseback. People aspired to be seated on a chair in the presence of a white colonial officer. During the 1857 military uprising against the British, a white army major reprimanded the army chief of a loyal Maharaja as the latter had his shoes on when he came to meet him. The chief was ordered to remove his shoes, and leave them outside the pavilion, as his own force looked on. A crude specimen of white racism was exhibited by George Bernard Shaw when he scoffed at the award of Nobel Prize in literature to Rabindra Nath Tagore. He expressed his contempt by deforming the latter's name. His statesmanship notwithstanding, Winston Churchill was cynical when Mahatma Gandhi was invited for talks with the Viceroy of India. He did not allow offloading of grain supplies from Australia, in India, during the 1943 Bengal famine. When the Indian Government sent him an account of starvation deaths, he questioned "Then why hasn't Gandhi died yet?" a revolting illustration of white racism.

White Europeans carried with them a streak of supremacy as they landed in foreign lands. They treated indigenous people with disdain and called them subhuman without souls. Hence, they were justified to treat them brutally. Europeans wanted trade with India and China, which were then richest countries of the world, but despised their peoples. In South America, Tenochtitlan, the capital city of the Aztec Empire of Mexico, was richer and surpassed any European city and its civilization. Timbuktu on the southern edge of African Sahara was known for its Islamic University and as trade centre for salt, gold and ivory. Natives of Africa were skilled potters and metal workers. They made sculptures with clay and brass; goldsmiths made necklaces, rings and bracelets. Europeans fell for gold, ivory, rubber and diamonds of Africa, which they called a country of apes. Nearer home, Native Americans, dubbed Indians, had well established tribes with their own customs. They wore clothes made from well finished deer skin and fibrous material, adorned with beads and shells particular to their tribe. They made decorated moccasins and jewellery of all kinds using precious stones, bones, shells, gemstones, and metals like gold and silver. Suffice to say natives of the non-European world were not cave dwellers who needed civilizing by white Europeans.

All colonial powers spilled blood to capture foreign lands. They overawed the outside world with their large ships fitted with cannons, their maxim guns, steel swords, galloping horses, and most of all their treacherous nature. The natives resisted their onslaught, but their rudimentary spears and clubs were no match against enemy armour. Europeans vanquished them and claimed their country as fruit of conquest. Another ruse employed was, to unilaterally declare countries and islands with indigenous populations as '*terra nullius*' or no man's land. This pretence was falsified by the High Court of Australia when it upheld rights of native people to lands of their country. Each European colony presented unique history of colonial guile. The Treaty of Waitangi in New Zealand, the Luderitz land deal in SWA, the Lochner concession of the Barotseland king Liwanika and Rudd concession involving Matabele chief Lobengula are few examples of perfidious dealings of Europeans with trusting natives. Colonial governments promulgated partisan laws which suppressed dissent and safeguarded interests of European settlers. They indiscreetly fiddled with the law to make their ends meet. For instance, Warren Hastings, the first governor general of India, and the newly appointed chief justice, connived to see that an innocent man, Nand Kumar was sentenced to death and sent to the gallows within days under an inadmissible procedure.

Colonials exploited colonies in different ways such as source of raw materials, precious metals, and exotic agricultural products, source of cheap labour and employment of their manpower to plum posts in the colonies. They wanted the colonies to produce raw materials for their domestic industry. Manufacturing was discouraged in the colonies by imposing export duties. Contrarily, duty was minimal on imported manufactures for promoting their consumption in the colonies. India clothed most of the world with millions of yards of high-quality cotton textiles. Gujarat and the Coromandel Coast of South India produced fabulous, printed calicoes which were popular in Europe for their uniqueness. Patola silk saris of Gujarat were world famous. The British deliberately killed the textile industry of India in order to benefit the Yorkshire textile industry at home and employ thousands of workers. Opium wars were thrust upon China to capture her ports for trade in tea, silk, and porcelain against silver dollars earned by scandalous sale of opium grown in India and Turkey.

Iberians were the first to milk their colonies dry. South America was home to advanced pre-Columbian civilizations. The Inca Empire in the Andean region and the Aztec Empire of Mexico were flourishing when the Spaniards raided them. The Inca had developed silver mining. It was Spain, which made the most of it. The mining of Mexican and Peruvian silver turned Spain into a super power at the time owning the famous naval fleet Armada. Portugal exploited Brazilwood which produced red textile dye favoured by the Royal Court of France. Brazil was the largest producer of sugar for the European market of the seventeenth century before other nations and neighbouring islands began competing with Portugal. Slaving was started to run sugar industry in the American continent. Similarly, slaves and indentured labour was employed to produce cotton and sugarcane in Australia. One has heard of fishing trawlers but in Australia, ships were used to capture slaves from neighbouring islands. The East India Company sent millions of pounds to the homeland by heavily taxing the native people. Unscrupulous company employees made loads of money by unashamedly exploiting the generosity of the Moghul king who had exempted the company from paying local taxes.

Some colonial officers were notorious for their cruelty. They had no hesitation in massacring thousands of natives. The book devotes one chapter to highlight their abhorrent conduct. Authors of some country-specific books highlight the devious ways of colonisers and their high-handedness but ignore unpleasant episodes. I have presented a sample of tyrannical rule of the mighty colonials. It covers several aspects of European administered world, which needed deserving recitation.

Introduction

The unsavoury period of colonialism is a thing of the past. Yet its effects are etched in the minds of those who experienced its depredations. Most books on the subject treat colonialism as a European event where nations claiming superior attributes captured foreign lands. The fate of original inhabitants of those countries, for whom colonialism was a scourge, is either understudied or has received cursory treatment. Colonials of Europe perceived natives as moronic, wretched, lazy, and even devilish to empathize with. Central theme of these books remained acquisition of colonies. There are honourable exceptions like The Fatal Impact by Allan Moorhead[1], A Commonwealth of Thieves; A Probable Birth of Australia by Thomas Keneally,[2] Let us Die Fighting. The Struggle of Herero People against German Imperialism by Horst Dreschsler,[3] Kenya by Norman Leys,[4] Imperial Reckoning, The Untold Story of Britain Gulag in Kenya by Caroline Elkins[5] to cite few examples. The authors strongly indict white supremacists but books are largely country specific. Forbears of the colonials belonged to the Mediterranean region of the post-medieval period where blood shedding was routine and slavery rampant. Spanish monarchs established the inquisition in 1478 when thousands of Muslim and Jew converts were burned at stakes and thousands more forced to migrate elsewhere. Spanish conquistadors, products of a violent environment disregarded the sanctity of life, they were unrepentant, and exercised unbridled power in the colonies they established.

At the time, southern Europe traded with countries of the East like India, East Indies and China for spices, silk, textiles and artefacts. Arab merchants carried the merchandise overland to ports like Constantinople and Alexandria. European merchants lapped up the merchandise and shipped it over to the flourishing markets of Venice, Genoa, Pisa, and Lisbon. Land-based trade collapsed in 1453 when Ottoman Turks captured Constantinople and the Levant. Portugal took the lead to find a route for ocean-based trade with the East. That step laid foundation of colonialism because empires followed the trade. Portuguese trade in gold and slaves had made Lisbon an enviable market for Western Europe. Other European nations followed Portugal and overtook it in trade and territorial gains.

Spain, envying of its western neighbour began scouting for seafarers who would discover a western sea route to the East. Queen Isabella of Spain sponsored the voyages of Christopher Columbus against one-tenth share in gold or other riches he acquired during his sojourns. Columbus miscalculated his drawings and landed in the Bahamas before touching the island he named Hispaniola and claimed it for Spain. He laid the foundation of the first European colony as part of the European colonialism. Spaniards like conquistador Hernando Cortes departed on an expedition to Mexico from Cuba. Few years later his cousin Francisco Pizarro launched his expedition to the Andes from Panama. While Cortes had some schooling, Pizarro was illiterate, but both had witnessed the plunder, murder and executions by burning at home. They held the notion that people outside Europe were pagans and infidels whose annihilation was sanctified by papal bulls. Both were fully tempered to be ruthless with natives of the foreign lands. They possessed canons and domesticated horses, both alien to the natives. They merrily used them to depredate lands they treaded. Spaniards subjugated the natives, plundered gold and riches and decimated civilizations of the Maya in Mexico and of the Incas in the Andes. Only the remnants of their temples and pyramids exist besides the pre-Columbian cyclical Mayan calendar that drew world attention in 2012.

Portugal had been a nation of seafarers. Its sailors like Vasco da Gama, Bartolomeu Dias and Pedro Alvares Cabral, who opened sea routes to the Indian Ocean, were keen seamen but heartless in adversity. Dutch sailor, Cornelis Houtman, sponsored by Dutch merchants of Amsterdam, was extremely cantankerous. English sailors of the early seventeenth century had also witnessed the squalid condition of their country, rampant counterfeiting, and thievery after rural poor migrated to the cities. Hence founders of colonialism were at best tempestuous and inclined to violence and mayhem. Moreover, they carried baggage of their perceived racial superiority and fixation for wretchedness of the natives in the target countries.

Years after the Portuguese reached Brazil, Spanish and French expeditions began exploring North America. Queen Elizabeth I and then

King James I of England and Ireland awakened to the prospect of Western Europe colonising the Continent. King James 1 chartered a London-based company to settle southern Virginia and a Plymouth-based company to settle northern Virginia. Earlier Sir Walter Raleigh, chartered by Queen Elizabeth I to settle North America, founded a settlement at Roanoke Island which failed. Later settlements authorized by King James led to the establishment of thirteen colonies under the flag of United Kingdom. The original inhabitants of these lands (named Indians) yielded space for white settlers after unsuccessfully fighting with the well-armed foreigners. The natives though docile, helpful and cooperative, were unacceptable to the white supremacists. The poor souls ended up in reserves. Britain, for her own faults, lost their first-ever colonies to the American Revolution. Independence of the colonies not only changed the map of America but also influenced what happened in the far away Australasia.

While Spaniards were outright conquerors, Portugal, Britain, Holland and France began trading with South Asia and the East Indies. Each one of them ended up acquiring colonies. Britain racked up prize catch of India and helped itself to become first rate world power. India which at the time held more than a quarter of world's wealth was reduced to a basket case by the time the British left that country. Portugal was overwhelmed by Britain and Holland because they owned strong naval fleets. Portugal was short of wood and resources to keep ahead of them. Hence British East India Company dominated trade in India and the Malaysian peninsula, and the Dutch pushed the Portuguese out of Indonesia. Latecomer France contented itself with small enclaves in India though it had a large empire in Africa.

European hegemony in South Asia and the East Indies is a saga of pretended supereminence, treachery, bloodshed, and plunder. British East India Company held the monopoly over trade in the East, behaving like a bully to force illegal merchandise (opium) on China. Manchu Qing government unsuccessfully implored the British government to stop smuggling opium into China. In desperation, China began confiscating the drug. That was a challenge to European sense of superiority. They ganged up to thrust the First Opium War upon China; then the Second Opium War; and finally, the Boxer rebellion. The United States and Japan also joined the campaign to humiliate the isolationist nation, dictate terms of surrender, and share the spoils. China, a premier world economy was made to shell out huge reparations including parting with chunks of her territory and opening the country for Europe and America to sell opium. An inward-looking China had never prepared itself to face a combined onslaught of ravenous nations.

Fifteenth century political and trade contacts of the Mediterranean region were confined to North Africa until Portugal established trading posts along the west coast of Africa. It was the Dutch who made the Cape of Good Hope their halting station on sea voyages between Holland and their East Indies capital of Batavia (now Jakarta). The halting station became an establishment which expanded in to the Cape Colony. The Dutch drove out indigenous people (Khoi Khoi). They disliked British soft handling of the natives and in protest left the Colony in their wagons for the interior of South Africa in what is known as the 'Great Trek.' Intrigues of the British South Africa Company solidified British hold on South Africa. France subdued Berbers and Arabs of Algeria in the north through bloody military campaigns to capture their lands. The farce of trading with Africa enacted in the November 1884 Berlin Conference is dubbed as Scramble for Africa. The continent was sliced without consent of the Africans. Germany entered the colonial race on a sordid note of mayhem and murder of the native Herero, Nama and other tribes. King Leopold II of Belgium got control of rubber yielding forests of Congo which proved to be a nemesis of the Congo natives. In fact, each European nation treated Africans expendable for no fault of theirs except the colour of their skin.

British colonisation of Australasia was curiously linked to the independence of American colonies which housed convicts exiled from Britain. It fell to the destiny of a faraway Australia to receive British outlaws. Nobody sought consent of indigene of the land before Captain Arthur Phillip arrived with first fleet of convict ships. Phillip established the first penal colony of Port Jackson (now Sidney) against strong opposition of the resident Gweagal tribe. Their leader Pemulwuy carried out guerrilla attacks on settlers and convicts until he was killed by the latter. The convicts played havoc with lives of the natives. They confiscated their fishing gear, turned them out of their pastures and abodes and carried away their women. Consequently, there was constant bloodshed through punitive expeditions when revengeful natives speared an odd white straggler. Another secret weapon wielded by the Europeans was infectious diseases like smallpox and tuberculosis which wiped out natives in no time[6]. In the end, surviving indigenous people ended up in reserves while outsiders occupied their lands. The British repeated this action in New Zealand with the relatively tough Maori natives. They managed them through missionaries who entangled the plain Maoris in the Treaty of Waitangi. The poor natives unwittingly lost their sovereignty and unsuccessfully fought for years to regain control of their country.

Europeans yearned to appropriate lands in foreign countries for white settlements. Their first action was to wrongly invoke the credo of *terra nullius* meaning that the land was empty and belonged to no one[7]. The British indulged in this farce in colonies of Australia and South Island in New Zealand. The purpose was to legitimize their colonising of new lands and appropriating lands which supported indigenous populations. The 1992 decision of the Australian High Court struck down the doctrine that Australia was *terra nullius*. The judgement conceded native title rights subject to sovereignty of the Crown. Tragically, natives had been pushed to extinction by the time original premise of the colonial government was quashed. In North America, the concept of manifest destiny was invoked to evict indigenous inhabitants (Indians) and occupy their lands. British South Africa Company of Cecil Rhodes hoodwinked native chiefs of South Africa into signing written concessions which led to their losing territories to the company. Land deal agents of German merchant Adolf Luderitz cheated native chiefs of south west Africa and got their entire land signed off. Morals and ethics were blatantly trampled by the colonials.

Great Britain held the largest colonial empire. It had a struggling economy in the sixteenth century when Iberians already possessed colonies. British monarchs were reluctant to risk money in ventures of unknown outcome. Britain encouraged private companies to venture into distant lands under the British flag. In this way it avoided losing anything should the adventure run into rough weather or fail. Once a colony stood on its own feet it opened doors for prospectors, entrepreneurs, adventurers, employees, and others looking for greener pastures. Colonial administrators and their compatriots provided land for businesses like, plantations, surface mining, and excavation mining. In

Australia droves of Europeans arrived and squatted on lands of natives who were evicted at gunpoint. A private company was floated in England to settle the whites in New Zealand. Colonial governments provided large swaths of land for white settlers to raise plantations for the export market. Large farming estates could not be run without labour. In mainland Africa, colonialists-imposed hut tax, which was to be paid in cash. Natives were left with only two options, work as wage labourers with white planters to discharge tax obligation or leave their land and disappear in the bush. In Queensland, Australia, labour recruiting vessels of ill repute ensnared young people from the islands of Melanesia. Cotton plantations of Brazil, Honduras, and colonies of the Caribbean employed labour from Africa. Undoubtedly a strong link developed between slavery and colonisation. It was the slave labour from Africa which helped Europeans to hold on to their colonies and in some cases the same people ousted them from the colonies.

Mercantile companies, who were forerunners of colonisation, were fixated on profits and did everything to that end. Shareholders wanted profits no matter what happened to the natives. Employees of the companies and individuals amassed wealth in different ways. They made money in the diamond mines of Kimberley in South Africa, plantations of the Caribbean and shared unscrupulous loot of the East India Company in India. These people returned home in style, purchased estates and membership of the British Parliament using their ill-gotten wealth. They were called *Nabobs,* a corrupted form of Moghul Nawabs. Some books highlight depredations of these individuals. Inhabitants of colonies helplessly watched the plunder of their country until they decided that enough was enough. They began voicing opposition to foreign rule that ravished their country. Colonial governments suppressed those voices in different ways. They concealed unfavourable information from the public by controlling the print media. Newspapers influenced public psyche. Hence, governments used every trick to rein in anti-establishment vernacular press. Censorship, prosecution of editor and publisher, and even confiscation of the press were common. Criticism of colonial administration was suppressed with a heavy hand. The government enacted draconian laws that impinged upon personal freedom. The laws it promulgated were often biased and against the natives. A native defendant could lose his life for a crime which attracted a short prison time for the white defendant. Native judges were not allowed to adjudicate on white defendants. Even competent natives could not aspire for 'white only' positions in the executive, judiciary, military, and police services. They were not trusted by colonial governments to man positions considered 'sensitive'.

Colonies were established and sustained by some ruthless administrators and military men who disregarded the right of life and liberty to the natives. They used brutal force to instil lasting fear in their minds. Had this fear lasted, Europe still would have ruled vast swaths of the world. Indigenous populations overcame the fear and took control of their own destiny. The author himself rejoices that moment. A question lingers if Europeans were ruthless supremacists or freebooters? One way to answer this question is to highlight what Europeans gained from their colonies and how much indigenous people benefitted from the colonial rule. Europeans milked colonies to the last drop. It was India's wealth that powered industrial revolution in Britain. Europeans nurtured their colonies to the extent that their own living and working was comfortable and hassle-free. They created infrastructure for their own needs, trained natives to the extent that they could help them in the day to day running of the country and serve as a link between the administration and the masses they governed. There were honest individuals and organizations with genuine concern for the welfare of the natives. Yet there were colonial officers who were too arrogant to be ignored by watchful natives. All nations, steadfastly worked for liberation from the colonial rule and after countless loss of lives, won their freedom in the post-Second World War period.

The above narrative split into separate chapters embodies the basic idea of the book.

Chapter 1
Europe's Eastern Trade and Colonisation

In the sixteenth century Portugal controlled the Indian Ocean and monopolized access to some of the richest nations of South Asia, Southeast Asia, and China. This region possessed long-established religions, political structures, and cultural mores when Portuguese sailed there as traders. These nations had traded in spices, silks, fine quality textiles, and gemstones through the Arab and Muslim traders. Turn of events that hit land-based trade, favoured sea-born trade. Portugal fully exploited the situation when it dominated sea lanes to the East. It built trading posts on the coasts of Africa, India and the East Indies. These posts corroborated the adage that, anywhere on the coasts of Asia, Africa and America, one can find a church, a fort, a geographical name or a family name linked to Portugal. Portuguese links with the East began on 20th May 1498, when Portuguese explorer Vasco da Gama arrived at Calicut (Kozhikode) on the west coast of India. A Gujarati trader based on the east coast of Africa helped him in navigating to the west coast of India. Da Gama met the local governor titled Zamorin at his residence, whose magnificence surprised the visitor. The governor was not impressed with presents the visitor could offer. Arab merchants present on the occasion made light of the offerings. The governor judged no advantage in a two-way trade with Portugal in part due to the hostility of the well-established Arab and Muslim traders. In the dockyard, Muslims massacred several of his men. In a fit of rage Da Gama bombarded Calicut killing many inhabitants. Terrified traders let him buy spices. Satisfied with the show of his force he sailed back home arriving in Lisbon on 10th July 1499 to a royal welcome. In December 1500, a punitive Portuguese expedition under Admiral Pedro Alvares Cabral arrived at Cochin. It had the mandate to punish Arab and Muslim traders he met on the way by sinking their merchant ships and butchering the occupants. After arriving at Calicut, Cabral trained his guns on the port city making the inhabitants and traders run for their life. The gun boat diplomacy worked, and the Portuguese were permitted to establish their mission at Calicut. In 1502 Vasco da Gama left on another voyage to India with a strong armada. Portugal wanted to display its naval might. On the way da Gama captured an Arab pilgrim ship, locked the pilgrims in the hold, and set it on fire. Near the coast he captured fishing boats, butchered their crew, chopping off their limbs and ears. Portuguese aggressiveness helped in browbeating coastal settlements because Moghul rulers did not guard them. Portuguese permanent settlements at Goa appeared after 1510 when Afonso de Albuquerque defeated the Sultan of Bijapur. Goa became the seat of Portuguese Viceroy who governed Portuguese overseas possessions in India and Africa. Portuguese conquered Calicut in 1513, Bassein in 1534, Diu in 1535 and occupied the towns of Tuticorin and Nagapattinam on the east coast of India. In 1541 they opened St. Paul's college at Goa. The Portuguese were able to strengthen their foothold because Moghul orders did not run everywhere in India.[1]

The next Portuguese ambition was to conquer the Spice Islands or Molucca Islands of eastern Indonesia. These islands were famous for producing nutmeg and cloves. In 1511, they raided and captured Malacca in the Malay Peninsula and established their post. Mahmud Shah, the sultan of Malacca fled to Bintan Island from where he tried vainly to regain Malacca. In 1526, arrogant Portuguese attacked Bintan Island and destroyed its capital town. The Sultan and his family fled to Sumatra. Back on the Malay Peninsula, Mazaffar Shah, elder son of the Sultan, founded the Sultanate of Perak which abounded in tin deposits. The other son founded the Sultanate of Johor which prospered as a trading post. The Portuguese for now controlled the Straits of Malacca, an important waterway between India and the Far East. In the meantime, British and Dutch explorers began sailing along with the winds because the ships used wind power, to the Moluccas.

The Dutch envied the lucrative spice trade and commercial hegemony of the Portuguese. They decided to watch Portuguese overseas commerce to break their monopoly over the spice trade. In 1592, Dutch merchants of Amsterdam sent a professional spy and known ruffian,

Cornelis de Houtman to Lisbon, on a mission of gathering information about the Spice Islands. Houtman found that Bantam (Banten) in Java was the best place to buy spices and establish a trade centre. On 2nd April 1595, Houtman sailed on a spice trade mission with four well-armed ships of the van Verre Company, forbearers of the Dutch East India Company. Houtman, after a distressful voyage which consumed 149 sailors, arrived at the Sultanate of Bantam in June 1596. The reigning Sultan of Bantam welcomed Houtman conceiving of him as an ally in the internal power struggle and against the Portuguese Sword of Damocles. Houtman signed a treaty with the Sultan but due to local disturbances could not strike the right price for the spices. The Dutchman lost his cool and in anger bombarded Bantam with canon fire. The natives were either stabbed to death or blown to smithereens with canon fire. Houtman moved on to the next island, Madura. The locals ignorant of the Bantam massacre arranged a traditional welcome for the visitors. The welcome party comprising the chief and natives moved in a flotilla of boats towards the Dutch vessels. The Dutch, unused to Eastern custom, panicked. They sprayed the party with canon fire. The natives were brutally slaughtered, and their boats sunk. Numerous natives were killed in hand-to-hand combat on the land. Houtman purchased pepper on his return journey but was menaced by the Portuguese on his way home. He arrived in Holland to a heroic welcome for achieving symbolic victory in denting the Portuguese monopoly over the Indian Ocean trade. Arrogant Europeans acted like a big brother to dictate who the East should trade with. Between 1598 and 1605, the Dutch launched twelve expeditions to collect riches of the East when Portuguese might was on the decline.[2]

In 1602, a multinational corporation, The Dutch East Indian Trading Company (VOC short for Varrenidgo Oostinidiche Compagnie) was floated. The Dutch government granted it 21 years monopoly of colonial activity in Asia. This company remained an unchallenged commercial power in Southeast Asia until Britain joined the competition. The VOC was so successful that it paid 18 percent annual dividends to its stock holders for nearly 200 years. In 1603 the company established her first trading post at Bantam. Enjoying local support, it seized the important trade station of Amboina (Ambon) from the Portuguese. Some company ships even sailed as far as Moluccas to collect precious cargoes of nutmeg, cloves, and mace at Amboina and Banda.

A significant event of the Dutch-Portuguese trade rivalry, in subsequently named the Dutch East Indies, was the emergence of another rival, the British East India Company. The Dutch were reluctant to share their booty of spice trade with other Europeans. Their territorial control increased after 1618, when Jan Pieterszoon Coen became governor-general of Dutch possession in the East. Coen was inclined to use brutal force to execute his plans. Abhorring Bantam as his headquarters, he stormed Jaykarta (Jakarta) with 19 ships, drove out native forces, destroyed the walled town, and built a new town named Batavia on the ruins of Jaykarta. In 1620, Coen attacked Banda islands famous for its nutmeg export. He detested 'puny' natives selling their produce to the British East India Company. Coen killed/ starved to death or banished the entire population of the islands to establish Dutch monopoly over the nutmeg trade. In 1623, the Dutch executed ten English settlers of Amboina and destroyed their trading post. This incident strained Anglo-Dutch relations, but the prudent British compromised and withdrew from the region to focus their attention on India. Consequently, the Dutch East India Company became the prime beneficiary of commercial and territorial gains in the present-day Indonesia. Interestingly, it was the trading companies who established European colonies in the eastern Hemisphere. That perfectly suited parent countries who were absolved of all expenditure and attendant risks in the venture.[3]

India and China excelled in sixteenth century Europe in riches, resources and manufactures of quality. It is claimed that at the beginning of the eighteenth-century India was a large economy with 25 percent of the world's gross domestic product (GDP).[4] India's textiles and spices and China's silk and tea were highly valued in Europe. The Portuguese and Dutch were the first Europeans to establish trade relations with these countries and reap rich profits. London merchants had witnessed booty of gold, pearls and ivory from a Europe-bound Portuguese ship coming from India. Lured by the rich haul, they pooled resources and launched a trading syndicate which came to be known as the British East India Company (EIC hereafter). Originally there were two companies of the same name which had merged in 1600 under the charter of Queen

Elizabeth I. EIC became the imperial face of Britain and was the one to force India and China into submission. The first Briton to arrive and stay in India was Thomas Stephens from New College Oxford. Stephens, a Jesuit priest, had joined Jesuit College in Goa in 1579. His letters to his father about India aroused considerable interest in Britain. Four years later some British merchants reached India by land. Their activities were hampered by the hostile Portuguese who loathed any other European power, particularly Britain, trading with India. But launching of the EIC boosted British resolve. On 31st December 1600 Queen Elizabeth I granted a 15-year charter to this company under the title "to the governor and company merchants of London trading in the East Indies". King James I made the charter permanent but subject to recall on a three year's notice.[5]

First four ships of the EIC arrived at Surat in 1608 and returned with valuable cargo seized from Portuguese ships in the straits of Malacca. Britain, who was at war with Portugal and France, had no compunction in robbing those nations. Naturally Portuguese abhorred the British presence in the Indian Ocean, much less in the Moghul court. The British envoy Sir Thomas Roe spent several months pleading British case seeking trade agreement with the Moghuls. He presented costly presents to impress the Moghul Emperor Jahangir but to the latter England was a small insignificant country to fuss with. Sir Thomas kept on trying for months together. Portugal's defeat at the hands of the British in the 1612 naval battle of Swally (Suvali) near Surat blunted the former's opposition and demonstrated British naval prowess. Moghul Emperor Jahangir granted Captain Best, commander of the English fleet, trading privileges. The British were permitted to set up a factory[6] at Surat, the main trading port of the Moghuls. Fortunes of the EIC were on the rise as they established another factory at Masulipatnam (Machhlipatnam) on the east coast of India. Madras (present-day Chennai) was made a presidency in 1653 and Bombay (now Mumbai), given to Britain as part of dowry of Catherine of Braganza by the King of Portugal, was made presidency in 1662. Calcutta (now Kolkata) purchased by the traders in 1690 also became a British colony. Within a short period, the EIC was on firm ground in India.

The Dutch East India Company (VOC) also competed for trading space in India. It established its factory at Devanampattinum in 1608. Fifty years later, they ousted the Portuguese from Pulicat and Nagapattinam towns. The Dutch however abandoned their Indian possessions in favour of Britain under the 1824 Treaty of Paris. In exchange, the British vacated Sumatra and other islands of Indonesia in favour of the Dutch. France, another contender for a stake in India, presented far greater danger to British supremacy in the country than other European powers. First French expedition sailed for India in 1615 under a letter patent from the French sovereign. In 1642, the French East India Company was established to contend with her British counterpart. A French expedition arrived at Surat in 1668 and established a trading post (factory). Next year another post appeared at Masulipatnam. In 1673 a major French settlement was established at Chander Nagar with the permission of Nawab Shaista Khan of Bengal. Two years later a Frenchman Francis Martin secured a small village Puducherry (later on Pondicherry) from the Sultan of Bijapur. This village which changed hands between the Dutch and the French was finally retained by the latter and designated as capital of French possessions in India. French ventures in India were purely commercial in the beginning. The vision changed when Joseph Francois Dupleix administered Chander Nagar between 1731 and 1741. Dupleix, who became governor-general of Pondicherry in 1742, envisioned a French Empire in India. During the First Carnatic War (1746–1748), the French under Dupleix seized Madras from the British. Interestingly Robert Clive, acclaimed as founder of the British Empire in India, was among the prisoners of war. Madras returned to the British after termination of the Austrian war of succession when, under the Treaty of Aix-la-Chapelle, the British got it in exchange for the French fortress of Louisburg in Nova Scotia.

The Moghul Empire of India declined in the eighteenth century amidst emergence of several power centres. Regional Nawabs of provinces like Bengal, Oudh and Deccan were virtually autonomous. Individually, these provinces were richer and larger than many European countries. Thus, Moghul hold over India gradually weakened. Marathas in the West and Sikhs in the Punjab established sovereign states. The French and British companies exploited the weakness of the Moghul rule to enter time-serving alliances with the local rulers. Both companies took sides in succession and territorial disputes of the native rulers. Dupleix extended French influence in southern India until he was challenged by an equally ambitious Robert Clive. The French government in Paris was cautious lest Dupleix's forward policy opened another front with the British in India. Unlike the British company, French overseas policies were governed from Paris. Dupleix supported Haider Ali of Mysore against the Nizam of Hyderabad who had signed a defence treaty with the EIC. The French and the British-backed rival claimants in the Second Carnatic War (1749–1754) fought over succession disputes in Arcot. Clive defeated Dupleix and allies. Huge financial losses were suffered by the French which led to recall of Dupleix from India. Europe's Seven-Years' War, in which Prussia and Britain were pitted in conflict against France and her allies, exacerbated Anglo-French rivalry in India. France was already confronting Britain in North America. Its side effect was the Third Carnatic War in India. In the beginning, France had advantage both in America and India but in 1756 British fortunes changed under the new British Prime Minister William Pitt. The EIC captured the French settlement of Chander Nagar in Bengal in 1757 and that of Pondicherry in 1761 but vacated them under the 1763 Treaty of Paris. Eventually, France was left with small enclaves on the east coast including Pondicherry (now Puducherry). French retreat ended European challenge to British supremacy in India.

The EIC took full advantage of titular Moghul successors of Aurangzeb. In 1711, the company earned exemption from custom duty from Emperor Furrukh Siyar in return for a paltry sum of three thousand rupees per annum. The company got authority to issue exemption passes to British merchants. Company officials freely misused this power. The EIC had its factories under a president and a council established at the Fort William settlement. It fortified these factories, ignoring orders of Governor Nawab Alavardi Khan of Bengal prohibiting such fortification by foreign traders. Siraj-ud-Daula, who succeeded his father Alavardi Khan, suspected British intentions. On their part the British distrusted the Nawab, who was a confidant of the French. The EIC secretly strengthened its forces and fortified Fort William. The young Nawab ordered both the French and the British to dismantle their fortifications. The British chose to ignore his orders. An incensed Siraj-ud-Daula attacked Fort William in June 1756, captured the British settlement of Calcutta, and renamed it Alinagar. Most British citizens had moved to the British fleet at Fulta. Those left in Fort William surrendered. According to an individual's account, Moghul troops captured 146 Britons on 20th June 1756 and confined them to a small poorly ventilated room. By next day 123 prisoners were found dead. Afterwards the incident was named the 'Black Hole' of Calcutta. The story of this episode, based on the narrative of one John Z. Holwell, has been contended. Some accounts give the number of detainees as 64 because most Britons had left Fort William. Historical accounts given out by conquerors often pander to the tastes of readers back home. Whatever the veracity of the incident, EIC held the Nawab of Bengal accountable for the occurrence. The company started planning a showdown with the Nawab while he was away to Purnea in Bihar. Absence of Siraj-ud-Daula from Murshidabad gave enough time for British reinforcements to arrive from Madras. Robert Clive and Admiral Watson arrived in December 1756 along with a combined force of 3000 men and artillery. Clive retook Calcutta and Hugli and forced Siraj-ud-Daula to sign the Treaty of Alinagar on 9th February 1757. The treaty granted the EIC duty-free transit of its goods through Bengal, fortification of Calcutta, and installation of the company's mint. This treaty was a precursor to the battle of Plassey and a step towards eventual British colonisation of India. The EIC began scheming to replace the young Nawab with a pliant person. To begin with Clive accused Siraj-ud-Daula of violating the Treaty of Alinagar. He reorganized his troops and struck secret deals with important functionaries of the Nawab's court. Mir Jafar, a relative of the Nawab and one-time commander of his forces, had fallen out with him. Clive promised to install him as the next Nawab if he cooperated in deposing Siraj-ud-Daula. Bengal forces were bribed through intermediaries and asked to remain passive during the battle, lay down arms at the first opportunity, and even turn against troops loyal to the Nawab. Thus, outcome of the impending battle was decided before a single shot was fired. Rival forces faced each other on 23rd June 1757 at Plassey — a village between Nawab's capital and Calcutta, the garrison town of the East India Company. Mir Jafar, despite Nawab's pleading stood aloof during the battle and so did other commanders Rai Durlabh,

Yar Lutuf and two thirds of Nawab's army. To the misfortune of Siraj-ud-Daula, the gun powder of his French artillery got soaked with rain at night. The British had adequately covered their ammunition against the rains. The Nawab, discovering treachery of his own officers, fled for his life. He lost to the British due to better strategy of his adversary and perfidy of his own court. "Had the supposed battle of Plassey actually been fought, it is far from certain Siraj would have lost it."[7] An elated Clive addressed Mir Jafar as Nawab – a title bestowed upon him as promised. Many in Britain disregarded the treacherous methods of Clive and questioned British sense of political morality which, of course, never became a corner stone of British colonial history.

An ambitious British oligarchy of Calcutta was soon disenchanted with Mir Jafar. He was dethroned in favour of his son-in-law Mir Qasim who promised large payments to the EIC councillors besides permanent transfer of the districts of Chittagong, Midnapur and Burdwan to the company. Soon, Mir Qasim got irritated with day-to-day interference of the company in Bengal administration. Finally, he fled to Patna to enlist support of Moghul emperor Shah Alam II and Shuja-ud-Daula, the Nawab of Oudh. Forces of the EIC pursued Mir Qasim and in October 1764, Major Hector Munroe defeated the combined Moghul forces at Buxur. Shah Alam II was obliged to sign the Treaty of Allahabad in which he ceded rights to civil administration and revenue management (Diwani) of Bengal, Bihar, and Orissa, to the EIC. In 1764, Clive was appointed governor-in-council of Bengal with a select committee of four persons. The British, with territorial concession over three provinces, virtually became master of 400,000 km^2 land area of India. In fact, the company of London merchants became founder of the British Empire in India. Even lowly officials of the company began acting as sovereigns with no holds barred. They became corrupt and oblivious of the plight of the natives now under their umbrella. Richard Becher, the company's resident at Murshidabad, who had several years' service in India, admitted that condition of the natives was worse than before the EIC got Diwani rights. Indian historians claimed that India was verging toward ruin.[8]

Clive used his second tenure to reorganize the company's territory and weed out corruption among company employees in the face of resistance from the Council. But the hero of Bengal's capitulation faced indictment back home. In his speech of 30th March 1772 during the parliamentary debates Clive asserted that Britain needed India for the lure of her wealth, for the benefit of trade, for her annual contribution of at least one and half million pounds to the British treasury, and to deny that country to France. Churchill in his 'History of English-Speaking Peoples' whitewashed Clive's assertion claiming that the EIC was compelled to acquire territories in India against their will and judgement. He wrote "Of India, it has been well-said that the British Empire was acquired in a fit of absence of mind."[9] No doubt this assessment of Churchill was never corroborated. With company affairs adrift, the British parliament took corrective action and passed the 1773 Regulating Act for functioning of the EIC in India. Another regulation, the Pitt India Act 1784, introduced parliamentary supervision over working of the EIC. Warren Hastings, governor of the presidency of Fort William in Bengal was designated governor-general in council of company's commercial and territorial interests in the East. The presidencies of Madras and Bombay were subordinated to the governor-general. Court of directors of the company wanted him to extract maximum amount of money from India for the stockholders. The EIC increased tax on peasants after gaining control of tax revenue in the 1770s. Land revenue collection, which was 817,000 pounds sterling in 1764–65, reached a figure of 2,818,000 pounds sterling in 1775–76.[10] Land revenue became big business of the company in India. In 1769 the EIC's Bengal Council, in a letter to directors, confirmed that EIC trade from hence was to be considered more as a channel for carrying your revenues to Britain.[11] Inability to pay revenues forced many peasants to abandon their land and work as labourers. The British gained both ways. They realized money through sale of land thus abandoned and got cheap labour for the British plantations. After the Bengal plunder began to arrive in London it ushered in the Industrial Revolution which began in the year 1760 and changed the world's life style forever.[12]

An annual remittance of over a million and half sterling was to be made from a subject country to the shareholders in England[13]. Hastings himself needed money for strengthening the company forces in order to face Marathas in the north and the French navy in the south. He forged alliances with native kingdoms for creating buffer zones between the British and Maratha dominions. His actions proved costly. Hastings turned to indecorous methods to collect money. He reduced the annual allowance of the Nawab of Bengal to one half and stopped annual payments of 300,000 pounds to emperor Shah Alam II as agreed to by Clive in lieu of Diwani rights over Bengal, Bihar and Orissa. Clive had also given away the provinces of Kora and Allahabad to the Moghul Emperor out of the territory of the Nawab of Oudh. Hastings sold these provinces to the Vizier of Oudh for 500,000 pounds. He also rented a British brigade to the Nawab of Oudh and supported the latter against advances of the Rohillas. In exchange the Nawab agreed to pay 40,000 pounds for the support and 21,000 pounds annually as mercenary money for lending the British brigade. The British extracted money from Indians in many more callous ways than the Moghul rulers. A Moghul nobleman felt that such heroic savages as the British were incapable of civilized statesmanship.[14]

Administratively, Warren Hastings was in a tricky situation. As governor-general he was responsible for actions of the Bombay and Madras presidencies which, though, acted independently. Madras troops attacked Mysore in league with the Marathas and Nizam of Hyderabad but faced defeat. The company had to submit to terms dictated by Tipu Sultan in the March 1784 Treaty of Mangalore. Warren Hastings asked authorities in Britain to punish the Madras presidency for this humiliation. Similarly, Bombay presidency intervened in the Maratha succession battle. The EIC at Bombay supported Raghunath Rao who ceded some territories to the company in the 1775 Treaty of Surat in exchange for protection. The Bengal Council at Calcutta rejected the deal and opted to face the Marathas. Bombay forces surrendered at Wadgaon and signed a treaty with the Marathas, surrendering all territories acquired by the company since 1773. Hastings rejected this treaty claiming that Bombay had no legal right to sign it. He dispatched a large force under Colonel Thomas Goddard. After a long stalemate Maratha Peshwa signed the May 1782 Treaty of Salbai. Peace prevailed for another two decades which gave the company enough time and space to meddle in affairs of South Indian Kingdoms. Indiscreet confrontation of Madras and Bombay presidencies with Haider Ali and his son Tipu

Sultan of Mysore, who enjoyed French support, cost EIC dearly. Hastings extorted money from vulnerable Indian states bound by treaties on the pain of British wrath and made up the loss. He forced Raja Chet Singh of Banaras (now Varanasi) to shell out 50,000 pounds over and above the annual rent of 225,000 pounds payable to the company. The Begam of Oudh, whom the company had appointed guardian of the young Nawab of Oudh, was forced to part with large sums of money under the garb of a loan.

The British government took steps to extract EIC out of its financial straits. Pitt's India Act of 1784 restrained the company from needless interference in affairs of the Indian rulers. Yet, EIC was anxious to avenge its reverses suffered in the battle against Tipu Sultan. In 1789, the Mysore king raided the British protectorate of Travancore. Charles Cornwallis, the new governor-general and company allies, encircled Mysore forces. Tipu Sultan who suffered defeat was forced to sign the 1792 Treaty of Srirangapatna compelling him to cede one half of his kingdom. Lord Wellesley (Richard Colley Wellesley), who succeeded Cornwallis, decided to eject the French and eliminate their ally Tipu Sultan. Accordingly, he contrived a defence alliance with the Nizam of Hyderabad which obliged the latter to disband his French- trained troops. In 1799 Wellesley ensured Maratha cooperation before attacking Mysore. The French themselves in the throes of a revolution deserted Tipu[15], who, heavily outnumbered and outgunned, died fighting. Tipu Sultan became the only king of that period in the history of India to die on the battlefield. The EIC divided the Mysore kingdom between the Madras presidency, the Nizam of Hyderabad, and five-year old Kirshnaraja Wadyar, the scion of the original ruler of Mysore. Wellesley took back Nizam's share of Mysore territory in lieu of money Nizam owed the company for stationing British troops at Hyderabad as bulwark against the Marathas.

Wellesley, a steadfast imperialist, devised novel instrument of subsidiary alliance when warring Indian states looked for protection through alliances. The British promised to intervene on behalf of the rulers entering a subsidiary alliance with the EIC. The company stationed a contingent of its troops to protect the signatory state on recompense. States who failed to pay for protection had to cede a piece of their territory to the company. Signatory State was barred from alliance or diplomatic relations with any other state or power. The treaties executed by Wellesley virtually excluded French intervention in Indian affairs. By the beginning of the nineteenth century, EIC controlled the East Coast, a part of the South West Coast and northern India from Bengal to Meerut excluding Oudh.

Wellesley annexed Carnatic upon the demise of its ruler in 1801. Later, Tanjore (Thanjavur) and Surat were seized. Wellesley warned Nawab of Oudh on his misrule. The Nawab offered to abdicate in favour of his son but continued to rule after his offer was not accepted. The Governor-General called his action insubordination and annexed one half of his territory. It is well said that civility takes a nose dive where might dictates what is right. The territory annexed included the contentious Rohilkhand region. Wellesley now turned towards the Maratha bastion of central and western India where Shivaji had established the Maratha Empire (Maratha confederacy) in 1674. Maratha power was at its pinnacle under Peshwas Baji Rao and Balaji Rao. They enjoyed unrestrained influence in and around their country before Ahmed Shah Abdali defeated them in the 1761 battle of Panipat. Thereafter Maratha confederacy became a loose confederation of the Peshwa's of Pune, the Scindias of Malwa and Gawaliar, the Bhonsles of Nagpur, and the Gaekwad of Baroda. Intense rivalry between these feudal states was an opportune moment for the British to intervene on behalf of the treaty-bound states. By 1818, the EIC finally conquered the dismembered Maratha confederation, Kutch, and Kathiawar. States that comprised present Rajasthan also accepted British supremacy. Belligerent policies of Wellesley demolished French and Maratha power in India. The EIC now mastered over 40 million Indians and ten million pounds of annual revenue. Lord Wellesley had incorporated more Indian territory than Napoleon did in his European expeditions. The governor-general took liberty of precipitate action seeking advantage of long communication time with London. Belatedly though, actions of Wellesley were debated by the Board of Directors of the EIC. They objected to his expensive wars. The Home Office was also unhappy over the 1804 disgraceful defeat of British forces in battles against Yashwant Rao Holkar. Hence, future adventures of this nature were put off and Wellesley was finally recalled.

The EIC did not limit itself to commercial interests of the London merchants. It nurtured political and territorial ambitions. It was watchful of any outside power entering strategically located Afghanistan. The company floated rumours of France inciting Persia to invade India linking it to close relations between Napoleon I and the Shah of Persia. The British premised that the 1807 treaties of Tilsit, marking France-Russian alliance, might also endanger their interests in India. In September 1808, Governor-General Lord Minto decided to forestall any Russian/Persian moves over Afghanistan by entering into defence alliance with front line states of Afghanistan, Punjab and Sind. He dispatched Mountstuart Elphinstone with 300 troops to Peshawar. The purpose was to coerce Afghan ruler Shah Shuja into signing a treaty against foreign invasion. Mountstuart was asked to warn Afghanistan of a possible attack by Persia and any aggressive designs of Sikhs against Afghanistan. Shah Shuja inked the treaty but was overthrown by his brother. The task of engaging the Sikhs into defence alliance was assigned to Charles Metcalfe. Ranjit Singh, the Sikh ruler of Punjab, did not share British concern over French/Russian designs on India. The crafty Britons condescended to browbeat the Sikh ruler. Colonel David Ochterlony issued a proclamation declaring cis-Sutlej Sikh states under British protection. In a show of force his troops crossed River Jamuna (Yamuna), gathered allied forces on the way and camped on the left bank of River Sutlej. The Sikhs reluctantly signed the April 1809 Treaty of Amritsar which confined Sikh kingdom to the right bank of River Sutlej.

By 1829, the EIC was turning up its nose against all Indian rulers. One gap in its armour was an access to the port of Karachi in Sind, it so badly needed to ferry troops and supplies for a push against Afghanistan and for trade and warfare with hinterland states of Sind and Punjab. Lord Minto deputed Nicholas Harkey Smith, a Bombay civil servant and Henry Pottinger a seasoned diplomat to pressurize Talpur Amirs[16] (rulers) into concluding friendship treaties with the British. These treaties disallowed passage of French troops through Sind. Another treaty, between the Amirs and Governor-General William Bentnick in 1832, opened roads and water ways of Sind to British merchants and traders. These treaties, though, excluded transit facilities to British troops through Sind should they invade Baluchistan or Afghanistan. In this way, Britain became the first European power to drag Afghanistan into the political games of the West. In 1814, Francis Hastings, who succeeded Lord Minto, dispatched 17000 troops under David Ochterloney against Gurkha rulers of the northern Himalayan region. The well-disciplined Gurkhas offered fierce resistance before Ochterloney captured their Malaun fort. The decisive battle of Anglo-Nepalese war was fought on 28th February 1814, when a 35000 strong British force armed with 120 pieces of artillery overwhelmed Gurkhas of General Amar Singh Thapa. The Gurkhas ratified the 1816 treaty of Sugauli ceding Kumaon, Gharwal, and Sirmur territories to the EIC. The British were so impressed with Gurkha valour that they began recruiting them in their military — a practice which is still prevalent. The British seized the town of Simla which later became summer capital of the British rulers. Maratha power, eroded by Lord Wellesley, succumbed to a series of wars during the tenure of Hastings. The governor general abolished the custom of Peshwaship and merged Maratha territories with the Bombay presidency. The EIC, with decisive say in affairs of the treaty states, became virtual rulers of India from Bengal to the left bank of river Sutlej and borders of Sind.

Saddled with unassailable power in India, the EIC turned its attention to Afghanistan and northwest India. Lord Auckland, governor-general in the 1830's, wished to restore British protégé Shah Shuja, then exiled to Punjab, to the Afghan throne. Russia also vied for influence in Afghanistan. The then Afghan ruler Dost Muhammad tried to win over the British, but Auckland persisted with Shah Shuja. In 1838, a friendship treaty was inked between the East India Company, Shah Shuja and the Sikh ruler Ranjit Singh for facilitating the return of Shah Shuja to Afghanistan. In October 1838, Lord Auckland issued the so called Simla manifesto which set forth conditions that would prompt British intervention in Afghanistan. Two months later, General William Elphinstone marched to Afghanistan with a combined force of 21000 British and native troops. He passed through Sind in violation of the 1832 treaty with the Amirs of Sind. British resident designate William Macnaughten also accompanied the invading force. British troops defeated the Afghan army and captured Kandhar and Gazni forts. Dost

Muhammad was deposed, and Shah Shuja was installed as ruler of Kabul in August 1839. The situation reversed when restive Afghan tribes rose in support of Dost Muhammad. British emissary Alexander Burns was assassinated. The harassed British, somehow, arranged a truce. A faction of Afghans, however, killed Macnaughten on 23rd November 1841. On 6th January 1842, Elphinstone arranged safe retreat of his demoralized force. But Afghan tribes waylaid the retreating column of 4500 British troops and hundreds of civilians. All of them were slaughtered except for the bloodied surgeon Dr. William Brydon, who survived to tell the tale. British prestige suffered a devastating blow.

The next governor-general Lord Ellenborough was desperate to redeem British honour by invading Kabul in strength using a shorter and hassle-free route. The least hassle-free route through Sind was out of bounds due to treaty with the Amirs. Ellenborough not only disregarded the treaty but also included seizure of Karachi, freedom of navigation through river Indus, and grabbing wealth of the Amirs in his wish list. He needed to invent an excuse to attack Sind. He accused the Amirs of hatching a conspiracy against the EIC. Ellenborough side-lined Sind political agent James Outram and asked Charles Napier to annex Sind. Napier began bullying the Amirs into signing a new treaty obliging them to cede the towns of Karachi, Thata and Bakkar. In further acts of belligerence, he asked the Amirs to close their mint. Adding insult to injury he attacked their Imamgarh fortress razing it to the ground. The harried Baloch retaliated and attacked British residency presenting Napier with much-needed excuse to attack Sind. Forces of Talpur Amirs were routed. In 1843 Sind was annexed to British India. The flimsy pretext to invade Sind received adverse notice in England. Lord Ellenborough was recalled. Napier admitted in his diary "We have no right to seize Sind, yet we shall do so and a very advantageous, useful humane piece of rascality it will be."[17] He admitted that war in Sind was impolitic and unjust, yet he was handsomely rewarded by the Court of Directors of the company for annexing Sind.

After Sind, the only territory that separated British India from Afghanistan was the Sikh Kingdom of Punjab, the last bastion of native power in India. The Sikh ruler Ranjit Singh had died on 27th June 1839. His successors were unable to control the domineering Sikh army and intriguing Punjab chiefs. The British seized upon this opportunity to conquer Punjab before reducing Afghanistan. The British encircled the Sikh Kingdom by make-break agreements with Afghan, Baloch, and Sind Amirs raising the bogey of Sikh intrusion in their fiefdoms. They even planned a similar deal with Dost Muhammad. On 11th December 1845, the British decided to cross the River Sutlej at Ferozepur. British troops were positioned in direct route of Sikh interests across the river. Two days later, the Governor-General Sir Henry Hardinge declared war on the Sikhs. A series of battles followed with heavy losses on both sides. The Sikhs fought bravely but were let down by their leaders Lal Singh and Tej Singh who had connived with the British. The Sikhs were made to sign a very debilitating treaty on 9th March 1846. Punjab had to disband a large section of Sikh army to alter its religious make up and give up hill areas in the north and territory beyond river Beas. Hardinge made certain that the Sikhs were in fetters.

Lord Dalhousie, who succeeded Hardinge, was physically weak but mentally a tough imperialist. His take on the future of Sikh kingdom differed from the London establishment who wanted a stable but pliant Sikh kingdom for a couple of years. On the contrary, Dalhousie advised his resident at Lahore that the British were still at war with the Sikhs. They forced the governor of Multan to resign on grounds of failing to meet excessive revenue demands made on him in a year of drought and poor harvest. An emissary was dispatched to install a new governor. A mob loyal to the then governor waylaid the emissary and killed him. This incident was a prelude to the Second Anglo-Sikh war. The British besieged Multan and it was General Gough who led the main strike. On 22nd November 1848, the Sikhs routed British forces at Ram Nagar. Gough's army suffered heavy losses at Chillianwala. A brigadier-general and a colonel were killed, and several units lost their colours. These losses aroused deep dismay in London. General Gough was about to be replaced by Charles Napier when the former redeemed British prestige by defeating Sikhs in the battle of Gujarat. The Sikhs surrendered on 29th March 1849. Although political opinion in London differed on the fate of Sikh Kingdom, Lord Dalhousie made the young Sikh ruler Duleep Singh sign the instrument of annexation.[18]

Free from the Punjab, Dalhousie attended to states thus far under indirect British rule. He annexed Satara on heir-issue provoking his doctrine of lapse. Oudh was annexed on the pretence of misrule. Harsh actions of Dalhousie and the over-bearing attitude of military top brass reverberated in the 1857 uprising against the British. In 1852, Dalhousie forced another war upon Burma (Myanmar) and made them to cede the province of Pegu along with Rangoon (Yangon) and other territories known to be a commercially important part of the country. The British conquest of Balochistan by 1870 completed their occupation of the Indian subcontinent bringing them face-to-face with Afghanistan. With the end of EIC rule in 1858, it was for Benjamin Disraeli to change the method of governance in India. The EIC believed in ruthless governance. Edmund Burke called them "the breakers of law in India." Disraeli's administrative set-up was more organized, nevertheless equally efficient in robbing one of the richest nations of the world until the British were compelled to leave the subcontinent in 1947.

Europeans Intrude into the Malay Archipelago. The sixteenth-century Portugal monopolized spice trade between Europe and Southeast Asia until challenged by the mightier naval power, the Dutch. The East India Company also joined the spice trade. In 1604, her ships commanded by Sir Henry Middleton arrived at Ternate, Ambon (Amboina) and Banda. They faced stiff opposition from ships of the Dutch East India Company (VOC). Despite Dutch hostility, the British set up trading posts at Sukadana (Kalimantan), Makassar, Jayakarta, Aceh and Pariman (Sumatra). In due course British and Dutch trade posts (factories) existed side by side at Batavia (Jayakarta), Bantam and Amboina. Malayan adventure of the EIC was halted by Dutch massacre of British nationals at Amboina. Governor-General Jan Pieterszoon Coen consolidated Dutch hold on Malay trade. He and Anthony van Diemen finally diminished British and Portuguese trade in the Dutch East Indies. The VOC was dissolved in 1800 and the territory held by it became a Dutch colony. The Dutch ruled what was to become Indonesia until the Japanese occupied it during the Second World War.

China was a prime trading destination for the EIC which held the monopoly over trade in the East. In 1711, the company opened its trade mission at Canton (Guangzhou) in the delta of Pearl River. This was the only Chinese port open for business with the foreigners. Chinese tea was the major import commodity in Britain besides a rising demand for Chinese silk and porcelain. The company started smuggling Bengal-grown opium into China to balance her trade deficit. Illegal contraband boosted British commerce to such an extent that the EIC required a half-way transit port for servicing her ships sailing between India and China. The Malacca Straits shipping lanes leading to China were notorious for piracy. The British began searching for a base in the Straits to secure and service transit ships. In 1771, British merchants of Madras (India) trading in the East, commissioned Captain Francis Light to explore Malayan waters. He was asked to study prospects of trade with Aceh, Kedah, and southern Siam, and establish a base in the region. When Light landed in Kedah, the ruling Sultan was fighting local insurgency. Light seized the fort from the rebels and offered protection to the Sultan on the condition that he allowed EIC to establish a trading post on the island of Penang. Lord Warren Hastings, the governor-general in Calcutta, however, scuttled the whole mission of Light.

British interest in sea lanes of the southwest resurfaced after independence of the American colonies. The next governor-general of Bengal, John Macpherson, commissioned Francis Light in the company's marine wing. He was also appointed superintendent of the new settlement he had proposed in Penang. Light, together with a small force and artillery, landed at Kedah coast in May 1786. He met the new Sultan along with customary presents and offered to guard Kedah and Penang coast, while remaining aloof of internecine conflicts. The Sultan agreed to enter a treaty with the British without grasping its fine print. Light got permission to establish a British base in Penang. Despite acquiring this important concession, the canny British refused to stand up for the Sultan when Kedah was threatened by Siam (now Thailand). Feeling betrayed the Sultan began courting other European powers for help in ousting the British from Penang. The ever-vigilant British pre-empted his move, attacked Perai on the opposite coast, burnt the Sultan's forts, and annihilated him. Their gun-boat diplomacy triumphed because the Sultan sued for peace. In the new treaty, he ceded the island of Penang to the British in exchange for an annual payment of six thousand dollars. In 1800, the Sultan was forced to part with the coastal strip of Perai opposite Penang. The annual payment was enhanced to ten thousand dollars. The acquired territory was named the province of Wellesley after Lord Wellesley, the then governor-general of Bengal. Its acquisition facilitated British hold on the Malayan Peninsula. The Dutch had seized Malacca from the Portuguese in 1641. In July 1810, Napoleon annexed Holland including her overseas possessions. It was a worrisome situation for trade prospects of the EIC. In August 1811, Governor-General Lord Minto invaded Malacca with a force of 12000 men and 100 ships. Malacca was captured after neutralizing the weak Dutch defence. This victory gave the British preeminent position in the Malacca straits. The EIC wanted to establish trading posts and secure shipping lanes of Malacca on both sides of the straits. In 1818, Lord Hastings approved the setting up of a trading post at the southern end of the Malayan Peninsula. He deputized Thomas Stamford Raffles, the lieutenant governor of Bencoolen (now Bengkulu, Sumatra) for this job. Raffles reached his favourite destination of Singapore, which was part of the Johor state under a local chief. Johor was facing a succession dispute between the siblings. Raffles favoured elder son of the then Sultan of Johor. The new Sultan Hussain Shah was obligated to sign a tripartite treaty between Johor, the local chief of Singapore, and Raffles, granting the EIC exclusive rights to set up a trading post at Singapore. The Sultan signed another treaty in 1824 ceding Singapore to the British in lieu of a cash payment and an annual pension. The British captured Malacca fort under the 1824 Anglo-Dutch treaty. The safety of shipping lanes of Malacca Straits became a joint Anglo-Dutch responsibility. In 1825, the British put together Penang, Malacca and Singapore to constitute the Straits Settlements as a British presidency of India under a governor based in Singapore. William Bentinck, the Bengal governor-general, visited the new presidency in 1827. The Indian connection was severed after the Straits gained a sizeable population. In 1867, the three settlements became a crown colony.

A young British adventurer, James Brooks sailed into Malayan waters when the EIC was fighting local pirates. Brooks had spent the first twelve years of his life in India before leaving for England. After the death of his father, Brooks decided to seek fortune away from England. He mounted his yacht with a heavy canon and, armed with small weapons, sailed for the Malayan archipelago. Brooks arrived in Brunei in late 1838 at a time when its ruler Raja Muda Hussain, was suppressing a rebellion of native Dyaks. On the plea of Sultan, he trained his gun at the rebels, and subdued them. Brooks also confronted pirates operating in the neighbouring waters. In gratitude, the Sultan of Brunei gifted him a piece of territory and bestowed upon him the title of Raja of Sarawak. Brooks intimidated natives with his armour and began nibbling upon Brunei territory and gradually created the state of Sarawak. The dynasty of this "White Raja" ruled Sarawak for almost 100 years. In 1846, the British compelled the Sultan of Brunei to cede them the island of Labanan for fighting piracy. In 1865, the ailing Sultan of Brunei leased territory of Sabah for ten years to the American Consul who in turn sold its rights to an American company based in Hong Kong. Ultimately Sabah ended up with the British North Borneo Company.

British overseas trade and territorial policy depended upon the political party that ruled Britain. General public was wary of increase in taxes whenever a new territory was added to the British Empire. Liberal Prime Minister, William Gladstone, disliked raising taxes and hence avoided imperial ventures. Staunch imperialists like Benjamin Disraeli opined that extension of Empire enhanced British commerce and standing among the European nations. Hands-off policy notwithstanding, liberal government of Lord Palmerston intervened in the succession dispute of Perak State and Larut War of 1860's between the Chinese miners. It was apprehended that British interests may be harmed with disruption in tin production of the Perak mines. Britain got a chance to intercede in succession battle upon death of the Sultan of Perak whose elder son was the natural heir. The British seized upon this God-sent opportunity to enhance their political stature in Southeast Asia. Perak dispute went in favour of Raja Abdullah. The new Sultan was obliged to sign the Pangkor Treaty of 1874 with the British. Raja Abdullah accepted to receive a British resident on his payroll whose advice would be mandatory in all matters except religion and culture. Perak also ceded Dinding and Pangkor islands to the British. This agreement legitimized British interference in indigenous states and pushed forward its imperial designs in the Malayan Peninsula. This treaty was used as model in treaties signed with Selangor and the Malayan territory which later became Negri Sembilan.

In the 1880's Fredrick Weld, the governor of Straits Settlements, tried predation into the indigenous Malayan States. Weld was determined to control actions of Malayan rulers by installing British residents in each state. In 1885, Britain recognized Johor as an independent state capable of self-rule and Emperor Abu Bakar its rightful ruler. Johor allowed the appointment of a British resident in the state with authority to veto decisions affecting British interests in the region. The British wanted a similar treaty with the unyielding ruler of Pahang, the third largest state of the peninsula and an important trading centre. Its Sultan Wan Ahmad resisted British interference for twenty years. The British abhorred the Sultan's move to sell large mining concessions to other European nations because that would threaten the British authority in the region. Moreover, the Sultan refused to accept British residents in his state. In 1887, a joint mission of Frank Swettenham and Weld failed to mellow the Sultan. Governor Weld drafted his cousin's son, Hugh Clifford, for the job. Clifford requested his friend the Sultan of Johor to persuade Wan Ahmed. He also did a bit of arm twisting by threatening the Sultan of recognizing his rival as the Sultan of Pahang. Further, the British accused him for the murder of a Chinese British at Pekan, in Pahang. Clifford employed this leverage and forced Wan Ahmed to accept a British resident for assisting him in administration and ensuring safety of the lives and property of the British subjects. Within a year, the sulking Sultan retracted his offer and began supporting Malayan chiefs opposed to British interference in their personal matters. The British subdued the 1891 disturbances of Pahang with reinforcements from India. Clifford pursued chiefs fleeing to Terenggamu Sultanate and defeated them. Some rebel leaders were exiled to Siam (Thailand). By a treaty signed in 1895, Pahang became part of Federated Malay States along with Perak, Selangor and Negri Sembilan.

In 1910, the British directly or indirectly ruled the whole of the Malayan Peninsula comprising Straits Settlements, a crown colony, protected Federated Malay States with a resident general stationed at Kuala Lumpur, and third component of the un-federated Malay States like Perlis, Kedah, Kelantan, and Terengganu acquired from Siam through the 1909 treaty. Although these states had a British resident, they enjoyed a large degree of independence. In reality the states could ignore dictate of the resident only at their peril. Johor was the only un-federated state with a written constitution and no British resident. Its next Sultan did accept a British resident in 1914. Sabah, on the island of Borneo, was a crown colony of the British North Borneo. The Sarawak territory remained with the Brooks family until the Second World War when Japan occupied the Malayan Peninsula. In 1946, the Malay Union was formed by uniting all British possessions of the archipelago except Singapore. The Union was dissolved in 1948 and replaced with a Federation of Malayan States whose ruler enjoyed autonomy under British protection. Discontentment with the British increased with time and an independent country of Malaysia was born in 1963.

Chapter 2
Discovery and Colonisation of the Americas

In 1520 A.D., Europe's population was 90 million while 400 million plus people lived in the non-European world spread over a number of either vaguely familiar or unknown continents. To the Christian world of Europe people beyond the Arab world, even if practicing well-established religions, were "heathen" and worthy of contempt. All trade with the East flowed through land-cum-sea route ending up in port cities like Constantinople and Alexandria. Monsoon winds linked the Red Sea with India. Indian and Arab merchants ferried their cargo to the Red Sea. From there it was either the camel caravans that carried the merchandise to port cities of the Mediterranean Sea or merchants floated the goods through the Nile to Alexandria. European merchants shipped them across the Mediterranean to Iberian, Greek, and Italian port cities. Cairo and Constantinople were the richest cities west of the Indus. This trade route became dysfunctional after Ottoman Turks seized important trading portals on the Mediterranean Sea. Demand of eastern goods like textiles, spices and silk necessitated exploring hassle-free shipping routes to the Indian Ocean, India and the Far East. This was the first step toward Europe's pursuit of colonialism. Discovery of the Americas was incidental to the above endeavour. Portugal, then a strong maritime country, was the leader in navigating along the African west coast and round the Cape of Good Hope. The Portuguese king Alfonso V requested papal sanction to intrude into foreign lands. On 18th June 1452, Pope Nicholas V, betraying promotion of militant Christianity, issued bull Dum Diversas authorizing Portugal the right to attack, conquer, and enslave "saracens, pagans, and any other non-believers" in the faraway lands. The bull legitimized slavery and therefore, linked Church and State. Ten years later, Portugal discovered and colonised the uninhabited Cape Verde Islands of the Central Atlantic Ocean. The Portuguese shipped African slaves to run plantations on these islands. In good time these islands became the centre of transatlantic slave trade. Portugal also focused on exploring sea routes to India and China for trading in textiles, spices, and silk. Expedition of Bartolomeo Dias to explore a sea route to India returned after rounding the Cape of Good Hope. King Manuel I sponsored an expedition of Vasco da Gama which sailed on 8th July 1497 and on 20th May 1498 reached Calicut on the west coast of India. In March 1500, he sent another fleet of ships under Pedro Alvares Cabral to enter a trade agreement with India. Cabral sailed too far west in the Atlantic and unintentionally arrived on the Brazil coast after touching the island later named Barbados. He claimed Brazil for Portugal. The Portuguese were so gratified with riches of trading with India that they forgot to occupy Brazil until 1531.

Once Portuguese settlers arrived in Brazil they founded the city of Sao Vincent (now in Sao Paulo state) in 1532. Some settlements moved to the north coast of Bahia (Salvador) and later into the Amazon Delta. This region was highly suited to labour-intensive sugarcane cultivation. The settlers enslaved natives for forced labour. Large numbers of natives died of European diseases they contracted and forced hard labour in sugarcane fields. The sugar industry of Brazil was so successful that Portugal monopolized all sugar imports to Europe. Increased sugarcane acreage and shortage of local labour prompted Portugal to ferry slaves from Africa. It set up small coastal posts for collecting slave labour. This move marked beginning of the misery of black Africa and advent of intercontinental slave trade of inhuman proportions. In Brazil itself, until the beginning of the nineteenth century, about 3.6 million Africans had ended up as slaves. In no time Brazil lost sugar monopoly to the Caribbean. Portugal began exploiting gold and diamond wealth of Brazil and thus exposed itself to territorial greed of other nations. Stronger countries like France, Holland, and Spain flocked to Brazil to exploit her minerals and timber. The natives suffered in proportion to greed of the European marauders. Forced labour and European diseases pushed them to verge of extinction. In 1555, France occupied a portion of the Portuguese colony. They were, however, evicted in 1567.

Spain Competes with Portugal: Spain, the other maritime Iberian nation, was also anxious to grab riches as well as land of the non-

European world. King Ferdinand II of Aragon and Queen Isabella of Castile sponsored the discovery voyage of Christopher Columbus to reach India through a westerly route. Miscalculations on the part of Columbus took him too far in the westerly direction. He was seeking the East, and the Americas, unlucky for her inhabitants fell in his way round the world.[1] The voyages of Columbus aroused rivalry between the two Iberian nations because Portugal claimed all the newly discovered lands on the strength of the papal bull of 1452. Spain approached Pope Alexander IV for an edict on lines of the one issued by Pope Nicholas V in favour of Portugal. The Pope, who happened to be Spanish, issued a papal bull in 1493 that granted Spain similar privileges overriding the 1452 papal bull and accepting Spanish claim over lands discovered by Columbus. Thus, for the first time, the Church and the Crown joined hands in claiming non-European lands. This union betrayed a thirst of conquest, evangelical thirst, conquest for glory and conquest for the sake of plunder.[2] In England, the Church often checked powers of the State. In Spain, there existed a centralized absolute authority because the Crown and the Church were often allied.[3] Spanish kings exercised strict control of all colonial activities as colonies were controlled from Spain. Commanders of all Spanish expeditions were always in touch with the Spanish Crown seeking guidance. Small wonder the king received a good part of plunder usually as gold. The papal bull of 1493 drew an imaginary line running south to the mid-Atlantic 100 leagues (480 km) to the west of the Portuguese island of Cape Verde. Portugal resented Spain obtaining lordship over a far larger expanse. The king of Spain, in an effort to avoid conflict between the two nations, agreed to revisit the division. In June 1494, both nations met at Tordesillas in Spain and redrew the dividing line 370 leagues (1770 km) west of the Cape Verde Islands. Portugal's claim was accepted to the east of this line which helped her to retain Brazil.

Spain nursed commercial and territorial ambitions though its official policy was to spread Christianity. While Portuguese became masters of spice and other trade in the east, Spanish explorers were busy discovering and mastering what lay in the west and southwest of Europe. The papal division entrusted Portugal with areas of long-established culturally secure societies, while Spain shared largely tribal societies with honourable exceptions like the Mayan and Andes civilizations of South America. Spanish conquistadors had no appreciation of advanced culture of the countries they plundered. They behaved like ruffians, yet believed in righteousness of their own cause, because 'God had condemned the natives to be annihilated'. The 1491expedition of Columbus funded by Spain was meant to discover a direct sea route to Asia, conquer new lands, spread Christianity, and compete with Portugal for a share in trade and wealth of the non-European world. Thus, began a competition between adventurous, yet ruthless and intolerant Iberian powers to exploit faraway lands by subjugating their natives. Their adventures portended what misfortune lay in store for innocent natives of the non-European world. Columbus sailed aboard flagship Santa Maria accompanied by two support vessels. On 11th October 1492 he arrived at the first island of the new world and named it San Salvador and claimed it for Spain. Three days later he unsuccessfully explored more islands for gold, reached Cuba, and finally landed in Hispaniola (Haiti). The natives received him cordially and helped him retrieve his vessel that had run aground. Columbus looked in vain for gold-domed pagodas and riches of the East as narrated by earlier voyagers. He was also misguided by natives wearing cotton, but he was nowhere near India. Yet he believed that he was in the East. His adventure did earn him a name for discovering the Americas. Columbus returned to Hispaniola in 1493 with 1300 colonisers. The first permanent Spanish settlement appeared only in 1496. Spaniards enslaved working-age natives and forced them to work long hours in mines. Poor natives scared of living among Spaniards, preferred death. In desperation, they jumped off cliffs, aborted foetuses and consumed poisonous concoctions to end their lives. Within few years Hispaniola was bereft of its minerals but not before most of her natives had perished in the process of mining them.[4] African slaves got introduced into the colony in 1501.

Spanish expeditions encountered several South American nations. In 1511, Diego Velazquez, assisted by Hernando Cortes, conquered Cuba. Velazquez became governor of the Island. In 1517, Francisco Cordoba reached the Yucatan Peninsula of Mexico which lay separated from Cuba by the Yucatan channel. In 1518, Velazquez sent Hernando Cortes to explore and conquer the interior of Mexico for the purpose of colonisation. Mexico, like other South American countries, was home to advanced civilizations like the Maya which peaked after 600 A.D. but declined within two centuries. Velazquez changed his mind and asked Cortes to abort his expedition. Cortes, disregarded the governor, and sailed for Mexico after collecting 508 sailors, three guns, and sixteen horses. He landed at the Yucatan coast in 1519 to a welcome from Indians of the Maya civilization. Burly white men and canons were too awe-inspiring to be ignored by them. Cortes met a marooned Spanish priest on the coast who knew enough local dialect to assist him in talking with the native chief. The chief fêted the Spaniards where Cortes met a Maya girl Princess Malinalli (La Malinche) who became his interpreter and advisor during the expedition.

Cortes received permission from the Spanish king, to establish the city of Veracruz. He interpreted this permission as royal approval of his expedition. Cortes marched towards the Totonac city of Cempoala where he learnt of the despotic rule of Montezuma II and the rich Mesoamerican kingdom of the Aztecs. Some local societies inimical to the Aztecs provided him with mercenaries. It was a forewarning for Montezuma who had learned of the arrival of strangers in his tributary city of Cempoala. In April 1520, Cortes proceeded towards Tlaxcala. After an initial and unsuccessful confrontation, Tlaxcalans, who hated the Aztecs for introducing excessive levies, received Cortes graciously and gave him thousands of soldiers and porters to trounce Montezuma. The Aztec king vainly forewarned residents of the large Aztec city of Cholula about the evil designs of Cortes. The Spaniards reached Cholula and invited all nobles and city leaders for a dialogue. As pre-planned, his men attacked and slaughtered all the invitees. Soldiers and mercenaries let loose by Cortes upon Cholula city killed more than six thousand, innocent citizens, looted riches and plundered city temples. Thereafter Cortes moved to the Aztec capital Tenochtitlan. No European city matched in size and splendour with this Aztec city of about 200,000 people. A group of noblemen came forward with splendid gifts, before Cortes descended on Tenochtitlan. Spaniards, dazzled by the richness of the city and its temples, were tempted to attack but were restrained by Cortes.

In early May 1520 Cortes learnt of Spanish ships sailing to Veracruz. These ships, captained by Narvaez carried Spanish troops meant to seize

Cortes on the orders of the governor of Cuba. Cortes, leaving a part of his force under his deputy Alvarado, proceeded to meet Narvaez. He promised Narvaez a part of the booty which the latter declined. In desperation Cortes overpowered Narvaez in a night raid after many soldiers of the Narvaez camp had defected. Cortes had to rush back to Tenochtitlan learning that Aztecs had besieged Spanish and Tlaxcalan forces. Aztec uprising was triggered after Spaniards massacred a large number of natives celebrating a national festival. Spaniards struck the gathering with massive force slaughtering all the nobles and priests present on the festive occasion. Even drummers and dancers were brutally mutilated. Thereafter Spaniards attacked, maimed, and slaughtered the crowd until the plaza was left with no living beings. Spaniards were themselves tired of carnage and weighted down by the spoils of their looting[5]. The Aztecs were taking on the Spaniards when Cortes returned to the palace. He escorted a shackled Montezuma to appeal that his subjects stop fighting. As soon as the king appeared before the crowd he was showered with stones by his angry subjects. His head was gashed, he knelt and then fell.[6] On 30th June 1520 an injured king either died of wounds or illness. He was most likely killed by the Spaniards. Ultimately Aztecs were overpowered after the blocking of communication, food and water supplies to the city. Thereafter, Cortes and his men plundered and destroyed Tenochtitlan. The Aztecs used to mine and refine gold. They were enslaved and forced to work in gold mines. Many natives escaped to the mountains. Every Spanish soldier got his share of slave labour and land. Slavery, unbearable physical work, psychological despair, and smallpox infections killed a large number of natives. Tenochtitlan lost close to half of its population. In many cases all members of the family succumbed to the epidemic. The deaths were too numerous to be handled by the Spaniards. They thought it fit to pull down the structures over the dead and be done with them. In this way a bustling and dazzling city lay dead along with her inhabitants. The present city of Mexico stands on its ruins. By 1680, the Aztec population had slumped from 1.2 million to 70,000 impoverished souls. Mesoamerica, altogether, suffered around 90 percent reduction in its native population. The marvellous city of Tenochtitlan, her temples, and Aztec civilization were lost to the world. Cortes became colonial administrator of New Spain.[7]

Spaniards decimate Inca Empire and civilization. The Inca Empire, which thrived between AD 1200 and 1534, was spread over the present-day Peru, northern Argentina, and parts of Bolivia and Venezuela. Incas, an agricultural society, practiced irrigated farming. They were innovative enough to build irrigation canals, masonry channels and used stones to build beautiful cities and construct roads. They were proficient in weaving cotton cloth which they wore. Although bereft of the written word, they had developed a counting system based on knotted strings for record keeping. They were well-versed in state business and had organized an efficient civil system to run the empire. The fame of Inca civilization of six million souls with its capital in Cuzco had crossed country boundaries. In 1510, conquistador Francisco Pizarro crossed the Isthmus of Panama along with explorer Vasco Balboa. Spain captured this Isthmus in 1519 and founded the city of Panama. The city became the centre of all future Spanish expeditions to South America. Pizarro, while he was mayor of Panama, learned about the Inca civilization of Peru. Barely five years after the demise of the Aztec Empire, Pizarro assembled an expedition to conquer the Incas. He took command with Diego de Almagro as his deputy. The expedition, consisting of 180 men, 37 horses and one gun, was funded by the vicar of Panama on the condition that he would receive a one-third share of lands, treasure and slaves gained by the expedition. Pizarro had received warm welcome from the Incas during his 1526 visit. Beaming with satisfaction, he sailed to Madrid and obtained Royal permission to conquer Peru and become its viceroy. The King agreed, but asked Pizarro to be gentle to the natives.

Pizarro sailed for Peru in 1531 at a time when the Inca kingdom had been weakened by smallpox epidemic, a disease introduced by early Spanish conquistadors. The disease had claimed its emperor Wayna Capac. Atahualpa and his half-brother Huascar sons of the late Inca emperor, were engaged in the succession battle. Pizarro waited for a few months before he marched into Cajamarca. Atahualpa who was the *de facto* ruler, learned of the expedition while himself on a mission of extending his empire. He returned and accompanied by unarmed court dignitaries and nobles visited Pizarro on 15th November 1532. Pizarro welcomed the emperor, praised his kingdom and posed to be on a diplomatic mission on behalf of the king of Spain. Soon a monk appeared with a book and crucifix in his hand asking the host emperor to accept Christianity and acknowledge King Charles V as his sovereign. A surprised Atahualpa retorted that he was not a Spanish vassal. The monk signalled the soldiers to fire on Inca nobles and others while their emperor watched helplessly. The horsemen charged and trampled women and children who were gathered on the occasion. Within half an hour the cream of Peruvians lay dead, and their emperor was prisoner of Pizarro. Atahualpa offered one room full of gold as ransom for his release. Pizarro accepted the ransom offer and began celebrating. Within half an hour an independent Peru had become Spanish.[8] The way it was conquered makes one blush for the race to which we belong.[9] Finally, in 1533, Atahualpa was baptized and then executed over charge of killing his half-brother. His kingdom was passed on to his brother Tupac Hualpa to be succeeded in the same year by Manco Inca with Pizarro remaining the *de facto* ruler. Three years later an independent-minded Manco fled to the mountains. Pizarro divided the plunder and lands of Peru among all conquistadors.[10] Slaves were also divided, and even lowly soldiers became masters of both land and slaves. The Spaniards treated the Peruvians so harshly that they revolted and fled to the mountains. Meanwhile, Spaniards fell apart. A war broke out between colonists and royal officials from Spain. Pizarro ruled for ten years but in 1541 he was murdered by followers of Almagro. Spaniards extended complete control over Peru by 1560. The short-lived magnificent Inca civilization had met its gory end at the hands of those who were chartered to spread Christianity in far-away lands. After two centuries of Spanish occupation, the population of natives declined from six million to less than one million. The Spanish conquests of Mexico and Peru presaged sixteenth century efforts of feudal Europe trying to bring down the non-European world.

In 1520, Ferdinand Magellan arrived in Chile during his circumnavigation of the globe. Diego de Almagro explored the country in 1535 but after finding no minerals returned to Peru. In 1541, Pedro de Valdivia crossed into Chile and found the city of Santiago. Later on, Chile was incorporated into the viceroyalty of Peru. Spain marked its presence in Venezuela which had been discovered by Columbus during his voyages. A permanent Spanish settlement was established in 1522. In 1542 Venezuela also came under the viceroyalty of Peru. Spaniards, who first visited Argentina in 1516, firmed up their control over the country. In a span of seventeen years a handful of Spaniards had spread themselves over territories more than equal in extent to the whole of Europe.[11] Consequently, by the first half of the sixteenth century, barring Portuguese Brazil, Spain ruled over most of South America. This nation had conquered South America with amazing rapidity. Hernando Cortes landed in Vera Cruz in the year 1519, and by 1521 became master of Mexico. Spain overran Peru, Quito, and Chile by 1532 and by 1535 it had occupied Venezuela. Ironically, population of natives in these lands declined with similar speed.

Europeans Enter North America: Inhabitants of the large continent situated to the north of Spanish acquisitions still enjoyed freedom. In the Europe, the Iberians knocked down sixteenth century mercantile ventures of their northern neighbour France but not its territorial ambitions. In fact, Iberian exclusion of fellow European countries from sea lanes of the southern hemisphere attracted France, Britain, and Holland to lands in the North. French interest in North America began with a desire to find northeast routes to the fabled riches of Asia. A French navigator, Jacques Cartier, under a commission of King Francis I, explored the interior of what is now North America. He sailed through Saint Lawrence River and claimed Lawrence River Valley for France in 1534. During his three-ship expedition of 1535, Cartier sailed up to the present-day Montreal. In both voyages he attempted but failed to locate eastern regions (China). During his third voyage of 1541, Cartier established a permanent settlement along the Lawrence River. His countryman Samuel de Champlain founded the French colony of Quebec in 1608 and governed the same until 1628. Eventually, European encroachers fell afoul of each other. The English attacked and seized Fort Quebec but returned it to France in compliance with the 1632 Anglo-French Treaty. In 1681, another French adventurer Robert Cavalier de La Salle, sailed down the Mississippi River up to the Gulf of Mexico and discovered a route for fur trade. Cavalier claimed the entire Mississippi basin for France in 1682 and named it Louisiana in honour of King Louis III. This basin lay west of the Mississippi River up to the Rocky

Mountains between the Canadian border and the Gulf of Mexico, reaching frontier lands of the viceroyalty of New Spain in the southwest. The French established trading colonies in Canada and Nova Scotia. They begrudged Spanish colonies abroad and sent colonists to north western coast of Hispaniola, abandoned by Spain. In early seventeenth century, French Huguenots fleeing religious persecution resolved to settle there and build colonies. These colonies were recognized by Louis IV and given the name of Saint-Domingo. Captain Alonso Alvarez de Pineda arrived in Texas and claimed it for Spain. Twenty years later, Hernando De Soto explored Florida and south-eastern America.

During the sixteenth century, Britons confined themselves to sea piracy and raiding Spanish holdings on the coasts of Spanish America. It was in the beginning of the seventeenth century that Britain joined continental Europe's colonial and mercantile ventures after the 1604 Treaty of London that ended sixteen years of war with Spain. Britain adventured into North America during the reign of Queen Elizabeth I, also called the Virgin Queen. She deputed Sir Walter Raleigh to establish a settlement. Raleigh landed at Roanoke Island off the coast of present-day North Carolina but his settlement failed. Yet this part of North America was named Virginia after the queen.[12] On 10th April 1606, King James I of England issued a letter of patent to two British companies, one of London and the other from Plymouth. The London-based company was chartered to settle southern Virginia between Connecticut and Wilmington, North Carolina.

The voyagers of the London Company comprised of 104 sailors who had survived rigors of travel and on 14th May 1607 made land fall at James Island. The survivors established the first ever foreign settlement of Jamestown on the bank of the James River, both named after King James. This colony received royal recognition in 1625. The Plymouth Company, which held charter to colonise lands between Delaware and Maine, set up Popham colony in the north on the Atlantic coast in 1607. This colony failed due to the extremely cold weather of Maine. The company folded up after two years. In 1620, a new charter was granted to its successor company, the Plymouth Council for New England. Hence the region comprising of thirteen English colonies earned the collective name New England. The Plymouth Company ferried a group of 102 settlers including 40 dissidents of the English church, called pilgrims, aboard the 180 ton ship the *Mayflower*. These people who landed at Cape Cod on 4th November 1620, were disillusioned during the winter months. Their low morale was boosted by tips for survival and words of comfort by one Native American. He advised them how to hunt and raise crops like corn. The native did not know that he was comforting their *bête noire*. He was also ignorant that indigenous people in South America and the Caribbean were victims of the same Europeans. He had no idea that one day they will usurp their country. In 1630, a group of Puritans, a name for dissenters of the Church of England, arrived in the present-day Massachusetts. This group led by John Winthrop set up the Massachusetts Bay Colony with himself as its governor until 1649. Within seventy years, the colony population rose to 100,000. In 1634, a group of Catholics settled at St. Mary's in the colony subsequently named Maryland. Roger Williams and his group who had differences with the Puritans of Massachusetts left the place and in 1634 established the Providence plantation in the present-day state of Rhode Island. The settlement became protector of Quakers in 1657 and a year later of the Jews who came from Holland.

Continental Europe in North America: A group of fishermen established the first settlement of Rye in 1623. Six years later the colony was named New Hampshire. It was in 1680 that the colony achieved an independent status. In 1633, a settlement of English Puritans and Dutch traders laid the foundation of what is now Connecticut which received independent status as a crown colony in 1662. The Dutch by virtue of their 1609 survey laid claim to Pennsylvania, originally a part of the Virginia colony. In fact, they established a trading post in 1629, but were thrown out by the English. Other Dutch possessions included the present-day New York, Delaware, and New Jersey, all part of what was then New Netherlands. The Dutch purchased Manhattan Island from the natives for a petty sum of twenty-four dollars and founded "Nieuw Amsterdam" as capital of the Dutch holdings. Later the English named the place New York. The Dutch were militarily weak compared to their French and English rivals. Consequently, they lost their acquisitions to the English. In 1638, the Swedes set up a permanent settlement of Delaware at Fort Christina near what is now Wilmington. The Dutch claimed the territory for themselves but had to yield the same to the English in 1664. In 1643 Swedes settled in New Jersey. The English followed them. Eventually New Jersey ended up as a Royal colony in 1702. The English settled in the colony of Carolina in 1653 but in 1702 divided it into North and South Carolinas. The last colony of Georgia was an outcome of the 1732 charter granted to 21 trustees by King George II.

Expatriate colonies of New England were largely self-governed with minimal interference from Britain. The English revolution of 1688 that created parliamentary supremacy over the Crown changed the equilibrium. The British parliament began to flaunt its authority over the American colonies. British settlers of the colonies resisted such patronage to the point of demanding independence from Britain. This situation dragged on until the mid-eighteenth century. The 1754 Anglo-French war strained British financial position prompting her to raise funds through taxes on the colonies. The colonists resented paying taxes without being represented in the British Parliament. They opposed the Stamp Act of 1765 insisting, no representation- no tax. Britain, on the contrary, forbade the colonies direct foreign trade that impinged on British shipping. It expected the colonies to produce raw materials for Britain and serve as a market for British products. The 1766 boycott of British imports was a striking act of defiance. The Townshend Revenue Acts of 1767 which imposed several taxes on the colonies became another irritant. Bostonians were most affected as they relied on trade. The Britain-Colonies divide culminated in the Boston Tea Party of 16th December 1773 signifying an open rebellion against the former. The war which broke out in 1775 in Massachusetts continued on different fronts and ended in October 1781 when Britain surrendered. The success of revolt of the colonies gave a rude shock to the British national pride. The nation had to be conditioned by the fact that independence is a natural sequel to colonisation.[13]Official hostilities ceased with the Second Treaty of Paris signed on 3rd September 1783. Benjamin Franklin secured important concessions including the recognition of an independent United States of America with the Mississippi River as its western boundary. Later, in the "noble bargain", France sold her 909,000 square mile territory to America for fifteen million dollars (Louisiana Purchase). Florida, which had returned to Spanish control, was later sold by Spain to the United States of America for five million dollars. In this way, this vast land belonging to her natives was supplanted by Europeans to create the United States of America.

American independence had far-reaching consequences. It forced Britain to seek another territory to exile her convicts. Their search resulted in Australia and New Zealand becoming English colonies. This event also opened Canada for those English subjects who owed allegiance to the English Crown. In 1897, George Burton Adams wrote that American independence short circuited any threat to the supremacy of the Anglo-Saxon race. According to him, "had England retained possession of their thirteen colonies it is scarcely possible that the immigrant labour and capital of Europe would have poured into our lands as they have. Our frontier settlements now may be nearing the Mississippi, but could hardly be beyond it, and it is more likely that all the territory of the second greater annexation would still be under the Latin race".[14] A relevant question is what would have been the shape of the political map of the world in the twentieth century? As a corollary, the American Revolution set the stage for Britain to acquire Canada and, by dint of her command on the seas, maraud her way into the non-European world and usurp a far greater territory and wealth than it had lost in the American Revolution.

The American Civil War posed a tough challenge to an independent United States of America. It threatened to divide the new nation between the Unionists (North) and the Confederacy (South). The roots of the conflict lay in the concept of human rights. Thomas Jefferson had included a potent statement in the preamble to the Declaration of Independence passed by the Congress on 4th July 1776. The statement "All men are created equal" was incongruous with slavery. The British Parliament had already abolished slavery in the British Empire through the Slavery Abolition Act of 1833.In the United States, the North, with comparatively smaller farms, and hence less dependence on farm labour, favoured abolition of slavery. On the other hand, the seven southern states, with large farms and plantations of cotton, fully exploited slave labour. Slave population of the southern states almost equalled their white population. These states seceded on this issue. Abraham Lincoln won the 1860 presidential election on the antislavery principle. The

North refused to recognize the secession. Conflicting stand led to the 1861 North (unionist) and South (confederate) Civil War. The Unionists forced the surrender of the confederate armies in 1865.

By 1890, the United States surpassed Great Britain in its industrial growth and overall economy but was weaker in ground and naval power. Hence it subdued any ambition of territorial expansion as witnessed in the 1884 Berlin Conference. Moreover, acquisition of territories abroad was inconsistent with principles of the republic. This renunciation did not last long. Emerging from the shadows of the Civil War, the country began to assert itself in international affairs in the last decade of the nineteenth century. Initially her concerns were limited to the immediate neighbourhood. In 1893, it had a hand in the overthrow of Hawaii's monarchy. The invasion of Cuba happened during the presidency of William McKinley, who had won with the support of business magnates. The American-Spanish conflict spilled over to the Philippines which was a Spanish colony. With the 1895 American-Spanish Treaty (Treaty of Paris) America got the Philippines for a payment of twenty million dollars.

The Filipinos regarded the treaty as a betrayal on the part of the Americans because they had helped them in the war hoping that they would earn freedom of their country. The U.S. President McKinley listened to the business lobby which wanted captive markets for the U.S. manufactures and the Philippines were to be one of them. On 15th May the President instructed U.S. general Wesley Merritt, later the military governor of the Philippines, that the U.S. would claim a wide degree of sovereignty over the Islands. The Treaty of Paris dismayed the Philippine freedom fighters. They swore in their leader Emilio Aguinaldo as President of the Philippines on 23rd January 1899. The United States refused to recognize the new government. Open hostilities broke out between the Filipino and American forces. Manila city appeared to be the bone of contention. Americans wanted the city at all costs. The President of the United States wrote to the Secretary of State for war directing all forces to take possession of the Philippine islands by right of transfer by Spain and by right of conquest.[15] The Filipinos were ignorant about American motives. The Americans went back on all assurances made to the Filipino fighters. Evidently America had embraced imperial ambitions. An anti-imperialist Mark Twain criticized his country for this turnaround. "But the master of the game (America) happened to think of another plan (rather than restoring Philippines to her rightful owners)-the European plan. Dewey (American general) acted on it. This was, to send out an army-ostensibly to help out native patriots put the finishing touch upon their long and plucky struggle for independence, but really to take their land and keep it."[16] American conduct of the war was brutal. This is vouched by accounts of American occupation of the Philippines between 1898 and 1912 when they used water boarding torture on the Filipino captives.[17] Filipino fighters acted like professionals and took good care of captured American soldiers. Back home the American public received incorrect information through official dispatches. It was similar to the conduct of colonial powers when they brutalized the natives. The American-Philippines War was projected as a race war, which it never was. A brutal radicalization was the American soldier's imagination of war as a hunting game. "It is lot of fun to hunt those black devils. We just shot niggers like a hunter would rabbits."[18] It turned out to be an extremist war when even non-combatants were also ordered to be shot on sight.[19] Blount called the American action in the Philippines a great wrong unwittingly done by a great, free, and generous people to another people then struggling to be free.[20]

The United States of America had no territorial ambitions to begin with. It attended the Berlin Conference but limited its interest to commerce. The U.S. was content to check further European access to the Caribbean and Latin America and their intrusion into the Pacific region. The economy of her nearest Caribbean neighbour, Cuba, depended on sugar export. The 1890 McKinley Tariff Act permitted duty-free export of sugar to the United States. Cuban sugarcane growers and labour highly benefitted from sugar export. In the nineteenth century Cuba accounted for one-half of the world's sugar trade. Most of its sugar was exported to the United States. The 1894 Wilson-Gorman Tariff Act imposed forty percent charge on all sugar imported into the country. This tariff hit the labour-intensive Cuban sugar industry creating huge labour surplus. Displaced labour joined Cuban rebels who were agitating against the Spanish rule. In 1895, a section of American press published inspired accounts of Spanish misrule to convince the American public that war was the only solution to rid Cuba of Spanish rule. Incidentally, an American ship, Maine, anchored near the Havana port blew up. Spanish inquiry deemed it an accident. America rejected the finding and blamed Spain for the loss of her ship. President William McKinley got approval from the U.S. congress to invade Cuba. General William Shafter led the campaign. Theodore Roosevelt, then assistant secretary for navy, resigned his job, organized a regiment of volunteers and led a cavalry assault on Spanish positions. Simultaneously, the United States launched naval action against the Spanish navy based in Manila, the Philippines. Spanish forces capitulated on 12th August 1898. It is during this American-Spanish war that U.S. soldiers employed water boarding against the adversary as an interrogation technique. American soldiers employed the same technique against Filipinos during the Philippine War.

A reporter of the New York Evening Post gave details of water cure in the issue of 18th April 1902. The native was thrown on the ground. His hands and legs were tied, and head was raised to make pouring of water easy. His mouth was stretched open, and the captive was forced to swallow gallons of water even by thrusting a bamboo stick into his mouth until his belly was swollen like that of a toad. Water was again squeezed out of him to repeat the process until the helpless victim agreed to cooperate. Spain signed the Treaty of Paris and renounced her control over Cuba. The U.S. lorded over the Philippines from 1896 to 1946. Theodore Roosevelt, who succeeded President McKinley, distrusted growing clout of Japan and Germany in the Pacific Ocean. An effective way to countermine their influence was to shorten American naval access to the Pacific by completing the Panama Canal thereby creating an Atlantic-Pacific link. This canal was planned through the Isthmus of Panama which was then controlled by Colombia. French builder Ferdinand Lesseps, the builder of Suez Canal, had to abandon this project in 1890 due to financial and sundry reasons. The United States tried to seek Isthmus on lease from Colombia, but the latter did not ratify the agreement. Roosevelt instigated rich Panamanians to demand independence from Colombia. He sent U.S. naval ships into the Caribbean signalling U.S. support for the Panamanian demand and indirectly sending a warning signal to Colombia. The latter freed Panama in 1903. In return, Panama granted the United States rights over the Isthmus for building the Panama Canal. The canal was completed in 1914. The canal-zone remained under U.S. suzerainty until a 1977 treaty declared the canal a neutral International Waterway. Colombia did not recognize Panama as a sovereign nation until 1921 when the United States paid 25 million dollars to the country as compensation and the U.S. Congress apologized for role of the then U.S. president Roosevelt in the affairs of Panama. Now for strategic reasons the United States marks her presence in the Pacific Ocean through several islands in the Americas and Oceania. Natives of this part of the world are either confined to reserves or are at the verge of extinction.

Chapter 3
Australasian Natives, the Innocent Victims

Dutch vessels bound for the Dutch East Indies often sailed past the west coast of a large unknown continent. The first Dutch ship reached shores of this continent around 1606. Over the years, Dutch mariners drew its vague outline and named it New Holland. Cartographic maps depicted a large blank space between New Guinea and the Van Diemen's Land. The latter landmass was so named by its discoverer Abel Tasman in honour of Anthony van Diemen the then governor-general of the Dutch East Indies. The Europeans were curious about the obscure unexplored large continent they called *Terra Australis*, a Latin name for land of the south. The Spaniards who had struck gold and silver in their South American colonies dreamed of similar deposits in this land. In 1768, Britain commissioned visit of Captain James Cook to Tahiti aboard Endeavour, a vessel fitted for exploratory work. Cook's mission was to observe transit of planet Venus across disc of the Sun, an event likely to occur on 2nd/3rd June 1769. His additional task was to charter the island and its surroundings, and secretly explore the large continent if it existed in the South Pacific.[1] The crew of Endeavour included officers, a surgeon, 40 seamen, marines and scientists like astronomer Charles Green and naturalists led by Joseph Banks, all from the Royal Society. Endeavour sailed for Rio de Janeiro in August 1768 arriving there by the year's end. After few months Endeavour sailed into Matavai Bay in Tahiti and stayed there until 9th August 1769.

After completing his Tahiti mission, Cook sailed in the direction of what is now New Zealand. He sighted its North Island on 7th October 1769. Two days later, Endeavour anchored at what Cook named Party Bay. Cook, Banks, and Swedish naturalist Daniel Solander disembarked. The curiosity of the natives gathered on the shore soon turned in to a ferocious affront. The visitors shot dead one native for his alleged attempt to seize their arms. Eventually the Endeavour departed but not before shooting a few more natives. Cook judged the island ideal for the settlement of Europeans. He symbolically claimed it in the name of the British Crown. It is not certain if Cook had a commission to claim any foreign land. Yet he chose to use prevalent doctrine of first discovery ignoring that the island was inhabited, and its natives had been trading with visitors from foreign lands. Cook spent the next six months in chartering the coastline of the islands (now North and South islands of New Zealand) before proceeding to search for the fabled land of the South. It was then March 1770. Approaching winter, shrinking rations, and repair needs, forced the Endeavour, to change course and sail for the closest European station. He sailed westwards, reached the east coast of what the Dutch called New Holland (it was yet to be named Australia) and then took course for the Dutch post of Batavia for ship repairs and to pick up rations. The Dutch had chartered a rough outline of the west coast of New Holland but its east coast was unchartered. Cook and his party sailed for this land on 1st April 1770. Nineteen days later the intended land was in sight and the crew found smoke emitting from several places. Two days later, five people of dark complexions were seen and then more. More natives and their huts were visible from the Bay where Endeavour was anchored. Unmistakably, this land was inhabited. Cook acknowledged in his journal, "I went on the boats in hopes of speaking with them accompanied by Mr. Banks, Dr. Solander and Tupia (a Tahiti native). As we approached the shore, they all made off except two men who seemed resolved to oppose our landing. Tupia gestured a friendly greeting but got an outraged response." Cook's party fired shots to scare them away. Next day a small group ventured forward but refused to accept gifts. The visitors found a small village where an old woman with children shivered with fear. She refused to accept gifts and wanted them to go away. It was 6th May when Banks and Solander discovered a large variety of plants near the bay. Gratified with the discovery, Cook named the place Botany Bay (probably Botanist Bay in the beginning). Moorland added a twist to the name: "It seems ironic that so innocent a name was to become synonym for all that was heartless and cruel, not only in this new country, but in Georgian civilization as well."[2] This place, a few years hence, was to host the first British penal settlement.

Cook engraved an inscription on one of the trees depicting his ship's name and date of arrival. He displayed the English colours every day. On 15th August, Endeavour sailed along the coast arriving at a safe place subsequently named Port Jackson[3] which is now Sidney. Endeavour sailed further along the coast and touched an island. Once ashore, Cook climbed the highest hill to get a good view of the East Coast of "New Holland". He surmised if any other European ever visited this side of the continent. Once again Cook hoisted the British flag to mark possession of the east coast in the name of King George III. He called the coast New South Wales (NSW) and proclaimed British possession of the territory by ceremoniously firing a volley of arms. Captain Cook did not claim the west coast discovered by the Dutch navigators, and hence did not pass muster as first discovery. Ceremony over, Endeavour sailed away to the relief of the natives who despised the presence of white intruders. Tragically their relief was cut short by what transpired in the far away North America.[4]

The eighteenth-century England, despite being in the forefront of the Industrial Revolution, was laggard in social and economic transformation. People of feudal England starving in the country side flocked to London in search of livelihood. Impoverishment was such that millions were desperate for a piece of bread. Desperation gave rise to petty crime. Georgian England was unforgiving. Urged by the rich and the mighty, tough laws were enacted against crime and cheating. Administration of law was illusory as fast-track courts decided punishment within fifteen minutes. The Bloody Code[5] in vogue between 1688 and 1815, provided capital punishment or harsh prison terms for even petty crimes. Opulent suburban rich were not ready to condone even minor crimes. Condemned prisoners were executed in the open outside London's New Gate prison. Lo and behold well to do people hired balconies of neighbouring buildings to watch the struggle of the condemned souls on the scaffold. Human dignity was the least concern for the English Society and a Christian nation of the times.[6]

James Bosewell, a Scottish lawyer and writer watched nineteen criminals including thieves, a forger, a stamp counterfeiter and others executed at New Gate.[7] In ten years between 1781 to 1790, courts sentenced 1188 people to death, of which 501 were hanged. The remaining got pardoned by the Crown. The Bloody Code prescribed death sentence or transportation for life in 222 offences. Even kids, as young as seven, sentenced for petty crime were hanged. Deprivation led to the clandestine manufacture of counterfeit currency and its circulation. Two young girls got snared in to this racket. Punishment for persons guilty of counterfeiting was burning on the stake. These girls found guilty of this crime were also sentenced to bear the burden of this barbarous law on their tender shoulders. Execution of one Catherine Hyland was stayed to complete her appeal for mercy. The *Times,* the next day, questioned if mankind must not laugh at long speeches against slavery when "we roast a fellow creature alive, for putting a penny-worth of quicksilver into a halfpenny-worth of brass.[7] Hyland got Royal pardon and approved for exile to Australia. Keneally described the end of the other girl (Margaret Sullivan) who was hanged for a short while before burning her at the stake.[8] How would English society of the day, so bereft of emotion, and of morbid conscience, treat Australian natives at their mercy, is not hard to imagine.

Some English counties legally transported thieves and lawless people for life. The statute of 1666 authorized transportation of such persons. The convicts faced execution if they dared to return to England. In the seventeenth and eighteenth centuries thousands of convicts arrived in the American colonies. Settlers bought a prisoner's labour, generally for seven years, at auction. Some 120,000 prisoners ended up in the colonies in this way. After independence, the colonies were out of bounds for English convicts. Without an outlet, British jails became overcrowded. A large number of convicts had to be confined to one small room. The overflow was interned in filthy and poorly maintained hulks parked in the Thames. Annoyed with the appalling conditions, British public demanded a solution to the problem. The government was forced to find a suitable place to transport her convicts. France had been colonizing Quebec in Canada since 1608. Thousands of Americans loyal to the English Crown had also moved to Canada. For this reason, Canada and on logistic grounds, Africa, did not find favour as places for penal settlements. Finally, the report of the Home Secretary Lord Sidney was accepted. On 18th August 1786, government settled for Botany Bay, the place suggested by Joseph Banks who had accompanied James Cook on his maiden voyage to Australia. Banks had convinced the government that Botany Bay was *terra nullius* or no man's land. James Cook and Banks knew that ancestors of the natives had arrived there thousands of years ago. The natives were as intensely attached to their ancestral lands as any other society on earth. They had been living among their own social groups based on their origin. It is now believed that their people settled in Australia more than 30,000 years ago and spread across the length and breadth of the country. Recent discoveries of rock art links the presence of humans in the continent to Palaeolithic times.[9] Cook believed that though the natives were wretched people, they led far happier lives than the Europeans. Their fun and gaiety, alas, disappeared from their lives once the First Fleet carrying British convicts arrived on Australian shores. Price grieved, "when Britain occupied New South Wales in 1788, she made no provisions for an aboriginal population which perhaps numbered 40,000; all she did was to instruct Governor Phillip to open intercourse with the natives and punish any colonists who wantonly destroyed them or disturbed their occupations.[10] (The estimate of native population given by price is on a lower side.) What actually happened was exactly the opposite. The natives were chased, hunted and killed with impunity, lending weight to the saying 'brutality abroad is matched by brutality at home.'

In 1787, Captain Arthur Phillip was chosen to ferry convicts to Australia, establish a penal settlement and function as its governor. Phillip captained the First Fleet comprising H.M. Sirius, six transport ships and three store ships, ferrying 800 convicts, 250 marines with their families, and twenty officials. First batch of ships touched Botany Bay on 19th January 1788. Upon investigation, Phillip found that the place lacked in fresh water and the adjoining land was unsuitable for robust agriculture. The native tribes, like Gweagal and Bediagal of the Eora language group, lived in Botany Bay. They were annoyed when foreign vessels appeared in the Bay. Pemulwuy of the Bediagal tribe, who was a fierce opponent of foreigners, was apprised of the development. Phillip knew of the hostile reception that Cook and his party received from these natives some 18 years ago. Hence, as soon as the ships arrived, the natives shouted at them to get out. Phillip counselled his men to be patient with them and start with locating a more wholesome site for the penal settlement.

Phillip dispatched a ship to Port Jackson, originally discovered by James Cook. The ship returned with good news of a land-locked harbour with a deep-water estuary and plenty of fertile hinterland. Phillip was setting sail when French explorers entered the Bay. The British considered the French their enemy. It was said that "before they (the British) learn there is God, they learn there are Frenchmen to be detested."[11] Phillip was relieved that French sailors were known to him and they had no intention to settle at Botany Bay. Fears allayed; Phillip sailed away for Port Jackson. He named the cove within the harbour, Sydney Cove after the British colonial secretary, Thomas Townsend (Lord Sydney). Phillip hoisted the British flag to mark British claim over the territory which became home to 161,700 British convicts until 1868. On 29th January 1788, Phillip met face-to-face with the natives who seemed in a sociable mood. A week later he assumed governorship of the settlement and of the entire coastal strip with absolute powers bestowed upon him by the Crown. In this manner Britain occupied a land thousands of miles away, which, by no means, belonged to it. Philip had claimed lands of Australian natives. In a way the natives were guests on the land they had lost without battle and without payment.[12] The natives were bewildered by this unforeseen development. They turned hostile after discovering that the visitors were there to stay. Natives saw white people only as usurpers of their lands and water channels but were unaware that they carried deadly germs their own bodies had never been exposed to.

Infectious diseases contracted from the Europeans killed natives in large numbers. Britons themselves did not foresee the impending calamity until April 1789 when they noticed scores of human corpses floating in the harbour. Dead bodies had smallpox pustules on them. Survivors were too weak to bury the dead. It was a repetition of how European diseases devastated native populations of the Americas, the Caribbean and all other pristine lands treaded upon by them. Charles Darwin, who toured Australia, wrote in his journal, published in 1839; "Besides these evident causes of destruction, there appears to be some more mysterious agency at work. Wherever the European had trod, death seems to pursue the aboriginal. We may look to the wide extent of the Americas, Polynesia, the Cape of Good Hope and Australia, and we shall find the same result."[13] Land around the Sydney cove settlement was infertile coastal sand, incapable of meeting the needs of the migrant population. Food was imported from England, Cape of Good Hope, or India. Governor Phillip found a better land upriver with fresh water, and fertile soil. The place was named Parramatta (Rose Hill) taken from the native name Barramatta. This place was home to the Drug tribe. Major Ross, a person of dubious fame, took over as commander of the colony. That appointment multiplied the woes of the natives. Within months, Ross began to defy orders of Governor Phillip on the premise that he is answerable only to the Admiralty.

Phillip was still sorting out his concerns when, on 3rd June 1790, Lady Juliana of the second fleet reached Port Jackson. It carried 225 female convicts along with few infants born on the eleven-month-long trip bearing witness to the sexual exploitation of female passengers. The fleet did not carry much-awaited food supplies. Other ships, which arrived few days later, carried male convicts so harshly treated by the contractors that 258 of them had perished on the way. Only 692 males and 67 females, most of them sick, arrived in Australia. A handful of them were dispatched to Parramatta for farm work. By 1791, the country side west of Parramatta was opened for settlement because the smallpox epidemic had almost wiped out the local Bediagal clan. On 27th March 1791, third fleet of nine ships carrying 2000 persons left for Australia foretelling the need for additional land to grow food. Phillip offered land grants at Parramatta and Norfolk Island to marines scheduled to return home, provided they stayed. The king of England had granted one hundred and thirty acres to every commissioned officer if unmarried and twenty acres extra if married. Every unmarried soldier was to get eighty acres and one hundred acres if married. Thus, by 1792, European population of Sydney rose to 1259 of Parramatta and associated farms to 1625, and Norfolk Island to 1172. These populations were settled on lands filched from the natives.

Australian natives deprived of their means of existence took to stealing food and cattle for their survival. Convicts exacerbated their desperation by seizing their fishing gear, canoes and even young women. Convict gunfire scared away all game that natives used to hunt with spears. Starving natives also took to hit-and-run raids. They were unable to face foreigners carrying lethal weapons. Governor Phillip made half-hearted efforts to assuage their sentiments, yet dispossessed and harassed natives retaliated by spearing stray whites crossing their path. Such violation attracted punitive expeditions against them. Poorly armed natives stood no chance against well-armed convicts who shot them mercilessly. After Parramatta another settlement was established at Toongabbie. It was on the 640-acre government farm where hundreds of convicts produced food for the colonies. In 1793, acting Governor Francis Grose granted 100 acres of land to John Macarthur, a lieutenant in the New South Wales Corps. Within few years, Macarthur expanded his estate and set up a sheep farm on 400 to 500 acres. He pushed a number of native clans westwards into unproductive lands. Natives retaliated against forcible occupation of their only source of living. They confronted heavily armed settlers but, after heavy loss of lives, retreated to areas rejected by the settlers as inhabitable.

Pemulwuy, a Carathi, was a prominent resistance leader of the Bediagal clan in the Botany Bay-Parramatta region. Each tribe had such persons who were supposed to be invincible and endowed with special powers. Pemulwuy resisted occupation of tribal lands from 1788 onwards until his death in 1802. Governor Phillip assigned official huntsmen in a resolve to make the natives sensitive to white man's supremacy. One huntsman was John McEntire, an Irish ex-convict who was notorious for his transgression against native women. Natives hated him intensely. In a reprisal attack Pemulwuy hurled a spear at McEntire seriously injuring him. An enraged governor dispatched a punitive expedition on 14th December 1790, with orders to bring back the heads of two natives and to capture ten of them for public execution. The expedition consisted of two captains and forty privates along with several non-commissioned officers. Unequal contest between heavily armed Europeans and naked unencumbered Indians was doomed to be short.[14] Captain Watkin Tench led the expedition to a native village but found it deserted. Another expedition failed in the same way. Meanwhile Pemulwuy's son Tedbury had joined his father in opposing white settlements on native lands. From 1792 onwards, both raided white settlements and government farms at Prospect, Toongabbie, Parramatta, Hawkesbury River, and other places. In a strong resolve the administration organized a punitive expedition comprising men of the N.S.W. corps and ex-convicts. The expedition chanced upon a group of natives which included Pemulwuy. In the faceoff, Pemulwuy received several buck shots to his head. He was taken to a hospital. The indomitable native, with bullets still embedded in his head, escaped from there and remained fugitive for several years. In 1801, Phillip Gidley King, Governor of New South Wales, declared Pemulwuy an outlaw. He also decreed that aborigines of the area could be shot on sight. Ultimately in 1802 two white settlers hunted Pemulwuy down. His head was sent to Joseph Banks in England for passing it on to physical anthropologist Johann Blumenbach in Germany for ethnic study.[15] Governor King described Pemulwuy as a terrible pest but a brave independent character. To label him a pest was grave injustice to a man, who for more than thirteen years fought unequal battles to save his ancestral land. Native resistance against white settlements faded away after Pemulwuy's death. His son Tedbury was captured a few years later. Moorhead adds a poignant note to the despair of natives. "They thought that their tribal hunting grounds were their own, and one day they found that this was not so, that they owned nothing, that they had virtually no rights of any kind, and they were aliens in their own country... Bewildered and resentful, they succumbed to listless serfdom."[16] It was beyond the capacity of white people to judge the agony of those who had lost everything.

Hopes of natives saving their lands in New South Wales dimmed with each passing day as more and more land-hungry free settlers, squatters, and bush rangers, poured into the area. Price empathized with the natives who faced the menace of white occupation, conducted in some cases by depraved invaders. The coastal aborigines (natives) withered away rapidly. Evidence on slaughter, land robbery and diseases is indisputable.[17] Starving natives endured brutal reprisals whenever they ventured to steal an odd sheep from the settlers. One such event led to the Waterloo Creek Massacre, also known as Australia-Day Massacre because it occurred on 26th January 1838. Lieutenant Colonel Kenneth Snodgrass, acting Governor of New South Wales, provoked this tragedy. Snodgrass, himself a squatter, owned a large herd of cattle which freely browsed on lands that were the life line of the local natives. He accused them of spearing his cattle and dispatched a punitive expedition of mounted police from Sydney under the command of Major James Nunn. This party of three troopers and volunteers carried out slaughter campaign for 53 days. A camp of gentle, advanced Kamilaroi tribe at Waterloo Creek was attacked and almost wiped out. Major Nunn himself boasted of hundreds killed. In another incident of 11th April 1838, natives resisted dislocation. They attacked a party of 18 employees of George and William Faithful who were searching new pasture land south of Wangaratta. Eight Europeans were killed. This was a reprisal attack to avenge the earlier killing of natives by the stockmen. Brutal punishment raids, called the Faithful Massacres, left several miles long trails of blood, burnt or buried natives as witness to the horrible crimes.

It was after the Myall Creek massacre of natives on 10th June 1838 that the law took cognizance of crimes by the Europeans. Governor Thomas Brisbane had abandoned the natives to their fate. The cruel conduct of the white settlers worsened. Brisbane proclaimed martial law in 1824 in a part of the Cape York Peninsula. Natives were killed like wild game. Trigger-happy settlers were further emboldened when Governor Ralph Darling authorized them to punish natives on their own. That was unlike Arthur Phillip's policy of treating them with amity. Darling was a votary of meeting force with force. A fall out was the Myall Creek massacre perpetrated by twelve stockmen at a farm near Bingara in northern New South Wales. The stockmen rounded up twenty-eight innocent natives including old men, women and children camping near the place where their relatives were working with station manager William Hobbs. In an orgy of cruelty natives were dragged to the nearest bush, killed, and their bodies were burnt. The incident came to the notice of the then Governor George Gipps who ordered a full investigation ignoring the resistance of the settlers. Eleven culprits were prosecuted but they got off scot-free due to the dubious role of the local magistrate. Seven of them faced retrial before chief justice James Dowling. They were found guilty notwithstanding strong defence arranged by the association of stockmen and land owners. They were sentenced to be hanged. The hanging of the condemned men caused an outrage in Sydney. That trial, however, reminded the white population that they were not immune to the English law. By this time diseases and indiscriminate killings by the Europeans had drastically reduced the native population. Native's hopes of retrieving their lands in New South Wales ended in 1861, when each free settler could choose up to 300 acres of land under Crown Lands Act 1861. This Act simultaneously barred the natives from the use of Crown lands.

In 1791, a Royal Navy surveyor George Vancouver obtained permission to study the south west coast of 'New Holland', what is now west coast of Australia. He found a spacious harbour, named it King George Third's Sound and claimed it for Britain. Ten years later, another English explorer Matthew Flinders who circumnavigated Australia, surveyed what is now the Great Australian Bight. Flinders arrived at Fowlers Bay in January 1802. The crew met local Nyungar tribesmen who seemed very amicable. Flinders chartered the entire coast up to Sydney and explored Van Diemen's Land. In his communications to London, he called New Holland, Australia, a name that stuck to the country. France, with an academic interest in the land sent two vessels staffed with scholars of the French Institute to explore the Australian waters. Voyage of Matthew Flinders was probably set out in response to that exploration.

Britain suspected its traditional adversary France out to settle unexplored parts of Australia. It instructed Governor Ralph Darling to watch French moves. Darling deputed Major Edmund Lockyer along with 23 convicts and 20 soldiers to establish a military post at King George the Third's Sound (now Albany). Lockyer was instructed to inform the French about British control over New Holland, should they attempt to set up a French settlement. In 1827, Lockyer was granted 2560 acres of land but by 1853 he expanded his ownership to 11810 acres. There is little doubt that he hounded out or outright killed the natives in order to occupy those lands. Another Englishman, James Sterling, surveyed the Swan River on the west coast and in 1829 founded the Swan River Colony. He promoted the idea of a free settlement colony in the Swan River area under his governorship. Lurking fear of the French made the Government to give over large parcels of land to persons like James Sterling, Charles Freemantle and Thomas Peel, to reward their service to Britain. Peel who had arrived from England with 300 people received 250,000 acres of land. These land allotments pushed out the natives to areas too poor in resources for their sustenance. Still, Peel lost no chance to provoke them into retaliation. About 10,000 natives lived on fertile lands of Western Australia endowed with good water resources. Inevitable skirmishes with settlers erupted in 1830. In 1832, Lieutenant Governor Sterling ordered all settlers to take suitable measures for self-protection because hungry natives were in a 'do or die' disposition. In April 1832, Calyute, a Nyungar resistance leader, accompanied by about two dozen of his tribe, raided a flour mill and stole flour. In retaliatory expedition enjoined by Peel, Calyute and two others were captured and publicly flogged at Perth. Calyute received 60 lashes and was imprisoned until 10th June 1834. After his release Calyute, aggrieved over his humiliation, raided Peel's place and killed his servant. Captain Sterling with a party of 25 settlers and soldiers ambushed a native camp. Out of 60 to 80 natives one half of males were killed. Calyute escaped but women and children were captured. Killing of natives continued unabated. In 1864, a punitive party, specifically instructed to avoid hostile course, had to be censored for shooting 18 natives to death. Yet in 1868 another punitive expedition killed four and injured up to eight natives unnoticedly.[18] Police, settlers, and officials continued the pogrom regardless of the law against killing the natives.

Victoria region of Australia was explored by George Bass in 1797, independently of Flinders. Port Phillip Bay was formally taken over for penal settlement and to deny any room to the French in Australia. In 1803, Lieutenant David Collins, one of the founders of the first penal settlement, led an expedition to Port Phillip. He worked hard to find a settlement at Sullivan Bay, but the site was abandoned due to harsh living conditions. Collins moved on to Van Diemen's Land. The British were anxious to settle this area to forestall any move by the French expedition that had surfaced near the coast. Britain detested the French presence even in those areas where monetary considerations prevented colonisation. Governor Richard Bourke sent a party of convicts to Western Port, a few miles east of Port Phillip. Their colony survived due to the perseverance of the James and Edward Hunty family who had moved there in 1834 without permission. Population of migrants in Port Phillip had risen to 90,000 by 1850 when it was accorded the status of a new district of the New South Wales.

Until 1851, distinguished Englishmen were in the forefront of usurping native lands. They either killed or pushed the natives to remote areas. John G. Robertson, a botanist turned pastoralist and squatter in the Wando Vale area, wrote in his journal of 1841 about the massacre of 51 natives at the hummocks known as Fighting Hills. The killers were the Whyte brothers of Portland Bay area and their three employees. The victims included men, women and children. Only one person survived the carnage. Curiously one of the killers, John Whyte travelled to Melbourne to inform Governor La Trobe of the massacre. No one was prosecuted for the crime. Even if the Whyte brothers had been prosecuted, they were bound to be set free because, at the time, natives could not testify in the courts of law. Discovery of gold in Victoria attracted large number of prospectors and pastoralists from other colonies. By 1854, people from Britain, Europe, America and even China swelled the local population to 300,000. The squatters, who owned cattle and sheep, cleared the land of what they called "human vermin" to make room for grazing their stock. Population of the natives slumped from 10,000 in the pre-settlement period to barely 2000 by 1863. Demoralized unfortunate natives ended up in reservations like Coranderrk. This 5000-acre hilly place was the last refuge of the Kulin natives of central Victoria. In 1867, government decided to sell this land and ask the natives to move elsewhere. Natives were now conscious of their rights and had gained the sympathy of some white residents. Anne Fraser Bon, widow of a wealthy pastoralist, protested that the government plan was meant to rob the natives of their hunting and fishing grounds. Such sympathetic voices were ignored. Kulin were denied justice to which they were entitled as British subjects.[19] They could only save one half acre of land under their cemetery.

Queensland was considered for settlement after settlers of the overcrowded New South Wales petitioned the governor to settle the worst convicts of the colony elsewhere. In 1824, Surveyor-General John Oxley selected Red Cliff Point in the Moreton Bay. This settlement was eventually shifted to Brisbane. In 1851 Queensland was made a separate colony. Here too convict population and new settlers began usurping lands where natives had lived for generations. Many natives perished while resisting land take-over and due to diseases, they contracted from the Europeans. The survivors were coaxed by laid-off members of the police force to join them in attacking the property of one prominent settler Horatio Wills. They murdered 18 white men, women and children including Wills. This act was tragic because the deceased Horatio Wills had full faith in the natives and employed them on his estate. Natives were agitated because some convict workers had seized their women folk for merry making. In the punitive expedition that followed, whites shot scores of native men, women and children, each one bragging about number of "niggers" they killed.

South Australia province was carved out of New South Wales after adding to it the unorganized territory between this province and West Australia. This area was home to 10,000 peaceful natives. They were left sulking when pushed out by the pastoralists. One native tribe of Nyungars regarded foreigners as invaders. Their title on native lands was compromised under the Foundation Act of 1834 which declared their traditional lands unoccupied wastes. Forced eviction evoked fierce resistance. Natives who attacked pastoralists bore brutal retribution. In 1850 there were 38000 European immigrants in the area when South Australia became Crown colony. Northern territory remained unorganized until 1863 when its administration was entrusted to South Australia. Population of the territory became a bit cosmopolitan due to influx of the Chinese labour and floating population of miners who included indentured labour from the tribal islands. The heterogeneous nature of the population gave rise to tension among natives due to molestation of their women. The natives who protested were killed.

Van Diemen's Land enacted wholesale pogrom of natives. In 1803, Lieutenant John Bowman landed here with 50 convicts and crew. They established the first convict settlement on the left bank of Derwent River. This settlement was abandoned the following year in favour of Hobart. Lieutenant David Collins came from England to select another site for a penal settlement. He also took charge of the Hobart colony. Van Diemen's Land, named Tasmania in 1856, became a major destination for British convicts. Pastoralist surge to the island increased its population to 75,000. Van Diemen's company was allotted 250,000 acres of land for colonisation. This land belonged to Tasmanian natives who were soon to be thrown out of their heritage. Land holders employed hardened criminal countrymen to secure their stock. These convicts carried away native women and gunned down retaliating natives. A station owner kept a harem of native women for himself and his men.[20] While stock keepers and convicts escaped punishment, British Law unfairly awarded death sentences to the natives. The latter always at the receiving end never forgot the Risdon outpost massacre of 1804. Even Governor George Arthur acknowledged that the Risdon massacre was the sole cause of trouble. This massacre was perpetrated upon 300 native men, women and children who were fired upon by soldiers while the former were chasing kangaroos. Though the natives were peaceable, military men lost their heads and shot about 50 people of all ages. This atrocity was the cause of future native reprisals against the settlers.[21] Perpetrator of the crime was the local in-charge Lieutenant William Moore, who on the morning of 3rd May 1804, while under the influence of alcohol, desired rifle practice on a moving object, i.e., fleeing natives. Hunting and killing of natives of Van Diemen's Land was nothing short of genocide. It was most shocking of all chapters in the history of British Empire.[22] Natives promptly retaliated and attacked solitary whites. In 1830, the governor asked the white population including convicts to cordon the colony from the East and shove natives towards the Tasman peninsula. This expensive operation nicknamed "black line" failed because convicts were disinterested in the job. In 1835, George Robinson, a preacher, persuaded surviving natives to move to Flinders Island. Price recorded the agony of homeless natives driven out of their abodes. "Every morning at sunrise parties of these unfortunates climbed a hill raised their arms, cried with tears on their faces bemoaning that the country belonged to them".[23] The governor was blamed for his insensitivity towards the natives and recalled. Tired and disillusioned natives had lost the zest for survival. Their population declined rapidly, and the last full-blooded Tasmanian passed away in 1876. New South Wales, Victoria, Tasmania, and South Australia, got legislative councils under the Colonies Act of 1850 but voting rights were restricted to the white males. In due course other colonies had their own parliaments. In 1890, the six colonies discussed a possible model and framed a constitution. Draft of the constitution was prepared and approved. It was adopted in 1901 when Australia became a federation. In 1911, Northern territory also joined the Commonwealth of Australia. Australia has since prospered but original inhabitants do not share this prosperity. The only relief to almost extinct native tribes came in 1992 when, in a petition by one Eddie Mbo, the Australian High Court with a five to one majority, overruled pretention of Australia being *terra nullius* at the time of British occupation. The natives had shed their blood to protect title to their land which was denied to them. Tragically, neither natives nor Eddie Mbo were there to rejoice this redemption.

Adams gave an interesting twist to the British colonisation of Australia when he connected American independence with the future history of the South Pacific and Africa. He argued that, had England still possessed most of North American continent, it was certain that Australia and New Zealand would have fallen to France and English occupation of Africa would have been extremely difficult, if not impossible. No colonist venture would have been made if England had not lost her thirteen colonies. It was an outlet for criminal population which she was seeking, and the colony she then established was the 'famous or infamous' Botany Bay.[24]

New Zealand. In 1642, a Dutch explorer Abel Tasman visited these unnamed islands. Dutch cartographers mapped these islands in 1645 and named them Nova Zelandia. During his 1769 voyage of the South Pacific, Captain James Cook named the islands New Zealand and claimed them for England. At the time, New Zealand was home to the people of Polynesian-Melanesian descent whose ancestors arrived there possibly from other islands few centuries ago. Gradually, the New Zealanders established a distinct culture. The British hesitated to lay outright claim over the territory because such an ambition required the straightway conquest or a land deal with the natives. The British colonial administration, conscious of the evils of penal settlements in Australia, refused to consider colonisation of New Zealand. The colonial secretary Lord Glenelg spoke of Great Britain having no legal or moral right to set up a colony in that country.[25] Moreover Britain refrained from warfare in a far-off place. European sealers lived in temporary stations for trade contacts with the natives. In addition to sealers, whalers, escaped British convicts, and crews of wrecked ships, built shelters along the coast.

Passing European vessels visited the Islands to obtain local timber for ship masts. They bartered goods for local flax. This small-time trade started a viable European settlement in the Bay of Islands. Behaviour of Europeans toward the natives was cruel and deceitful. One Samuel Mersden, a chaplain of the London Missionary Society in Sydney, landed in New Zealand in 1814. He founded the first Anglican mission, but failed to influence ways of native worship. Another clergyman, Henry Williams, joined Mersden in 1823. By 1850 they succeeded in gathering a sizeable following among the natives. New Zealand natives called 'Maoris' addressed the whites 'Pakeha'.

Maoris were settled in different islands of the country and localities depending on their lineage and social structure. Native tribes commonly fought each other over their jurisdiction. These fights were settled with less lethal traditional weapons until Europeans introduced them to muskets which took heavy toll of native lives during intertribal conflicts. In 1821, Hongi Hika, chief of the largest native tribe of North Island Ngapuhi bought 300 muskets from Sydney while returning from a visit to England sponsored by Mersden. His tribe used muskets to browbeat various tribes around present-day Auckland. In 1822 Ngapuhi tribe invaded Waikato forcing Te Rauparah and his tribe of Ngati Toa to migrate towards South Island. In 1824 Ngati Toa leader Te Puhi Kupe also travelled to England and on return bought arms from Sydney.[26] Meanwhile, the power of Ngapuhi declined with death of Hongi Hika in 1828.Te Rauparah used muskets to spill a lot of blood in the South Island. His campaigns against other tribes lasted several years. South Island was a stronghold of Ngai Tahu[26] tribe. Hence Ngati Toa suffered much loss of life. In retaliation, Te Rauparah conspired with English captain John Stewart of brig Elizabeth, who hid his armed men in the vessel, and attacked the Ngai Tahu tribe as soon as the vessel anchored at Akaroa harbour near their village. Dozens of the tribe were killed and their chief Maiharanui was handcuffed and detained along with his family in the captain's cabin. They were butchered and cooked while the crew watched.[27] For his part in the conspiracy, Stewart was promised cargo of flax. This was first instance of a European vessel and its crew aiding in deception and intertribal bloodshed in New Zealand. John Stewart was arraigned in Sydney as an accomplice to the murder of natives, but he escaped conviction.

Tribal warfare encouraged gun running between Sydney and land speculators from Australia and England who had joined in the plunder of New Zealand. Land speculators treated the resentful Maoris maliciously. British Government disliked actions of these land sharks and misdemeanour of John Stewart. At the same time, the British were wary of lurking French missions. Protestant missionaries relieved anxiety of their government. In 1831, they persuaded the Maoris to petition the British government for keeping the French out of New Zealand. In 1823 the governor of New South Wales responded by appointing James Busby, a civil engineer, as British Resident to the Bay of Islands. Busby had no administrative powers or force at his command beyond some control over local chiefs, missionaries and European settlers. He had no capacity to control the lower class of settlers or to stop them from selling firearms and liquor in exchange for Maori girls.[28] Maori chiefs themselves resented any notion of British lordship over them. But their fortunes took an ominous turn. Edward Wakefield, a disgraced British colonial enthusiast, who had helped in white settlement of South Australia, founded the New Zealand Company in London. He prodded the British Government to colonise New Zealand claiming it to be the best place for the white people. The then government in London showed no zeal because it preferred commerce over territory. Undeterred, Wakefield purchased a vessel Tory, and on 5th May 1839 dispatched it hurriedly to New Zealand. It had prospective settlers onboard led by his brother William Wakefield. The Home Office failed to abort the move in time. The vessel landed unhampered at Wanganui on 20th September 1839. The visitors established a settlement at Petone on the Hutt River. British colonial secretary was obliged to enforce some sort of order in the new settlement. He appointed Captain William Hobson as lieutenant governor of the New Zealand territories under the governor of New South Wales, Australia. Hobson was also asked to persuade Maori chiefs to accept British sovereignty on at least a part of New Zealand and accept the British queen, as their sovereign. In 1890 a French naval frigate arrived at the Bay of Islands. Its commander involuntarily disclosed French plans for the South Islands. In a pre-emptive move Hobson annexed South Island by right of discovery.[29]

On 22nd January 1840, another party of 150 settlers arrived aboard Aurora. William Wakefield had purchased 200,000 acres of land from Maori chiefs like Te Rauparah for their settlement. Purchased land was located on both sides of Cook's strait in North and South Islands. The deal safe-guarded possible blockage of transaction by the British government. Town of Willington was founded on the southern tip of North Island. Several shiploads of immigrants landed there. Hobson used the clout of the missionaries, who had since reconciled to colonisation of the country, in persuading Maori chiefs into signing a treaty with Britain. Missionaries prepared a draft of the treaty in English, and then a Maori version was prepared for the Maori chiefs by missionary Henry Williams and his son. Maori translation of the treaty was signed on 6th February 1840 at Waitangi by 46 Maori chiefs including Hone Keka of Nga Puhi tribe of North Island. Subsequently more Maori chiefs came forward to put their mark on the document as a token of their signature. The Treaty of Waitangi which became the basis of British occupation of New Zealand contained only three articles. The most important clause implied that Maoris transfer their sovereignty to the British queen. Maoris contested the treaty as soon as they perceived the literal meaning of the clause. Simple-minded Maoris were given to understand that the treaty guaranteed them continued lordship over their lands. The treaty also provided that should any tribe wish to sell their land, the British held the sole right to purchase it. Both parties contested these clauses based on their own interpretation of Maori and English versions of the treaty.

Wakefield began to establish a kind of self-rule in his settlements, but Hobson regarded his actions treasonable. In a quick move on 21st May 1840, the Lieutenant Governor declared British sovereignty over New Zealand and in 1841 made Auckland its capital. The Treaty of Waitangi stirred up passions when settlers needed more land, but Maoris refused to oblige them. Settlers invoked the English version of the Treaty of Waitangi to be challenged by the natives. In reality Maori chiefs had put their sign mark on the dotted line of the hastily drafted Maori version of the document on assurance of the missionaries. Moreover, all chiefs were not party to the treaty. Some of them were never approached and others had refused to sign it. Maoris claimed absolute ownership of their lands. They declared that under no circumstances they could sub-serve anyone much less a white queen. The settlers swore upon the English text of the treaty. English version legitimated their otherwise illegal settlements, based upon contrived consent of the natives and Crown's power of pre-emption vested in the treaty. Edward Wakefield even sneered at the so called treaty's web of imbecility.[30] Joseph Somes, deputy governor of New Zealand Company ridiculed the treaty: "We have always had very serious doubts whether the Treaty of Waitangi made together with naked savages by a consul invested with no plenipotentiary powers, without ratification by the Crown, could be treated by lawyers as anything but a praiseworthy device for amusing and pacifying savages for the moment."[31] The English version was indeed a clever device to pacify the easily-exited Maoris who now believed that the language of the treaty was manipulated to hoodwink them. The draft was translated by missionaries the way they comprehended the Maori language. Little wonder Maoris continued to affirm never having signed away ownership of their lands.

In 1840, the population of the English settlement of Port Nicholson rose to 40,000. After 1860, its location was changed to present-day Wellington. Land-hungry settlers let loose their cattle on native lands. The Maoris who venerated land, resented this action. Nevertheless, the British government was obligated to accommodate new arrivals. It ignored controversy over the Treaty of Waitangi, and appropriated more and more Maori lands regardless of native resentment. Disputes erupted to the point of open defiance by the Maoris. Hone Heke, the Nga Puhi chief and signatory to the treaty of Waitangi chopped off the British flagpole at Kororareka (later Russel) to show his defiance. This action was repeated whenever the flag was replaced until, in 1845, British troops moved against this chief on the North Island. Hone Heke challenged the British for two years before he was defeated due to treachery of a pro-government Maori chief. Land speculators continued to nibble on Maori lands. Land deals carried out between 1844 and 1847 incited uprisings against the Europeans. Maoris accepted trade relations with Europeans but were determined to save the lands they held sacred. In fact, Maori lands were not held by individuals but by the respective tribes. The natives of South Pacific Islands and the Americas also considered their landed heritage sacred and hence indivisible into personal property. Europeans wrongly declared their lands *terra nullius*. The 1846 Royal Proclamation of land use abolished Maori claim over lands. In 1848, Governor George Grey purchased 20 million acres of land for the Canterbury settlement. Within ten years commissioners purchased the entire South Island to extinguish its native title and exert Crown's claim over country lands. Maoris retaliated by espousing nationalistic feelings. In their 1854 assembly at Manawa pa in the southern Taranaki region of Northern Island, they resolved to get rid of white supremacy in their lives and have their own king with stature equal to the British queen to deal with whites on equal terms. In 1858 they crowned Te Wherowhero Potatau as Maori king or Kingitanga for stopping the alienation of Maori lands. Meanwhile Governor Thomas Gore Browne struck a deal with a Maori chief in respect of land near the mouth of the Waitara River. The Maoris objected to the deal because they held that land rights were vested in the tribe and not in an individual. Wiremu Kingi, Maori chief of the Te Atiawa tribe who had participated in the election of the Maori King, opposed the Waitara land deal and defended word of Maoris not to sell their lands. He, in alliance with King Wherowhero, opposed the Waitara purchase. The Governor perceived Kingitanga movement and opposition to Waitara purchase, acts of rebellion on the part of a section of Maoris. In July 1860 he persuaded Maori chiefs, not part of Kingitanga, to attend a conference; swear allegiance to the Crown and join in opposing Kingitanga. Browne coaxed white settlers into opening a war front against the Kingites over the issue of Waitara land deal. It was too late when George Grey returned as governor because battle lines had already been drawn. Punitive expeditions alienated moderate Maoris who joined ranks with Kingites. Still 2000 Maori fighters stood no chance when pitted against 10,000 well-armed regular troops and an equal number of white colonists. British superiority in men and arms decided the outcome in their favour. The Maoris lost one and a half million acres of land between 1863 and 1866. The governor expelled all those Maoris, who refused allegiance to the British queen, from British held territories. In 1865 a native land court was established to legalise individual claims to the tribal community lands. This was a clever action to divide the Maori community and to facilitate land purchases by white settlers through the court. Maoris again took up arms because they held their lands so sacred that they would lay their lives down to protect them. They chose guerrilla warfare against their adversary. In 1869, they stood up to the British in a pa (fort) near a village Orakau in the Waikato district. British forces relentlessly shelled this fort. Besieged Maoris ran out of ammunition. In desperation they began pelting stones and pieces of wood towards the British. British General Duncan Cameron asked them to surrender but defiant Maoris shouted back that they will fight forever. Finally, beaten by thirst and hunger, the Maoris opened gates of the Pa. About one half of besieged men, women and children escaped while the other half lay dead from artillery fire.

General Trevor Chute, who succeeded General Cameron, wanted complete annihilation of what he perceived a tribal aberration among them. Thus, an aggressor became arbiter of native heritage. It was a difficult task because natives were fighting for their "sacred" ancestral land. Twenty thousand whites of various denominations, fought for twelve years against them, often escaping certain defeat. In the end, however, Maoris, worn out by struggle against their formidable foe, were subdued to the advantage of "Pakeha", who remorselessly usurped native lands. By 1896, the white population of New Zealand exceeded 700,000. Appetite for land grew correspondingly. Despite clear cut civil cases, Maoris could not protect sovereignty over native lands as guaranteed by their version of the Treaty of Waitangi. Ever since this treaty is a favourite subject of discussion whenever rights of natives are debated.[32]

Tahiti. Tahiti, though a small land mass, was a conspicuous member of the Society Islands lying in the South Pacific Ocean. Like Australasia, it escaped the prying eyes of the European nations for centuries. Beginning with the 1567 voyage of Spanish navigator Alvaro de Mendana, who discovered the Solomon Islands, Spanish ships sailed past the Society Islands in search of the then mythical southern continent. A Spanish ship sighted Tahiti in 1606 but Spain had no interest in the Island. English captain Samuel Willis was the first European to touch Tahiti shores on 18th June 1767. His ship HMS Dolphin anchored at the Matavai Bay. Natives, who gathered there though surprised to encounter a white man, were friendly. But for reasons best known to them, they attacked the crew when they came ashore. They were beaten back. The natives regrouped on 26th June. Willis ordered a barrage of canon fire from the Dolphin. Thereafter he destroyed the canoes and houses of the natives. Willis claimed the island for Britain in the name of King George and sailed away opening the island for future English voyagers. On 2nd April 1768, a French explorer Louis Antoine de Bougainville visited Tahiti. He made the island famous in Europe through narratives of his voyage and description of the Islanders. He called the natives innocent and very different from the corrupt Europeans. Bougainville was ignorant of the earlier visit and actions of British Samuel Wallis. He too claimed the Island for his own country. On 13th April 1769, British explorer, James Cook reached Tahiti on a mission of the Lord of Admiralty for viewing transit of Venus on 3rd June 1769, followed by a search for the famous southern continent. Those were the times when France had lost her territory of Quebec in the seven-year Anglo-French war. Both nations were scouting for new colonies. British invariably tiptoed French expeditions to thwart possible colonisation moves on their part. Cook apprehended this when he was camped at Matavai Bay. He left for the second part of his mission wishing that natives were left alone from the curse of colonialism.

Tahiti was home to Polynesians who arrived there during the early centuries of the Christian era. Their earlier home might have been the Tonga and Samoa Islands and even present-day Philippines and Indonesia. Tahiti society included several tribes each having a highly respected ruling family. They were a happy lot before foreign ships began visiting the Islands. Europeans exposed them to a variety of infectious diseases and vices like alcohol and prostitution which were alien to them. Tahitians were not immune to European diseases like typhus, smallpox, influenza etc. These diseases killed so many natives that by 1797 their population was reduced to 16000. The population picked up again after touching bottom. In 1907 it rested at 30,000. After Cook, Lieutenant William Bligh reached Tahiti on 25th October 1788 aboard the Bounty. The crew spent several weeks on the island and one of the crew even married a native girl. In 1797 preachers of the London Missionary Society followed these sailors. Within few years they disturbed the traditional ways of Tahitian life. In 1834, two French missionaries also landed in Tahiti on a mission to convert non-Christians as well as Protestants to the Roman Catholic faith. Consequently, Tahitian society had to contend with adherents of two conflicting Christian faiths. French priests braved well-entrenched English missionaries who held sway over the local government. George Pritchard, the British Chancellor to Tahiti Queen Pomare intervened on behalf of Protestant missionaries. On 12th December 1836, the queen expelled French missionaries from Tahiti. King Louis Phillip of France responded immediately. He dispatched a frigate to Tahiti capital Papeete carrying an ultimatum to which the queen meekly acquiesced. Pritchard and Protestant missionaries tried hard to recover the lost ground. They persuaded Queen Pomare to address an appeal to Queen Victoria seeking British protection. The French king swiftly reacted to this move and dispatched another warship to Tahiti in 1839. The French demanded that the queen surrender. Protestant missionaries lost official support when Queen Victoria refused to intervene. Finally, native chiefs had to choose between France and Britain. In 1841 they assembled without reaching a decision. The chiefs met again the following year. Meantime more French troops had landed in Tahiti. The chiefs sent a message to French Admiral Abel Du Petit-Thousars seeking French protection. At the time, the British consul to Queen Pomare was away in England. He returned and waged a war against the French. Pritchard forced the queen to abjure French authority. In November 1843, Admiral Thousars lost his cool, landed French troops, took possession of the Island, deposed the queen, arrested Pritchard and had him expelled from Tahiti. Religious intolerance of English missionaries forced Thousars to act on his own. Queen Pomare became an unwilling victim of attrition between the two European nations. She took refuge on the British ship. Unhappy natives took up arms against the French until 1855, but superior French arms mowed them down. A helpless Queen Pomare refused to return to her land. Tahiti remained a French protectorate until 29th June 1880. Finally, king Pomare V was compelled to accept French sovereignty over Tahiti and her dependencies. In 1946 Tahiti and the whole of French Polynesia, comprising 118 islands became French territory with Papeete as the capital.

Chapter 4
Europe's Trespass to Plunder China

An overbearing imperial West outflanked, choked and pillaged a sovereign nation simply because it refused to trade with them. China at the time was possibly the richest nation on earth in terms of gross domestic product (GDP) with a self-sustaining economy. In fact, China and India together accounted for more than half of the world's wealth. These were two great civilizations of the world before the Westerners intruded on their lives.[1] China had advanced in ship building and her sailors reached distant lands when it decided to abolish long-distance trade. It was least interested in Japanese or European goods. Quing dynasty (1644-1912) was isolationist. It exported tea, silks and porcelain to Europe but shunned Western goods because it had no demand for them. China had the capacity to buy European products, but her government persisted that all Western products were inferior and there was no purpose to trade with the West.[2] Commercial aspirations of British merchant companies like William Jardine and James Mathason induced the East India Company (EIC) to sell opium to the Chinese for reducing trade imbalance caused by imports of tea. China, famous for her tea, began its cultivation as a medicinal beverage between A.D. 400 and 600. Outlet for her tea was Portugal who monopolized trade between China and Europe from her bases of Goa in India and Macao Island (Macau) in the southern China Sea. Britain became fond of tea after 1664 when King Charles received a gift of two pounds of Chinese tea. In due course tea became an important trade commodity owing to its popularity in England and Europe as a relaxant.[3] By 1669, the East India Company (EIC) became sole tea importer into Britain. Gradually annual tea imports into Britain exceeded 800,000 pounds. EIC bought tea from China but her own merchandise did not find a good market in that country.[4] Britons also fancied Chinese silks and porcelain. All British imports were against British silver whose exodus could not be balanced because China avoided imports claiming that she was self-reliant and had no appetite for 'inferior' quality British goods. In essence, China shunned close contact with foreigners especially traders, and EIC was a company of traders. Maximum liberty allowed by China was to trade with Portugal from the Portuguese enclave of Macau some 75 miles downstream of Canton (Guangzhou). China relented following consistent pressure of western nations to open access to Canton (Guangzhou) port in the Pearl River delta. China introduced a strict regimented protocol. The port could not be accessed by ships hoisting foreign flags and all foreigners required a passport before proceeding to Canton. The EIC was however allowed a trade mission consisting of twelve super cargos (trade supervisors) based in the Canton port. The company spent as much as 100,000 British pounds per annum to operate the facility. Her super cargos operated only through authorized Chinese merchants or Co-hongs (Hongs for individuals). Hongs acted on behalf of the Chinese government. EIC ships had to anchor at Linton Island, where they were inspected by Hongs who levied and collected custom duty. In practice Linton Island located in the estuary of Pearl River was the British trading post with storage facilities.

Burgeoning imports of tea, silks and porcelain into Britain, compared with nominal export of goods to China, caused huge trade deficit and exodus of British silver. China did not want any British goods but silver for her tea.[5] On the other hand the EIC was obliged to bring back equivalent quantity of silver it expended in China. To the discomfort of the company, the value of gold and silver inflated while the price of tea it sold to Europe increased only marginally. The British government required a steady supply of tea as a source of revenue because British exchequer levied 100 percent tax on its import. Britain collected around three million pounds tariff enough to meet 50 percent of expenses of her naval fleet which was then the best in the world[6]. The EIC which held the monopoly on all Eastern trade, and hence on all tea brought into Britain, was anxious to bridge annual trade deficit with China which exceeded 250,000 pounds sterling by turn of the nineteenth century.

The EIC found that the Portuguese earned huge profits from opium they smuggled out of Goa and into China. The company calculated that the operation of clandestine opium trade through smuggling would solve their balance of payment predicament. It controlled vast plains of India where opium poppy could replace food grain crops grown by peasants to feed their families. Company minions commanded peasants to shift to poppy cultivation for producing opium. Peasants were forced to sell each gram of opium they produced at a price fixed by the company. The company ensured that every particle of the produce was handed over to her. The drug was annually auctioned at Calcutta (Kolkata) at a huge profit. A chest of Bengal opium which cost the company 280 Indian rupees was sold for upwards of 900 rupees leaving a huge margin of profit. Such was the pace of opium cultivation in India that, within 15 years, revenue receipts of the EIC increased from 78,517 pounds sterling in 1834–35 to 3,309,637 pounds sterling in 1849–50.[7] Thus the great Christian nation embarked upon producing and smuggling this deadly poison into the unwilling country.[8] The EIC-licensed ships smuggled opium into Linton Island from where it was taken over by the Chinese smugglers who clandestinely sold it to the Chinese public. The EIC earned income both from tax on Indian growers and from auction of the contraband in Calcutta. By 1839, company opium out of Patna and Benares (now Varanasi) was highly valued in China. The EIC devised an ingenious method to smuggle her opium into China while maintaining an unsullied reputation with senior Chinese officials. This perfidy was performed through third-party trade. The company issued licenses to Indian peasants to grow poppy and supply the produce at a price fixed by the company. The EIC auctioned opium in the Calcutta market for four-fold of the amount it spent in procuring the contraband. This windfall to the company was at the cost of poor Indian peasants. The profit that ran into millions of pounds sterling was a major source of income for the company next only to land revenue. Both Britain and the EIC benefitted from the illegal opium trade. The company earned 39,000 pounds sterling from opium in 1773, but her annual income surged to 250,000 pounds a decade later.

Production and sale of opium remained a valuable adjunct to the company revenues and a means to tighten her grip over India. Between 1806 and 1809, the Chinese public bought seven million pounds sterling worth of the company contraband. Consequently, the balance of trade between China and Britain was reversed. Chinese imports of opium, copper, cotton etc. exceeded its exports of tea, silk etc. by 2,500,000 pounds sterling.[9] This scandalous operation was run very smoothly. By

1830 China was the only available source of tea.[10] Country merchants, usually British, who ran the trade between Calcutta and China, purchased company opium in open auction at Calcutta. Consequently, further disposal of opium was left to the country merchants while the EIC abjured all responsibility. Country merchants shipped opium to China in private ships plying under license of the EIC. These ships sailed to Linton Island north of Hong Kong. The Hongs inspected the ships to determine the nature of the cargo and custom duty to be levied while the ships were anchored at Linton. Company officials certainly knew about the cargo but left it for settlement between merchants on both sides. The Chinese officials settled and pocketed kickbacks per chest of opium. British merchants were ever cautious. They kept their hulks anchored offshore until Chinese traffickers transhipped the cargo in connivance with the local officials.

Country merchants like William Jardine and James Matheson who loathed Chinese trade protocol, wanted a free-trade regimen. As preeminent smugglers, they audaciously proclaimed that opium use gave comfort and benefit to the hard-working Chinese. The EIC instructed its super cargos to ignore them and, instead, respect Chinese rules and regulations. The company wanted to keep the Chinese in good humour while clandestinely selling around 4000 chests of opium annually. Opium sale accounted for 75 percent of the EIC trade with China. Gross amount of opium revenue in 1908–1909 was 5,885,000 pounds and net revenue 4,645,000 pounds sterling.[11] Annual imports exceeding her exports by two and half million pounds was a great drain on China's revenue, reason being the clandestine import of opium. Strachey opined that real objection of the Chinese were not to the import of opium but to the necessity of paying for that in silver.[12] Subsequent events do not support this view. Country merchants (in fact opium smugglers) sold silver coins, earned in China to the EIC in Calcutta against bankers' draft payable in London. The company super cargos took Chinese silver to London and collected bullion required for running the opium trade. This jugglery whitewashed the company's dirty money and its black deeds. In fact, the EIC feigned her inability to interfere in drug trafficking. However, their false posturing did not convince the suspecting Chinese officials.

In 1833, the British Parliament revoked EIC's monopoly on trade with China. Britain constituted a trade commission on the pattern of the company's select committee. The commission comprised a chief superintendent and two deputies besides the subordinate staff. All except the chief were drawn from the company. The new arrangement worked as long as trade went smoothly. The snag came when the British government appointed their own chief superintendent in the person of William John Napier. The latter was personally chosen by King William IV for this job. An over-confident Napier considered himself the King's Commission, somewhat higher than the position he held. He presumed that Chinese protocol followed by country merchants did not apply in his case. Accordingly, after landing at Macau on 15th July 1834, he sailed for Canton without obtaining the mandatory passport. He arrived in Canton and addressed a letter to Governor Lu Kun, the imperial representative at Canton. This was another transgression of the Canton trade protocol which forbade direct contact between foreigners and senior Chinese officials. Governor Lu informed his Emperor of Napier's breach of protocol. He ordered Napier to leave Canton and prohibited all British trade from 2nd September 1834. Consequently, Hong merchants stopped dealing with the British. Napier took the Chinese actions offensive and a slight to Britain. He wrote in his diary how it was easy to force the Chinese to open their ports for trade by deploying a blockading squadron.[13] Napier implored foreign secretary Lord Palmerston (Henry John Temple) to force China into accepting his official authority. Although Palmerston was himself a votary of gunboat diplomacy, he counselled restraint on the part of the chief superintendent. Still, Napier believed that a naval force would settle the matter. He ordered British frigates to fire on the Chinese Bogue forts that guarded entry into the Pearl River thirty miles south of Canton. The aggression failed and Napier retired to Macau where he died after a brief illness.

Charles Elliot, a former navy captain, succeeded Napier as chief superintendent. At this time China resolved to curtail opium smoking and prohibit smuggling of the contraband into the country. In March 1839, Emperor Daoguang appointed Lin Zexu as Imperial Commissioner at Canton expressly to eradicate the menace since the number of Chinese opium addicts had grown to two million. Lin ordered Chinese merchants to hand over their stocks of opium. Tons of confiscated opium was burnt in their presence. Foreign merchants were ordered to shift their opium stock away from Canton lest it is confiscated. Foreign merchants decided to defy the orders. The EIC itself was determined to ply this illegal trade. Moreover, the company had expanded the cultivation of poppy in the fertile Malwa belt of central India, and China was the most lucrative market for this contraband. On her part China had firmly resolved to stop this scandal. Commissioner Lin even appealed to Queen Victoria and the British government to end opium smuggling on moral grounds. He questioned the young queen how should the world feel if people from another country sell opium to her subjects and seduce them to smoke it. Britain ignored the appeal. In desperation Lin ordered confiscation of all ships and detention of the foreigners. Captain Elliot relented. He asked British merchants to surrender their stocks of the contraband promising them full compensation from the British government. Heeding his advice, merchants handed over 2000 chests of newly arrived opium to the Chinese. The merchants, however, refused to sign a bond to shun opium trade in future. Lin ordered methodically dumping the confiscated opium into the river at low tide. S.L. Baldwin (Ms) who spent twenty-two years at a mission in China in her *Missionary Point of View* called the event "Opium Tea Party."[14] She was highly critical of the English and American merchants involved in this illegal trade.

Troubles were mounting for China. Inebriated British sailors murdered a Chinese national at a time when opium trade had strained relations between China and Britain. Lin demanded custody of the culprits for trial in a Chinese court. Elliot argued that the seamen could only be tried under British jurisdiction. A trial was held but the convicts were supposed to receive punishment after they arrive in England. Lin regarded the trial a farce and sought surrender of the seamen. As a pressure tactic he stopped food supplies to the British ships anchored at Macau. Elliot asked all British subjects to leave Canton and sent for naval reinforcements from Calcutta. Britain considered Elliot too lenient in facing the Chinese. He was recalled. Elliot's recall was possibly engineered by the influential Jardine and Matheson Company who favoured gate-crashing China. In fact, they were the main instigators of the ensuing quarrel between China and England.[15] The British argued that seizure of their opium and its destruction was unpardonable. On 4th

September 1839, gunboats and merchant ships of Britain armed with cannons, attacked vulnerable Chinese junks. China was under the impression that the Canton system of trade was secure enough without any naval support. Hence Chinese navy consisted merely of light-weight wooden vessels sans heavy artillery. It could not resist the iron-hulled British ships ten-times heavier than the Chinese junks. Steamship Nemesis and other British ships equipped with heavy artillery and maxim guns could overawe the Chinese navy. The British flaunted their overwhelming naval strength to impose their will on the Chinese. British public opinion was systematically turned against China for allegedly non-cooperation in trade while keeping the company's illegal opium trade under wraps. Tempers flared in the British House of Commons. A man of liberal ideas, William Gladstone, castigated British government for what he called hoisting the British flag for an unjust and iniquitous war simply to protect illegal trade of an obnoxious contraband. The press as well as the Church expressed outrage. Foreign secretary Lord Palmerston offered shameless justification that British action was meant to correct the balance of payments.

Skirmishes broke out after a British frigate arrived in early November. Poorly armed wooden Chinese vessels were sitting ducks for the British navy guns. Still, for the sake of sovereignty, China opted for an unequal war. In June 1840, another expeditionary force commanded by Sir James Gordon Bremer left Singapore for China. Shallow-draft steel-hulled Nemesis of the EIC also joined the expedition. Enfeebled China refused Bremer's demand for compensation. The British marched ahead, and in January 1841 captured Bogue forts guarding the mouth of the Pearl River and high ground near Canton. Major General Huge Gough arrived in August with a mixed British Indian force to block Yangtze-Kiang River to force the Chinese to negotiate. China was defeated at several fronts. The British occupied Shanghai by the middle of 1842. In deep desperation, China sued for peace. On 29th August 1842, Chinese negotiators signed the unequal Treaty of Nanking (Nanjing) under the shadow of guns.

The Nanking Treaty (Treaty of Ports) forced China to open five ports of Canton; Amos (Xiamen), Foochow (Fuzhou), Ningpo (Ningbo), and Shanghai to the British; allow them to directly deal with any Chinese merchant; pay 21 million silver dollars as reparation for the war, pay for loss of British merchandise (mainly opium that was dumped into the river); compensate for loss of money due from the Chinese merchants; and compensation for the imprisonment of British subjects. China ceded Hong Kong to the British. The treaty did not mention opium trade, yet open access to treaty ports meant uninterrupted smuggling of the contraband. The western powers and Japan began to humiliate China. Independent British thinkers castigated opium smugglers and the British government for violent assaults on China's sovereignty. In their annual meeting, the Quakers condemned opium trade as a "great reproach of this professedly Christian nation." The Christian missionary Baldwin lamented British treatment of China. She asked, "other great protestant nation the United States": "Have we observed the Golden Rule toward a friendly nation?" Not by any means. We just bowed assent to what England did. Our merchants shared in the traffic and iniquitous indemnity forced upon China; and after the Chinese government was compelled to admit opium as an article of trade, every chief American tea firm save one, had its opium treasure-vault and made its greatest profits on sin".[16] Lord Palmerston influenced by William Jardine justified British bellicosity falsely stating that China was not sincere in its objection to opium smuggling. Atlantic Monthly carried an article "Truth about the Opium war". It referred to the British assertion that it had the righteous cause. It pointed out that opium was not the cause of war but arrogant and insupportable pretentions of China that she will hold commercial trade with the rest of the mankind, not on terms of equal reciprocity, but upon the insulting and degrading forms of relations between the landlord and vassal.[17]Arguments of the above author were controverted by another Briton Joseph Alexander.[18]

The First Opium War did not fully gratify British vanity. Britain's aim was to open all Chinese ports for international trade, free access to merchants and missionaries to the Chinese interior, and abolition of import levies. The Europeans and Americans did not merely mean to force the Chinese to trade with them in opium. They also wanted China to trade with them in general.[19] Britain urged renegotiation of the Nanking Treaty citing above British motives. An added and exceptional demand was to legalize opium import into China and allow the British ambassador to reside at Peking (Beijing) which was then a forbidden city to the foreigners. These demands were bizarre and humiliating for the government of the Qing dynasty. An incident on the open seas added to the discomfort of the Chinese government. In October 1856, Qing officials intercepted a ship "Arrow" registered in Hong Kong, to arrest a local pirate who owned the ship. The ship was flying the British flag though its registration had long expired. Chinese officials pulled down the unauthorized flag. The British consul, Harry Parks, regarded the incident an insult to their flag. Prime Minister Palmerston supported the Consul, but a number of cabinet ministers described any action morally wrong. A vexed Palmerston recommended dissolution of the Parliament. Behold subverted mindset of the British public at the time! Palmerston won the next election on this issue. All those who protested against British high-handedness, lost their seats. China had to bear brunt of morbid British conduct at the time. In 1856, a Second Opium War broke out over the Arrow incident. British forces attacked Canton through the Pearl River, captured it and burnt Chinese establishments. France also joined Britain after a French missionary lost his life in Guangxi. The war ended in 1858 when Beijing and Tianjin fell to the invaders. Chinese negotiators were forced to accept demands hurtful to their honour, sovereignty, and above all economy of their country. On 26th and 27th June 1858, they reluctantly signed the Treaty of Tianjin (Tientsin Treaty of 1858) yielding to the following; (1) Britain, France, Russia and the United States were allowed to establish their diplomatic legions in Beijing, (2) Ten additional ports would be opened for trade, (3) Western ships would freely operate in Yangtze River; (4) All foreigners including Christian missionaries would be allowed free access to the country; (5) The Qing government would pay indemnity to Britain and France and compensate British merchants for the loss of their property. Russia and the United States who were neutral observers at Tianjin also got same concessions as the belligerent European powers. China refused to ratify the treaty in view of wide-spread public outcry against its terms. The Emperor tried to exert his sovereign authority by preventing entry of foreign diplomats into Beijing. Foreign powers found enough excuses to enforce their writ. They attacked Taku (also Dagu) forts. A joint Anglo-French expeditionary force was assembled in Hong Kong. It attacked

Beijing in 1860. Chinese army was overrun. The city was plundered for days together and turned into smoke. British and French troops scaled the Summer Palace, looted and burnt it. Lord Elgin, who later became viceroy of India, ordered the complete destruction of the palace in retaliation for imprisonment of British diplomats. Allied forces spent three days in stripping the palace bare of its priceless artefacts dating from ancient Chinese civilization. The plunder lasted well into 1860.[20] The complex of palaces was burnt. Some of the looted gold and wealth was distributed among the troops, with commanders garnering the lions share. Europeans had no qualms for native sentiments when they looted and destroyed a part of their heritage. Incidentally, some of the looted statues and figurines were now returning to China.

A demoralized China again sued for peace and ratified the 1858 Treaty. Christian missionaries had the freedom to work in China. The Nanking and Tientsin treaties established Western hold on coastal China so tight that China would be forced to trade with the West on their terms. Doors were opened for free entry of opium into the country. Americans annually dumped 100 tons of Turkish opium into China, Britain brought in 5000 tons every year. Opium became an important revenue source for British India which was now directly controlled by the British Parliament. Between 1861 and 1893 China meekly obeyed diktats of foreign powers ceding them control of several territories. Russia captured the Amur River area in 1858 and two years later a maritime province of China. Japan began forcing Korea out of Chinese influence, defeated China in the 1894–95 Sino-Japanese war, and annexed Formosa (Taiwan). Subsequent to Japanese victories, Western powers too began to grab concessions from the helpless nation. France, Germany, and Russia forced their way into China through concessions.[21] In April 1865, M. Berthemy, the French envoy at Beijing, compelled the Chinese to sign the so-called Berthemy Convention granting French missionaries all kinds of land rights in China. The imperial government yielded to issue a decree granting French Bishops the same rank as viceroys and governors of Chinese government. It implied that missionaries could settle local disputes with natives at their own level rather than appeal to the Chinese government. "Behold the Christian Catholic Bishop holding court, examining witnesses, sentencing, punishing at his pleasure, ever favouring, as we too sadly know, his natives against the heathen and to him the worse Protestant heretic."[22] In 1898, Britain obtained Kowloon area on a 99-year lease and Germany got Jiao Zhou Bay on a similar lease from China. Germany had concessions in the Shandong Peninsula. Russia obtained rights, to construct Trans-Siberia railway line, through Manchuria. In short, foreign powers completely humiliated and emasculated post-war China. Woodbridge *et al* commented on the scramble for concessions; "China was being cut up like a melon."[23]

Chinese public was deeply hurt by the economic and political domination of foreigners and religious aggressiveness of the Christian missionaries. The oppressive environment bred militancy against both the government and the foreigners. A nationalist uprising spearheaded by a secret religious society (The Righteous Harmony Society) emerged and took up arms against foreigners and native Christians. The Westerners dubbed its members 'Boxers' from their clinched fists signifying protest and defiance. Boxer movement was born in the Shantung province for protection of the peasants, against robbers in times of famine. The movement lacked clear direction and objectives beyond its emphasis on general physical and moral development of the common people of China. Boxers decried increasing influence of foreigners on Chinese life, calling it corrupt and perilous. They bracketed together, British and American missionaries, German and Russian railway workers, engineers from France surveying new routes or opening mines, as plotters against peace of the Chinese civilization. Within ten years after 1885, the movement turned into a new crusade targeting Catholic missionaries. The latter had seen better days, in the aftermath of the opium wars. They now faced Boxer outrage. Berthemy Convention had opened their entry into the Chinese interior, allowed to buy land, and reside in China permanently. Protestant missionaries were relatively recent arrivals. Anti-missionary movement gained momentum. According to a 30th May 1899 report in the *New York Times*, Boxers killed nine Methodist missionaries and a large number of Chinese Christians. Heeding a warning issued by foreign powers, Empress Dowager outlawed the Boxer movement and imposed the death penalty on the rioters. The *New York Times* of 31st May 1899, named the Chinese action a farce and the promulgation on Boxer movement more as an excuse than in condemnation of the movement.

The Foreign powers refused to appreciate the brutally wounded psyche of the Chinese people and predicament of the Qing government. Traditionalist Chinese like Prince Tuan opposed any change in the order of Manchu rulers being imposed by the West. Boxers, who had sneaked into Beijing, gathered sympathizers in the public as well as in the government. The Chinese government was in a catch-22 situation. Foreign legations were in a combative mode but the Chinese government chose to ignore their warning. Foreigners flexed their muscle in the north China waters. They moved their guards from Taku to protect legations in Tianjin (Tientsin). The violently emotive boxers demanded the foreigners to quit China and leave their country to them. On 28th May 1900, they burned several railroad stations on the Tianjin-Beijing route. On 10th June they ransacked British summer legation. A Japanese diplomat was assassinated the next day. On 13th June, German minister Baron von Ketteler was killed while on his way to a meeting at the Chinese foreign office. The same day allies sent an international response force of 2000 men commanded by British Admiral Edward Seymour for the relief of Beijing. On 14th June, the Boxers began torching churches and shops selling foreign merchandise. The International relief force had to return to Tianjin under pressure from fierce Muslim troops of the Chinese army. On 17th June, foreign naval forces captured Taku forts. The Chinese government declared this an act of war and waived its neutrality vis-à-vis the Boxers. On 19th June, Empress Dowager Cixi, who ruled in the name of Emperor, declared that her country was in a state of war. Foreign legations were ordered to leave Beijing within 24 hours. The legations ignored the order. The following day combined forces of the Chinese government and Boxers began a siege of Beijing and by the second of July the barricades were pushed close to the foreign legations. Captain John Myers, as head of American, British and Russian forces, attempted to push back the barricades. Although Captain Myers was wounded in the effort, foreign forces succeeded in breaking the siege at one point. Still the siege of legations continued until 14th August when a 20,000 strong international force of eight- nation alliance, under Lt. General Alfred Gaselee, arrived from Tianjin. Allied forces captured Tianjin on 14th July and Beijing a month later when Chinese defenders, who had steadfastly maintained the siege for 55 days, were defeated. But the siege finally ended when Indian troops of the International Expeditionary Force arrived under the command of German Field Marshal Graf von Waldersee.

Field Marshal Waldersee was deputed by German Chancellor Wilhelm II. Due to his rank, his allies acknowledged him as the commander of allied forces. Kaiser's incendiary speech to the departing German soldiers, though variously interpreted, reflected his disdain of the Chinese. "When you come before the enemy, let him be struck down; there will be no mercy, prisoners will not be taken… let the name of Germany be known in China in such a way that a Chinese will never again dare even to look askance at a German". Incidentally, German troops arrived too late to take part in the warfare, but they were not behind in looting, and mopping up the country side. By 18th August, 33,343 foreign troops gathered at Taku before leaving for Beijing where they paraded on 28th August. The Chinese government pleaded for peace after the siege of Beijing. Prior to that on 19th July, when allied forces were in an assault mode, China appealed to the U.S. President William McKinley for intervention to which the latter agreed. China withdrew her troops from Beijing. Allied troops began the mopping-up operation. German soldiers, true to their Kaiser's words, flattened all villages in their way. All the inhabitants, Boxers or not, were bayoneted. An orgy of looting by soldiers, civilians and even missionaries continued in the towns. For a year long, Beijing, Tianjin and other major towns were controlled by foreign troops under the command of Waldersee. German post cards of the time depict an orgy of German violence unleashed against the Chinese. By 7th September, Boxer rebellion was effectively putdown throughout China. The Chinese sued for peace from a servile position.

The United States demanded the territorial integrity of China while preserving commercial interests and safety of U.S. citizens. Secretary of State John Hay advised European powers and Japan to occupy Beijing jointly until a viable Chinese government, capable of underwriting new treaties, was in place. After the initial hesitation, the allies agreed to talk to plenipotentiaries of the Chinese government. American representatives at the talks insisted that all those who supported Boxers, irrespective of their official status should be punished. China accepted the demand and handed over high government officials of the Emperor's court to the allies. Ranks and offices of several princes were abolished through an edict making them answerable to the allies. American advice and cooperation of the Chinese government worked. Britain and Germany agreed to guard China's integrity while protecting their gains of the earlier treaties. Negotiations were held at Beijing and it was agreed that (1) China shall impose the death penalty on guilty princes and officials; (2) Taku and other forts on the Chinese coast shall be demolished; (3) China will not import arms and war material into the country; (4) All foreign legations will be allowed permanent guards; (5) Boxers shall be suppressed throughout China for a period of two years. An imperial proclamation shall be issued to this effect; (6) Indemnity imposed on China shall include compensation for the death of Chinese staff of the foreign legations. In addition to the above, China committed herself to erect a memorial to Baron von Ketteler and apologize to Germany in the presence of a prince. China also promised reparation for the death of a Japanese diplomat. The indemnity imposed on China was 450 million teals (333 million dollars) payable over the next 39 years along with interest. The above sanctions, resulting from the Boxer uprising, meant abject humiliation for the already harried Manchu dynasty. A nation trying to protect itself from the illegal opium trade found itself in a position of extreme submission. Europeans along with the United States, Russia and surging Japan were in the driver's seat. They subjugated mainland China short of dismembering it. All of them scrambled for concessions like economic exploitation; free trade and trading concessions; religious freedom and extra territorial rights. They claimed areas of their own influence. France carved colonies of Cochin China, Tonkin and Annam (all parts of present-day Vietnam). In 1887, it declared a protectorate over Laos thereby securing for herself all the territories which collectively came to be known as Indochina. Britain which had seized Hong Kong after the First Opium War in 1860, now attached Kowloon Peninsula to it. Germany claimed Shantung Peninsula to facilitate her trade with the interior China. Japan occupied small islands and captured Taiwan, besides imposing hegemony over the Korean Peninsula. Russia secured agreement for the construction of 800-mile rail link through Manchuria in order to shorten distance between

Vladivostok in the East and Central and Western Siberia with all attendant benefits. "Every major Chinese river was patrolled by gunboats of her invaders. Hobson's apotheosis of imperialism in the crowning form of a captive China ready for extensive exploitation by a condominium of the western empires seemed the logical next step."[24] In his anti-imperialist critique Mark Twain singled out Germany. "The Kaiser went to playing the game without first mastering it. He lost a couple of missionaries in a riot in Shantung... China had to pay a hundred thousand dollars apiece for them, in money, twelve miles of territory, containing several million inhabitants, and worth twenty million dollars."[25] The concessions extracted by the Europeans badly bruised Manchu dynasty which fell to the revolutionary military uprising of 10th October 1911. Thankfully, the Chinese mainland never came under European rule. The Europeans and Japan were however relieved that the country began to break up into kingdoms of independent land lords, just as India had done after the death of Moghul emperor Aurangzeb. Finally, the Chinese Communist Party under the leadership of Mao Zedong (Mao Tse-tung) came to power. China has since progressed by leaps and bounds and has salvaged the prestige it had lost to the then overbearing Western powers.

Chapter 5
Pan-European Slicing of Africa

The Portuguese arrived at the Sierra Leone coast of Sub-Saharan Africa during time of Prince Henry the navigator (A.D 1474–1479). In 1482 they constructed Elmina Castle (Sao Jorge a Mina) at the coast of Ghana as a trading post. Portugal's monarchy fully backed adventures of discovering new lands for advancing overseas trade. Pope Nicholas V through his papal bull *Romanus Pontifex* of 1452 sanctioned Portugal's monopoly over African coastal trade, exploration, and enslavement of "infidels". Under this authority, Portugal indulged in slave trade in addition to trade in gold, ivory, and minerals. Elmina castle rose to become a famous slave trading station. Before long, trans-Atlantic slave trade introduced Africa to other European nations and the Americas. In 1485 Portugal discovered the Cape of Good Hope and pioneered the discovery of sea trade routes from Europe to the Indian Ocean. Her vessels sailed past the Cape of Good Hope which remained their port of call until 1652. The position reversed in the seventeenth century when the Dutch mastered those sea lanes and founded the first phase of colonisation in Africa.

Ships of the Dutch East India Company (VOC) sailing for India and the East Indies frequented Table Bay, an inlet to south west of the Cape. In March 1647, Dutch vessel, the Harlem, was wrecked on the Table Bay. Marooned sailors erected a sand shelter where they stayed until their rescue a year later. This shelter was first temporary European encampment on the Cape. Dutch sailors survived the ordeal thanks to customary hospitality extended by the Khoi Khoi African tribes of the area. The Dutch abused the friendliness of the natives when they built a halting-cum-trading post at the Cape in the form of a mud fort. Unsuspecting friendly natives soon discovered the difference in their way of life and that of the Europeans.[1] This gulf eventually spelled doom for them. Soon a group of 90 settlers under the command of Jan van

106

Riebeeck arrived for permanent settlement on the shore of the Table Bay. Their colony came up in 1671, after they seized lands of trusting Khoi natives of the Cape, whom the Dutch called Hottentots. They fenced this land to keep out the Khoi Khoi claiming that they had conquered this land. More settlers arrived to increase the population of the Cape to 1500. Of necessity, the Dutch began filching more and more land for the new arrivals and for growing vegetables and fruits to restock vessels bound for the East Indies. Dutch soldiers even talked of killing or expelling natives from their pastures, capture their cattle, and use those lands for planting more orchards.

The British captured the Dutch bastion of Cape Town in 1795. As was their wont they wanted to deny a sea route between Europe and the East to the French. Cape Town was briefly returned to the Dutch but, recaptured in 1914 for good. This town had remained an important transit and restocking station for visiting ships of the Dutch East India Company for many years. Later on, it became capital of the Cape Colony and finally of the Republic of South Africa. The Dutch and some French and German residents of the Cape took to ranching. They seized pastures and cattle of the natives. European farm commandos captured cattle of even well-off Hottentots. Destitute natives began stealing stray cattle of the Dutch farmers who had earned the synonym of Boers or Afrikaners. Reprisals led to bloody wars that took a heavy toll of native lives. Thousands of their cattle were appropriated. Boers sold dairy cattle to English settlers and purchased fire arms with the proceeds. These arms were used to browbeat, poorly armed natives. In this way Boers ousted the Hottentots and the Bushmen from the Khoisan (Southwest Africa) territory, captured their lands and forbade them from owning any farm land. Extreme privation led to the Khoi-Khoi-Dutch Wars of 1658, 1779–1781 and Xhosa-Dutch wars fought between 1779 and 1801. Deaths from these wars and small pox infection contracted from the Europeans drastically reduced Khoi Khoi and Xhosa populations.

British settlements like Albany and Port Elizabeth of the Cape Colony appeared in the early nineteenth century. In 1814, the British took over administration of the Colony, introduced English in schools and courts and treated the natives more humanely than the Boers would digest. Boers also disliked customary dealings with the natives. British administrative steps caused distrust between the two European communities. The *Times* (London), described the Boer dilemma. "Sooner than endure such repression and misgovernment of the British any longer, they would go out into wilderness and found a new home for themselves in the most uninhabited lands beyond the Orange River."[2] The Boers sent out advance parties in preparation for their famous 1834-35 trek. A similar trek of a section of the native Zulu tribe began slightly ahead of the Boers. These natives loyal to chief Mzilikazi (Moselekatse), a lieutenant to the ferocious Zulu king Shaka (Chaka), escaped along with their chief. They were fierce fighters who devastated Bechuanaland for gathering more recruits while keeping clear of advance parties of the Boers. The Zulus settled in the Matabeleland country (part of the present-day Zimbabwe) beyond Limpopo River and far away from the revengeful Shaka. Following a signal from the advance parties, some 12000 Boers drove out of the Cape colony in ox wagons in search of a new home in the north, distant from prying eyes of the British. In November 1837, 1000 Boer wagons reached Natal and established a colony. Boers attempted to buy peace with the Zulu chief Dingane who had succeeded his half-brother Shaka. The latter however massacred the 69-member Boer delegation along with their leader Pieter Retief. On 16th December 1838 infuriated Boer leader Andries Pretorius attacked Dingane killing 3000 Zulu warriors and wounding so many more that the water of the Nicome River turned red with blood of the slain. Thereafter, this tributary of the Buffalo River was called the Blood River.

In 1839, Boers found an independent republic of Natalia on the coast of Indian Ocean but could not sustain it for long in the face of British confrontation. Boers defeated British forces in 1842 but gave up when reinforcements arrived from London. In 1843, Britain annexed the young republic. After annexing Natal, the English commenced at once the same policies which had driven the Boers out of their first homeland. Natal became part of the Cape Colony for administrative purposes until it gained the status of a colony. Dutch settlers of the colony were permitted to manage their own civil and judicial matters. Still, a large number reloaded their wagons and headed for the Highveld region of the Orange River where they established the Orange Free State. A section of Boers crossed the Vaal River and found the South African Republic or

Transvaal. Britain recognized Transvaal in 1852 and Orange Free State in 1854. Circumstances however, worked against the Boers. Jacobs, young son of a Griqualand[3] farmer found a shiny stone on the south bank of the Orange River near the Hope town. This 21.25 carat stone came to be known as the Eureka diamond. Two years later, a native was noticed wearing a large stone as a charm. It was subsequently recognized as the 83.5 carat Star of South Africa. The diamond was found in the area which lay within natural borders of the Orange Free State close to the confluence of Orange and Vaal rivers. Subsequent explorations found that the area was rich in diamonds. These discoveries activated mining in the Kimberley region that attracted hordes of Uitlanders.[4] The Boers claimed that the Griquas had sold the rights of the area to the Orange Free State. But Cape Colony also laid its claim to the area. Another claimant was Griqua leader Nicolaas Waterboer. Governor Robert Keate of Natal, the arbiter, ruled in favour of Waterboer, who had already placed his territory under British protection. Thus, the British elbowed out Boers from the diamond mines. Through this circuitous way they annexed Griqualand and territory adjoining the Cape Colony.

The Boers inept in human relations were constantly at odds with their African neighbours. As a part of diplomacy, the British customarily resolved their disputes. Mindless conflicts ruined Boer economy rendering them ineffective against the calculating and aggressive British. In 1877, Britain annexed the Transvaal on the pretence of protecting interests of British diamond workers. Actually, Britain wanted to control the diamond business and trade under pretext of ending the Boer-Zulu conflicts. The British ignored Boer protests against their uncalled-for arrogance. Desperate Boers decided to resist the British under leadership of Vice President Paul Kruger of the Transvaal Republic. Both parties confronted each other in November 1880. On 8th December 1880, Boer leaders Paul Kruger, Piet Joubert and M.W. Pretorius met at Paarde Kraal and commanded "Burgers"[5] of the Orange Free State to rise up against the British. A force of 8000 to 10,000 fighters gathered for the cause. The First Anglo-Boer War erupted on 27th February 1881. Boer forces drubbed the British at Majuba Hill inflicting upon them heavy casualties. The British government of William Gladstone was forced to reaffirm the independence of the Transvaal republic at the London convention of

1884.

Boers were still adjusting to the consequences of the discovery of diamonds in their territory when, in 1886, gold deposits were discovered in Witwatersrand. These deposits, just thirty miles from the Boer capital of Pretoria, triggered a gold rush. Hordes of prospectors thronged to what is now Johannesburg. Gold rich Vaal reefs reignited British interest in Transvaal. In due course, English prospectors (Uitlanders) outnumbered the Boer (Afrikaner) population of Johannesburg. President Paul Kruger hesitated to franchise all Uitlanders lest they vote out the Boer government. On the other hand, concept of universal franchise favoured Britain who was secretly supporting the demand. Cecil Rhodes, premier of the Cape Colony was fomenting trouble for the Kruger government. His confidant Dr. Leander Starr Jameson, who administered his South African Company, prematurely plunged into action. On 29th December 1895, he raided the Transvaal with a posse of armed men expecting disgruntled Uitlanders to rise in revolt and join his expedition. Unresponsive Uitlanders ruined Jameson's raid and prospects of British intervention. Boer government rounded up the raiders and handed them over to the British for suitable punishment. An ashamed British government asked Rhodes to resign his job and imprisoned Jameson. British action was meant to placate English critics for a while. Rhodes and Jameson were not only back on their jobs but were eulogized by their countrymen for their role in extending the frontiers of the British Empire in Africa. Britain was determined to capture Transvaal gold. It amassed troops from her colonies as far as Australia and New Zealand and deployed them on borders of the Boer republics. On 28th August 1899, Joseph Chamberlain, the British colonial secretary, issued an ultimatum asking Transvaal to confer equal rights upon all Uitlanders of Transvaal. British stringency on this issue heralded the Second Anglo-Boer War. The United States of America decried British belligerency. On 20th October 1899, Michael Davitt, an Irish member from East Mayo and a peasant leader, speaking in the British House of Commons on supplementary estimates for the war, affirmed that the United States would not side with Britain in the Anglo-Boer War. He cited a report in the *Washington Post* that indicted the British government for meddling in domestic affairs of the Transvaal republic. He quoted the paper that

Britain wanted diamond and gold mines and nothing more indecent and outrageous could be found in the history of any country pretending to be an enlightened Christianity. On 25th October, Davitt announced his resignation from the House of Commons asserting that the war, for the meanest and most mercenary aims, would be known as the greatest crime of the century.

Paul Kruger, noting that the British were craving for a war, offered to discuss the citizenship issues with Alfred Milner the British high commissioner in South Africa and governor of the Cape Colony. Milner, an inflexible and ardent imperialist, turned down the offer claiming that a war was inevitable. The British ignored Boer ultimatum to withdraw forces from their borders which was a clear signal for the Second Anglo-Boer War. The war was fought between 11th October 1899 and 31st May 1902. The Boers besieged British garrisons for 118 days before British General Redvers Buller broke the siege. On 15th November 1899, Winston Churchill, then war correspondent for the *Morning Post*, was taken prisoner. He escaped and wrote about British offensive. "Sooner or later in a righteous cause or a picked quarrel... for the sake of our Empire we must fight the Boers."[6] Michael Davitt in his book "The Boers Fight for Freedom 1898–1902" published in 1902, records a dispatch from Pretoria which is at variance with Churchill's escape narrative. The Boers were depicted far more humane than their adversaries. The siege of Kimberly and Mafeking was broken after several attempts. Field Marshal Lord Roberts replaced General Buller. More than 40,000 troops along with guns were deployed for assaulting Bloemfontein, capital of the Orange Free State, which had sided with its sister republic of Transvaal. The Boers wilted under the British onslaught. Britain annexed the Boer republic on 28th May 1900 and named it Orange River Colony. In late 1900, the Boers began resistance through guerrilla warfare. British counter campaign was brutal to the extent of following a scorched earth policy. Thousands of Boer homesteads were destroyed and crops burnt in order to seek surrender of the Boer fighters.[7] Boer families were interned in concentration camps where thousands of internees died of malnutrition and disease.

Paul Kruger addressed the joint session of Volksraads for the last time on 7th May 1900 calling the British invasion a devilish act. He emphasized that Britain was bent upon attacking Transvaal even if they had agreed to franchise all Uitlanders after a year's stay in our Republic. He regretted that neither Chamberlain nor Salisbury acknowledged his proposition. Transvaal republic was annexed on 1st September 1900 and named Transvaal Colony. A Boer delegation visited The Hague in a last-ditch effort to save their Republic. Boers beseeched all nations for help lamenting ruthlessness unleashed by the British upon their exhausted fighters. They appealed in the name of justice and humanity to save their country. Their appeal went unheeded given their poor record vis-à-vis African natives and the European reluctance to intervene against a belligerent Britain. Americans were somewhat sympathetic in those days of presidential elections. The *Times* claimed that sympathy expressed by American politicians for the Transvaal Boers was never more than platonic and will soon fade away and forgotten.[8] By 1902 the Dutch, who were the first to establish a colony in South Africa, lost all their possessions. Boer efforts to hold on to their Republics cost them 30,000 lives besides internment of 120,000 civilians men, women and children in British concentration camps. Ironically, Europeans fought each other for territories which actually belonged to the Africans.

British aim in Africa transcended diamond and gold mines. They yearned to lord over the continent. Imperialists like Cecil Rhodes spearheaded this endeavour. Rhodes believed that to be born an Englishman was like winning a lottery. This fanciful belief in Englishman's superiority entreated Britons to appropriate maximum foreign territory for themselves. Rhodes even visualized recovery of the United States of America for the British Empire. His frontal organization, the British South Africa Company (BSAC) assumed a role similar to that of the East India Company in South Asia. Rhodes mused over a mission of seizing African territory in between the Cape and headwaters of the Nile. Success of his mission rested upon forestalling other European nations. He dreaded the prospect of 40 million of his countrymen engaged in civil war over the question of bread and butter unless new lands were acquired for surplus population and new markets found for British manufactures.[9] For people like him treachery, double dealing, military aggression, deportations, and dubious treaties were legitimate instruments to overcome obstacles in annexing states of the African chiefs. In 1884, Britain annexed Basutoland (now Lesotho) and declared Bechuanaland (now Botswana) its protectorate. John Mackenzie, a Scottish missionary of the London Missionary Society, assisted in these acquisitions. Mackenzie spoke about the rights of African natives simultaneously persuading them to seek British protection in order to keep them away from the basically Calvinist Boers[10].

The BSAC pined for the vast Ndebele land (Matabeleland) and the one inhabited by the Shona-speaking tribes of the Zimbabwe plateau (Mashona land). Rhodes expected rich harvests of gold and other minerals especially from the Mashonaland region. Moreover, it fell on his much-endeared north-south African link. Rhodes, then a member of the Cape Colony parliament, met the Matabele chief Lobengula in 1888 but failed to extract any favour from him. Lobengula distrusted all white men other than Christian missionaries. A wily pursuer, Rhodes won over an English missionary John Moffat to speak for him with the Matabele chief for a mining concession for his company. Lobengula trusted Moffat's word. He agreed to sign an agreement with Rhode's company. The chief was assured that at any time no more than ten white men will work in his kingdom. Contrary to Lobengula's perception, an associate of Rhodes, Charles Rudd, tricked him into signing a mining concession that divested the chief of all his lands. Armed with the concession, Rhodes obtained a Queen's Charter authorizing the BSAC to govern all its territorial acquisitions in Africa. Rhodes had plans to locate British industries on lands between the Zambezi and Limpopo rivers, but Rudd Concession did not permit settlement rights over Ndebele lands. Hence the British company decided to attack Mashonaland, force Lobengula to intervene, defeat him in the battlefield, and capture his Kingdom. The plan fructified with least effort. Lobengula's warriors fought with fervour but were cut down by superior British fire power. For the first time the British deployed the Maxim gun for combat in Africa. British flag was raised over the Ndebele capital of Bulawayo on 4th November 1893. By 1899, the BSAC controlled both Matabeleland and Mashonaland. In 1901 these territories north of Limpopo River were merged to form Southern Rhodesia (now Zimbabwe) with its capital at Salisbury. Queen's Charter did not specify northern limits of Rhodes territories leaving him with room for further expansion. Emissaries of Rhodes in

Nyasaland signed treaties with the Barotseland king Lewanika who ruled over a vast territory in the northwest across the Zambezi River. This area was under British radar through a Scottish missionary David Livingstone. Incidentally, Ndebele and the Portuguese both menaced Barotseland Kingdom. French missionary Francois Coillard persuaded King Lewanika to seek British protection. In the end a Rhodes emissary, Frank Lochner, prevailed upon Lewanika to sign an all-encompassing concession on 27th June 1890. The concession granted BSAC rights over minerals, and related activities, and import of arms into his kingdom. In return, Lewanika was promised an annual payment of 2000 British pounds. Before long, Barotseland kingdom became a British protectorate watched over by a Resident. As in other British protectorates, Lewanika's powers were drastically curtailed. Britain also came to control land resources of his kingdom. In 1900, this territory was named northwest Rhodesia and in 1911, it was merged with northeast Rhodesia to form northern Rhodesia (now Zambia) with its capital at Lealui.

Christian missionaries facilitated the colonisation of Africa. The missionaries were the first to arrive, strike roots amidst natives, and win their trust. They persevered to influence social, cultural and political ethics of the natives. In a way they cleared path for trading companies to jump in. The British South Africa Company, the Niger Company, and the East Africa Company established colonies in Africa. This arrangement absolved home governments of any financial risk should the venture fail.[11] Robert Moffat of the London Missionary Society set up a mission in Bechuanaland in 1822. In 1845, an explorer David Livingstone established a church and a school in the region. The missionaries gathered a sizeable following among native tribes like the Barolong and Bamangwato. These tribes always feared the Europeans and native chiefs of the neighbouring Bechuanaland. While Ndebele claimed the northern part of their territory, the Boers encroached upon lands of the Barolong tribe. Boers of Transvaal also levied taxes on them. The British regarded Bechuanaland an obstacle in their hassle-free access to North Africa. They waited for the chance to capture this territory. The Barolong chief, a convert to Christianity, appealed for British protection in exchange for allowing English freebooters to settle on his lands and engage in business. In 1876, Bamangwato chief Khama III also sought protection of the British queen through the governor of the Cape Colony. These missionary-inspired overtures led to the British occupation of Bechuanaland territory clear up to the border of South West Africa. On 31st March 1885 Bechuanaland was proclaimed a British protectorate because Germans had occupied the nearby South West Africa (Namibia).

In the North, several political and economic consequences followed the Suez Canal project. Said Pasha, the then ruler (Khedive) of Egypt, sanctioned its construction through the French company of his engineer friend Ferdinand du Lesseps. The canal was completed in 1869 at a huge cost to Egypt. Said Pasha was unable to bear the financial liability. In 1875 he sold 44 percent of Egypt's shares to Britain to discharge the debt. Britain, with a respectable stake in the Canal, liked to secure the canal-zone. In 1882, Britain and France sent warships to Alexandria in support of the Khedive, who was facing the Urabi revolt led by Ahmed Urabi. Britain bombarded Alexandria, suppressed the revolt, and in 1883 appointed Evelyn Baring, the Earl of Cromer, as Controller General in Egypt. The Earl virtually ruled over Egypt until 1907. Following its sway over Egypt, Britain targeted Sudan which formed a segment of the British envisioned north-south link. In 1882, Sudan was under the control of a rigid Muslim sect called the Mahdis, who controlled headwaters of the Nile as well as northern access to Cairo from the South. In 1884, after a nod from Britain, General Charles Gordon toured Sudan, to report on Mahdi insurrection and to help evacuate Egyptian troops and civilians stranded there. Gordon was besieged in Khartoum and was killed before he could be rescued. Britain decided to annihilate the Mahdis to avenge Gordon's death, and control Sudan. In 1892, the haughty British General, Herbert Kitchener, was Sirdar (chief) of the Egypt army. British troops were also stationed in Egypt. In 1896, Kitchener led heavily armed British and Egyptians troops against the fanatical, though poorly armed Mahdis. The latter were brutally cut down by the artillery and gun fire of the combined force. Britain occupied Sudan and Kitchener briefly took over as its governor general.

The Suez Canal considerably shortened the shipping distance between Britain and India. Britain was, therefore, anxious to secure this route by exercising her authority over countries, like Kenya, which embraced the east coast of Africa. For good measure, British rule in

Kenya and Uganda was meant to protect the Suez Canal and the Cape of Good Hope sea routes to India and keep other European nations away from source of the Nile. The British East India Company's Charter to operate in the Kenyan territory helped it to lay claim to this territory at the Berlin Conference. Kenya became a British protectorate of East Africa in 1890 after the company ceded its control to the British government. A wholesome climate and rich agricultural land attracted English and other European settlers to the area. By 1930 some 30,000 Europeans settled amidst one million ethnic Kikuyu natives. Charles Eliot, the first governor of Kenya, initiated the policy of white supremacy when he invited white settlers to Kenya to occupy lands of the Masai natives and turn the interior of the country into a white man's country. In time, the natives found themselves reduced to the status of roving cultivators on the very lands of their ancestors. They were barred from producing cash crops like coffee lest they compete with the European planters. The natives were forced to pay hut tax regardless of their paying capacity. The purpose was to impoverish them to the degree that they abandon their lands and work for European farmers to make a living. Hut tax was a major source of revenue for the British but an irritant to the natives. More land seizures took place while the European population swelled to 80,000. Although resistance to colonial expansion was crushed, Africans harboured lingering resentment against deprivation. Pent up indignation led to the Mau Mau uprising followed by a civil war between 1952 and 1960. Thousands of natives perished in the struggle. It was revealed in the House of Commons that British administration in Kenya often hanged to death as many as 50 Mau Mau sympathizers each month.[12] Of the 800 hangings from 1953 and 1955, 200 persons were hanged for associating with freedom fighters and 320 for possession of arms, even a couple of bullets[13]. At last Britain conceded national elections. The African National Union of Jomo Kenyata won elections to the legislative council ultimately leading to the independence of Kenya in 1963. In 1877, Protestant missionaries supplemented British quest for the territory now called Uganda. Shortly, there were European settlements clear up to the shores of Lake Victoria. The territory became a British protectorate in 1894 but its geographical boundaries were drawn in 1914 after merger of other units. The country earned internal self-government in 1961 and independence in 1962.

British quest for a Cape to Cairo link materialized only after the First World War when a large part of the German protectorate of German East Africa, outside Rwanda and Burundi, fell to the British share. This area, named Tanganyika, which later on became Tanzania upon merger of Zanzibar, also lay along the east coast of Africa. As for the west coast, Continental Europe's interest had begun with slave trade. British became interested in the region in 1787 when a proposal was mooted to settle destitute Africans of London in what is now Sierra Leone. The proposal fructified in 1792 through the Sierra Leone Company. Several hundred black settlers were shipped to the new settlement aptly named Free Town after the freed slaves. This settlement was the second British colony in Africa. The settlers comprised British loyalists from Nova Scotia who had sided with Britain during the American Revolution. These people were far more conscious of their rights than a majority of their African compatriots. Between 1807 and 1896, an African institution governed affairs of the colony. Later on, it became a British protectorate. Britain exploited this mineral-rich nation. However, in 1898 people revolted against the imposition of hut tax. The uprising was suppressed with a heavy hand but resistance against outside rule continued until Sierra Leone won independence in 1961. Other British colonies on the west coast were Gambia, Ghana and Lagos territory of Nigeria all of whom were governed from Free Town. A prized British possession on the west coast was Nigeria. Britain had acquired this country through the agency of one George Taubman Goldie, founder of the United African Company. He, like his compatriot Cecil Rhodes, was a staunch colonialist. He laid claim to the Nigerian territory at the Berlin Conference holding that the British flag flew over the Lower Niger. His claim was accepted despite French reservations about boundaries of the claimed territory. The Royal Niger Company ruled over the acquired territory until January 1900. Thereafter, its control was transferred to Britain. Northern and Southern Nigeria were governed as separate protectorates until 1914 when they were merged to form the British colony of Nigeria. The country was given a federal structure in 1954. The nationalist movement that erupted after the Second World War eventually led to independence of Nigeria in 1960.

French colonies of Africa: For ages, foreigners violated North African coastal lands. As early as 1517, Ottoman Turks held jurisdiction over Algiers and coastal Algeria. Barbary Corsairs, who inhabited the Algerian coast, were pirates who continuously menaced European ships. In 1808, France drew a plan to invade Algeria. The plan materialized on flimsy grounds. Hussein Dey, the governor of Algiers had mockingly slapped French Consul with a flyswatter during an argument over payments outstanding against French merchants. Charles X, the king of France, regarded the episode an insult to French pride. In 1830, General Louis Victor-Auguste de Beaumont attacked and captured Algiers. French control stimulated the influx of French farmers and businessmen who settled in the northern part of Algeria along the Mediterranean coast. Actual colonisation began in 1840 after French soldiers were allotted lands for free. The government encouraged French civilian settlements by constructing villages and allotting parcels of land to each colonist. By 1847, there were 110,000 colonists. Thousands of Algerians were forcibly evicted from their lands in order to accommodate these colonists. As a result, Muslims, who constituted 90 percent of Algerian population, had a stake of hardly 20 percent to Algeria's income, but paid 70 percent of direct taxes and 45 percent of the total tax collected. The extremely deprived and exploited population rose in revolt to protect their rights. One prominent resistance leader was Abd-el-Kader who led the insurrection. Thousands of Algerians perished demanding freedom from the French rule. The National Liberation Front, which spear-headed freedom movement, claimed 1.5 million deaths, yet France accepted a figure of 350,000 killed during the insurgency. The first figure was derived from the estimated native population of four million which declined to 2.5 million in 1890. In 1962, when Algeria became independent, her European population was close to one million among the native population of about eleven million people. So much bad blood existed between the communities that, except for a handful of Europeans, all the rest had to leave Algeria.

Since the occupation of northern Algeria, the neighbouring territory of Morocco was under the French radar. France restrained itself for many years fearing adverse international reaction and due to the unsettled internal situation of the territory. Meanwhile, France regained colonial spirit in competition with other European nations. Besides, political economists like Paul Leroy Beaulieu had warned that France would slip to the level of a second-rate power unless it built a colonial empire.[14] Therefore France joined other European nations who longed to capture some part of Africa. On the initiative of Portugal, Chancellor Bismarck of Germany invited Europeans and the United States of America to a conference held at Berlin on 15th November 1884. The conference was not for the sake of Africa or Africans. Europeans were there for land grabs and to spread 'their' civilization with the Maxim gun. The agenda of the conference ended up in legitimizing the partitioning of Africa into areas of influence for the purpose of trade and tapping natural resources by participant nations. Surprisingly no native African king or chief was privy to Europe's unethical machinations. The reason was weakness of the African political system which was in no position to counter cunning European designs. Portugal produced a map meant to meet her own ambition of acquiring African territory lying between her east and west territories of Angola and Mozambique. Britain rejected this depiction because it interfered with its plan of linking the Cape with source of the Nile River. The participants agreed on the principle of effectivity which allowed each European nation to claim territory under its actual control through a treaty with the native chiefs or if its flag flew over the territory. This permitted a nation holding territory on the sea coast to claim the hinterland which produced goods for trade. Under this clause King Leopold of Belgium obtained exclusive rights over one million square miles of the Congo Basin. By the end of the nineteenth century, this territory, called the Congo Free State generated eight-million-dollars-worth of commerce contributed mainly by rubber, palm oil and ivory. Between 1899 and 1906 Leopold collected 13,700,000 dollars-worth of rubber. The king obtained rubber and ivory by allotting quotas to the villages. Those who did not meet the quota were brutally flogged. This horror was endured by most natives of the Belgian Congo. King Leopold, in a will dated 2nd August 1889 bequeathed his sovereign rights in the State in favour of Belgium.

The Berlin Conference formalized deliberations, but conflict of interest arose over slicing Africa into areas of influence. At the time of the Berlin Conference, hardly 10 percent of the area was with the

Europeans, but before the First World War the Africans themselves, controlled hardly 10 percent of Africa. Every European nation had its own interest in holding a part of Africa. The Industrial Revolution was turning out many products requiring steady markets and Africa was such a place. Britain, France and Germany had strong industrial base but Industrial Revolution had bypassed Portugal.[14]Another reason was acquiring what Africa could offer. Palm oil in Nigeria, minerals in South Africa, and the strategic location of Kenya and Uganda for the protection of Suez route to India, and competition for expansion, dominated European minds. Britain warned Portugal to keep out of territories that ultimately formed Rhodesia and Nyasaland (presently Zambia, Zimbabwe and Malawi). The lowly Portugal gave into British demand. France wanted to extend her possessions of Senegal, Mali, Niger and Chad up to the Nile River in order to link Niger and Nile rivers for the purpose of trade. The French were jealous of British hegemony over Egypt. They dispatched General Jean Baptiste Marchand to raise the French flag over an area around Fashoda and up to waters of the Nile. Marchand took 12 French officers and 150 Senegalese riflemen and left in a hired boat through river Ubangi. He arrived at the edge of the Sudanese desert, traversed through the inhospitable terrain finishing his 14-month long track to Fashoda in November 1898. Enforcements from the French outpost of Djibouti were supposed to join Marchand's expedition. However, Ethiopia refused to allow passage to French troops through its country. Consequently, Marchand was left with too little force to challenge the British. The ever-alert British got wind of the French intentions. Their commander Herbert Kitchener and a force comprising 100 Cameroon Highlanders and 250 Askaris (native African soldiers) armed with field guns and Maxim guns sailed through the Nile for Fashoda. A flotilla of gun boats was also stationed next to the Fashoda Fort. Marchand saw the writing on the wall. After a polite interaction, both sides agreed to leave resolution of the situation to their respective governments. French government advised Marchand to back off from Fashoda. Prolonged negotiations followed in London and Paris. In the end, French influence was restricted to the west of headwaters of the Nile. The British conceded their claim over Sahara as well as western Sudan. The Fashoda incident, a diplomatic victory for Britain, reaffirmed her fiefdom over Egypt, Sudan and the Nile water way.

France, restrained from eastward expansion, turned towards territories in the African northwest. By the end of nineteenth century, it had occupied three million square miles of African territory against 2.76 million miles held by Great Britain. Of course, the bulk of French colonial possessions comprised low productivity lands of the Sahara Desert and adjoining lands as against much productive British colonies in terms of agricultural production and mineral resources. France renewed efforts to capture Morocco. It engineered border skirmishes as a prelude to intervening militarily. France was on solid enough ground to attack Morocco when eight Europeans were murdered at Casablanca. General Antoine Drude was commissioned along with 2000 French troops for military action. They occupied part of Casablanca. Other Europeans also wanted their finger in the Moroccan pie. Finally, in 1904, the country was divided into areas of French and Spanish influence with the former getting a larger cut. On 4th March 1910, Mulai Abdel Aziz, the Sultan of Morocco, placed his country under French protection. In the bargain, Britain got a free hand in Egypt, Italy in Tripolitania and Spain in southern East Africa and northern Sahara. French colonial empire in Africa included countries of northwest and central Africa comprising Algeria, Morocco, Mauritania, Mali, French Guinea, Ivory Coast, Burkina Faso (Upper Volta), Dahomey (Benin) Niger, Chad, French Togoland and Djibouti (French Somali land).

Germany became the third largest colonial power in Africa. The first German Chancellor Otto Bismarck worried over the country's economic downturn and prodded by Hamburg merchants and traders joined the race to capture African lands and markets and thereby remain in competition with fellow Europeans. *London Globe* of December 1884 described German mania for colonial adventure. "So deeply are the people imbued with a vague but enticing vision of wealth to be won in Africa that thousands of young men are longing and waiting for an opportunity to seek their fortune in the new Eldorado.[15] Still German endeavour during the scramble for Africa was spearheaded by non-state actors like Carl Peters on the east coast and by Adolf Luderitz on the southwest coast of Africa. These territories were granted German protection *ex post facto* by Chancellor Bismarck. The society for German colonisation run by

Carl Peters signed treaties with native chiefs of the east coast and thus earned territorial rights over those lands. Germany granted imperial charter to Peters in 1885 and recognized his acquisitions as protectorates of German East Africa. Native population of this highly productive territory was deeply conscious of their rights. Consequently the 2000-odd German population faced resistance to their occupation from the Hehe tribe led by its popular chief Mkwana. Germans curbed this movement and suppressed the Maji Maji rebellion of 1905. African resistance ended in 1907. By that time 75,000 Africans lay dead[16]. In fact, Germany established her position in East Africa only after winning the confidence of the local chiefs.

In 1883, Adolf Luderitz, a wealthy German merchant dispatched his agent to the southwest coast of Africa. The agent sailed to a place named Angra Pequena by the Portuguese. This area was inhabited by the Nama tribe. The agent met the local Nama chief, struck a land deal with him, and set up a trading post. Luderitz entered into similar land deals with other native chiefs and in all acquired one quarter million acres of land clear up to borders of the Cape colony. These land transactions were facilitated by missionaries of the Rhenish Missionary Society operating in the area since 1829.[17] German approbation of Luderitz acquisitions was conveyed through a German warship that sailed to Angra Pequena. Chancellor Bismarck granted German protection to the territory on 24th April 1884. On the strength of above land deals, Germany presented a solid case in the Berlin Conference about effective occupancy of lands on the east coast and the south west coast of Africa. Later on, German colonial society took over these territories. German South West Africa became a settler colony where interests of German settlers directly clashed with those of the natives who were cattle herders and whose very existence depended upon their lands. Unlike the British, Germans were novice in colonial diplomacy. Chancellor Bismarck favoured smooth international relations and hence preferred a conciliatory approach towards the natives. His colonial administrator in Africa, Theodor Leutwein was firm and acted diplomatically while expropriating maximum possible land for the German settlers who always craved more and more land. Land greedy colonists, however, regarded Leutwein too soft towards the natives. Leutwein's policy received set back in 1890 when Emperor Wilhelm II replaced Chancellor Bismarck. The Kaiser, a grandson of the British Queen Victoria, was a hard-line colonialist striving to expand the German Empire in Africa and the Pacific Ocean. His choice of new chancellor Leo von Caprivi modernized and strengthened German navy to support the expanding Empire. The Kaiser, on his part instructed Schutztruppe to ruthlessly crush any resistance to German advance into the interior of Africa. Between 1891 and 1894 local Schutztruppe, comprising German officers and soldiers aided by African recruits, launched 54 expeditions against the Africans. Every native African suspected or declared a rebel was executed on the spot. Germans had an unrelenting hatred and extreme thirst for revenge. The orders were to make a clean sweep, hang them, shoot them to the last man and give no quarter[18]. German policy in South West Africa Colony was to clear the territory of natives, and use their lands for raising plantations and establishing German settlements through the genocide of Herero and Nama tribes, who were themselves agricultural people, is an abhorrent event of German colonial history. The great German naturalist Dr. Carl Schillings admitted that within a few years Germany slaughtered 200,000 natives in the colonies. German brutality in her colonies was widely publicized in the 1920's and 1930's as political propaganda to perpetuate the myth that other colonial powers were more civilized, and gentle toward their African subjects[19]. At the dawn of the twentieth century, the German flag fluttered over her colonies of Togo, Kamerun (Cameroon), German South West Africa (Namibia) and German East Africa (Tanzania) occupying 2.6 million square kilometres of African territory. Within 30 years this flag came down as German colonies were distributed among the victors of the First World War under mandate of the League of Nations.

Portugal, once presided over an overseas trading empire encompassing the coasts of Africa and India, the East Indies and China. It was another player at the Berlin Conference. Portugal held tenuous control over 800,000 square mile area of Mozambique, Angola, Guinea Bissau and Sao Tome islands. It exploited human and natural resources of these territories to the hilt. Portuguese used conscripted African labour to run plantation farms. Labour from mainland territories worked the plantations of Sao Tome and Principe islands. Unabated exploitation led to civil unrest and Africans began to assert their right to be free. The civil wars that erupted in rural areas continued for a number of years. About 50,000 Africans lost their lives when Angola got her freedom following the 1974 Leftists coup in Lisbon. All Portuguese colonies won freedom by the 1970's. Another colonial power, Italy occupied Eritrea in 1890 and Somali land in 1889. A decade later Libya came under the Italian flag. Italy lost her overseas possessions in the aftermath of the Second World War. Spain occupied small coastal territories of Spanish Morocco and Spanish Sahara (or Western Sahara) awarded to her at the Berlin Conference. In short, through a compact arrived at in a single conference, the Europeans appropriated between themselves 28 million square kilometres of African land without the consent of its natural heirs. The only territories to escape European onslaught were Ethiopia and Liberia.

Chapter 6
Perfidious Treaties that Helped Colonisation

Europe of the day acquiesced acts of fraud, conspiracy, deceit, and malice, in pursuit of colonial endeavour. Europeans occupied foreign lands in the name of discovery which it never was or the lands being *terra nullius* which those never were. They stooped to contemptible levels to expand their domains and to outsmart their competitors. There were critics at home who loathed the disgraceful acts of their compatriots, but governments at that time regarded treachery a part of the game. Perfidious acts of European powers were revealed when they scrambled to gain maximum territory in Africa. Land agreements with native chiefs opened doors for future territorial expansion in the African continent. Christian missionaries, particularly those of the London Missionary Society, working in the countryside for long, had the ear of native kings and chiefs. Natives, strange to the English language, relied on these missionaries when dealing with the foreigners. One particular missionary John Mackenzie who was once deputy commissioner of Bechuanaland spoke for the rights of African natives. He was critical of what Cecil Rhodes stood for. At the same time, he helped Britain to expand her African territory. He believed that Africans were incapable of self-governance but needed to be protected.[1] Missionaries interpreted the essence of the agreement before the chiefs were asked to put their mark on the document. Alas, the role of the interpreter was often dubious. He would cleverly use metaphors and analogies presumably to remove any apprehensions of the African party, but in practice to dupe native chiefs into signing the agreement. African belief in the spoken word often led to their undoing. For example, drafts of documents, which native chiefs of the Nigerian Delta signed, often originated from the foreign office in London. The chiefs learned the essence of contents and implications of the written word from what translators chose to let them know.

Sometimes the verbal assurance of British agents and missionaries were enough to convince the native chiefs or kings into placing their sign or signatures on the document. It was acceded that in colonial Africa the so-called consent to agreement or treaty was usually obtained either under duress or by duplicity.[2]

A mention of acceptance of sovereignty of the British Crown in the document was sufficient for colonial officers to claim control over all that was previously the sovereign right of the concerned chief or king. Often-times duplicity or duress worked in seeking the consent of native chiefs and kings. Carl Peters on the East coast of Africa and Franz Adolf Luderitz on the coast of South West Africa (SWA), tricked native chiefs into signing deals which led to appropriation of almost all of their territory. John Mackenzie disclosed how prospectors dispossessed native chiefs of their lands by making them drunk and getting them to sign the document.[3] Natives were even ignorant of the actual territory they controlled and signed away their rights to territories they never controlled. In Swaziland, Mbadzeni, who became king in 1875, signed so many overlapping concessions with colonists and prospectors that the total area of Swazi territory that he gave away exceeded the area of his kingdom[4]. Swazis who believed in the 'word' bemoaned that the papers killed them. The British annexed his territory once they learnt of gold deposits in the Kingdom. Mbadzeni's successors struggled to get back lands ceded by the former, until the time Swaziland became a free nation.

A famous act of trickery was put through in the Zulu Kingdom of Matabeleland – a territory surrounded by the British in Bechuanaland, by the Portuguese in East Africa, and the Transvaal state of the Boers. Matabele state was suspected to have gold deposits. Inevitably, prospectors from Britain and other European nations thronged the kingdom seeking mining concessions from the Matabeleland King Lobengula. The king was wary of the Europeans. Cecil Rhodes, a staunch imperialist, who had entered the Cape Parliament in 1881, was himself seeking mining concessions for his British South Africa Company (BSAC). In the back of his mind, he yearned to expand British control in Africa. Rhodes believed that Matabeleland abounded in gold reserves. He briefed a shareholder that once they got Lobengula's territory the rest would be easy because his territory was the only block to central Africa.[5]

He visited Bulawayo, the capital of Matabeleland, to meet Lobengula. The Zulu King shunned him. Rhodes decided to seek the assistance of John Moffat, a son of Robert Moffat of the London Missionary Society who had been on friendly terms with Lobangula's late father King Mizlikaze. Moffat was at the time assistant commissioner at Bechuanaland and had been to Bulawayo on official business. Moffat successfully persuaded Lobengula to meet with the British agents. Rhodes sent his agent Charles Rudd along with two others. One of them Francis Thompson, nicknamed 'White Zulu,' was fluent in the Zulu language. The other was James Rochfort Maguire, a friend of Rhodes from the Oxford days. Rhodes had inkling that Matabeleland, and Mashonaland, over which Lobengula claimed his sovereignty, had rich deposits of precious metals, and hence ideal for prospectors and settlers from England. He wanted to trap the Zulu king in a written agreement before occupying his territories. An added gain was to keep Portugal and the Boers of Transvaal at bay. Rhodes knew that Lobengula had confided in Charles Helm of the London Missionary Society that he distrusted the presence of British and other foreigners in his kingdom. John Moffat was, however, able to convince him that a mining concession in favour of the British would dissuade other concession hunters he was so wary of. An indecisive Lobengula was shown a draft of the mining concession whose essence was translated to him by Helm who was present during negotiations to watch out for the interests of the natives and to witness the deal. Helm, who was affiliated with the British South Africa Company, was hardly an honest broker. The concessionaires Rudd, Maguire and Thompson were all Rhodes men out there to trick the Zulu king into signing the deal. Thompson assured Lobengula that the treaty being signed was a sort of friendship treaty. All the dice were now immaculately loaded against the Zulu king. Agreement to which Lobengula was bluffed into putting his mark on, as signature of the king of Matabeleland, Mashonaland, and adjoining territories, granted complete and exclusive charge over all lands with metals and minerals in the kingdom dominions and principalities with full powers to do all what was necessary and enjoy full profit and revenues thereof. Lobengula was to receive one hundred pounds sterling per month, one thousand Martini Henry rifles with cartridges and a river steam boat from the grantees. The

Zulu king had his apprehensions about several clauses of the agreement, but Thompson put his doubts to rest one by one through sign language and metaphors familiar to Lobengula. He was verbally assured that not more than ten white men will undertake mineral exploration at a time and the British will abide by laws of the Matabele kingdom. The latter clause was clearly omitted from the written text. Thompson knew how to communicate with Lobengula in figurative language and convince him without disclosing the exact intent of the treaty. For example, he told Lobengula that, why would the British offer him guns if later they were to seize his kingdom. The treaty called Rudd Concession was signed on 30th October 1888. Charles Helm certified that the document was fully interpreted and explained before signatures of all participants including the sign of Lobengula were affixed on it. There were doubts in Britain about the status of the witness signees and absence of powerful *Indunas* as party to the agreements. These doubts were removed when Hercules Robinson, high Commissioner of South Africa, termed the agreement valid.[6] It is surmised that Rudd Concession was one of those frauds which paved the way for British settlement in the Zimbabwe.[7]

Contents of the concession, which appeared in the newspapers of South Africa, trickled down to Bulawayo. The news was lapped up by rival concession hunters who met and communicated contents to the king of Matabeleland. They convinced him that mention of land and other terms in the treaty amounted to surrender of his kingdom in favour of the British South Africa Company. Lobengula found himself hoodwinked in to signing for more than simple mineral rights. He disowned the treaty and dispatched emissaries to present his case before the British queen. Meanwhile he refused to accept guns. The promised boat had not been delivered yet. The queen on her part skirted the real issue and instead advised the Matabeleland king to cooperate with the British in keeping other European powers out of his kingdom. Rhodes armed with Rudd concession obtained the Queen's Charter for the BSAC to control and administer Matabeleland and other areas associated with the Lobengula's kingdom. Rhodes bought out residual concessions in Mashonaland to terminate the occupancy status of the territory. In the summer of 1890, Rhodes deputed Fredrick Selous, an employee of his company to guide an expedition to Mashonaland avoiding the Matabeleland territory. A

British flag was hoisted at the present site of Salisbury signifying possession of Mashonaland in the name of Queen Victoria. Lobengula in an effort to assert his authority on Mashonaland sent his warriors to attack an assembly by the Mashona tribe while remaining clear of the British. His adventure offered the British an excuse for confrontation. The high commissioner for South Africa ordered British forces to annihilate the Matabele and push them out of Zulu territory. Christian missionaries supported the British in the Matabele war and the Shona uprising. Lobengula had 3000 fighters but they were outgunned with superior weapons, the most lethal being the Maxim gun which could discharge 500 rounds a minute, fifty times faster than the fastest rifle available.[8] Confrontation with Lobengula was a part of the conspiracy in which the latter lost half of his fighters. Rhode's deception helped his mission of establishing the colony of Rhodesia on the ruins of the Zulu kingdom. A desperate Lobengula fled to the north and little later succumbed to an attack of smallpox. British occupation of Zulu and Shona territories was justified as a fruit of conquest.

Lochner Concession: This concession was also pulled out by the BSAC with a sleigh of hand. Rhodes arrived in England in 1889 with Rudd Concession under his belt. On that basis, he acquired British government charter to rule, police and win more territories across Bechuanaland and north of the Molopo River. The BSAC began casting eyes on neighbouring African lands after Rhodes became premier of the Cape Colony. Barotseland which lay on the southwest of the present country of Zambia included rich plains of the Upper Zambezi River which was home to the Lozi people and twenty-five subservient tribes. This territory was administered by a litunga (king). Lozi nobles had proclaimed Lubosi (Lewanika) as litunga/ king in August 1878. He was dethroned briefly in September 1884, but he reclaimed his position in November 1885. Litunga Lewanika, who ruled over a kingdom spread over 250,000 square miles, had experienced rebellion in pockets of Barotseland. Necessarily he feared internal disorders and outside dangers from the Ndebele in the South, the Portuguese in the East and West, as well as from the Boers, and British intentions over his kingdom. Playing safe, Lewanika's friend King Khama III of Ngwato in the then Bechuanaland (Botswana) and a convert to Christianity, had accepted

British protection. Khama advised Lewanika to accept similar protection. The Barotse king however faced opposition from *Indunas* (leaders) of his kingdom. The latter feared losing their traditional authority and eventually the kingdom. Even Matabele King Lobengula, who felt cheated by Rhodes' men, offered a brotherly hand to Lewanika in facing the Europeans. The Lozi king had, however, decided to seek British protection. Francois Coillard of the Paris Evangelical Society, whom Lewanika held in high esteem, had worked in his kingdom since 1885. Coillard also advised the king to accept British protection. On Lewanika's request, he wrote a letter to Sir Sidney Shippard, the administrator of Bechuanaland, conveying Lewanika's desire. The letter was ignored by the British, but it did arouse the interest of the concession hunters. In April 1989, Henry Ware arrived in Lealui on behalf of the Nind Consortium of Kimberley to seek mining rights from Lewanika. He made sweet promises even alluding to British protection to convince Lewanika into signing the so-named Ware Concession on 27th June 1889. Rhodes purchased this concession for a payment of 900 pounds sterling. The concession laid some restrictions in pursuit of Rhode's goal of exploiting the resources of the Barotseland kingdom and eventually annexing it. He deputed Frank Elliot Lochner, formerly of the Bechuana police, to secure a revised concession. Lochner was assisted by an emissary of Khama in Lealui. Francois Coillard and Adolph Jalla, the two missionaries, acted as interpreters. Khama's emissary silenced dissident *Indunas* with the threat of harsh retribution from Khama and warned them to think twice before opposing Lewanika. On his part, Lochner hid his duplicity and falsehood in impressing upon Lewanika that he was negotiating a concession and offer of protection as a British emissary. He conversed in such a way that even Lewanika's trusted advisers and official interpreters Jalla and Coillard were taken in. They understood that Lochner represented British government and the treaty to be signed was between King Lewanika and the British government.

Lochner compounded his duplicity and fraud when he presented King Lewanika with gifts purportedly sent by the queen of England.[9] Lewanika not only gracefully accepted the gifts but in return handed over Lochner a pair of some of the finest ivory tusks for the queen. He vainly awaited the queen's acceptance of the gifts for a couple of years. Lochner presented a draft of concession he had drawn up. During deliberations, Lewanika excluded territories inhabited by his Lozy tribe. He was so much charmed with the prospect of winning the friendship of the British Government that he signed the document 'Frank Lochner Concession'. This concession granted mineral extraction and trading rights over Barotseland to the BSAC for a period of ninety-six years. Lewanika was to get annual mining royalty of two thousand British pounds plus guns and a promise of promoting education among his people and a promise of seven-year British protection. These commitments never materialized. Yet the BSAC was enjoying the provisions of the agreements. A frustrated Lewanika remonstrated with Coillard against British inaction. He denounced both Jalla and Coillard as cheaters and agents of the British. The missionary himself suspected that Lochner had misled them on his relationship between the British government and the BSAC. An anguished Coillard let off his steam by addressing a letter to Cecil Rhodes protesting that his agent did not come out clean on the status of his company vis-à-vis the British Monarch. Lewanika also protested to London that the BSAC had misrepresented facts. British government did not respond but he was told by George Middleton and other interested traders that the British Government had nothing to do with the workings of the BSAC. This episode shattered the dream of Lewanika about coming under British protection. The Lozi king was convinced that the missionaries and his interpreters had wrongfully led him into yielding his country's sovereignty to a commercial concern.

Finally, the BSAC posted Major Robert Thorne Coryndon as British resident of the company. Coryndon arrived at Lealui on 27th September 1897, almost seven years after the signing of the Lochner Concession. He had been instructed by the BSAC to insist upon revising the terms of the concession in consultation with Captain Arthur Lawley, the administrator of Matabeleland. Coryndon told Lewanika that the BSAC could not meet its monetary commitment due to unsuccessful mining in his kingdom. He impressed upon the king to modify the royalty clause. On 21st June 1898, an agreement was signed at Victoria Falls between Lewanika and Arthur Lawley, with Coryndon as a witness. The agreement could not be ratified in England. Another concession with similar provision was finalized between Lewanika and the BSAC in

October 1900. Annual royalty payment was scaled down to eight hundred and fifty British pounds. In 1909, through another clause, the king authorized BSAC to give land grants and farming rights to the Europeans throughout the kingdom except the Barotse Valley, homeland of the Lozi people. Colin Harding, who later became commandant of the Barotseland police, signed as a witness to the agreement. Harding expressed amazement that Lewanika gave so much for nothing. He claimed that the full contents of the new agreement were not divulged to the king before he witnessed the agreement. George Middleton, a missionary turned trader, who turned up after the Lawley deal, termed it an immense sale of whole country. He goaded Lewanika into petitioning the British government into seeking annulment of treaties and placing his kingdom under the direct protection of the queen. The king was so naïve that he continued granting concessions to the BSAC through simple exchanges of letters. Ultimately Lewanika and his kingdom received Imperial protection, but this event marked the end of Lozi autonomy. The agreement laid the foundation of future British colony of Rhodesia (subsequently the Republic of Zambia).

Fraud and Betrayal Marked Onset of British Empire in India: British rule over India was neither a consequence of bequest nor of a clean conquest. Queen Elizabeth I of Britain chartered the East India Company (EIC) floated by a group of London merchants, to trade in the East, win territories, maintain an army, and run a judicial service for people associated with the company. This mercantile company lost no opportunity to secure trading concessions and checkmate rival European merchant companies in India. The company and its workers amassed wealth through fraudulent use of duty exemption granted her in 1717 by a weak Moghul ruler Furrukh Syiar. With this wealth, the company gratified her investors in London, built fortified trading posts along the Indian coast and recruited mercenary and regular forces. The French were their main rivals in the rich province of Bengal, where they had a strong bastion of Chander Nagar. The EIC had her trading post or factory at Fort William. Nawab Alivardi Khan, the autocratic governor of Bengal, objected to fortification of factories by the foreigners and illegal use of privileges granted to the companies. While the French were willing to fall in line, the imperious EIC disregarded his orders and continued its illegal activities. Siraj-ud-Daula, who succeeded Alivardi Khan in 1756, was young and impulsive but a pragmatic ruler. He sent his emissary Narayan Singh to the British factory of Fort William at Calcutta (now Kolkata) demanding that the company stop fortification of their factory forthwith, desist from misusing custom-free privileges, and not to shelter fugitives of the Bengal Court.

The EIC ignored the warning of Nawab Siraj-ud-Daula. A slighted and alarmed Nawab acted against the company and seized its factories at Kassim Bazar and Fort William, Calcutta. He renamed the latter place Alinagar. It is alleged that forces of Siraj-ud-Daula interned around 143 British nationals in a small poorly ventilated room where the majority of them succumbed to the ordeal. English press of London reported an acerbic narrative of half-baked information received from India. Later historians named the episode "Black Hole of Calcutta". The news of British ignominy reached Madras in August 1756 through Charles Manningham, a representative of Roger Drake of the Bengal Council, who pleaded for a strong reprisal against the Nawab. In their letter of 13th October 1756 sent to Fort William, the Council at Fort St. George in Madras (Chennai) spelled out the object of the expedition. Five war ships, 528 infantry, 109 artillery men, 940 sepoys (Indian soldiers) and 160 lascars (Indian sailors) constituted the expeditionary force which left for Calcutta on 15th October 1756. Colonel Robert Clive and Admiral Charles Watson of the Royal Navy led the expedition which arrived at Fulta in Bengal on 15th December 1756. Composition of the force showed that it was a combined action of the EIC and the British government. Clive, aided by deadly gun fire captured Calcutta, Hoogly and the French factory of Chander Nagar. This success salvaged British honour. Clive restored the name of Calcutta. The young Nawab was forced to sign a treaty of friendship on British terms. He agreed to compensate the company, its military, and Calcutta merchants, whose business were allegedly disrupted. The reparation amounted to twenty million rupees or roughly two million pounds. The Nawab was obliged to grant the company some tactical advantages, over and above the privileges it already enjoyed.

Once in the commanding position the EIC began scheming to install a pliant person as governor of Bengal. The mercantile company now assumed a kingmaker's role.[10] Its Select Committee which met on 23rd April 1757 resolved to overthrow Siraj-ud-Daula and install a new Nawab. Out of two names of Mir Jafar Ali (Mir Jafar) and Yar Lutuf Khan or Yar Lutuf, they opted for the former. Mir Jafar, a close relation of Siraj-ud-Daula, was unhappy with the Nawab who had side-lined him in favour of Mir Madan Khan as paymaster (Bakhshi) of his forces. Ever since, Mir Jafar had hobnobbed with other courtiers of the Nawab and with some company men to see the back of Siraj-ud-Daula. The EIC took advantage of the discord. On 5th June 1757, it deputed William Watts, its man at Kassim Bazar, who was well-versed in both Bengali and Persian, to sound out Mir Jafar for a deal. Five days later Clive and Watson jointly met Mir Jafar to plan to oust the Siraj-ud-Daula from Nawabship of Bengal. Nitty-gritty of the conspiracy was worked out by Watts along with Clive's men like Jagat Seth (Mehtab Chand) a Marwari banker. Amin Chand (Omi Chand, as the British understood his name) a leading merchant in the good books of the Nawab, mediated between the company and Mir Jafar. The deal was that Mir Jafar will replace Siraj-ud-Daula and he in return would hand over French possessions to the EIC, compensate the company for war damages and share Nawab's treasury with company officers and co-conspirators like Rai Durlab, a former Diwan of Bengal and Yar Lutuf. Jagat Seth was asked to reimburse Nawab's forces for desertion in the ensuing battle. Rai Durlab was verbally promised a five percent of Nawab's wealth as reward for staying aloof in the battle along with his force.

While a division of spoils was under discussion, Amin Chand demanded three million rupees and five percent of all treasure that should be found and a quarter of Nawab's jewels as his share, besides a written stipulation that Mir Jafar will keep his word. He threatened to disclose the whole affair to the Nawab unless that was complied with immediately. Clive desperately needed Amin Chand's cooperation to keep the conspiracy under wraps. He kept him in good humour but inwardly decided to outwit him in his own cunning way. Clive told his men to prepare two documents of the deal.[11] The one on red paper would include Amin Chand's name among beneficiaries but the real document on white paper would exclude his name. Fictitious red document was to bear signatures of Clive and Mir Jafar to allay fears of Amin Chand. A vigilant Amin Chand when presented with the red document demanded that Admiral Watson should also sign it. But Watson, who smelled a rat, refused to sign the document. It is alleged that he allowed his name to be added by another hand.[12] Clive had no qualms of conscience. He asked company employee Henry Lushington to forge the Admiral's signatures on the red copy of the document. Nevertheless, the Admiral was unhappy over this disgraceful act. But morality did not bother the Victorians.[13] Assured of betrayal on the part of Siraj-ud daula's men Clive dared the Nawab on the battle field. On 23rd June 1757, he confronted the forces of Siraj-ud-Daula at the village Plassey near Murshidabad. The Nawab tried in vain to win back Mir Jafar along with his 16000 men. True to their plan, Yar Lutuf, Rai Durlabh, Amin Chand and Jagat Seth remained passive spectators in the war. In this way effectively two-third of Nawab's force was out of action. Despite these desertions, Nawab's forces under Mir Madan and Mohan Lal stood their ground. They were turning the tide when Mir Madan was killed by a cannon ball. A sudden monsoon shower had soaked through unprotected gun powder of the Nawab's French artillery. But the British had kept their powder dry by covering their ammunition. Fight was now unequal, because Nawab's artillery became ineffective. British pounding of his positions unnerved Siraj-ud-Daula who fled the fight. He was subsequently captured and executed. British triumph in the all-important battle that founded their empire in India, was more like a negotiated deal. Clive visited Mir Jafar to congratulate him as new Nawab of Bengal. The EIC emptied the Murshidabad treasury to the last rupee to extract the promised money from Mir Jafar. Still, available money was insufficient. It was agreed that the shortfall will be collected in instalments and in-kind payments through jewellery and precious metals. Mir Jafar ceded Diwani (revenue collection) of 24 Parganas district to the company. Lord Macaulay recorded that booty coined in silver was sent in boats to Calcutta. There were 75 boats each carrying a chest with one lakh (100,000) silver rupees.[14] Clive claimed two hundred and eighty thousand rupees as his share being a member of the select committee, two hundred thousand as commander-in-chief and a further sum of sixteen lakh rupees as a special gift from Mir Jafar. His total booty was equivalent of 234,000 British pounds sterling. Other members of the select committee and army also received their share.[15] However, Indian collaborators were shown the door because the treasury was empty, and Mir Jafar still needed money to meet his commitments. Amin Chand insisted on having the amount promised in the written document. Clive confronted him with the real copy of the document which did not mention his name among the beneficiaries. Upon learning that he was hoodwinked the hapless merchant lost his mind[16] and fainted. He left on pilgrimage, never fully recovered and died a few months later. An Indian gentleman of that day might expect double-dealing from his fellow countryman but would never expect an Englishman to break his word. Clive's actions, including the deposing of Siraj-ud-Daula and the tricking of Amin Chand, were dubious. The whole episode, another dishonourable ruse of the honourable company, embellished her moral depravity. The irony is that listless Moghul rulers of India let it pass unnoticed.

Luderitz Land Fraud: European nations-built forts/posts along west coast of Africa during the busy days of slave trade. In second half of the nineteenth century, these nations shifted their focus and began vying for a chunk of African territory for purposes of commodity trade, mineral prospecting and colonisation. The first German Chancellor, who had thus far shunned imperial ambitions, also joined the race. He promised German protection and letter of patent to those German merchants who acquired lands in Africa and administered them in the name of Germany. Two German adventurers, Franz Adolf Luderitz and Dr. Carl Peters took the lead. Luderitz, a tobacco merchant from Bremen, secured the chancellor's assurance before opting to prospect minerals in Africa. In 1882, Luderitz and his partner Heinrich Vogelsang traced a landmass on the west coast of Africa which looked unclaimed. Their understanding was incorrect. Since 1851 a Cape Town-based trader Aaron de Pass had been working on the Guano deposits of the area. In 1863, his company de Pass, Spence and Co. had signed a deed of land sale with the then native chief David Christian. The agreement granted the company mining rights on the coastline between Angra Pequena and Baker's Cove and a stretch of hinterland, excluding the Bays. Unaware of this deal, Luderitz sent Heinrich Vogelsang for acquiring land in this Nama territory for mineral prospecting and trade. Vogelsang landed at Angra Pequena on 10th April 1883 and travelled on foot to Bethany, headquarters of the Nama chief. He met the ruling chief Joseph Fredricks II in the company of Johannes Heinrich Bam, a Rhenish missionary known to the chief. With assistance from Bam, he bought from the Nama chief an area along the coast, in a radius of 8 km (5 miles), including Angra Pequena Bay against payment of one hundred pounds in gold and 200 Westley Richard rifles. Even this small sum was not paid in cash but in the form of goods, prices of which were fixed by the Germans. Nama chief was also urged to keep the earlier deal of his predecessor David Christian with the British firm, under wraps.

This initial transaction gave the Germans a foothold on the African west coast. German flag was raised over Angra Pequena on 12th May 1883. Vogelsang struck another deal with Nama chief which turned out highly scandalous because it exploited the ignorance of Joseph Fredricks II. This deal signed on 25th August 1883, mentioned that Bethanie people had sold a 20 geographical mile wide strip of land extending from the mouth of Orange River up to 20° South latitude, to Luderitz against a promised payment of 500 pounds (equivalent of 10,000 German Marks) and sixty rifles.[17] Later on the horrified Nama chief claimed that Vogelsang had shown him the area he sold on the map with a compass. Actually, Vogelsang had rendered Nama chief inebriated with a liberal dose of drinks to make the confused chief believe that German geographical mile and English mile meant the same thing. Joseph Fredricks had surmised that the transaction was about a worthless stretch of coastal desert. Further he was assured that Luderitz was only interested to explore minerals in that sand. Based on the German interpretation of the contract, the Batheny chief had parted with a major chunk of fertile territory of his people. The trick lay in mention of the geographical mile, which though obsolete and rarely used, was 7.4 km long compared with 1.6 km length of the English mile Joseph Fredricks II was familiar with. Missionary Bam who acted as interpreter and signed the deal as a witness knew that the Nama chief was ignorant of the vast difference in the two units of length. Still, he did not caution him. In this manner Germans had acquired the 148 km wide strip of land instead of a 32 km wide strip the Nama chief had actually agreed to sell. The chief had been tricked into selling not only more than half of Bethany territory but also a part of the territory supposed to have been acquired by the British firm de Pass and Spence of Cape Town. Although it was his partner who struck the fraudulent deal, Luderitz knew that Vogelsang had hoodwinked Joseph Fredrick by concealing the difference between the two units of length. He acknowledged this fact in private. As regards territory claimed by de

Pass and Spence, the British and German governments discussed the issue and reached a settlement wherein Luderitz retained most of the contested territory.

Joseph Fredricks II, after he failed to seek amends from Luderitz, brought the fraudulently executed deal to the notice of Dr. Gustav Nachtigal, German council general for the west coast of Africa. Nachtigal asked the chief to give his complaint in writing signed by witnesses to the deal with Luderitz. Nachtigal understood the reprehensible role played by missionary Bam who did not explain what was meant by the word 'geographical' mile. He deleted the word 'geographical' in the treaty and retained mile, only to signify English mile. Nachtigal was to carry the document to Germany for amendment but he never reached Berlin.[18] He died at sea on 20th April 1885 off Cape Palmas. The deal remained as penned despite subsequent efforts of the Bethany people who were the real owners of the property. As in the first Luderitz deal, Joseph Fredricks II was never paid the promised cash. Instead, he was paid in trade goods where the price was fixed by the Germans themselves. On 24th April 1884, Bismarck declared all Bethany territory a German protectorate. For all intents and purposes Namaqualand came under German rule. Luderitz purchased additional land from other Nama tribes promising them lands in the interior of Africa, knowing fully well that those lands belonged to the Hereros. Theodor Leutwein, governor of SWA, from 1894 to 1904, acknowledged that land acquisition treaties of Luderitz were of dubious nature.[19] Usurping African lands fraudulently left ugly scars on the native psyche. Their discontent, whenever surfaced, was brutally suppressed. By 1907 legislation, African natives of German colonies were barred from owning land and cattle. Their movement was curtailed. These measures were undertaken to ensure regular availability of cheap labour for the agricultural estates of the white settlers.

Chapter 7
Natives Lose Their Lands in the Americas, Africa and Australasia

Manifest destiny and ethics are incongruous. Ethics never bothered Europeans when they ran over the non-European world to expropriate its lands and resources. They sheltered their actions under laws that they proclaimed and legal rights they invented. Europeans justified occupation of foreign lands invoking the self-declared doctrine of discovery and unilaterally declaring the land being *terra nullius*. Colonial powers developed legal systems to extinguish land titles of the natives in their colonies. Sometimes they entered in to dubious treaties and agreements. The *modus operandi* was to claim significant sovereignty over the occupied territory while relegating sovereignty of the indigenous peoples to their mere usage of lands.[1] The papal bull of 1452 originated the first phase of European colonisation and land grab. It authorized Portugal to hold non-Christian world by conquest and to spread Christianity. Papal bull Romanus Pontifex of 1455 was used by Catholics and non-Catholics alike to capture lands of the natives in the Americas and countries of the South Pacific region. Christopher Columbus had already laid Spanish claim on Hispaniola before the Pope bestowed similar authorization upon Spain in 1492. The British jumped on the bandwagon proclaiming that a Christian nation was duty bound to bring Christianity to the 'heathen'. The 1606 Charter granted by King James I to London and Plymouth companies was a religious mission invested with the idea of establishing settlements on foreign soil. Cushman, a leading pilgrim on ship of the Plymouth Company persuaded fellow pilgrims to sail for America to convert the 'heathen' of that land. He promised that land being empty will make their settlement lawful. He assumed that this distant land mass was *terra nullius* despite an obvious presence of the natives. In Western eyes, conquest and assumed discovery sanctioned occupation of foreign lands. All occupied lands had indigenous populations. Europe also swore by the inane doctrine that proprietary right to foreign lands vested in the sovereign by the right of conquest. Europeans settled abroad under this proposition and then evicted the natives from their heritage. Westward expansion of the United States was treated as divine wish. Wells made interesting comparison of acquiring territories by the United States and England. "While England never did a meaner thing in respect to the acquisition of territory than did the United States in 1848, when under a claim of might and a higher civilization, she robbed, without justification, and at full swoop, poor Mexico of more than half of all its territory."[2] It could be a matter of degree but every colonial power used the meanest methods to grab foreign lands. To cite one case, the English invaded and annexed the state of Sind in India. Their military chief admitted that they had no right to seize Sind, but it was a useful piece of rascality.

Largest land grab occurred in the Americas. Iberian church pioneered encroachment of lands in the newly conquered world. By 1600, the Catholic Church owned over one-third of land in the Jesuit estates of the Spanish and Portuguese America. In the early 1700s, the Dominican plantations of Central America, employing some 1000 native Indians and 150 black slaves, enriched Iberian economy.[3] European adventurers and conquistadors claimed foreign lands in the name of their mother country regardless of the presence of its rightful owners. They affirmed that expropriation of lands accompanied conquest. The British, who supplanted Moghul rule in India, claimed that proprietary right to lands of India vested in the Sovereign by the right of conquest. They charged the cultivators as much as one half of agricultural produce as land tax. All common property lands, like grazing grounds and forests were declared Crown lands.

In North America native Indians were threatened overtly or covertly to sell their lands at nominal price. Other lands were expropriated under the English law or on ecological reasons. In the end, the Indians were the losers. In the early 1600's English settlers depended on these very Indians for their survival. As the European population increased and the population of Indians declined, foreigners gained the upper hand. In the end the colonists captured almost all the land of the country and the natives were consigned to reserves. The Indian Removal Act of 1830, passed during the presidency of Andrew Jackson, authorized their forcible removal. Indians were relocated west of the Mississippi River in an area that now forms the state of Oklahoma. Most unfavourably affected was the Cherokee nation. Over 4000 out of the 15000 relocated Cherokee perished due to exhaustion, hunger and diseases during the journey they called the *"Trail of Tears"*. Muscogee, Seminole, Chickasaw, and Choctaw were the other nations who were forced out of their abodes. Within seven years, 40,000 Native Americans of south eastern states had to leave their homeland at bayonet point.[4] Thousands of them died protecting their heritage. The survivors bowed out into designated reserves, chiefly to the west of Mississippi River. Majority of the Indians ended up in reserves under the Indian Removal Act. Most badly treated were the Sioux Indians of Minnesota, 38 of whom were hanged on 26th December 1862 under sanction of the U.S. President Abraham Lincoln. Their crime was that they protested against rotten grains supplied to them and disregarding their other living needs. The Sioux had signed the treaty to entrust a million acres of their land and move in to reserves on the promise that their living needs would be taken care of by the State. Between 1828 and 1838, twenty-five million acres of their land was occupied by white settlers after the natives were pushed in to the reserves. Forcible occupation was justified as white man's manifest destiny. Another 90,000 natives were rendered landless under the 1887 Dawes Act. Thus, natives who once possessed the vast country were confined to 2.21 percent land area of the United States of America. Major expansion of the United States occurred at the cost of Mexico which lost about one half of its territory. Similarly, natives of a number of Caribbean islands vanished leaving behind their inheritance to the European intruders.

Natives of Africa, Australia, New Zealand, and islands of the Oceania lost their revered lands to colonialism of the eighteenth and nineteenth centuries. Land was a key to European rule and a strong purpose of being in the colonies. The history of expropriation of lands of African natives begins from 6th April 1562 when Dutch Captain Jan van Riebeeck anchored his vessel carrying 82 men at the foot of Table Mountain near the present-day Cape Town. He was on a mission to establish a strong base, raise fruits and vegetables, and procure animal products for stocking Dutch vessels bound for the East Indies. Riebeeck found native pastoralists, whom the Dutch called Hottentots, very friendly because they helped him build a mud fort at the Table Bay. The natives cheered all ships that passed the calling station, unmindful of the evil designs of their human cargo. Gradually the calling station grew into a small settlement. Once settled, visitors began casting intrusive eyes on the pastures and cattle of the natives in their vicinity. They even talked of killing them to capture their cattle and pastures. Eventually the natives were forced out and their lands seized to grow fruits and vegetables, using the very natives as slave labour. Natives rose up in defiance. Beginning 1659, they fought incessant battles with the foreign intruders. But neither Hottentots nor Bushmen stood any chance against the sturdy and well-armed Dutch. Eviction of African tribes from their ancestral lands accelerated after French Huguenots and Dutch Calvinists came and settled in the Cape area. Descendants of these Europeans took to farming with the help of dispossessed natives taken as slaves.

After the British occupied the Cape in 1795, they confiscated native lands and allotted those to white settlers of the Colony. Native tribes, as everywhere else, considered lands community endowment and inalienable. They were shocked when their lands were given over to the Europeans for permanent settlement. The original owners were left with only two options of either becoming tenant farmers or moving out of the area. Dutch pastoralists, called Afrikaners or Boers, who lived on the periphery of the Cape Colony, constantly looked out for new pastures in the interior. Boer movement into their domain was vehemently opposed by the Bantu-speaking Xhosa tribe, who were sturdier and more belligerent than the other African tribes. Beginning 1779, the Xhosa fought nine wars with the Europeans in a span of one hundred years. Land grab ventures of Boer settlers of the Cape Colony continued until the early nineteenth century. In 1811, the Boers and the British launched a joint expedition against the Xhosa and seized their lands on the Great Fish River to settle four thousand British colonists. At the end of the sixth Xhosa-British war of 1834–1836, all Xhosa lands up to Kei River were declared Crown property. White settlers joined hands with British forces of Governor Benjamin D'Urban to fight the Xhosa. They occupied Xhosa lands and seized thousands of Xhosa cattle. By this time Boers and Britons fell apart, and the former opted to embark on the Great Trek. During their trek Boers overran solitary African tribes, seizing their lands as well as cattle.

In East Africa, the British declared grazing lands as Crown property and brought in white settlers to raise large plantations. They induced dispossessed natives to work on white-owned plantations as wage labour. The British had problems in accomplishing the same in the Gold Coast colony where best agricultural lands were declared Crown lands to encourage European settlers.[5] In 1891, Chief Justice Hutchinson of the Gold Coast was asked if the government could take over all waste lands. The chief justice opined that all land occupied or unoccupied had an owner in the traditional African law. The British had to take the legislative route to acquire the lands of the natives. The government promulgated the Crown Lands Bill of 1896 and the Lands Bill of 1897 which threatened traditional system of land tenure. The Aborigine Protection Society opposed it. Colonial office disallowed the Bill after a delegation of the Society visited London. This Bill was designed to vest the queen with all wastelands, forest lands and minerals in the colony. It was eventually withdrawn. In 1909, the British promulgated Private Location Act which closed land renting opportunities to the Africans. Prior to this Act, 40,000 Africans lived in the Cape Province. By 1931, their numbers dwindled to mere 7000.[6] The 1913 Native Land Law Act restricted 84 percent native population to just 13 percent land area reserved for them. The purpose was to destroy any economic independence of the Africans.

African natives were made to depend upon white settlers for sustenance. According to the South African Native Affairs Commission (1903-5) African economic independence was a threat to the survival of European dominance. Therefore, there could not be any equality in terms of land ownership.[7] No African was permitted to buy land in the non-reserved 87 percent land area of South Africa. Africans outside the reserve could neither buy nor rent the land of the Europeans.[8] They had no option but to become agricultural tenant labour. The whole country was under a mere 16 percent white population that lived on large farming estates. By the 1920's South Africa enacted laws restricting African access to farming land. They could either become share croppers or slave labour on the estates of the white settlers. Above acts and regulations virtually cut off African natives from the lands they had lived upon for generations. They could seek life outside reserves only as tenant farmers or in servitude on white estates set up on their own lands by the British, the Boers and the Portuguese.

Europeans, who participated in the Berlin Conference of 1884–1885, faked concern for African welfare and against slaving. Actually, it was a gathering for spoliation of Africa. German Chancellor Bismarck repudiated colonial ambitions but, soon enough, Germany joined European nations in claiming her own share of protectorates like German East Africa, South West Africa, (hereafter SWA) Kamerun (Cameroon), and Togoland. Similarly, other powers carved out chunks of African territory based on the strips of land they held along the African coast. In this manner sitting thousands of miles away, Europeans thrust hegemony on a population which was not even represented at the conference. Armed with self-proclaimed legitimacy of the protectorates, each colonial power began appropriating African lands to establish white-run farming estates. Natives resented alienation of their pastures and agricultural lands. Their resistance was crushed with proclaimed laws and punitive expeditions. By 1914 colonial governments had curbed all resistance to land acquisition. Africans had learnt that that they cannot challenge white man's firepower. The British began colonizing Kenya in 1885. An advertisement was placed for white settlers who could use fertile land in Kenya to produce cash crops. In 1920, 10,000 British were settled on fertile highlands where they got 600 to 1500-acre parcels of land on a 999-year lease. Around 60,000 acres of Kikuyu land was acquired for this purpose. The Kikuyu tribe vainly rose in protest against confiscation of their lands. The tribe had to move over whenever white settlers demanded more land in the fertile elevated region. Europeans benefitted from expropriation of best African lands in two ways. They became owners of highly productive lands and economic insecurity thus created for the Africans compelled them to do labour at their estates. Eviction from ancestral lands ended their traditional communal land tenure systems.[9] Thousands of natives perished resisting superior British forces. The Masai people lived in the Rift valley. Oxford-educated first British Governor of Kenya, Sir Charles Eliot, had no compunction in modifying his opinion of the Masai in deference to need of the time.[10] When white settlers cast their eyes on the fertile Rift Valley grazing grounds of the Masai, Eliot justified appropriation of the territory questioning the right of wandering tribes over large tracts of land merely because they had acquired the habit of spreading over far more land than they could utilise. Many in Britain objected to seizing the lands of the natives. Eliot in his letter to Lord Lansdowne, the British foreign secretary, denounced the Masai and those who defended and exaggerated African claims over land rights. He clung to the view that the Masai should not be allowed to stand in the way of European development.[11] In 1903 the East Africa Syndicate was given a lease of a block of 500 square miles of land in the fertile Rift Valley.[12] Hapless Masai ended up in distant reserves in Kenya and Tanzania. Eliot turned Kenya into white man's country after displacing Kenyan natives and bringing in white settlers in their place.[13] White settlements were to be the backbone of Kenya's economy. Kenyan Africans were discouraged from developing their own areas. Government scaled up taxes to compel destitute Africans to do labour in public works. In 1915 the colonial office accepted the demand of the white settlers for greater security of land tenure. The increase in tenure of land lease from 99 to 999 years was a step in this direction.[14] Out of 224,960 square miles area of Kenya, 16000 square miles was alienated to the European settlers. Similar land grab occurred in South Africa, Southern Rhodesia, Zambia and Malawi.

Europeans imposed restrictions on land use by the Africans. They were allowed to own least productive lands in Kenya, Rhodesia and the Belgian Congo.[15] White settlers were free to set up large estates on crown lands, but the same privilege was denied to the natives. The British created a category of Crown lands by alienating grazing grounds after declaring them waste lands. They succeeded in executing this ploy in East Africa but the same was strongly opposed in Gold Coast. British policy created enough work force of natives for working on white-owned estates because cattle rearing natives had lost their source of livelihood. In 1904, the Natal government barred Africans from purchasing Crown land. They were also prohibited from buying lands held by the European settlers. The South African Native Affairs Commission (1903–1905) admitted disparity in the right to land ownership between the white and native populations. The British South Africa Company drove Africans into reserves so that the bulk of territory vacated in Northern Nyasa Land (now Malawi) could be used by white settlers for their plantations. Settlers expanded their estates after the First World War. Eventually land owned by the Europeans *per capita* rose to about 800 acres, while per capita land with the natives was barely six acres. In colonial Zimbabwe 4700 white farmers held 41 million acres while four million native peasants possessed only 39 million acres of land. Alienation of lands held by the Africans created a large work force of natives for the European-owned plantations. Loss of land entailed economic hardships to the natives who were further burdened with poll tax, hut tax, and other restrictions. Economically weak natives had no choice but to accept cheap labour at European farms to discharge their taxes and feed their families. Governor Sir Charles Eliot, a votary of white Kenya, admitted that taxation was the only method to compel natives to seek work. Inherently, Africans resented the large white estates established on their lands and the monopoly granted to them to grow commercial crops like cotton and coffee which enjoyed a large export market. Landless Kikuyu peasants drifted toward the anti-colonial Mau Mau uprising between 1952 and 1960 to fight not only white settlers and the British government, but also native British loyalists who assisted land transfers favouring the white settlers. The British produced a crop of loyalists in all their colonies by bestowing small favours. Kiwanuka called them collaborators.[16] Landed natives were only allowed to grow crops like beans, rice and maize, which found limited local market. Colonial government unabashedly justified this disparity before the 1929 Native Reserves Commission on the premise that Africans required just ten acres of land to produce staple crops to feed their family, but Europeans needed in excess of five hundred acres to raise commercial crops. Another sad effect of the expropriation of lands of the natives was the Mau Mau uprising in Kenya that consumed thousands of African lives.

European estates in all the colonies continued to expand at the cost of the displaced Africans. In northern Nyasaland, the natives apprised the Native Reserves Commission that they were threatened by the expansion of settler estates.[17] One A. Harvey, in partnership with two other Europeans, established a 300-acre farm in 1911. In 1920, he acquired another 500 acres. By 1929, he owned 1000 acres, 700 acres of which were bought by him.[18] Evidently Europeans felt no bar in extending their farming estates, but Africans were prohibited from doing the same. In 1920 when European settlers already owned 10,000 acres land *per capita* in Southern Rhodesia (Zimbabwe), the government decided to acquire more land from the Africans who hardly possessed twenty-three percent of the total land. In northern Rhodesia (Zambia) per capita land with the Europeans was 130 times larger than what was owned by any African.[19] In 1980, Zimbabwe's white minority commercial farms were spread over nearly one-half of the country's agricultural land. In 1994 white settlers of South Africa who formed less than 10 percent of the country's population owned 87 percent of her agricultural land.

Germans wrote the bloodiest tale of land grab in South West Africa. The local Herero and Nama were agricultural people who survived on cattle rearing. Germans decided to settle Europeans in fertile lands then occupied by the above tribes. Naturally, the natives resisted their eviction from lands they had always lived upon. This was enough of a pretext for the Germans to conquer the territory militarily and settle this land issue once for all in their favour. The Herero were determined to defend their land. Their women shouted Herero land is our land.[20] But General von Trotha led a military expedition to oust Herero and Nama tribes from their lands. The brutally executed expedition amounted to their genocide in which they were all but wiped out. The Germans had broken the resistance power of the Herero and Nama people for years to come. Some of their people fled to the neighbouring countries for refuge. Following this expedition, an Imperial decree issued on 26th December 1905 declared all Herero land, and subsequently all lands of the Nama tribe, Crown territories. These lands were passed on to the white colonists. Justification for seizing grazing lands from the natives was that the colonists wanted them for grazing their own stocks.[21] On 1st October 1904 an extermination order of von Trotha appeared stating that all Herero must leave the land.[22] On 18th August 1907, the governor of SWA issued ordinances that permanently barred Africans from owning land and rearing cattle, the only livelihood they had ever pursued. In this way, one-third of all good quality land was seized from the Africans. Poor natives who were supposed to be under German protection were, instead, rendered paupers and stateless in their own country. Similarly, in 1896, Germans declared all land out of active cultivation (native pastures) in Cameroon (Kamerun), as Crown property, and given over to the European planters. The 1910 ordinance of German Togoland declared all land classified as waste land to be State property. In this manner the Germans dispossessed the natives of their lands they used for pasture and agricultural crops and transferred the same to the white settlers.

The Portuguese, who pioneered Atlantic slave trade in Africa, were notorious for their slave-run farming estates and plantations in their mainland colonies of Africa, Sao Tome and the Principe Islands. Portuguese created an estate system of land tenure in the colony of Mozambique. All land outside individual ownership, was declared State property and allotted to white settlers. A mere 2.7 percent white population occupied 48 percent land south of the Save (Sabi) River. Lands, where Africans raised their livestock, were reserved for alienation through a system of concessions. Out of this pool, corporations and even white individuals with means to develop lands were given land grants from 10,000 hectares up to 50,000 hectares (100 sq. km to 500 sq. km area). Displaced natives sought work in the Rand mines of South Africa. Thus, a large section of the native population was reduced to the status of vassals or labour force for the white estates. Native tribes, who had thus far lived on community lands, lost their right to live on them and raise their cattle.

France seized a part of coastal Algeria from the Ottoman rulers and began expropriating Arab lands. In 1832, the Duke of Rovigo, who headed the French military in Algeria, began settling colonists over land forcibly seized from the Arabs. Legislation was formulated to dispossess the natives of their lands and thus reduce them to the status of vagrants.[23] Two years later, France annexed all occupied territories then populated by two million Algerians. In this way the French expropriated 168,000 hectares (about 420,000 acres) in Algiers district alone. Through a decree issued in March 1843, all religious (*waqf*) lands stood confiscated. The 1843 decree, declared all uncultivated lands, excluding land deals prior to 1830, as State property. A subsequent decree of October 1844 permitted Europeans to buy the above lands. The large native population was left with merely 30,000 hectares (75,000 acres). France confiscated

1.25 million acres of tribal land in the aftermath of the 1871 Kabayle resistance movement. In this way European colonists had monopolized three million hectares of the best lands. In 1954, European population of Algeria was 11.5 percent out of 9.5 million total population of the country, yet they occupied 75 percent of the irrigated crop land. Of the agriculturist population, 3.5 percent Europeans owned 22 percent of best agricultural lands with an average of 90 hectare (225 acres) per person compared with 32.5 acres per capita with the Algerians. French arbitrariness reduced 85 percent of the previously sedentary population in the affluent part of Algeria to nomadic existence. Many native peasants migrated to the neighbouring countries.[24] Economic security of native population of the colonies was shattered when Europeans seized their best agricultural lands. Colonialists created export bias that favoured white settlers who held monopolies on commodities like tea, coffee, cocoa, sugar and cotton, and enjoyed captive European markets. Land grab policy of colonial nations also broke down the traditional community structure of the natives.

The African nation where natives were reduced to most deplorable conditions was the so-called Congo Free State of King Leopold II of Belgium. Leopold decreed that all lands of the Congo, except small patches of land under actual cultivation, were property of the State. After monopolizing all forest and uncultivated lands, he granted large parcels of lands to European corporations on the stipulation that Leopold received one half of the turnout of those lands. He put aside 112,000 square miles of area under best rubber forests as his personal property. Besides rubber, these forests yielded ivory from elephants both of which had great demand in the West. Leopold forced native labour to collect both commodities. They were required to collect designated quantities of rubber and ivory and deposit them at the collection centres. At the end of the day failure to meet the allotted quota meant inhuman corporal punishment, dismemberment of limbs and even death. Corporal punishment and inhuman exactions wiped out about one-fifth of the native population. Congo Free State earned so much infamy that Belgium had to annex the territory in 1908. It was then named Belgian Congo.

Wholesale seizure of lands of the native populations occurred in countries of Australasia, turned by the British into white man colonies.

In 1770, Captain Cook demolished the right of natives over their ancestral heritage when he wrongly claimed that 7.6 million square kilometres plus country of Australia was *terra nullius*. He had full knowledge that the country was inhabited. Until 1788, when Captain Arthur Phillip arrived with a shipload of English convicts, the natives were masters of all land and natural resources of that country. The land was considered common property of a tribe never to be divided. It was preserved and, in fact, venerated, treated as a community property never to be parcelled. Similar common property custom prevailed in New Zealand and probably in other indigenous societies of the colonised countries. The English disregarded this tradition and extinguished the right of natives under their own concept of law. Sir William Blackstone, a British jurist and author of several commentaries, saw no rule by which laws of England became laws of a territory which was not a "desert uninhabited" country when the Crown acquired sovereignty over that territory by discovery and occupation as *"terra nullius."* Britain applied its own concept in her colonies. In the Mbo case, the Australian high court accepted that the strong assumption of the common law was that interests in property which existed under the native law or custom were not obliterated by act of the State establishing a new British colony but were preserved and protected by domestic law of the colony after its establishment. The natives were happy in their tribal life, rearing cattle and collecting food from the land and fish from the waterways. Their life pattern was imperilled when thousands of British settlers, convicts, prospectors, and squatters, began forcing themselves on their lands ignoring their inherent right to their heritage. Natives resisted foreign occupation but their traditional weapons like spears were ineffective against combined force of the colonial armed police, convicts and new settlers. White settlers connived with the colonial government and killed natives indiscriminately for the sole purpose of forcing them out of the lands they themselves wished to settle upon. Surviving natives were pushed into inhospitable areas and left to fend for themselves. Fifty years later only a handful of wretched natives were seen in the Sydney area. In Tasmania, a military campaign was launched to either eliminate or force the natives to abandon lands they were living upon. Surviving natives were captured and shipped to a remote island. Out of productive lands, thus cleared of natives, 250,000 acres were allotted to van Diemen's Land Company. In the end remaining natives were confined to the reserves. More than two centuries later, in 1970, a native Eddie Mbo successfully challenged the British premise of Australia being *terra nullius*. In 1992, the Australian High Court overturned the status of *terra nullius* and accepted the right of the natives to ownership of their lands. The Australian parliament enacted the Native Title Act in 1993, whereby legal position of the indigenous land holders was codified. Acknowledgment of the native's rights over lands of Australia, demolished the only British argument for occupying that country and seizing lands which had sustained native populations for centuries.

New Zealand, twelve hundred miles to the southwest of Australia was also declared *terra nullius* by the British when they first registered their presence in the South Island. They entrusted the administration of the Island to the governor of New South Wales. At the time New Zealand was home to well-organized communities of the Maori tribe. Christian missionaries, who pre-dated British intrusion, helped the latter in gaining a foothold in the new country. In the meantime, a private company began shipping prospective English settlers to the island and signed land deals with some local chiefs. The colonial government in Australia was alarmed at this development. It sought the help of local missionaries to persuade the Maori in to signing a treaty with the British. It was a race against time to forestall the efforts of the private company. Missionaries prepared draft of a treaty, later called the Treaty of Waitangi. The treaty was drawn in the local Maori language. Its essence was explained to few chiefs without explaining its import. The treaty invested all lands in the native community, but the natives were obliquely made to accept the sovereignty of the British Crown. Natives were not briefed about what they were surrendering by accepting sovereignty of the British Crown. When confronted with the English version of the treaty, Maoris found it at variance with what they were made to understand by the missionaries. The British had begun acquiring, lands from the individuals. Maoris protested to the extent of open hostility on the premise that the Waitangi Treaty was misinterpreted. A disputed land purchase by Governor Gore Brown at the Waitara River led to the Maori-British wars of 1860's. By 1861, colonial government had purchased about two-thirds of the territory of New Zealand, largest purchase being in the South Island. British made all purchase under the Native Land Act of 1860 which permitted individual ownership of land. This was done under the pretext of a sovereignty clause under which the Crown usurped community rights. This act took lands out of communal ownership then prevalent in the country and facilitated the government as well as individuals to purchase lands through surreptitious deals. Consequently, by 1895, Maoris lost almost 95 percent of their land. They also suffered a huge loss of lives in unequal and prolonged wars fought with the colonialists and due to diseases, they contracted from the Europeans. Maori population which was about 100,000 in 1840 declined to 42113 in the 1896 census. European population, hardly 2000 in 1840, rose to 100,000 by end of the Maori wars, and touched the figure of 700,000 in 1896. Meanwhile, the Treaty of Waitangi remained a disputed document. By 1930 the Europeans had firm control over the non-European world. Post First World War colonies of Germany and their allies were taken over by other European nations. Colonial occupation of lands remained unchanged with 84 percent of global land surface under white nations.

Chapter 8
Slavery and Colonisation: The Connection

The institution of slavery dates back to ancient times but the master-slave relationship is not fully defined. Hierarchical rank and social standing of a person was measured by the number of slaves under his command. Slaves were supposed to submit to their master completely. Ancient societies accepted slaving of the vanquished, and this practice prevailed in all major civilizations. Ancient treatise on state craft written in the fourth century BC by Kautilya incorporates rules regarding slavery and labourers. Slavery of that period was, however, different from the slave trade practiced by the Arabs and the Europeans. Enslaving resulted from indebtedness, punishment for crimes, or in wars when the victor enslaved the defeated army and general public. In medieval times, returning conquistadors took vanquished people to their country and sold them. In tribal wars, a defeated tribe was reduced to slavery *en masse*. War time slavery was oblivious of ethnic and religious distinctions. Actually, it was one form of social dominance. Victors of religion-inspired invasions butchered all able-bodied males of their foe. Their women were taken prisoners for harems and domestic slavery. In A.D. 712 Hajjaj bin Yusuf, the governor of Iraq sent his son-in-law Muhammad bin Qasim with a large army of religious zealots against the Hindu rulers of Sind in India. To begin with, Qasim killed most defeated Hindus but subsequently pardoned many on the condition that they pay a religious tax. On his return journey, he herded thousands of Indians as slaves including young ladies of royal blood and took severed head of the Hindu ruler as a trophy for Hajjaj. Mahmud of Gazni invaded India seventeen times between A.D. 1000 and 1025 to plunder the country. Besides looting the treasure of demolished Hindu temples, he took thousands of Indians as slaves and sold them in markets of central Asia. Around one million Christian slaves were brought into the Muslim world during the Tatar raids of the thirteenth century and Ottoman wars of the fifteenth century. Most of them belonged to the coastal villages of Portugal, Spain and Italy. Similarly, victims of Barbary piracy captured along the Mediterranean coast were sold in markets of North Africa. Between 1500 and 1730 there were 25,000 captives in Algiers. Some 7500 men, women, and children were held in Tunis and Tripoli.[1] Irish Catholics suffered disgrace of slavery at the hands of English church at home and on British sugar plantations in the West Indies.

Slave trade where humans became a commodity began in the seventh century. Gilbert Murray an English scholar and educator approved it in terms of a worldwide division of labour among breeds of men, the inferior work going to the inferior races, the higher work to the higher and more highly paid races.[2] The inference is too simple to hold water. Arabs and Christians practiced slavery for several hundred years regardless of the race. A slave dynasty ruled India for a century. The watershed area for slaves started from Zaire in west-central Africa extending through Tanzania, Kenya and Sudan. Arab traders shipped black Africans from this area to locations in the Muslim world now represented by Kuwait, Iran, and Turkey. In India, African slaves from the East Coast were employed as guards by the rulers. Slave trade was plied through overland caravans of slaves across the Sahara to North Africa after the Portuguese and other European nations showed up on the East Coast of Africa for the same purpose. Annual trans-Saharan trade amounted to around 6000 to 7000 slaves. Between A.D. 650 and A.D. 1900, millions of hapless Africans of the Sahel and other regions were enslaved and marketed like a commodity. Upper Egypt had separate dealers for white and black slaves. Slave trade caused degradation of the African peoples.[3] It was pressure of the British Anti-slavery Society that 1877 and 1895 Anglo-Egypt anti-slave trade conventions were held to end this abhorrent trade.

Slave trade on a large scale began with the trans-Atlantic shipping of slaves to meet the growing demand of labour in the European colonies. Portugal, a maritime nation of modest means but geographically a close neighbour to Africa, arrived on the coast of Guinea for the purpose of trading in gold, pepper and ivory in the mid-fifteenth century. It became the first European nation to establish slave trade and dominate it until beginning of the eighteenth century. West coast of Africa with its myriads of lagoons and waterways was an ideal place to capture and haul Africans from the interior to the coastal ports. Gold coast area came to be known as the Slave Coast. Portugal acquired 150,000 slaves between A.D. 1450 and 1500. Some of them were transported to her new colonies of Madeira and Azores for sugarcane and wheat cultivation. The rest were sold to Italy and Spain.[4] Portuguese operated out of the Lagos slaving centre from where they shipped slaves for their own colonies and for sale to other colonial nations in the Americas. Slaves were needed for sugarcane cultivation in the Portuguese colonies of Sao Tome and Principe established in the Gulf of Guinea in 1522. Elmina Fort built in 1482 on the coast of present-day Ghana became an important slaving centre as well as trading post for gold. The Dutch East-India Company seized Elmina Fort in 1637 and used it as capital of Dutch Gold Coast and a base for shipping slaves to the Americas. The Portuguese fort of Benguela built in 1587 to the south of Luanda in Angola, also became a busy slaving centre. Portugal lost control of these slaving centres during the wars with the Dutch. It is during this period that the Dutch developed taste for slaving and then on became an important trans-Atlantic slave shipping nation.

Trading in slaves was a very lucrative business. Besides monetary gains, slaves helped Europeans fully exploit their colonies and enrich themselves. Profits and the indispensability of slaves boosted trans-Atlantic slave shipping. The first direct shipment from Africa arrived in Hispaniola (now Haiti and Dominican Republic) in 1578. A decade later Spaniards obtained a shipment of slaves in their failed effort to establish a colony in what is now North Carolina State of the United States. Brazil became an important destination of slaves because by 1545 Portuguese needed slave labour for their gold mines and sugarcane plantations. They found native labour sluggish due to diseases they contracted from their colonial masters. Thus, trans-Atlantic slave trade between Niger Delta and Amazon Delta picked up in the sixteenth century. Around 1620, English, French, and Portuguese ships began ferrying slaves from the Congo River Coast to destinations in North America. Slaves were procured by African chiefs and rulers in the interior and brought to the slaving ports. There were professional slave catchers along the coast who helped in this abhorrent trade. Moreover, Europeans managed to install those African chiefs/rulers who were prepared to do their bidding. The Portuguese even launched military expeditions to capture slaves. Slave trade had several dimensions. African chiefs needed guns as a bulwark against their rival chiefs. They bartered slaves against guns, alcohol, horses and even cloth. Slaves were shipped to the West Indies where they were sold to the Spanish colonies and in central and South America. Spanish monarchy prohibited direct trading in slaves. During his third expedition Columbus proposed that gentle native Caribs of the West Indies should be sold as slaves to finance the government. In 1494 he shipped five hundred slaves from Hispaniola to markets in Spain under the pretext that these idolaters needed to be baptized.[5] Slave shipping companies used earnings to buy sugar, coffee and tobacco for the European market. On another Trans-Atlantic run between North America and Africa, ships carried rum and other products of the New England colonies. These commodities were bartered for slaves in Africa. Sugar and coffee bought against slaves were taken to New England and sold to producers of rum. In this manner 70 percent of the African slaves ended up in the Americas.

Several slave trading companies appeared on the horizon because this profitable trade required very little investment. The Dutch and French entered this trade in the 1650's to ferry slave labour needed for exploiting their colonies in the Caribbean. The Dutch, on the back of their maritime and economic strength, were preeminent in shipping slaves to the New World. As early as 1619, Dutch traders sold 20 Africans to the colony of Virginia. Dutch West India Company chartered in 1621 was a foremost slave trader in the slaving history. By 1650 it shipped 30,000 African slaves to Dutch Brazil. Between 1705 and 1805 Rhode Island merchants sponsored 1000 slaving voyages to West Africa. In the East, between 1626 and 1662, Dutch East India Company annually exported between 150 and 400 slaves from the East Coast of India to its bases in Batavia and Malacca. By the middle of the seventeenth century, slaving companies owned by the Swedes, Danes and Germans were also in the thick of this trade. Britain's entry into this field could be accidental but it was tempting. In 1562, Admiral Sir John Hawkins of the Royal Navy, during the reign of Queen Elizabeth I, was sailing towards the Caribbean when he waylaid a Portuguese ship carrying 300 African slaves. Hawkins traded pirated human cargo in Santo Domingo islands in the West Indies for hides, pearls and sugar. In 1564, Hawkins in partnership with Queen Elizabeth I, whose ship he hired to fortify his fleet, jumped into the world of slave trade. He piloted the first slaving ship to Spanish waters in 1562–63. In a short time, British slave merchants captured 40 percent of the slave trade. They shipped 2.5 million African slaves earning some 12-million-pound sterling in profit. Hawkins captured 400 tribesmen from the West Africa coast and took them to the Venezuelan coast amidst Spanish opposition. He sold them at great profit. He and his brother Sir Francis Drake supplied slaves to the Spanish colonies breaking Spanish law that prohibited the purchase and sale of slaves in their colonies. Spanish colonists were in dire need of slaves. Hawkins and his brother imposed their cargo over Venezuela under a threat and earned a handsome income. Enriched, Hawkins returned to England as a celebrity. Later, the Royal African Company set up in 1672, regularly traded in slaves. This company shipped 120,000 Africans to Western destinations including North America. The English built Fort James on the mouth of Gambia River (site of Banjul, capital of Gambia) as its famous slave trade centre. Other English slave embarkation centres that came up on the African West Coast, included Cape Coast Castle and Accra. The British retained only four of them after 1807 and used the rest for other trade and to act as watchdog against slave trading companies of other nations. This British company had dominated slave trade until it was abolished. At its height English shipping was transporting 300,000 slaves a year and her share in the abominable trade was one half of more than 11 million Africans who were shipped across the Atlantic.

Each European nation held a fort/castle or a collection centre along the 300-mile coastline of present-day Ghana. There were 46 posts for holding slaves prior to their shipment. Some slave holding stations like Cape Coast Castle, Elmina Castle/Fort and Fort Jago have attained status as world heritage sites. Ouidah, on the coast of Dahomey (now Benin), had slave trading forts of several nations from where one thousand slaves boarded each month. It has several monuments including 'the Door of No Return' in the form of an arch to empathize with those who passed this door for the last time. Slaves brought to these centres by slave traders were screened for health. Healthy persons were branded with a hot iron rod by the purchaser company. The sources of slave supply in Africa were mainly the native chiefs who scouted for slaves in their territories. The captives were bartered with shipping companies/slave traders for goods like fire arms, printed cotton cloth and cookware. The companies spent a pittance to procure a slave but earned up to 160 pounds per slave in the colonies. No wonder their effort was to procure maximum number of slaves. One way to fatten their kitty of slaves was to pit one African chief against the other. The triumphant chief enslaved the tribe of the vanquished chief and sold it to the slaving company. About one half of total slaves were accrued from such conquests. The other half comprised petty criminals, defaulters in debt or those who earned the wrath of their ruler.

In 400 years beginning the 1450's, twelve million Africans were enslaved. Another five to six million died during enslaving operations in the interior of Africa, during transport to coastal stations, during trans-Atlantic voyages, and finally at the hands of their ultimate masters in the colonies. The processes of capturing slaves, branding prior to sailing, loathsome conditions of their travel while in crammed confinement, and finally treatment at the hands of their masters were so inhuman that many captives preferred to embrace death. Slave traders, however, took this colossal loss of life in their stride. The number of Africans deaths during transport to destinations in the Americas and the Caribbean equalled African deaths during their capture in Africa. William Bosman, chief factor of the Dutch West India Company, who operated from the West Coast of Africa between 1682 and 1702, described slave trade analogous to trading in any other commodity. He claimed that the act of branding and the method of inspection of slaves was nothing more than exhibiting ownership and inspecting the quality of a commodity. Slave traders considered slaves sub-humans who could be punished like domestic animals. But cruelty involved in these processes did not go unnoticed. "The slaves were stripped naked and strictly examined by European surgeons both men and women, without the least distinction or modesty; those who were approved as good were marked with a red-hot iron with the ship's mark. After arrival in the colonies, they were disposed of to planters, again exposed naked, without any distinction of sexes, to the brutal examination of their purchasers. Families were separated and children torn apart from their parents, sisters clinging to their brothers, daughters to their mothers and wives to their husbands."[6] Sure enough, the hapless creatures presented a gruesome picture of civilized Europe of the day!

Slavery and Colonisation: Iberians were the first to begin slave trade to augment the work force in their colonies. Brazil, discovered and claimed by the Portuguese, became an important market for African slaves. Portuguese colonists, who started large sugarcane plantations along the Atlantic coast of Brazil, absorbed all imported slaves. Agricultural plantations had made slavery indispensable. Portugal, on the strength of these plantations, monopolized the sugar markets of Europe for 200 years until it faced stiff competition from sugar producing countries like Barbados. Sugarcane, a labour-intensive crop demanded many hands. The Portuguese imposed slavery on the natives who were undernourished and overworked. They were treated cruelly and punished when unable to work for extended hours. Their death rate approached staggering proportions. Europeans and African slaves had a huge impact on the natives. They brought with them diseases and thrust their religious practices and culture on the natives of the colonies. Surviving native labour was so debilitated and, hence inefficient, that the Portuguese had to import African labour. They brought slaves from Mozambique which was under their control since the early sixteenth century. Commercial production of sugar accelerated after 1550's when sugar mills were constructed along the Atlantic coast. In the seventeenth century the Dutch supported the sugar industry with abundant supply of slave labour. By 1600, black Africans constituted one half of the population of Brazil because about 40 percent of all African slaves that arrived in the Americas, ended up in Brazil. Although Portugal had a small share in the slave trade due to her weak maritime and economic strength, it was the slave labour which established this nation in the New World. Portugal continued shipping slaves into its colonies of Sao Tome and the Principe Islands under the garb of contract labour to flout the ban on slavery. In 1865, a joint Anglo-Portuguese Commission on slavery objected to shipping of African labour to the cocoa plantations of the above islands. Judice Biker, Governor of New Guinea, disclosed the sordid drama that accompanied the purchase of slaves from the interior of Angola and their arrival in Sao Tome islands.[7]

Spain, the other Iberian nation that conquered Cuba in 1511, the Aztec empire of Mexico in 1524, was master of Peru, Venezuela and Chile by 1535. Spaniards also depended on slave labour for operating their plantations and mines in their colonies. Spain had a black population which was part of her early expeditions to Mexico and Peru. Later these blacks were employed for mining in Hispaniola until 1520. Spain lost her interest in the colony when it was depleted of gold and her interest shifted to the newly conquered Mexico where silver was discovered in 1520. The 1493 papal bull granted Spain the right to colonise the new world on the condition that it converted indigenous people to Catholicism. The bull allowed enslavement of natives should they refuse conversion or subsequently revert to their previous religious beliefs. The conquistadors manipulated stipulations in the bull for enslaving the natives of other lands. Queen Isabella, however, explicitly asked to set all the natives free. Orders of the Pope and Queen Isabella protected the natives against slavery when Hernando Cortes overwhelmed the Aztec Empire. Spaniards baptized large number of natives but, lacking follow-up, they reverted to their indigenous religious practices. This was enough of an excuse for the conquistadors to enslave them. When Cortes granted large tracts of land to his compatriots, natives living on the land accompanied as slaves. Spaniards used them for farm and domestic work. Spanish Dominican priest Father Bartolome de Las Casas challenged this form of enslavement. He instead, proposed that people from Africa should be imported and put to farm work.

Although Spanish monarchs did not favour slavery, the colonists needed slaves to run Mexico's silver mines. About one half of the native Mexican population had vanished during the Spanish conquest of the Aztec empire. The survivors, who were forced to work in the mines, were prone to infectious diseases contracted from the Europeans. As a result, the natives became sluggish workers. King Charles I relented at last and permitted colonists to import hardy African slaves. In 1508, the first shipment of slaves arrived in the Spanish colonies. Between 1519 and 1560 Spanish territory of Mexico imported about 120,000 salves. Up to 1810 another 80,000 Africans joined the labour force in other colonies.

Close to the late 1700's the slave population of the West Indies exceeded that of free citizens. Colonists of other European nations also depended upon imported slave labour for their plantations and mines. French buccaneers came to Hispaniola after Spain abandoned a part of this colony. In 1659 France finalized her presence on the western part of this Island. In 1697 Spain recognized French control over the territory of Saint-Domingue (Saint Domingo) and Tortuga through the Treaty of Ryswick. Afterwards, French buccaneers took to dairying and raising tobacco. They felt the labour shortage because the native Taino population had almost vanished during the Spanish occupation of Hispaniola. Shortage of labour was exacerbated when French colonists and farm syndicates opted to grow labour-intensive high value crops of sugarcane and coffee increasingly in demand in Europe and North America. The French government shipped about 1.25 million African slaves to Hispaniola and the French Antilles. Dominican plantations employed thousands of native Indian and black slaves. A major portion of imported labour was absorbed by Saint-Domingue plantations leaving a small portion for the French Antilles. By early 1700, Dominican planters which employed thousands of Indian and black slaves enriched Spanish economy.[8] Nearly 150,000 Africans died during shipping, the huge mortality implied the horrible conditions of shipping captive Africans. Requirement of slave labour in Saint Domingue increased in direct proportion to export of sugar and coffee. At one time this French colony supplied 60 percent needs of coffee and 40 percent requirement of sugar to Europe. The place became fabulously rich by back-breaking work of slaves notwithstanding the shabby and brutal treatment of their masters. In 1788, the black African population of the French Caribbean rose to 693,000 compared with 56,000 French citizens. The blacks refused to be cowed down and revolted against the French in 1791. There were continuous wars between French forces and a combination of blacks and Mulattos. Finally, this most important French colony won its independence in 1804.

In 1492, Spain seized the island of Barbados which they discovered while sailing to Brazil. Spain forced the native islanders (Caribs) to work as agriculture and mining labour. Within a few decades a majority of natives died of contagious diseases and due to maltreatment of their masters. Bereft of labour support, Spain abandoned the island for anyone to occupy. In 1627 the British began settlements in this colony after Captain Henry Powell arrived there along with 80 settlers and 10 slaves. By 1630, Barbados sugar was poised to dominate the Caribbean sugar industry. British colonists cleared forest lands to raise cotton and tobacco crops. These commodities along with sugar had a growing market in Europe. Demand for agricultural labour far exceeded available workforce. Moreover, thousands of native Caribs had perished during the 1647 fever and hundreds were executed by arrogant planters. The British attempted to bridge the labour gap by importing Celtic people from Ireland. Following the Nine Year's War, Britain sold fifty thousand Irish people including prisoners of war, as indentured labour to the American colonies and the West Indies. Thousands of Irishmen, who participated in the 1641 rebellion, were transported to Barbados and Bermuda under orders of Oliver Cromwell — a staunch baiter of Catholicism. Subsequently, the Celtics served in the British militia. Labour shortage accentuated as more colonists arrived and began growing plantations. Rich English businessmen of the eighteenth century owned large sugar plantations. They financed Dutch merchants to ship thousands of slaves from the west coast of Africa. In 1645, Barbados had 6000 Africans and about 40,000 Europeans. Forty years later, the population of Africans rose to 46000 while that of Europeans declined to 20,000. Barbados lost her sugar producing supremacy by 1720 when the Leeward Islands and Jamaica became prominent sugar producers.

Colonial settlers, especially farming syndicates, of the Caribbean, could not have flourished without the sweat and blood of the African slave labour that filled the gap left by native societies who had vanished from the face of earth. All colonial nations enjoyed the fruits of slavery. For example, in 1768, out of 104,000 slaves arriving from Africa, English colonies shared 53,100; United States, 6,300; French colonies, 23,500; Dutch colonies, 11,300; Portuguese colonies, 8,700; and the Danes, 1,200. Colonial powers considered slave trade like investment in any other business. Between 1735 and 1763, British alone shipped 13,000 slaves annually from her trading post on the west coast of Africa which later became part of the colony of British Gold Coast.[9] Slave trade, with her meagre investment needs, but proportionately far greater out turn, formed an important link in commerce between the colonies and the colonial countries. Colonial powers produced alcohol, fire arms, cookware and recycled cloth procured from India. All these goods had great demand in Africa where slave traders and native chiefs exchanged them against slaves they had captured from interior parts of Africa and handed over to slaving posts of the Europeans. Slaves were sold to planters in the colonies where they endured back-breaking labour and produced sugar, indigo, raw cotton, tobacco and coffee for their masters. Slave ships carried slave-produced commodities to destinations in America and Europe. Each transaction was lucrative business. Rum produced in the American colonies was exchanged for procuring slaves from Africa. In this way the sweat and blood of the slaves nurtured colonial economies.

Tales of abominable slave trade and infinite cruelty inflicted upon the natives (especially in Congo and Peru) and Africans everywhere, tumbled out of official and unofficial reports. Common Britons abhorred the way the natives were treated by the conquistadors, and revolting methods they employed during capture of Africans and their shipment to the western destinations. A group of evangelized Protestants joined the Quakers to campaign against slave trade under the well-known English philanthropist and abolitionist William Wilberforce. In 1787, his emancipation society purchased one district from a native chief of Sierra Leone to serve as a home for the freed slaves. Governance of the place was handed over to the Crown in 1807. Other nations also despised slave trade. In March 1807, the 20-year-old struggle of Wilberforce fructified when, following Royal assent, an Act was passed to abolish slave trade in the British Islands. Yet slave trade did not disappear. It was revealed in the House of Commons that the number of those unhappy beings dragged from their homes and sold to everlasting slavery might not be less than 200,000 annually. In Brazil and Cuba alone 140,000 slaves landed annually. Besides, 40,000 captives lost their lives during sea voyage. A law similar to the one in Britain became operative in America in the beginning of 1808. Both countries abolished slave trade but could not stop slavery. Britain dismantled her slaving ports on the west coast of Africa retaining only four of them. Between 1808 and 1860 Britain seized 1,600 slave trading ships and set free 150,000 Africans. British posts did benefit Britain during the Berlin Conference of 1884 because the country could claim British protectorates on the strength of its presence in the area. Britain had reconciled to the Slavery Abolition Act of 1833, but Americans fought the 1861–1865 Civil War on the issue of abolition of slavery.

Chapter 9
Instruments of Strangle Hold: Muzzled Press

Europeans occupied foreign lands not for discharging 'white man's burden' but to upsurge their own political, economic and military power. They perpetuated domination by keeping the natives ignorant of their rights through control of print media and enactment of laws aimed to suppress opposition to the alien rule. The seventeenth to mid-nineteenth-century Europe was by no means wealthy in comparison with India and China. The latter countries accounted for more than 50 percent of the world's gross domestic production. Early phase of neo-colonialism was, therefore, trade and economy orientated. Europeans got the chance to milk Asian wealth. Lord Curzon, viceroy and governor general of India (1898–1905), admitted that without India, Britain will drop straight away to a third-rate power. Accordingly, Europeans experimented with different approaches to retain hold over their colonies in the early years of colonisation. France and Portugal, half-heartedly, tried an assimilative approach, whereby natives of colonies were to be integrated with the mainland. They ended up running their colonies through authoritative rule emanating from their European capitals. Contrarily Britain, the omnipresent colonial nation, believed in distancing herself from her subjects. It claimed that the natives comprised 'lesser nations' ordained to be kept at a lower pedestal than the superior Anglo-Saxon race. The East India Company (EIC), which laid foundation of the British colonial empire, came to India as a mercantile company, but altered its course due to greed and in competition with other European nations. It began to acquire and govern foreign territories it had traded with. In her largest colony of India, the motive was profiteering and robbing the country of her resources. The company, and later the British government, would not let go of the hen that laid golden eggs. They held on to the country through instruments of suppressing the freedom of the press and enacting laws that curbed native dissent and curtailed civil liberties.

The EIC governed her territories in a despotic manner during the consolidation phase. Its governor-in-council and governor-general-in-council, behaved like autocrats answerable to no one. The staff picked up by the company was young, just out of school, but entrusted with despotic powers and temptations of office which were sour grapes for them in their own country. In no time, they faced criticism of their own countrymen in India, and in the Great Britain. Newly established English newspapers would scrutinize the functioning of the company employees thereby adding to her anguish. In 1776, William Bolts, a former employee of the EIC, set out to publish first-ever English newspaper in India to uncover the misdeeds of company employees. The paper never saw the light of the day. Bolts was deported and put on first available ship sailing out of Calcutta (Kolkata). In 1780, an Irishman James Augustus Hicky became first publisher to bring out a newspaper named *Hicky's Bengal Gazette*/original *Calcutta Advertiser*. This Journal, being sensational, attracted a large number of subscribers from Bengal. Misdeeds of Governor-General Warren Hastings, chief justice of the supreme court at Fort William, Elijah Impey, and other unscrupulous company officials provided enough printable matter for this paper in the fluid political situation of the time. *Hicky's Bengal Gazette* highlighted abuse of power by Hastings in connivance with Impey. It did not spare even Lady Hastings. As a result, Hicky was fined five hundred rupees plus a jail time of four months. The sentence did not deter him from raising a barrage of questions from the jail. Inconvenienced, Hastings issued a public notice on 14th November 1780, stopping circulation of *Hicky's Bengal Gazette* by mail. Hicky was fined a hefty sum of five thousand pounds sterling and his wooden press and type were confiscated. Hicky remained in jail in 1781 because he could not furnish bail money. In this manner *Hicky's Bengal gazette* died within two years of its birth. His deportation alarmed nascent news media, but it did not stop criticism of British despotism. B. Messink and Peter Reed started the next paper, *India Gazette* or *Calcutta Public Advertiser*. They were pliant publishers and their paper survived for several decades. In 1784, the colonial establishment commenced *Calcutta Gazette* or *Oriental Advertiser* in order to put across the company side of the story. In the end this publication became the *Calcutta Government Gazette*. The very next year, one Thomas Jones began publishing a paper, *Bengal Journal*. This paper was circulated free of cost because it carried government advertisements. In 1786, *Calcutta Journal* and the *General Advertiser* were launched. Other Calcutta-based newspapers that appeared in the eighteenth century were *Asiatic Mirror* and *Commercial Advertiser of Calcutta*, *Friday Morning Post* and *General Advertiser,* and *the World.* These papers were weekly or monthly, appearing on different days of the week. William Duane, editor of *The World,* published stories narrating the maltreatment of natives by the colonial administration. Sir Philip Francis, an adversary of Warren Hastings, fed Duane with news which appeared in his paper. Later Duane published an incorrect report about the demise of Lord Cornwallis. John Shore, the then governor general, ordered deportation of Duane and he left the Indian the shores on 30th May 1794. In 1799, Charles MacLean, a Scottish writer and founder of the *Bengal Harkaru,* got into trouble with the EIC for writing an article on the conduct of a magistrate. Governor General Wellesley accused him of animadverting and censoring conduct of a public officer. He was deported to England. MacLean continued his tirade against the aggressive policies of Wellesley and his haughtiness against the natives. Eventually, the governor general had to resign and leave for England.

Press censorship of sorts existed since 1795, but strict scrutiny of print media began after 1795 when the Marquess of Wellesley was governor-general of India. *Asiatic Mirror* inadvertently spurred an impulsive Wellesley into action against the print media. The governor-general was enraged because the editor of the paper, Charles Bruce, quoted an estimated strength of European and native troops during the campaign of Wellesley against Tipu Sultan of the Mysore kingdom. Within a month, in May 1799, Wellesley introduced rules for regulating press in India. New regulations required newspapers, under pain of penalty, to exhibit the name of the printer, publisher, proprietor and editor, and submit all matters to be printed for pre-censorship. Marquees of Hastings abolished pre-censorship but continued other regulations. Editors were made responsible for the matter they published. Power of the governor general to deport combatant and non-conformist editors remained intact. This power was used by acting Governor-General John

Adams for deporting James Silk Buckingham, who edited *Calcutta Journal,* the first daily newspaper of India. He was charged for criticizing the native armies, sovereigns, and the Indian population. On 14th March 1823, Adams issued a new licensing order which was more stringent than the regulations of Wellesley. This order was followed by a more elaborate order of 5th April 1823 which spelled regulations to prevent the establishment of printing presses without license and, under certain circumstances, restrain the circulation of printed books and newspapers. The purpose was to reign in the print media. Educated Indians and respectable citizens had begun to criticize inequities of the British rule through the print media. This criticism spurred the company to impose press censorship. Sir John Malcolm, a former military general, statesman, and once governor of Bombay (1827–1830) warned that free press would encourage nationalistic feelings incompatible with the English rule.

Calcutta residents appealed for a repeal of the 1823 order, but it was only in 1832 when press censorship was removed on the eve of renewal of the EIC Charter. In 1835, (Lord) Charles Metcalfe, the provisional governor-general of India and an advocate of liberty of the press, restored freedom of the press and abrogated the licensing system. The Indian press became as free as that of England.[1] The English press of Fort St. George, Madras (Chennai) and that of Bombay (Mumbai) were more cooperative. In 1785, *Madras Courier,* the first weekly newspaper was established by Richard Johnson. It published government notices and remained in circulation for many years. Its editor Huge Boyd started an independent newspaper, *the Hircarrah* in 1791, but it closed after the death of Boyd in 1794. Robert William launched *Madras Gazette* in 1795. In the same year John Goldingham established the *Government Gazette.* Both newspapers enjoyed government patronage. Thereafter, one G. Humphreys ventured to publish the *Indian Herald* without seeking mandatory permission. He was arrested and deported. A Bombay newspaper, *Bombay Herald,* established in 1789, was renamed *Bombay Courier* in 1791. It was followed by the *Bombay Gazette.* These newspapers survived on government advertisements because the English-reading population was yet small. Hence the majority of the English press, except few papers of Calcutta, towed the government line.

Rustam Caresajee was the first Indian to establish a printing press in 1780. But it was only in 1822 that the first vernacular newspaper *Bombay Samachar* was launched. In the same year, a Persian weekly *Meerut-al-Akbar,* edited by Raja Ram Mohan Roy began publication from Calcutta. A Bengali daily, *Sambad Privar,* appeared on 14th June 1839. In 1863, *Indian Daily Mirror* became the first ever English newspaper to be edited by an Indian native. Bengal became home to several Bengali-language newspapers; some of them being highly critical of the EIC administration. Company officials largely ignored contents of the vernacular press because circulation of native language papers was insignificant in relation to the native population. Gradually natives, particularly the English literate, imbibed ideas that militated against company misrule. Public disaffection against the EIC spurred demand for native-language newspapers. Editorial policies that criticized the company boosted the sale of vernacular newspapers. Vernacular press, softer towards company administration, was called 'toady' because natives had no stake in company administration. Hence, they openly expressed their alienation and resentment against injustices and humiliation through the only medium they had access to. Company administration became increasingly touchy to criticism appearing in the native press. It would not tolerate even a justified comment on the British government under whose nose the EIC misgoverned the country. Agitation for free press arose in Calcutta and Madras (Chennai). In Madras, the *Courier* was hauled up in 1818 for reprinting an article from the *Morning Chronicle* (London) that attacked treatment of Napoleon at St. Helena. It also published material supposedly approving revolution in Spain. The Madras government was forced to shut down the *Courier* on insistence of Lord Bathurst the secretary of state for war and colonies.[2]

Insensitive and intolerant company rule turned the native press into increasingly nationalistic. It voiced native concerns about deposition of the Nawab of Oudh (Awadh) and *sepoy* protests against supply of greased cartridges. Two months after the 1857 uprising against the company rule Lord Canning, the governor-general, promulgated the Vernacular Press Act of 1857 to rein in the native press. Harsh measures were brought to bear on the vernacular newspapers. The editor had to choose between abject surrender and closure of his newspaper. Canning insinuated that vernacular press promoted sedative feelings to an audacious extent. About a dozen Bengali language newspapers bore brunt of this act. The only English newspaper to be rapped was the *Harkaru*. Overall English press, both in India and England, spewed venom against the *sepoys* (native army men). With native press either completely gagged or locked out, the only source of information about the 1857 uprising against the British was the biased English press or correspondents of foreign newspapers like the *Times*, London. British public was fed with unconfirmed tales and exaggerated accounts of atrocities on British citizens in some towns of northern India. Voices of reason were drowned in furore of the sensitized British people thirsty for Indian blood. They never came to know that British led forces perpetrated disproportionate vengeance on the innocent population of India, because history is written by the victors. British authorities in India were hell-bent to decree rules and regulations meant to stifle native outrage over large scale killings of natives in towns and villages of northern India. Post 1857 era was, therefore, a period of despair and despondency for the Indians who faced unjust retribution. Oppressive laws were enforced, and state machinery was empowered to orient, regulate and monitor printed matter, and confiscate any matter they considered objectionable. Regulatory measures were to bear on the published matter through the Press and Registration of Books Act 1867. Overtly the Act meant to keep a record of published works. The purpose was to discipline the newspapers. They were required to publish names of the owner and editor printed clearly along with date of publication. Newspapers towing the official line were rewarded but, nonconforming news media were castigated through the judicial system and their licenses to publish were cancelled. This was particularly true for the vernacular press. On 10th August 1876, Sir Arthur Hobhouse, law member of governor-general's council, remarked that even English papers bring the government to contempt. He referred to an article in the *Friend of India,* taken from the *Statesman* that charged the British with taxing or rather plundering India for the benefit of England, with a violence of language and appeals to divine and human wrath which certainly would excite rebellious feelings. Company administration had failed to soothe injured Indian psyche. The advocate-general advised that charges of poisoning one nation and emasculating another are seditious.[3]

Simmering public resentment led to the Indigo Riots of 1860 in the Bengal province. People revolted against inhuman treatment of the peasants by English indigo planters. English planters enticed and often forced peasants to plant indigo instead of food crops but gave them an extremely low price for the produce. The plight of peasants was voiced by a nationalist newspaper *Hindu Patriot*. The editor had to bear the ire of planters. Their court case fell through because it was outside jurisdiction of the presidency court at Calcutta. The government began mulling over the prospect of launching her own newspaper to publicize Government policies and her benevolence toward the subjects. This idea was a nonstarter. The viceroy, Lord Mayo brought in Act XXVII of 1870 intended to curb attempts to "excite feelings of disaffection to the government." The punishment was transportation for life or imprisonment and fine. Public outcry was further fuelled by a Bengali play, *Neel Darpan,* which depicted a pitiful picture of cruelties unleashed on the indigo workers. Government retaliated and promulgated the Performance Act to curb such publicity. Memories of the indigo revolt still lingered in the minds of Indians, when in 1876 Edward Robert Lytton (later Lord Lytton) took over as viceroy and governor-general of India. A national scholar but a pathetic administrator, his actions hurt both the Indians and India's treasury. He abolished import duty on British textiles which mortally hit the already suffering native textile industry. His expenditure on the Second Afghan War was completely wasteful. While the hyped Russian threat proved imaginary, its cost to India was huge both in blood and money. Lytton introduced the Arms Act, mandating Indians to have a license to own a fire arm; a condition which did not apply to the Europeans. In 1877, he organized Imperial Durbar at Delhi to proclaim Queen Victoria as The Empress of India. This glittering show was attended by 84000 guests. It cost the Indian exchequer a huge sum of money at a time when India had been hit by a devastating famine which claimed several million lives. Indian press criticized the actions of the governor-general. Lord Lytton called the native language press mischievous scribblers preaching open sedition. Within hours of receiving the nod of an obliging colonial secretary, Lytton had his council pass the Vernacular Press Act IX of 1878 (an act for the better control of publications in the Oriental languages). On 14th March, it obtained the status of law. Summing up the debate of the Legislative Council the Viceroy remarked, "I should have rejoiced had it fallen to my lot to enlarge, rather than restrict the liberty of the press in India; for neither the existence nor the freedom of the press in this country is of native origin or growth."[4] The Act empowered magistrates to demand bonds from publishers of vernacular newspapers affirming their promise to shun printed material that appeared seditious and inflammatory to the government. A kind of censorship was introduced. A press commissioner was appointed to oversee government concerns about both Vernacular and English papers. Police could seize any published matter which it considered unworthy of circulation. The publisher risked confiscation of bond money as well as his printing press. Government closely watched Bengali language newspapers like *Amrita Bazar Patrika, Soma Parkash, Sulabh Samachar, Halisahar Patrika* and *Dhaka Parkash*.

The Press Act 1878 continued to impose strict restrictions on 170 vernacular newspapers until it was repealed. Under this act, newspapers were required to submit all print matter and proofs to the police before it was published. A government officer scrutinized proofs of the matter. Newspapers regarded errant, were fined and their editors and publishers faced terms in jail. Since this Act did not apply to the English-medium newspapers, in an overnight transformation, *Amrita Bazar Patrika* became an English-medium newspaper. British Parliament ignored appeals, of well-meaning Indians and Britons, against the Act. William Gladstone, a Liberal member, denounced the Act in the House of Commons. Gladstone, after taking over as the British prime minister, advised the new viceroy of India Lord Ripon to repeal it. The Act was revoked in 1882. This action infuriated Anglo-Indian community of India who viewed it as 'pandering' to Indian extremism. Founding of the Indian National Congress in 1885 provided forum for nationalistic Indians to mull over problems of the Indian community. The government became apprehensive and as a counteractive measure undertook stringent press regulations. In 1898, Indian criminal procedure was fortified by adding sections on sedition and treason. Newspapers propagating ideology of the Congress protested against this measure. A section of the party called for boycott of government posts and foreign goods. Indian

172

National Congress got a shot in the arm in 1905 when Lord Curzon, the then viceroy, decided to partition Bengal. There was agrarian unrest in the Chenab colony of Punjab following the Punjab Colonisation Act (1906). Indian opinion against the Bill was constantly mocked at by the Anglo-Indian paper *Civil and Military Gazette* of Lahore using invectives like "babbling B.A.", "serfs", "beggars on the horse back" etc. against the Indians. Sir Denzil Ibbetson the lieutenant governor of the Punjab regretted the tone of the articles but refused to prosecute the paper. On the other hand, two Indian papers of Lahore were prosecuted. Of these, *INDIA*, for republishing a letter from America (purportedly by exponents of the *Ghadar* party in San Francisco) containing seditious appeal to the Indian troops. Its editor Pindi Das was sentenced to five years and the proprietor Dina Nath to two years of imprisonment. The other paper *Punjabee* was prosecuted for its comments on the death of two Indians forced to do free hard work (*begaar*) for an official. Its proprietor Lala Jaswant Rai was sentenced on appeal for a fine of one thousand rupees and six months imprisonment.[5] The Indian Statutes book added five Acts between November 1907 and August 1910 to strengthen laws against sedition, political crime and press offences. A new law, the Newspapers (Incitement of Offences) Act was passed in June 1908. This Act empowered the executive to suppress newspapers considered to incite violence. During the passage of this act, Viceroy Lord Minto indicated the need for further regulations to control the press. Magistrates were handed powers to confiscate printing press and the government was authorized to terminate the license of a newspaper. Within fifteen days of the passage of this act, seven printing presses were confiscated. The Indian Press Act of 1910, that followed, was even more stringent for better control of the press. It imposed strict restrictions on all publications. Publishers were asked to furnish a security deposit of five thousand rupees, which was liable to forfeiture for publishing objectionable material. Further offences carried heavier penalty and confiscation of the press. Local governments were also empowered to declare any book, newspaper or other document wherever printed forfeited, if it contained prohibited matter. Such matter included incitement to murder, or acts of violence or similar inferences, suggestions etc. There was political unrest in India after the First World

War in which thousands of Indian troops died fighting for the British. In 1915, the nationalist leader M.K. Gandhi arrived in India from South Africa. This event triggered an undercurrent of public resentment against the foreign rule. The Rowlatt Act passed on 10th March 1919 aggravated tension in the Punjab. There was an outrage against British policies in northern India resulting in several deaths in Delhi. Kalinath Ray, fearless editor of the Tribune a popular English newspaper of the Punjab, criticized government high-handedness. Police closed the office of the Tribune for three days to conduct search operations. The commissioner court at Lahore convicted Ray on 28th May 1919 for allegedly exciting disaffection toward His Majesty and the British government. He was sentenced to two years rigorous imprisonment. Following public protests, the sentence was reduced to three months simple imprisonment and a fine of one thousand rupees. The Press Association of India prepared a memorandum for circulation in England detailing the history of suppression of press freedom in India from an Act of 1867 down to that of 1910 which gave the executive the power of arbitrary control over presses, newspapers, books and other publications. The regulations threatened the very existence of Indian press.[6] British government passed the Indian Press (Emergency Powers) Act in 1931 when Gandhi announced the Non-Cooperation Movement. This act, which revived provisions of the 1910 Press Act, empowered local government to forfeit any security deposits of the newspapers. The Act accorded sweeping powers to the government for curbing propaganda related to the Civil Disobedience Movement. These measures, although meant to suppress public discontent, turned the press more vocal and masses more restive. The Press Law was enlarged and made a part of the Criminal Law Amendment Act of 1932. The amendment authorized civil administration to demand heavy security deposits from the newspapers. A paper could be seized should the authority decide that the publication carried objectionable material. Section 4 of the Act included a whole range of print material liable to be declared objectionable. Under this act, both printer and publisher of the *Bombay Chronicle* had to deposit three thousand rupees each. Similarly, the printer and publisher of the *Ananda Bazar Patrika* had to deposit one thousand rupees each. A security of six thousand rupees each was to be deposited by *Liberty* of Calcutta, *Amrita*

Bazar Patrika and the *Free Press Journal,* whose security was forfeited by the Bombay government. The Foreign Relations Act 1932, prohibited publication of any matter likely to affect British relations with other countries. The freedom of the press was effectively thwarted by the British administration to muzzle public voice against the foreign rule. This Act was passed by the Assembly on 2nd April 1932.

Press in the African Continent: Britain was well grounded in the art of colonialism before it began to consolidate her possessions in Africa. The Africans, unlike the Indians, had become politically more astute by that time. Several European nations were competing for their own piece of colonial pie in Africa. Nevertheless, it was the British colonies where the press played a singular role in awakening nationalistic feelings among Africans and subsequently for freedom from foreign rule. The newspapers in Africa appeared by 1800. The first paper published was *Official Gazette* of the Cape Colony. It was bilingual (English and Dutch). The *Cape Town Gazette* and the *African Advertiser* started by two slave dealers, Alexander Walker and John Robertson, began as a government mouth piece but later joined the struggle for freedom of the press. The reason for the change was commercial. The paper criticized Britain's antislavery position and accused her of being soft towards African natives who were despised by the Boers. The paper had to close its shop because it lost its patronage of the Boers for its supporting policies of Cecil Rhodes. In 1829, press censorship was removed and the newspaper became free to comment on government policies. Within a year, the first Dutch language paper *De Zuid Afrikaan* was launched. First African language newspaper *Umshumayeli Wendaba* was started in 1837. It was only in 1876 that the first Afrikaans language newspaper *Die Afrikaanse Patriot* appeared with Christoffel Joseph Brand as its editor. This paper promoted Afrikaner interest. The first lasting English newspaper, *the Herald,* began publishing in 1845 and the other enduring English newspaper, *the Cape Times,* appeared in 1876.

It was the western-educated Africans and returnees from America and the West Indies, who established printing presses and began publishing newspapers with nationalistic and patriotic overtones. *New Era* was the first African-operated newspaper that came out in May 1855 through efforts of William Drape, a West Indies Creole. *New Era,* an outspoken critic of policies of the colonial government, provided a forum and rallying point for anti-government forces. Although this paper had a limited circulation, its criticism of government policies appealed its readers but annoyed Governor Stephen Hill of Sierra Leone. The governor blocked government advertisements to the *New Era,* but Drape was undeterred. Hill prepared an ordinance, meant to enforce new regulations on printers and publishers of Sierra Leone. Newsmen were instructed to provide sureties approved by the chief justice ahead of printing and publishing a newspaper. Copies of the ordinance were sent to the colonial secretary Henry Labouchere. Hill admitted that the background of the ordinance was a newspaper of a West Indian Creole whom he referred to in a demeaning language. Labouchere failed to foresee likely implications of such an ordinance. He "unhesitatingly sanctioned both law and a minor amendment that soon followed it, and unwittingly created a monster, the consequences of whose activities embarrassed him and his successors."[7] The obstinate governor took a number of vindictive actions. Finally, a repeal of the law vindicated Drape's stand. The governor was humiliated but escaped a recall. Drape's perseverance encouraged other West African newspapers to fight government arrogance. It was only a fleeting glow of freedom because colonial government enacted more laws similar to those they had applied to rein in the press in India.

Accra Herald was the first truly African owned and influential newspaper of the Gold Coast, West Africa. It was launched in 1858 as a hand-written paper by Charles Bannerman. After two years, it was renamed *West African Herald.* Bannerman, a lawyer by profession, criticized a court judgment of 1862. He was charged and imprisoned for contempt of court. The paper had low readership in the Gold Coast, hence it was moved to Sierra Leone but again brought back to the Gold Coast. It maintained its reputation for fearless criticism of the government. Two-thirds of its readership of 300 consisted of native Africans. In its sixteen years of publication, it stimulated the launch of several native-owned newspapers. In 1859, a Yoruba language newspaper, *Iwe Iorhin,* was founded by an African missionary. African-owned newspapers expressed ideals and aspirations of the Africans and watched their rights as well. Native elite regarded expression of such aspirations a ladder to political power. For example, in 1897, *Gold Coast Aborigines* newspaper was started to oppose the Lands Bill of 1897. The Bill was opposed by the Aborigine Rights Protection Society formed for this purpose. The paper closed its publication in 1898 after the bill was withdrawn. The British, to a large extent, tolerated what was being published because their interests lay more in trade than political gains. Editors of local newspapers, who enjoyed freedom of expression, articulated ideals of self-governance and political consciousness. Gradually, many native businessmen and nationalists established their own newspapers. One Herbert Macauley launched the *Lagos Daily News* in 1925. In 1937, the *West African Pilot* was founded by Nnamdi Azikiwe who became first president of independent Nigeria. The U.S. educated Azikiwe inspired several native leaders like Kwame Nkruma (first president of Ghana). Another nationalist newspaper, *Nyanzh Times* was founded by Jomo Kenyata, who later became president of the independent Kenya.

Relationships between native newspapers and the colonial government were not always hunky dory. After 1920, the African native press began articulating opposition to foreign rule. As a counteraction, the government gathered support of the English press owned either by Europeans alone or in partnership with the anglicized Africans. English press was required to trumpet virtues of the colonial government and its benevolence toward the native population. In 1874 James Brew a nationalist, founded the *Gold Coast Times*. Its publication was suspended. It reappeared in 1885 as the *Western Echo*. The paper was so critical that it earned wrath of Governor W. Brandford Griffith. James Brew escaped prosecution because his son was advocate to the then queen.[8] The nationalistic newspapers like *Gold Coast,* published since 1891 by John Mensah Sarbah, and *Gold Coast Independent* established in 1895 by James Bright Davies, castigated the colonial government for its failings and overbearing attitude towards the native Africans. Government issued sedition ordinance No. 21 of 1934, in the Gold Coast. It prohibited Africans to publish and possess a newspaper or document containing seditious words or writing. A failure to show to the satisfaction of the court that at the time he was found to possess such material he was not aware of its content, was an offense. It was under this Act that Kwame Nkruma was charged for sedition in 1950 and jailed.

In 1787, the British began to settle the black poor of London in the colony of Free Town, Sierra Leone. Later the Sierra Leone Company shipped several hundred freed African slaves from the United States. American charitable organizations purchased the colony of Liberia where 1200 freed American slaves were relocated at Christopolis. This place was renamed Monrovia after the American President James Monroe. Many freed slaves from America and the West Indies, who returned to Liberia and Sierra Leone, were engrained with ideas of freedom and self-governance. They were educated and skilled in various trades. One of them, Charles Brown Force of America, who arrived in Monrovia in 1820, possessed a hand-operated press gifted to him by the Massachusetts Colonisation Society of Boston. He started a paper the *Liberia Herald* in 1826, but he did not live long. John B. Russwurm revived *Liberia Herald* in 1829 and remained its editor from 1830 to 1834. Russwurm was a Jamaica-born Mulatto educated in Canada. Several editors succeeded him. One Edward Blyden who edited *Liberia Herald* from 1855–56, was an anti-colonial thinker. He is regarded as the father of pan-Africanism and the founder of African nationalism. An important newspaper, *Lagos Times* and *Gold Coast Advertiser,* began publication in 1880. It criticized colonial policies and published opinions from the Gold Coast and Sierra Leone-based newspapers. John Payne Jackson, a Liberian by birth, is credited to be the first full-time journalist of Africa. He started a newspaper, *Lagos Weekly Record,* in 1890. This paper regularly criticized the high-handedness of the colonial administration while feeding nationalistic ideas to its African readers. His attitude alarmed the colonial government. In October 1903, William Macgregor, governor of Lagos Colony, passed the newspaper Ordinance (No. 10) modelled on the Indian Penal Code of 1860, and 1894 Press law passed in Trinidad. This law required a newspaper to furnish a bond, a deposit of two hundred and fifty pounds, one or two sureties and registration of its printer, publisher and editor, before it was allowed to publish. This ordinance failed to silence criticism of colonialism. Herbert Macauley, an exponent of the African nationalism, criticized the rule of Walter Egerton, who had succeeded Fredrick Lugard as governor of Lagos, in the *Lagos Daily Times*. Macauley hated any tirade of British press against the African chiefs, barristers and public at large. In 1905, he published impetuous criticism of British administration over imprisonment and deportation of two African tribal chiefs.[9] In his pamphlet of 1909 entitled *Governor Egerton and his Railway* he charged the administration of corrupt practices. This publication caused wild demonstrations against the British rule. The governor, a strong advocate of the Lagos to Ibadan railway line, did not take kindly to opposition of his project. He issued the 1909 Seditious Offences Ordinance, which forbade any published or unpublished criticism which spread disloyalty and disaffection toward the British King. Offenders risked prison terms up to two years and a fine. This ordinance was also a transplant of the Indian Penal Code. Fredrick Lugard, who returned in 1912 to take over governorship of both southern and western Nigeria, detested journalists like John Payne Jackson, who spread nationalistic feelings among the Africans. Lugard defended the ordinance with the colonial office arguing that, due to unrestricted license to publish, the African press undermined authority of the government and vitiated public order. Lugard became governor-general of unified Nigeria in 1914. In 1916, he enacted a criminal code which made it riskier for anyone to criticize or malign government policies. The 1917 Federal Newspapers Ordinance made press restrictions even severer. British rule over her colonies was therefore, marked by intimidation of the press. African rulers also took a leaf out of the British book and placed restrictions on newspapers critical of their rule. President Charles King of Liberia strangulated press freedom through the 8th February 1924 Bill, which prohibited publication of any material critical of the State. Offenders faced prison terms up to two years and fines of up to one thousand dollars. President William Tubman jailed inconvenient editors. One journalist was put behind bars for fifteen years.

Unlike the British, the French colonial rule was a direct rule from Paris. The French policy of "Assimilative Association" lessened the chances of confrontation with the native people. Their colonial empire, extending over 12.3 million square kilometres on different continents, comprised natives of colonies which were not on the same page as the local colonial administration. *Government gazettes* were issued as official publications to enunciate government policies and official approach towards the native population. Later on, private Frenchmen,

French colonists, and missionaries of Dahomey (Benin) started their own newspapers. *L'Echo du Dahomey (1905)* and *L'Independent (1910)* catered to literary tastes. Press criticism of French colonialism surfaced in 1920, when returnees from Brazil started newspapers, *Le Dahomeen* and *Le Guidedu*. They formed the core of Dahomean elite. A Dahomean intellectual wrote a critique "Africa in Revolt" in 1858. In Senegal, French journalist Jean Daramy d'Oxoby founded *Le Democratic du Senegal* in 1913. It was the first newspaper from a French colony in Africa which criticized French colonialism. Laws of France mainland applied to its colonies. Thus, French laws of 1881, based on the freedom of press and publication were transposed on her colonies. That, with few exceptions, curtailed the criticism of French colonial policies. Gradually, however, views of educated West Africans of nationalistic consciousness began to appear in the French colonies. African native-run newspapers too began to express nationalistic feelings. In 1927, the monarchy exerted strict control over the press in the form of censorship. A bureau of censors was established for this purpose. Publication of uncensored newspapers was banned. Filtered news was passed on to readers of the newspapers. Some 365 newspapers appeared in the post Second World War period. A number of them criticized French colonial rule.

Portugal, another colonial power in Africa, arrived on the continent for exploration and trade purposes. Obviously, this country of meagre resources wished to hold on to her colonies of Angola, Mozambique, Guinea Bissau and Cape Verde for economic reasons. Thus, majority of population in the Portuguese colonies was oblivions of what was happening in the contemporary colonial world. Spain, once a great maritime power could not retain her Latin American colonies for long due to geographical reasons and the emergence of stronger powers like the United States and Great Britain. The first Spanish language newspaper published outside Spain, *El Misisipi* appeared in 1808 from New Orleans, Louisiana. This paper demanded independence. Other newspapers that followed also played activist roles and spread the word against the Spanish rule. Spanish authorities could not act against them because these papers were published in the United States.

Chapter 10
Instruments of Stranglehold: Despotic Laws and Flawed Justice

Natives of colonies could not live-in a repressed state for long or be paralyzed with fear of the foreign rulers. They began voicing opposition to foreign rule. Colonialists handled them in ways outright unfair and brutal. They enacted laws to execute authoritative colonialism, counter native opposition, curb dissention, and force people into submission. A biased judiciary of their own ilk or inclination helped them to exert full force of the law on native populations. Thomas Babington Macaulay once governor-general of Bengal's council, minced no words when he, in his speech of 10th July 1833 in the House of Commons, called an early tenure of the supreme court in India, as the terror of Bengal, the scourge of native population, the screen of European delinquents, and a convenient tool of the government for all purposes. Some acts and regulations targeted native peoples and were open to prejudiced interpretation by the judiciary. On the contrary, white colonists flourished under benevolent laws, usurped native lands, and enjoyed privileges of cheap and even free labour. Native protests were crushed ruthlessly. Native media was the only forum where natives could air their grievances. Media deplored the plight of their countrymen often at the cost of prosecution under draconian press laws. Pent-up reactions to injustice stirred public anger against foreign rulers. For instance, the British Navigation Act of 1651 and the acts that followed were meant to regulate trade in the American colonies to the advantage of Britain and a way to hit Dutch shipping. Even though colonists were their own kith and kin from the British Isles, Britain had no compunction in promulgating such acts. The final provocation was an effort to enforce British parliamentary authority over the colonies. American resentment boiled over, and Britain had to pack up after the colonies won the War of Independence.

Stringently executed repressive laws were the bane of the non-white colonies and tribal communities. The British East India Company, (EIC) the Dutch East-India Company and the British South Africa Company, who were in the vanguard of colonialism, took refuge under these laws to hold on to their colonies. These companies drew power from the charters awarded them by their home governments. They established laws, rules, and regulations like sovereigns, to perpetuate their rule. Colonial administrations, placed thousands of miles away from their home government, acted whimsically in the absence of oversight-until telegraphic lines facilitated quicker scrutiny of their actions. The insatiable greed of white settlers for resources of the colony conflicted with hereditary rights of the native residents. The EIC came to India as a trading enterprise and gradually outmanoeuvred her European competitors. The 1813 Charter of the company, which terminated its monopoly over trade in the East except for tea and China trade, started an uncontrollable influx of capitalists, merchants, planters, and adventurers into India. The charter empowered the company to permit the Englishmen to settle and hold land in India. Company administration exploited the proviso and accommodated new arrivals at the cost of natives and previously tranquil environment of the country. What a tragedy it was? Moghul noblemen evidently felt that such heroic savages, as the British, were incapable of civilized statesmanship.[1]

The EIC Charter was renewed every twenty years after a review of its performance by the British Parliament. The first Royal Charter authorized the company to enact laws for governing her Indian establishment. The company established a governor-in-council and her own courts. In March 1773, the British Parliament authorized the first supreme court at Calcutta, and Sir Elijah Impey as chief justice with jurisdiction under the English law over British subjects in Bengal, Bihar and Orissa. The court, however, arrogated itself to administer English law against Indian citizens of Calcutta. Arbitrary adoption of this law, to adjudicate cases against the Indians, was betrayed when a respected Indian Brahman, a former member of the Moghul aristocracy and a confidante of the Bengal council, Raja Nand Kumar,[2] was handed down the death penalty and executed within days of pronouncement of the sentence. Nand Kumar had brought up charges of bribery against

Governor-General Warren Hastings in the Bengal council. He dared to do so, because three out of four members of the Bengal council lent him their support. One of them, Philip Francis, even fought a dual with Warren Hastings over corruption charges. An outraged Hastings boycotted council proceedings and conceived a conspiracy to annihilate the poor Indian. Three days later, one Mohan Prasad surfaced with charges of forgery against Nand Kumar. That was clearly a contrived move of Hastings. On 15th June 1775, Elijah Impey, three other English judges and a jury of twelve Englishmen, pronounced Nand Kumar guilty and condemned him to death. The sentence ignored the facts that, the alleged event of forgery was four years old; forgery was not a capital offence under the Indian laws; and the sentenced person was an Indian subject outside purview of the English law.[3] This clear case of judicial murder came to life in the House of Commons during impeachment proceedings against Warren Hastings and Elijah Impey. But life of an Indian was inconsequential for a majority of the British parliamentarians.

Laws of the EIC exempted European subjects settled in India from jurisdiction of the native courts. This proviso had the approval of the British Parliament because the Charter Act made European subjects, irrespective of the nature of their crime, outside the purview of Indian laws and courts. Europeans could be tried only by His Majesty's courts in Calcutta (Kolkata), Bombay (Mumbai), and Madras (Chennai). This duality concealed a biased handling of law-and-order cases by the company because its courts in the *mofussil*[4] (country courts) lacked authority to prosecute European offenders of various crimes. Those European offenders, who were neither company employees nor Indian subjects, could not be brought to justice even for serious crimes by virtue of the dual system of law and the then faulty judicial standards. Native victims seeking to litigate against European perpetrators of crime failed to get justice. Financial constraints and long distances from the countryside to the Presidency towns made it impossible for poor Indians to litigate in the Presidency courts competent to hear cases against the Europeans. The estimated cost of litigation in the supreme court at Calcutta was fivefold of that in *mofussil* courts of the company. The justice system was also heavily weighed against the poor natives. John Basil Cochrane, revenue administrator of Nagapattinam, was acquitted of murder charges due to the duality of the company law. Cochrane had ordered the flogging of his native employees so severely that one of them Vaidyananda, succumbed to his injuries. In June 1784, Muttaya, a relative of the deceased, petitioned Fort St. George (Madras) that his brother-in-law Vaidyananda had died following corporal punishment inflicted on him by Mr. Cochrane. The complainant alleged that Vaidyananda was confined in the "guard" because he owed money to the accused. Cochrane refused to release him against the surety bond offered by the local people. Instead, he ordered the *sepoys* to flog the victim continuously for four hours. Four days later, Vaidyananda died of the flogging. Muttaya contended that the natives knew about the highhandedness of Cochrane but were unwilling to bear the ordeal of going to Madras and depose before the Fort St. George Council. The witnesses, however, gave their statements about the commission of crime under the native oath. In 1787, the all-English jury at Madras disregarded their oath but accepted a version of Cochrane in that he only reprimanded a dishonest employee. Cochrane was found 'not guilty'. On top of it the new governor Sir Archibald Campbell, gave him a local job during pendency of the case against him.

European planters exploited the dual law to their advantage. In 1824, Dacca circuit judge informed the court of directors of the EIC that European owners of indigo factories in his district had employed bullies to extract outstanding produce from indigo growers, and even to corner produce of the neighbouring growers. Prevalent law offered no protection to the exploited peasants. This lacuna was freely exploited by the Europeans, because only European magistrates or judges exercised jurisdiction over the European subjects. These judges had to be justices of the peace; a position only open to the Europeans. In his note of 19th February 1829, British colonial administrator Charles Metcalfe condemned the company's system of laws which smacked of racism and uncertain judicial administration. He demanded true legal equality and justice for all.[5]

A motion tabled in the House of Commons on 28th June 1831 asked for an inquiry into the operations of the EIC before its charter was renewed. The motion emphasized defects in the company laws and their execution. Hence the 1833 charter of the company created a governor-general and his legislative council to conduct the company's affairs in India. A law member was added with powers to legislate and receive complaints against the Europeans. Thomas Babington Macaulay, who was appointed law member, was also made president of the First Law Commission. In the new charter, civil courts of the company were also empowered to adjudicate upon cases involving the Europeans. Macaulay introduced a bill into the legislative council abolishing privileges granted to Europeans in the *mofussil* for approaching the supreme court in civil matters. Tumultuous protests erupted in Calcutta against the bill. Angry protesters even suggested the lynching of Macaulay. In a petition addressed to the Governor-General Lord Auckland, barristers and English newspaper editors claimed their birth right to be governed by the English laws. Their demand was at odds with opinion of the British jurist Sir William Blackstone that with no rules, laws of England became laws of a territory which was not "a desert uninhabited" country when crown acquired sovereignty over that territory by discovery and occupation as *terra nullius*. Some members opposed greater powers to the Indian magistrates. They argued that the very existence of the British in India depended upon exclusion of the natives from military and political power. The law member Thomas Macaulay emphatically defended equal justice for all. He argued that racial distinction meant something less than justice for the natives and something more than justice for the European subjects in India. The company, therefore, refused to relent and the legislative council passed the bill on 9th May 1836. Europeans dubbed the bill *Black Acts* because it brought them under jurisdiction of the company courts.

Governor-General William Bentinck permitted the appointment of Indian natives to the criminal courts as subordinate magistrates. In 1843, during the tenure of Lord Ellenborough, the position of a deputy magistrate was thrown open to the Indians. The Second Law Commission of 1853, besides endorsing views of the First Law Commission, recommended uniform substantive civil law on the pattern of English law and amalgamated civil and *sadar* (main) courts in the Presidency towns. The commission also recommended uniform judicial procedure in all courts of British India. Thus far, *sadar* courts did not exercise jurisdiction over cases involving Europeans, and the supreme court held similar positions over Indian natives residing outside Calcutta. The European community strongly opposed recommendations of the Second Law Commission.[6] Earl of Albemarle presented petitions on behalf of the Europeans of Bengal. The petitioners contended that European capitalists, who had contributed substantially to the prosperity of Bengal, resented new laws and would withdraw their investment. Smitten by racial superiority complex, the Europeans of Bengal wanted exemption from criminal jurisdiction of the country courts presided over by Indian judges. They shuddered to contemplate a white man appearing in a court presided over by a native judge.

In 1858, a central legislative council came up at Calcutta, when direct rule of the British sovereign and British parliament was established over India. The number of European offenders in India rose in proportion to the rise in their population. The famous Indian Penal Code of 1860 was soft on European criminals. It stipulated that a life- term in their case could mean a maximum prison term of ten years. The Code of Criminal Procedure of 1861, an Act passed by the legislative council of India, decreed that no person other than a justice of peace shall commit or hold on bail, any European British subject for trial before the supreme court. This code awarded the death penalty to Indians convicted of murder but bestowed legal superiority upon Europeans through privileges like the right to trial by a jury in which half or more jurors had to be European British subjects or Americans. Europeans could be tried by only English judges or magistrates. In this manner, the whole judicial procedure heavily weighted in favour of the Europeans and to the detriment of native victims. Wherefore, Europeans assaulted and maimed Indian natives with impunity. Brutal assaults of British planters passed muster under the Whipping Act of 1864, which legitimized barbaric whippings inflicted upon natives as a form of punishment. Indians loathed this Act, as well as Act 1 of 1853, which permitted the whipping of juvenile offenders. In 1894, whipping was included in the list of punishments for prison-based offences under the Prison Act of 1894. Provisions of these Acts were applicable only for Indians and not for Europeans. For this purpose, a triangle was erected outside the court of each magistrate. In July 1909, Sir Henry Cotton asked a pointed question in the House of Commons about this inequality. The discriminatory justice system disadvantaged Indians, because native Indian judges could not adjudicate cases involving the Europeans except in the Presidency towns of Calcutta, Bombay, and Madras. Privileges granted to the Europeans based on birth, struck at the roots of efficient and swift administration of justice. In 1883, Lord Chancellor admitted in the House of Lords that his experience of cases appealed to the Privy Council showed that, in respect of integrity of learning, of knowledge of soundness and satisfactory character of judgments arrived at, judgments of native judges were quite as good as those of the English."[7] Sir Ashley Eden, the lieutenant governor of Bengal, was dissatisfied with the existing judicial process. Shortly before leaving India, he asked his secretary to send a note to the viceroy proposing an amendment in the criminal law to bring European offenders under jurisdiction of the Indian magistrates. He reasoned that a European joint magistrate who is subordinate to native district magistrate was empowered to try cases which his immediate superior could not try. He wanted this irrationality to be removed.

One Bihari Lal Gupta, who had joined the Indian civil service in 1871, prepared a note against the dual system of criminal procedure which denigrated native judges. This note along with Sir Ashley's letter formed the basis of the bill which was drafted with the consent of Lord Ripon, governor-general and viceroy of India. Its purpose was to mitigate *lacunae* in the justice system. On 9th February 1883, this bill meant to amend the code of criminal procedure, was introduced into viceroy's council by Courtney Ilbert, a law member in the viceroy's legislative council. The bill called the Ilbert Bill was meant to empower native judges/magistrates in the colonial service and define criminal jurisdiction in cases involving Europeans living in the *mofussil* outside the three Presidency towns. The bill intended to prevent battering of native labour by European planters and merchants operating in the countryside. Taking undue advantage of the prevalent law, native landlords had begun hiring European goons for battering their labour because the former would escape punishment. Wherever native magistrates possessed powers to try European offenders, they could impose only nominal fines and imprisonment. For serious cases, European offenders had to be committed to the high court, which was almost out of reach of the poor victims.

Lord Ripon decided to remove the anomalous situation in enforcing law and order in the *mofussil*. Of the provincial governments he consulted, the proposal was apathetically received in Bengal and Bihar, home of few debased European planters of Cachar and Western Dooars. The Anglo-Indian community also disagreed with Lord Ripon's move to introduce self-government at the municipal level, because that meant empowering the natives. Lockwood Kipling, the father of Rudyard Kipling, reflected resentment of his compatriots by proclaiming the well-meaning governor-general, a "terrible calamity." The Ilbert Bill gave its detractors an opportunity to air their perceived sense of superiority over the Indian natives that they wanted to preserve headlong. The English press of Calcutta was galore with invective-laced language of 1858 vintage against the natives. The *Englishman* of Calcutta published an anonymous letter insinuating that Indian magistrates will mentally torture wives of the Englishmen appearing in their courts. The paper also carried a critique in which Lord Ripon was portrayed as an ass and a *Brahmani* boy listening to Calcutta babus. The critique, reproduced by *Civil and Military Gazette* of Lahore added a few unsigned verses at the end. The Ilbert Bill was named ma-bap[8] legislation (ma-bap used by subservient Indians to address their masters). Rudyard Kipling denied authorship of these verses, but those were suspected to be a joint work of the Kipling father and son duo.[9] Indignation was pervasive among European officials and non-officials. It was a case of the pot calling the kettle black. The North American Review of April 1858 on page 500 recorded, "Be as it may, it is beyond question, that while our ancestors, whether we call them Saxons or Celts, were painting their naked bodies, and were as ignorant of letters as the rudest tribes of negroes discovered by Dr. Livingstone in his African travels, the *Hindoos* were in the enjoyment of a high state of civilization." Even members of the Indian civil service, the most loyal class of government servants, were loath to support Lord Ripon. The then, lieutenant governor of Bengal, Sir Augustus Rivers Thompson, openly vented his social prejudice.[10] In his letter of 22nd June 1883 to the Government of India he mentioned that the majority of European officers disfavoured the bill. He argued that the bill would not help the natives. He downplayed the intelligence of the Indians selected to the covenanted service saying that they come from the same competition of the Subordinate Selective Service, and that their training in England would not enable them to occupy positions of higher responsibility.

The nonofficial European community boycotted entertainment functions and insulted the viceroy at the entry to the government house. On 28th February 1883, in a meeting of the Defense Association presided over by J.J.J. Keswick, a conspiracy was hatched to overpower sentries at the government house, whisk the viceroy, put him on a steamer at Chandpal Ghat and send him to England via the Cape.[11] In a protest meeting held in the Town Hall in Calcutta, speaker after speaker ridiculed the 'Bengali babu'[12] who dared to seek equality of the law with the English. A false sense of European superiority over the natives was brazenly touted through several resolutions. First of them moved by J.J.J. Keswick, president of the Bengal Club, and head of the Jardine and Skinner Company, called any amendment of civil criminal procedure code unnecessary because it took away the much valued and prized privilege of European subjects, imperilled their liberty, and would deter the investment of British capital in India. Keswick asked the audience if a three or four-year training in England would make native judges like Europeans that they could adjudicate against the Europeans. He asked the cheering crowd if an Ethiopian can change his skin or a leopard his spots.[13] How come native judges demand power to sit in judgment on a lion-hearted race? Another speaker, James Branson-a barrister, who later became senior acting magistrate, thundered that a jackass wanted to lick the lion which was not dead and that natives should dread its awakening. The worst part of the proceedings were insinuations such as native judges falsely implicating English ladies to force them for sexual favours. An alarmed European of Madras lamented that European ladies would be torn from their homes on false pretences and tried by men who did not respect women. News of agitation labelled 'white mutiny' reached England through J.C. Macgregor, a barrister and a correspondent of the Times, London. In fact, the campaign against Ilbert Bill was led by the European barristers and businessmen of Calcutta. Within a month of introduction, most English newspapers led by *Englishman* of Calcutta, began lambasting the Bill. Racial bigotry of British Indians was apparent when a native magistrate convicted a British on charges of brutally assaulting a native. Britons called the charges factitious, demanded a reversal of the sentence, and censuring of the magistrate. They threatened that unless their demands were conceded the British would not feel safe in Calcutta and would opt to leave India along with their capital. The *Times* in its editorial reported the disgraceful behaviour of the English residents of Calcutta.[14] It published accounts of a Town Hall meeting requisitioned by the Bengal Chamber of Commerce. An English lady did not object to the skin colour of an Indian but to the colour of his mind[15] — an envious viewpoint indeed. Defense officers also joined anti-native censure. In a meeting of the Defense Association held on 22nd March 1883, James Furrell, editor of the *Englishman* of Calcutta, proposed drafting a separate petition to the British queen on behalf of the English women in India.

Lord Ripon harassed by bigotry of his own countrymen, pulled back and watered-down provisions of the original bill. Anomalies were not only restored but provisions became extra cumbersome. This compromised Act III of 1884, and allowed district magistrates and session judges to try English defenders themselves. In the case of native judges and magistrates, European defenders could ask for trial by a jury consisting of at least half of them to be Europeans or Americans. It became mandatory to commit cases of serious penalty to the high court. The compromised bill embodied bias against the native judges which Sir Ashley and Lord Ripon had sought to remove. A disillusioned and disappointed Lord Ripon left India in 1884. He was acclaimed by Indian crowds of Calcutta but reviled by most Europeans. Open and shameless display of intellectual and moral bankruptcy by the English residents of Calcutta, did awaken the Indian masses to fight for their own rights. Racial bias against Indians had percolated to all levels of the civil and military administration. It was during the viceroyalty of Lord Lansdowne (1884-1894) that an Irish soldier Thomas O'Hara and his fellow soldiers of East Kent Regiment at Dum Dum left their barracks without leave and in a drunken state shot dead a villager on the outskirts of Calcutta. The poor fellow had failed to supply them with local brew, *toddy*, because he did not have it. This felony came to the notice of the viceroy and the two Britons were put on trial. In February 1890, the trial judge committed them to sessions of the Calcutta High Court. The jury of eight Europeans and only one Indian convicted O'Hara and acquitted the second defender. The judge, Sir John Norris had made it clear that penalty for murder was that of death. This news caused a sensation among the European community. Military authorities sought opinion of the advocate general of Bengal who opined that the trial judge committed error of procedure. Evidence of the third soldier should have been recorded to find out if he was an accomplice in the crime. A full bench of Calcutta High Court found the objection valid and quashed O'Hara's conviction. All four soldiers were retried for the breach of regimental law and given brief imprisonment for absenting without leave. The Indian community was outraged. An English newspaper, *Hindoo Patriot*, commented that Europeans are above the law and British-born subjects may murder "black bastards" with impunity. London press picked up news of the trial. A question was raised in the House of Commons about fairness of the Indian judicial process. Finally, the official response was escapist, non-interference in the normal course of law. The viceroy was helpless. He was aware of the fate of his predecessor. His office ordered a pension for the widow of the deceased. The moral of this episode was that highest powers in India, as well as in England, could not rein in racial bias against the Indian community.

Managers of the Assam tea gardens were notorious for exploiting and ill-treating native labour, which they called coolies. In fact, they were the law unto themselves. Sir Henry Cotton, chief commissioner of Assam, detested their arrogant behaviour. The managers either got their labour by kidnapping or by enticing labour to migrate to the tea estates from the neighbouring provinces. After landing in the tea estates, they were made to enter into contracts. Once bound by the contract, they were treated as slave labour, underpaid and harshly treated. Sir Henry, who served in Assam from 1896 to 1902, had himself seen several labourers dead or dying in the ditch by the road. He tried his best to improve service conditions of tea estate labour but faced resolute resistance of the European management who considered natives unworthy of pity. On 27th July 1901, Horace Lyall, the manager of Chubwa Tea Estate of Assam, was miffed at some labourers, and asked ten labourers to lie face down on the ground and then ordered them to be severely beaten. Three labourers and a woman had their arms broken as a result of the beating.

One labourer succumbed to his injuries. Lyall was arraigned and charged for causing grievous hurt under section 307 of the Indian Penal Code of 1860. The trial was conducted by the deputy commissioner of Nowgong. The jury, consisting of three Europeans who happened to be fellow planters and two submissive natives, acquitted the offender. The deputy commissioner called the jury verdict a travesty of justice. The chief commissioner regarded the verdict a pro-planter bias and asked the deputy commissioner to commit the case to the Fort William High Court. The High Court convicted Lyall for simple hurt and sentenced him to one-month imprisonment and fine of one thousand rupees. The European Defense Association was outraged. It petitioned the viceroy for remission of the sentence. Lord Curzon refused the petition. Sir Henry Cotton was so dejected that he preferred to quit his job and left for England.

Lord Curzon, though a staunch imperialist and a votary of the superiority of English race, had to engage with the perverted thinking of his countrymen in India and Britain. Soon after taking over as viceroy of India in 1899, he found all-pervading racial bias against the Indians. An aristocrat, Lord Curzon was not to be brow-beaten on the path of fair play. There were instances of his brush with civil and military judiciary. In one case, three members of the famous British regiment, the 9th Lancers, who arrived from South Africa on 9th April 1902, asked their native cook, named Attu, to procure a woman for their pleasure. Attu refused to oblige them. He was severely thrashed by the troopers. His ribs were broken, and he got blows to his face and back of head. Attu lay unattended one whole night and the next day, he was carried on a stretcher to the hospital where he died after nine days. Before his death he deposed in the hospital that it was the men of 9th Lancers who assaulted him.[16] Police visited the crime scene, which was splattered with the victim's blood. Lord Curzon was shocked that the regiment did not conduct a proper investigation. Relatives of the victim petitioned for justice because the regimental inquiry was a sham. Curzon was convinced of the spuriousness of inquiry because none of the inquiry officers understood a word of local language. The regiment did not include a doctor or a police officer in the inquiry. Curzon wanted to put an end to the hushing up of such cases. On his intervention, the commander-in-chief asked Lieutenant General Sir Bindon Blood to conduct a fresh inquiry. To astonishment of the viceroy, Sir Bindon denounced the deceased as a drunkard and liar and recommended extra-sentry duty for the erring soldiers. An enraged viceroy over-ruled the general and had the whole regiment punished. The king of England was angered at Lord Curzon's action, simply because the sons of dukes and earls were on rolls of the regiment. The nobility looked for a chance to humiliate the viceroy. They got the chance to vent their ire in 1903, on the coronation 'Durbar' of Edward VII, the king of England, when the 9th Lancers, dukes and duchesses slighted the viceroy in different ways.

Lord Curzon was unfazed. He detested injustice and believed in punishing the guilty despite the virulent protests of the Englishmen in India. He cowered on occasions but largely stuck to his guns. Assam tea gardens were notorious for ill-treating their bonded labour. Labourers were not allowed a leave of absence even for legitimate reasons. In 1902 the European manager of a tea garden in Cachar, P.W.B. Bain, mercilessly thrashed a labourer to death with a stirrup as the blows had ruptured his spleen. Bain also ordered the brutal flogging of two women accused of absence from work. Bain was tried at Cachar by sessions and a jury of five Englishmen who were his fellow planters. He was acquitted of charges of grievous hurt, amounting to culpable homicide but convicted for causing simple hurt and sentenced to a six-month imprisonment. Lord Curzon was very upset. He ordered an appeal to the Calcutta High Court against the acquittal on a serious charge. The appeal was heard by a bench comprising Mr. Justice Handley and Mr. Justice Banerjee. They ordered a new trial by another judge of the high court, Mr. Justice Sale. The judge did not conduct a jury trial but based on the previous evidence, ruled that charges of grievous hurt did not stand against the accused. Even he expressed astonishment that the defendant was convicted at all, even for a minor charge. The conviction of Bain enraged the whole European community. A leading Anglo-Indian newspaper charged Lord Curzon of callousness towards his own community. Fearing uproar, the chief commissioner of Assam advised the viceroy not to seek intervention of the high court. To the annoyance of the viceroy, he arranged to shift the prisoner to Calcutta where he could get better jail facilities than those available at Cachar.[17] Curzon felt disgusted at the whole affair. On 25th March 1903, he sent the whole case file to the India Office in London. J. Arthur Bain, brother of the prisoner appealed to the House of Commons against the sentence on the plea that it was a simple case of assault on the worker who had run away from work. The House of Commons took up the case on 30th March 1903. Lord George Hamilton, the secretary of state for India, replied that it was up to the local government to ask the high court for retrial in another district and disposed of the case. Burke and Quraishi quoted a letter of 5th August 1903 to the secretary of state in which Curzon grieves that managers of tea gardens were drawn from the most inferior class of Englishmen, who have no knowledge of local language and they have profound contempt for the natives.[18] The British justice system in India was so stuck in racial mire that even the viceroy of the colony was helpless against the judiciary, the British officials, and the white supremacists in India and Britain. Curzon had no choice but to change rules governing labour work on the plantations. He lamented the racial prejudice of his countrymen in reply to an address presented to him on 20th July 1904, in the Guild Hall of London. "Unless we persuade the millions of India that we will give to them absolute justice and man to man equality before law, freedom from tyranny and injustice and oppression, our empire will not touch their hearts and will fade away."[19] Simmering discontent against the British rule in India vociferously surfaced in days of the First World War when thousands of native troops lost their lives. Indian statesmen questioned the morality of India's involvement in far-away conflicts. The British government was alarmed by the nationalistic rhetoric. It enacted Indian Regulation Act of 1915 to curtail revolutionary thinking among Indians. The Act was employed in conspiracy case against the revolutionary *Ghadar* party in 1915. Lord Curzon's words proved prophetical when the above Act became precursor to the 1919 Rowlatt Acts meant to curtail public dissent. These acts allowed internment of persons without trial. Newspaper headlines termed them Black Acts. On 13th April 1919, Jallianwala Bagh massacre in Amritsar occurred in the aftermath of this Act. The process of British exit from India had begun.

The colonial justice system in Africa: The British introduced laws of the Indian Penal Code, the Criminal Procedure Act and Police Act of 1860 in their protectorates and colonies in Africa. They could choose between the English law and the Indian laws when they began administering East Africa in 1895. The British commissioner Sir Arthur Hardinge, who was an army commander in Bombay between 1881 and 1885, preferred the simpler Indian code. In fact, laws of India had already been introduced in Zanzibar since 1867. In 1884 additional Indian Acts were extended to Zanzibar. Among these acts were the Indian Lunacy Act, the Indian Penal code of 1860, the Indian Whipping Act of 1864, the Indian Succession Act, the Indian Contract Act and the Indian Evidence Act. For the sake of administration of Justice, these acts made British subjects of Zanzibar a part of her Majesty's Indian Empire. By an order of 1897, twenty additional Indian laws were introduced in Kenya and more followed. Similarly, in 1900, Indian Acts were introduced in Uganda. Thus, the laws of India covered much of criminal judicial work in the British colonies of Africa. An increase in the population of British settlers in the colonies generated opposition to the Indian laws. The plea was that they were product of authoritative colonialism and hence were unsuitable for adjudication of disputes between the English subjects. Under the sustained pressure of the European settlers, the Indian laws yielded space to the English laws in 1839. South Africa had two sets of laws, the indigenous or customary laws practiced by the native rulers and the English law. The Pass Law, that covered the native population, was most degrading. It was introduced by the Dutch in 1760 in the Cape Colony. It was meant for Africans moving between white towns and the black countryside. They had to carry this pass as a token of authorized movement. British occupied the Cape Colony in 1795. Two years later, Earl George Macartney governor of the Cape Colony, introduced a regular Pass Law for excluding African natives from areas occupied by white colonists. A series of Pass laws followed for the same purpose. The 1923 Pass Law of South Africa regulated movement of African natives from their designated habitations into white areas. Every native was required to possess this document issued by the Native Affairs Department and produce it on demand under Act 38 of 1927. An 1809 law required all the Khoi Khoi (natives) including their women folk to have a fixed place of abode. In case, any Khoi Khoi needed to move between white and black parts of the colony, he or she needed a pass from a local official. Besides forced segregation, white colonists used pass laws to evict natives from their lands and force them to work on their farms and plantations.

In 1938, Sir John Harris, organizing secretary to the Anti-Slavery Society and Aborigine Protection Society, visited South Africa on a fact-finding mission. He found thousands of natives imprisoned, not for any crime on their part but for Pass Law offences. The Native (Urban Areas) Act of 1923 completely barred Africans from entering urban areas.[20] This Aact also affected contract services and the use of alcohol by natives in the identified areas. It dehumanized family relations of the natives. Khoi Khoi women employed for domestic work by the colonists were housed in their backyards while their husbands lived in segregated places. Husbands risked prosecution for trespassing, should they be caught for stealthily visiting their wives at night. This law was reframed as Native (Urban Areas) Act of 1945, with the same objectives but an added provision that natives could live only in specified areas. The purpose was to ensure that farm and industrial labour was available where needed, and it was easy to impose and collect tax from the Africans. Section 147 of the same Act authorized the governor-general to specify areas where aforementioned labour could reside. These areas were out of bounds for the unemployed natives and the defaulters faced prosecution. In this respect, the Act was an extension of the flagrantly discriminatory Native Labour Regulation Act of 1911, which disallowed native labour from walking out of a contract while settlers could break the contract at will. This Act gave virtual license to the colonists to bash the native labour. The Native Land Act (No. 27) of 1913 specified areas where the natives were allowed to hold free land. Ironically, two-thirds of the native population was allowed 7.5 percent land area of the country, while white colonists, just one-fifth of the population, appropriated for themselves 92.5 percent of the country land. The Act disallowed the natives from becoming share croppers in order to force them to work for the colonists. The Germans during their brief colonial stint also promulgated compulsory labour laws in the German East Africa till they lost their colonies after the First World War.

White colonists of East Africa took coercive as well as legislative routes to grab maximum land. They used similar tactics to secure native labour to run these enterprises after establishing large farms and plantations. Natives were heavily taxed to ensure that economically weakened natives were left with no choice but to work on the white-owned estates to pay off taxes and feed their families. Those who opted to be tenant farmers were required to obtain written permission of the landlord before they switched to another employer. Violators were given corporal punishment. In 1840, natives who left their station without permission were hunted down under the Bushrangers Act. Labour contracts included children of the labourer. Thus, a whole family worked as bonded labour. The natives were thrashed over petty matters. Those natives who ran away to escape unbearable lashings, but were captured by the police, awaited more stringent punishment. The Native Service Contract Act of 1932, which legalized whipping of African lads under eighteen, was meant to make children subservient to their masters. The Master and Servant Acts of the eighteenth and nineteenth centuries were designed to exploit cheap native labour. The South Africa Identification and Registration Act of 1957, was a variation of the Pass Act. Africans had to get registered and obtain a registration book and an identity card which they were supposed to carry with them to avoid criminal liability. Village chiefs were responsible for ensuring adherence to this requirement. Between January 1958 and July 1965, five thousand Africans were convicted under this Act.[21]

Racial prejudice pervaded all European colonies in enacting laws and administration of justice. British colonies in Africa practiced dual system of jurisprudence. African courts for the natives were supervised by colonial administrators. White colonists were tried through a jury system that invariably favoured colonists against the natives. Of all British colonies, the colonists of Kenya were notorious for inhumane treatment of African natives. These settlers dispensed rough justice to native servants on their own convinced that no harm will ever come to them in the courts. Kenya magistrates and juries were averse to convict a white defendant when the victim was a native.[22] The 1911 case of Galbraith Cole is an abhorrent example of their debased mentality. Cole voluntarily admitted to shooting dead a native he suspected of stealing his sheep. His claim was far from truth because he had shot the man before he found his dead sheep. The friends of the victim lodged a complaint with the police after they found his body on the premises of Cole. They vehemently contradicted Cole's contention that the victim was a thief. Notwithstanding the confession of Cole and testimony of the victim's friends, the white jury of Nakuru High Court acquitted Galbraith Cole.[23] There were men of clear conscience in the British society. Leys, who joined the colonial service in Kenya as a medical officer in 1904 narrated this episode to T.E. Harvey, a member of the British Parliament. On 13th July 1911, the case came before the House of Commons. Ramsay Macdonald, leader of the Labour party asked the secretary of state for the colonies if he was aware that Galbraith Cole had admitted murdering the man and in spite of that, the jury, after few minutes deliberation returned the verdict "not-guilty". In reply, the undersecretary of state, without admitting the fact, explained that they had not yet received the report of the governor of East Africa Protectorate. On 22nd August, the secretary of state for the colonies, Lewis Harcourt, read a report of the judge and ordered Cole's deportation from Africa. Harcourt was annoyed that British settlers raised hue and cry against the deportation orders of their compatriot, who happened to be a pioneer settler. Ultimately the tamed colonial secretary did not obstruct legislation meant to combat stock theft. Hence, the Punishment Ordinance (1909) and the Stock and Produce Theft Ordinance of 1913 combined, gave extensive leeway to the colonial government to levy collective punishment as heavy fines on the family of the accused and as well as his community. The Collective Punishment Ordinance of 1930 repealed previous ordinances. This ordinance empowered the governor to impose fines on all or any inhabitant found to collude with 'criminals' as also failed to prevent them from escaping and for suppression of evidence in the court. The governor's decision was final and not subject to appeal in a court of law. The 1929 Tribal Police Ordinance allowed the imposition of a fine on specific communities for financing police patrols.

Soon after the end of First World War, Galbraith Cole was permitted to return to East Africa amid partying by his friends. The Cole story did not end with his return. It took an interesting turn when the Indian Community in East Africa got entangled in the episode. A community newspaper reported the story but mistakenly referred to Cole's brother as the culprit. The brother sued the editor of the newspaper for damages to his reputation. The court ordered the editor to pay two thousand pounds as damages to the litigant. Although Galbraith Cole had shot and killed a native, most white settlers were not perturbed because they regarded Africans sub humans who needed battering to discipline them. Whenever a native died of flogging, settlers raised a fund for defence of the perpetrator. Africans were often flogged to pulp with a hippo-hide strap regardless of its impact on the victim. A sensational case of flogging a native to death appeared in the East African Standard of 11th August 1923.[24] One white settler of Molo in Kenya lent his mare to a friend for reaching a railway station. The farmer sent his native servant Kitosh along to walk the mare back without himself riding the animal. A neighbour informed the farmer that Kitosh had a ride on the mare. The infuriated master began hitting Kitosh with a whip of ox hide and then ordered his servants to lash the servant in turns until he fainted. Kitosh was revived by throwing a bucket of water on him. His legs shackled and hands tied behind his back, he was thrown into a store room. Flogging had rendered Kitosh deaf, and he died by the next morning. The medical report gave injuries from lashes and kicks as the cause of death. The farmer was tried on 1st August 1923 by an all-white jury in the High Court at Nakuru. He was found guilty of grievous hurt but not of his death. Two doctors from Nairobi also testified that his will to die, and not the flogging, was the cause of death. Accepting this strange logic, the farmer got away with two years of imprisonment. However, the case rebounded in the British House of Commons. The colonial secretary informed the House of his writing to the governor of Kenya condemning the verdict. He admitted to injustice meted out to natives and spoke about abandoning the jury system. The Archbishop of Canterbury, speaking in the House of Lords on 20th May 1925 conceded that scandalous cases of cruelty against the natives did occur in Kenya. In 1920 Lord Delamere's friend A.E. Atkinson had a dispute over the proceeds of ivory with some tribesman. Atkinson attached a slow fuse to a keg of ivory and asked the tribesmen to inspect it while he excused himself to go away. The powder exploded in their face. The white jury refused to convict him despite plenty of evidence to hang him. Leys gave a very poignant explanation that men do not kill their servants unless they hire them as animals which are not supposed to exhibit signs of hurt or seeking compassion while being hit.[25]

The colonial justice system in Australia: Indigenous people or the natives of Australia were the worst sufferers of asymmetrical application of the English law. The basic cause was the declaration that Australia was *terra nullius* that barred natives of any rights emanating from the motherland. Consequently, Australian natives became victims of a burgeoning settler population. Local authorities and settlers forced out natives from their traditional hunting grounds and sources of food and shelter as well as fishing waters. White stock holders and ex-English convicts regularly seized native fishing boats for their own fishing. Disillusioned, the natives vented their anger by spearing stray white settlers. Pangs of hunger tempted them to steal an occasional sheep or goat for food. The government and the settlers organized sanguinary punitive expeditions. Scores of natives were shot dead to avenge even a single white death. Governor Darling of New South Wales and Van Diemen's Land (1824–1831) permitted settlers to take care of their own defence, thereby giving them a license to kill the natives and seize the lands they lived upon. The native's only recourse to seek justice, the courts, held no solace for them. They were denied the right of evidence in the court because, being ignorant of the English language, they could not swear as witness and face the English law. The case against, one Nathanial Low, heard in the Supreme Court of New South Wales on 18th May 1827, illustrates the kind of justice delivered to them. On 26th June 1826, some desperate natives attacked a station in retaliation and fled after killing two persons. The local police waylaid a native they called Jackey Jackey[26] at Wallis's plains and brought him before Lieutenant Low at Martland. Low ordered four policemen to take the captive behind a bush where he was tied with a tree and shot. Governor Ralph Darling ordered an inquiry into the killing. Thomas Farnham, the prosecution witness, testified in the court that he was at the scene and witnessed the killing. Dr. Robert Wardell, barrister and editor of "*the Australian*", cross-examined the witness. Wardell questioned the jurisdiction of the court in the matter because the victim was a native and an enemy of the Crown rather than an English subject. He argued that the deceased was not governed by the English law and got the deserved treatment. The chief justice, Francis Forbes, disagreed with the contention of Wardell, arguing that both the defendant and victim were British subjects. Dr. Wardell and another lawyer, William Wentworth, claimed that the witness was a worse character whose testimony could not be relied upon. The jury of seven military men, and one from the navy, met for five minutes and returned to deliver a "not guilty" verdict. The *Sydney Gazette* of 21st May 1827, reported on this case. It criticized the jury and opined that objection to jurisdiction of the court was taken on two grounds: namely, abstract principles of law of nations as applied to the subject before us and to the Act of parliament not giving jurisdiction. In this way, natives were killed with impunity because English law and an English jury failed to convict the offenders. The only case when whites were sentenced to death pertained to the 1838 slaughter of 28 native workers at a farm managed by one William Hobbs. The case was heard on 15th November 1838, by Justice James Dowling of New South Wales. The prosecution witness was George Anderson, the station hut keeper, who was present at the site. Justice Dowling reminded the all-white jury that law made no distinction between a white man and a native. After a twenty minutes deliberation, the jury returned the verdict 'not guilty'. Later a juror confided that he could not convict a white person for killing of blacks who he felt were no more than a set of monkeys deserving to be exterminated. The attorney general brought out more charges for the second trial held on 29th November 1838. A key witness this time gave a clearer version of the incident including the kind of arms used in the massacre. On the following day, the offenders were found guilty and sentenced to death by hanging. There was a loud uproar in the settler community. *Sydney Morning Herald* wrote that killed black animals were not worth the money colonists had to pay for the silly court documents. Except for the above case, the law of the jungle prevailed in respect to the right to life and property of the native Australians.

If European settlers were brutal with native Australians, they also did not spare Pacific Islanders recruited as labourers. The newly formed colony of Queensland required farm hands for cultivating cotton and subsequently sugarcane, a task beyond the capacity of white labour. The 1862 Coolie Act empowered the governor-in-council to admit foreign labour for this purpose. In 1862, a Sydney entrepreneur named Robert Towns acquired a few thousand acres on the Logan River under Queensland government regulations for growing cotton crops after the Civil War in America threatened cotton supplies to the Manchester mills.

He established his cotton plantation at Townsvale. Towns sent a labour recruiting vessel Don Juan, to Melanesia in the South Sea. The first batch of sixty-seven Melanesian labourers landed in Queensland in 1863. These non-white labourers were called Kanaka, in some European colonies. Melanesians were mistreated in spite of several legislative measures. Robert Towns needed them for growing the cotton crop whose price in the world market had soared due to the American Civil War. Towns shifted to sugarcane cultivation once cotton prices settled at the previous level in the post-civil war period. Other settlers also began labour-intensive sugarcane cultivation. Between 1864 and 1904 about 600 vessel-loads ferried 62,000 labourers to Queensland from South Sea Islands, mostly from the Solomon Islands and New Hebrides (now Vanuatu). These labourers had been coaxed, coerced at gun point, forcibly captured, or cheated into boarding so called recruiting vessels. They were shipped to Queensland in a manner similar to the Atlantic slave trade. This act of kidnapping Melanesians for sugarcane cultivation in the Queensland took the name of "black birding," which involved cheating, kidnapping and forced capture.

The notoriety of labour transport vessels forced the Queensland government into passing the Polynesian Labour Act in March 1868. The Act required the presence of a government agent aboard the 'recruiting' vessel, followed by an inspection of recruits by a land-based magistrate in Queensland. Some recruiting vessels ingeniously escaped thorough inspection courtesy of the accomplice interpreters. The Islanders, exasperated of treachery and blood-shedding on the part of the recruiting parties, began attacking lone Britons. In 1872, British Parliament intervened and passed the Pacific Islanders Protection Act (also known as the Anti-Kidnapping Act) requiring all recruiting vessels to provide proof of consent of the recruited persons. It became mandatory for recruiting vessels to be licensed and the law prevented recruiters from seeking protection of the Roman law. The law was further strengthened in 1875 with the appointment of a high commissioner for the Western Pacific Islands in order to oversee labour recruitment. The 1880 Pacific Islands Labourers Act repealed the 1868 Act. Employment of Kanaka labour was restricted to tropical agriculture and by the 1884 Act, their employment was restricted to three years, and offering of incentives for recruitment was banned. The 1885 Abolition of the Island Labour Act was passed to prohibit the import of Island labour beyond 1890. In fact, the Act provided for the repatriation of Islanders and many of them were shipped back. Unable to cope with labour demand however, Queensland government repealed the 1885 Act through the 1892 Pacific Island Labour Act.

Queensland government failed to prevent brutality unleashed by recruiters on the Melanesians despite its legislative measures. Rogue recruiters continued with unauthorized recruiting methods. The government of Premier Samuel Griffith appointed a Royal Commission to investigate labour recruitment practices in the Melanesian Islands after regulations failed to curb the menace. The commission, which examined 500 witnesses, noted atrocious iniquities in the labour trade, brazen treachery, wickedness, and the brutal methods of recruiters. The islanders were coaxed into recruiting vessels to obtain tobacco and other rewards. Once close to the vessel, their canoes were deliberately toppled. Drowning natives were caught from the sea and thrown into the hold. Young islanders were often fired upon during sea or overland raids. An unaccounted number of them were killed in the process. Details of barbaric acts of the crew of the labour recruiting vessel *Hopeful* emerged during the criminal trial which commenced in November 1884 in the supreme court at Brisbane. It transpired that Captain Shaw of the *Hopeful,* Williams, the boatswain; and recruiting agent McNeil were determined, at all cost, to return with the vessel full of labourers. *Hopeful* began recruiting work at Moresby where the crew forcibly dragged unsuspecting natives into boats despite their refusal to be recruited. The interpreter was promised handsome reward should he coax a sufficient number of young men onto the vessel. Abhorrent bloodshed followed at Ferguson Island where a number of native canoes sailed close to the vessel for trade. Two boats were lowered from the *Hopeful*, one each under McNeil and Williams. Sensing trouble, the Islanders beat a hasty retreat towards the shore at speeds faster than the *Hopeful* boats. Failing to close in on the native canoes, McNeil fired at the native steering the canoe and killed him. The man next to him was also hit and he fell overboard. The canoe overturned and sank while natives jumped into the sea. Four of them were picked up by McNeil before they drowned.

Natives on the boat chased by Williams also jumped into the sea. Five of them including a small boy, were picked up by Williams who knifed a drowning man. Thus, eight natives were captured at Ferguson. The next halt of the *Hopeful* was Normanby Island where crew spotted a large number of natives. The natives took to their heels upon noticing white armed pursuers. A seaman, Preston, shot two of them and Williams killed another of the party. McNeil, enraged over their flight, torched their homes and shot dead two natives who emerged from the bushes. A large number of natives were subdued and made to board the vessel. In this way, all the so called "recruits" had actually been killed or kidnapped against their will. The crew of *Hopeful* faced trial in Brisbane. It was impossible to know the number of natives killed by the crew. Nevertheless, they were found guilty of kidnapping and murder. Five crew members were sentenced to jail terms ranging from seven years to life. One received a death sentence. The European population was shocked and outraged. They did not expect white men to be so severely sentenced for crimes against non-whites. The governor used his prerogative of mercy and commuted the death sentence to life in prison. In the end all the executive council, except Governor Sir Samuel Griffiths and another member, voted for commutations. A disgusted Griffiths was convinced that labour recruiting should be altogether abolished. He appointed a commission which recommended the return of all recruits to the islands. The governor concurred despite protests from the growers. There was agitation for the release of the crew of the *Hopeful*. The government of next premier, Boyd Moreland, set them free in 1890. The result of the Commission of Inquiry and subsequent trial exposed the charade of justice to the innocent victims of Melanesia.

French justice system in the colonies: France, the second-largest colonial power at the time, practiced an arbitrary system of jurisprudence in her colonies. France had a centralized system of governance because her colonies were an extension of Paris-rule under the laws of France. The colonies had a dual set of rules: one of traditional African law and the other of the French law, applicable to French citizens. The division between two sets of French nationals, i.e., natives and whites, became confused with time. France, in their first West African colony of Senegal, experimented with 'assimilation', a policy meant for close integration of

French colonies by imposing French culture on the natives. These 'black French' were to be awarded French citizenship (the *Evolues*)[27] with all attendant rights. In the last years of the eighteenth century, France created four coastal communes of Saint Louis, Goree, Dakar, and Rufisque where inhabitants comprising white French, Metis (mixed black and white) and blacks were granted special privileges. In 1815, privileges were curtailed for non-whites, but in 1845 all inhabitants of these colonies received full French citizenship and the right to elect deputies for the French National Assembly. Louis Napoleon abolished these rights. In the French colony of Algeria, a sizeable population of European settlers opposed integration of natives into the French society. Consequently, France used the option of association for governing the native population. This policy was a ruse for authoritarianism. A very liberal law governed French citizens, but others labelled as 'subjects' were placed under Code de Indigent.[28] The code allowed French administrators summary powers to unleash tyranny under the garb of adjudication. It consisted of defined offenses whose numbers varied in different colonies ranging from minor infractions like disrespect towards French officials and insulting the French flag, to major crimes like murder. The code in Ivory Coast listed 54, and in Algeria, 33 infractions which were not part of the French law, but punishable when the natives were involved. African society was divided into administrative units for the governance and hence consisted of different tiers, the lowest being the village. The French appointed a village chief, not based on his standing in the community, but on the basis of his loyalty to the colonial rulers. The chief was responsible for collecting taxes, conscription of labour for public works as well as private farms of French men. Always scared of being replaced, the village chiefs attempted to obey the colonial rulers with the utmost loyalty. Several villages constituted a canton, whose chief was a native appointed on the same considerations as the village chief. He supervised the functioning of village chiefs and could be asked to act on committees or tribunals. The main administrative and judicial unit was the circle, which consisted of several cantons. The circle commander, essentially a French citizen, exercised absolute authority over his domain. His decisions were subject to the approval of the district commander. Circle commanders could inflict any sentence they fancied on native offenders. District commanders were answerable to the chief commissioner or governor of the colony who in turn was under the tight control of the governor general.

The circle commander had a large supporting staff which included African officers of police and military units assigned to the circle. The chiefs of villages and cantons enforced customary law as ordered by the circle commander, who had the final word on the interpretation of law and its enforcement. The natives were relegated to the position of passive subjects liable for harsh punishment should they exhibit signs of political awakening. In their case, prosecutors and investigators were the final arbiters. Customary courts convened by village or canton chiefs, dealt with legal matters. Since customary law differed between circles, it was African officials who advised the circle commander about oral traditions, but it was the commander who decided punishment at will. Customary law was abolished by the end of colonial rule.

Justice system in the German colonies: Heavy-handed approach prevailed in all European colonies but the Germans excelled in earning notoriety. It is probable that the records of German colonies were interpreted after these were mandated to South Africa, Britain, and France in the aftermath of the First World War. In 1918, administrator of the protectorate of South Africa, E.H.L. Gorges, hastily compiled a 'Blue Book', narrating atrocities committed by the Germans. Events narrated in the book were contested a year later by Germany claiming that the author did not authenticate eye-witness accounts. Germany claimed that Britain exaggerated recorded events to justify her own claim over the South West African Colony. German Chancellor Otto von Bismarck called the 1884–1885 Berlin Conference not for a political division of Africa but for regularizing trade with the African continent. In the end however, Europeans claimed their own areas of influence based on occupancy as determined by the physical presence on the African coast, trade with the interior, treaties with native chiefs, and the presence of colonial country flag. Bismarck refrained from direct German colonisation but let German merchants rule areas they acquired in Africa, rather than sending German bureaucracy, military, or civil officials overseas. He, however, promised to protect settlements which came up in the course of trading. Consequently, Germany did not create a colonial force. In 1884, traders and trading companies, through their African acquisitions, provided Germany with the basis to claim colonies of East Africa (subsequently Tanzania), South West Africa (present Namibia), Kamerun (Cameroon), and Togo. Unlike other colonies, Togo, which was declared a German protectorate in 1884, was directly administered from Berlin. True to their profession, merchants began making a quick buck. In addition to her mineral resources, Africa offered potential for growing coffee, cotton, millets, and sugarcane. There was plenty of ivory and rubber to collect. Colonists needed manpower which was in plenty all around. But natives who led a satisfied life in their own way were forced to work for German colonists. Most effective method employed by the European colonists was to levy a poll tax or hut tax to be paid in cash by the natives. Natives, thus far used to a barter system, had to work on German farms to earn cash, which was barely sufficient to pay taxes. Forced labour, flogging on various accounts, eviction from lands, confiscation of their livestock, and violation of their women, goaded the natives to rise against the foreigners. Thus, within a few years, there were reports of insurrections beyond the control of merchant companies. The German government intervened through her "schutztruppe" which very soon earned notoriety for the atrocities it heaped upon the Africans. "Schutztruppe" consisted of German officers, some subordinate ranks, and *askaries*. The latter were local natives. From a beginning with about 3000 men, it more than doubled in size when native unrest spread far and wide.

Germany appointed commissioners/governors to administer two main blocks of German territory created by German merchants. German civil and military officers depended upon African mercenaries for suppressing native uprisings. Their expedition unleashed brutality and wanton destruction. Even in peace time, twenty-five lashes had become synonymous with German rule in SWA. Field officers were law unto themselves under the tacit approval of the Kaiser. They often bypassed the governor/commissioner of the territory who bore the ultimate responsibility for maintaining law and order. The 1888 Arab-inspired revolt along the east coast and the *Maji Maji* revolt in the interior, especially the latter threatened newly established German rule. The overbearing attitude of German officers in SWA culminated into revolt of the cattle-based society of the Herero people whose cattle and grazing grounds were being expropriated. An immediate cause of uprising was the inept handling of a dispute involving a goat.[29] German district chief Lieutenant Walter Jobst sent for the Bondelswart chief Jan Abraham Christian. The latter did not respond because it was a case between African natives and thus well within his jurisdiction. Jobst felt slighted. On 25th October 1903, he marched to Warmbad with a posse of men to arrest Jan Christian. He ordered his men to drag Jan Christian from his home like a common criminal. Embarrassed in front of his own people, Jan Christian tried to wriggle out of the hold when he was shot at point blank. The horrified tribesmen retaliated, and Walter Jobst was killed in an exchange of fire. The Bondelswarts did not take murder of their chief lying down. They revolted against the Germans under the leadership of Johannes Christian, brother of the slain chief. The Germans mustered the support of Nama chief Hendrik Witbooi and temporarily put down the uprising. Very soon, Hendrik Witbooi sensed the German game plan of playing one African tribe against another and joined the resistance movement. He was killed in 1905, but resistance against German occupation continued under Jacob Marengo who ultimately died in the Kalahari Desert during a skirmish with a British armed force in September 1907. His death broke the back of the Nama resistance against German occupation. The dispossessed and harassed Hereros around Windhoek revolted in January 1904 and fought a war of survival against the well-armed Germans who were commanded by their ferocious general Lother von Trotha from June 1904 onwards. Von Trotha turned it into a war of races and led his campaign with the owed purpose of exterminating the Herero and Nama tribes. By late 1904 most of the Herero tribe lay dead in the Omaheke desert. Theodore Leutwein, governor of SWA between 1894 and 1904, did not subscribe to von Trotha's scorched earth policy. He admitted that the Germans did not take a single prisoner during the expedition.

Justice system of German colonies was only meant for the Europeans. Professional judges adjudicated in cases against the whites, but it was the German field officers who dished out a kind of summary justice to African natives. As a result, Africans suffered degrading and brutal corporal punishments, and executions, often without reference to higher authorities.[30] Even German settlers arrogated themselves the right to manhandle their African labour for what they called paternal chastisement. A German farmer Ludwig Cramer of Black Nassob in South West Africa brutally assaulted African women labourers. Two pregnant women miscarried, while two died of the beatings. In 1912, he was charged of assault and battery in eight cases and sentenced to a prison term of one year and eight months. On appeal, his sentence was reduced to a jail term of four months plus a fine. His wife, Adelheid Cramer, a writer who participated in some of her husband's assaults, criticized the court judgment while justifying deeds of her husband. In Togo, the penal code of April 1896 entrusted absolute authority to German district officers to punish the natives by flogging, sentencing them to hard labour, and imposing fines. Even station leaders (stationsleiter) were a law unto themselves so much so that they maintained harems by browbeating natives. World-wide shortage of long-staple cotton prompted Germany to grow export quality cotton in Togo. It sought technical assistance from the government of the United States. Accordingly, a team of scientists from the Tuskegee Institute of Alabama set up a cotton experiment station at Trove, a group of six villages about sixty miles inland from the Lome seaport. The natives took it another form of foreign imposition. They already opposed the foreign occupation of their country and, hence, detested any foreign enterprise. In retaliation, the Germans burnt five native villages in 1895, and killed a large number of natives of the Ewe tribe, and even shipped decapitated heads to Germany. The agitated natives refused to work for the cotton station. German leader of the district ordered village chiefs to produce 450 labourers for field work at meagre wages. Labour was also harnessed to pull ploughs and wagons in the place of animals who did not survive animal trypanosomiasis caused by the tsetse fly. The same labour situation repeated itself in 1903, when a cotton school was proposed for Notse, a conglomerate of seven hutments north of Trove in Atakpame district. German station leader, Schmitz, marched to Notse with a posse of policemen. He ordered the police to round up the natives. Police produced forty elderly men in chains because the other natives had disappeared into the bushes. Station leader caned them with twenty lashes each and then put them on road construction work despite injuries they had sustained[31].Several men died of the dual trauma of the caning and the hard work beyond their physical capacity. By 1904, the school was made functional, but no trainees came forward, except two volunteers. The trainees had to be conscripted from neighbouring districts in the initial years. The German treatment of the native Ewe and Akawa tribes was so harsh that many of them escaped into the nearby English colonies. Migration and indiscriminate killings almost halved the two and a half million population of Togo within a span of twenty years.

Treatment of natives in the German colony of Kamerun (Cameroon) was no different than the other colonies. Germans entered a treaty with the native Duala tribe promising that their right to lands under their occupation will be honoured. Duala right was recognized through a government ordinance of 5th September 1904. Incidentally, Duala had settled on resource-rich riverine lands which were also coveted by German settlers. In 1910, the German Parliament approved a plan that proposed to uproot the Duala people from their lands to make room for wholly German settlements. The plan, which was against the German treaty with the Duala, was resisted by the tribe. Their leader, Manga Bell, led a fierce resistance against the expropriation of the natives' lands and the imposition of poll tax. He was captured and hanged on 8th August 1914. Germans brutalized the people of Akawa tribe in the same manner. Their homes were burned down in order to drive them out of their ancestral abodes. German colonies were called flogging colonies, notorious for the use of *kibok* made of hippopotamus hide. The former Governor Leutwein of German SWA acknowledged that Africans were denied justice. German colonial records debouched that. While fifteen Africans were executed for the deaths of six Europeans, the courts which adjudicated against whites for the deaths of three Africans, awarded the culprits prison terms of two years, one year and three months.[32]

Justice system in the Portuguese colonies: The Portuguese pioneered incursions into the New World in pursuit of adventure, commerce, and proselytism. They reached Brazil, but did not occupy it. Portuguese discovered African coast and established trade posts (forts) for slavery. At a later stage, broadly for commercial reasons, Portugal began establishing colonies. It had a year's long presence on the African coast before venturing into the interior of Africa and claimed colonies like Angola, Mozambique and Guinea Bassau. Portugal wanted to administer these colonies on the assimilation pattern of France but, like the latter, did not succeed beyond creating a small class of "Assimilados" who never got the promised rights. The reason was that Portuguese colonial policy came to rest upon maximum exploitation of her overseas colonies. Specific Portuguese civil law and African customary law prevailed in her colonies. African settlements or *regidoria*, governed under customary law, were under an African or Portuguese official or *regulo* chosen by the settlement. Villages in each *regidoria* had a native headman. Colonies were treated as overseas provinces of Portugal but were singled out for authoritarian centralized administration. The Colonial Act of 1930 engineered by dictatorial Oliveira Salazar made Portugal and her colonies interdependent, thereby fulfilling his dream of a vast empire. Under this arrangement, it was mineral, agricultural, and manpower resources of the colonies, which were exploited for the sake of Portugal. Portuguese administration and chartered companies joined hands in milking them. The lands of Africans were occupied to establish plantation estates to be run with conscripted African labour used like slaves. Chartered companies even sold African labour to plantations of the neighbouring English colonies. Angolan contract workers uprooted natives for a kind of slave labour in the cocoa and coffee plantations of Sao Tome and the Principe islands in the Gulf of Guinea, some 150 miles from mainland Africa. By 1908, 70,000 Angolans ended up as slave labour in the Sao Tome plantations. Women of these labourers were preyed upon by the master, irrespective of their age and marital status, thereby fuelling native resentment. Labourers were treated as property and had to work as per the wishes of the slave owners.

The overbearing conduct of the Portuguese created simmering resentment against foreign rule. Portugal ignored European powers who resolved to terminate their colonial rule in the wake of Second World War. It also ignored the United Nations Declaration of 1960 which demanded colonial powers to cease control of foreign lands. Consequently, the natives of Portuguese colonies intensified armed resistance. Portugal did not swerve. It committed 80 percent of her military power to combat insurgency. British South Africa aided Portugal in combating native resistance. In Angola, military commanders like

Fernando Robles became known for their ruthless retribution against the natives who had killed Portuguese settlers. Rebel captives were decapitated, and their heads were impaled on stakes. Angola achieved independence after a 15-year struggle which consumed 300,000 native lives. On 3rd February 1953, close to one thousand plantation workers of Sao Tome, who protested slave labour were killed in what is known as the Batepa massacre. Bloodshed triggered a resistance movement against Portuguese rule. Finally, Sao Tome achieved independence in 1975. The same year, Mozambique, where administration was largely run by private companies, saw the end of Portuguese rule.

Chapter 11
They Embodied Terror for the Natives

Governor Edward John Eyre. Edward Eyre was only 17 when he landed in Sydney to seek his fortune in Australia. A greenhorn in any specific trade, he promenaded unknown parts of Australia. Soon he took to driving cattle overland from Sydney to the English settlements in remote parts of Australia where animals fetched good prices. After enduring harsh desert conditions, he was able to delineate a stock route from Adelaide to King George Sound by the Great Australian Bight. During this adventure he gained the friendship and admiration of the natives who lived in those dry areas. He worked with them and became familiar with the tribal way of life. Eyre landed the job of resident magistrate and protector of the aborigines in the Murray River area. In this job he resolved disputes between the natives and white settlers. His experience allowed him to predict that progress and prosperity of the white race in Australia will follow the ruin of the natives.

His sympathetic approach towards the problems of the Australian natives earned him many admirers in England. His good work was rewarded with governorship of the Saint Vincent islands followed by the position of governor-in-chief of Saint Vincent and Antigua islands. In 1865 Britain captured the Spanish colony of Jamaica and settled it with residents from other British colonies. Several Englishmen established plantations in that colony. Even a number of Mulattos[1] like George William Gordon, who was son of a white attorney and a slave native, owned plantations. The blacks, descendants of African slaves in the colony, were treated very harshly. A mere 2000 out of a population of 436,000 had voting rights. They had no rights on lands. Droughts made their lives miserable. Eventually they began protesting against the white colonists. During this period in 1862, Eyre was appointed governor of Jamaica.

Edward Eyre was chosen for the West Indies due to his background in amicably solving problems between the natives and the English settlers in Australia. Strangely his demeanour underwent a marked change in Jamaica. Blacks of Jamaica led by a local leader Paul Bogle, a Baptist deacon, walked 45 miles to the Spanish Town to present their grievances to Governor Eyre. The governor refused to meet them. The secretary of the Baptist Missionary Society in Jamaica tried to intercede with the colonial office on their behalf. Eyre forestalled their petition to Queen Victoria for permission to cultivate Crown lands. Angry and disappointed Jamaicans began detesting the colonial rule and started resistance movement against the administration. They were in a sinister mood when on 7th October 1865 the court of petty sessions ordered a native boy to pay a fine and expenses of a trial for assaulting a woman. The magistrate ordered the arrest of a black person named Geoghegan who exhorted the boy to pay the fine but not expenses. Other black persons present in the court including Paul Bogle intervened and rescued the man. On 9th October 1865, arrest warrants were issued against Bogle and others. The following day police arrived at Stony Gut to arrest Paul Bogle. Several hundred of his supporters came out of his church and overpowered the policemen. The latter were however, released and assured that Bogle and other wanted persons would present themselves in the court at Morant Bay the next day. Meanwhile, custodian of the court Baron Maximilian Ketelholdt arranged volunteers of the citizen force to guard the court on 11th October 1865. He informed the governor of impending disturbances around the court. Paul Bogle arrived with a large restless crowd at the court. Ketelholdt's volunteers panicked and opened fire killing a few among the crowd. In retaliation, the blacks (Jamaicans) killed 15 white officials including the custodian. The court was also burned down.

Governor Eyre considered disturbances at Morant Bay court as a law-and-order problem. His superiority complex overshadowed the next move. He dispatched one hundred troops to Morant Bay against the poorly armed Jamaicans who had no mind to confront the raiding force. Leaving out Kingston, the entire Surrey County was placed under a one-month-long martial law. On 13th October 1865 Eyre himself travelled to the area in a revengeful mood along with additional fifty troops. He ordered punitive expeditions. Brutal repression, summary trials and hangings started the next day. Military commanders began sending startling reports to the colonial office in London. On 17th October military plundered every hut within a quarter of a mile of the Long Bay and killed twenty blacks. Every black man, within a mile of the expedition route, who failed to stand at the approach of troops, was shot.[2] Upwards of sixty people were killed in this manner. Those taken prisoners were subsequently shot. Eyre had witnessed similar punitive British expeditions against the natives in Australia. He acted with pitiless ferocity executing some four hundred and fifty rebels.[3] Soldiers celebrated at the sight of indiscriminate floggings. J. Francis Hobbs, colonel of the Sixth Royals who commanded white troops, admitted, that on 19th October, he shot eleven prisoners brought to him, because he did not know what to do with them. A soldier boasted that they slaughtered all men, women and children they came across. *New York Herald* grimly headlined "Eight Miles of Dead Bodies."[4] A Jamaican newspaper of early November 1865 reported that the water of Morant Bay had become unwholesome due to stagnant bodies it carried.

Governor Eyre returned to Kingston on 17th October and ordered the arrest of William Gordon, a *mulatto* skilled businessman having no connection with the disturbances. Gordon was arrested in Kingston and shipped to Morant Bay with the express purpose of bringing him into jurisdiction of martial law. News of atrocities on the blacks and the arrest of William Gordon raised public outcry in England. Radicals in the British Parliament were highly indignant. Edward Cardwell, the colonial secretary, called for copies of court martial proceedings from Governor Eyre. He was concerned about Gordon. He advised Eyre not to execute him until he was found guilty of crimes which deserved death.[5] Nevertheless Gordon was tried under court martial on 20th October and three days later, summarily executed. Altogether 439 black Jamaicans were killed straightway and another 354 including Paul Bogle were arrested and executed without trial. Six hundred men and women (including pregnant ones) were flogged. One thousand homes of blacks were torched to the ground. Sir Frederic Rogers, the under-secretary of state for colonies, admitted that it was terrible to see human nature naked.[6] Eyre faced outrage of the church. Baptists, Methodists and anti-slavery groups united under the banner of Exeter Hall to plead the case of the Jamaican blacks. They bluntly denounced Eyre and the barbarism of the British army. Black Christians were followers of the Baptist Church, and so were Paul Bogle and William Gordon. A Jamaica committee headed by John Stuart Mill, an economist, political theorist, and a member of Parliament for Westminster from 1865–1868, and naturalists like Charles Darwin, Herbert Spencer, and T.H. Huxley brought out charges against Eyre. A rival group headed by historian and essayist Thomas Carlyle, a known intellectual of the Victorian era, and writers like Charles Dickens and Charles Kingsley eulogized Eyre.[7] Carlyle believed in racial hierarchy in human society in which white North-western Europe was at the top and Africans at the bottom. He lamented that Eyre had not shot the whole black population of Jamaica and cast them into the sea. Public at large, considered Eyre an indiscriminate murderer, but a section of the press, the Anglican Church, politicians, men in uniform and English planters praised judgment of Eyre which saved 15,000 white lives. The Crown commissioned the court of enquiry, headed by Sir Henry Storks, to enquire into the episode. It revealed that black leaders acted with preplanning but there was no general conspiracy against the British government. The future of Eyre was doomed. He was dismissed and recalled to England in 1866. A banquet in his honour awaited him. The grand jury refused to indict him for murders. Only a handful of parishioners in Jamaica favoured raising funds for presenting him with a testimonial for his services. Eyre was tried for murder twice but cases against him never arrived at conclusion. In 1874 he was retired on a governor's pension.

Field Marshal Thomas-Robert Bugeaud: Thomas-Robert Bugeaud born in 1784 in rural France rose to be a contentious military administrator. He joined the service in 1804 during the reign of Napoleon I. In 1811, he was sent to Spain as battalion commander but lost his job four years later when constitutional monarchy was established. Bugeaud returned to his father's estate where he experimented on innovative farming. Adventurous part of his career commenced after King Charles X of Bourbon dynasty was over-thrown in favour of Louis Philippe. The new king admired the military passion of Bugeaud and entrusted him important assignments like a marshal of the French army. He displayed firmness and a tactical acumen when Philippe appointed him governor of the Fortress of Blaye where Marie de Berry, Duchess of Bourbon, was interned. The Duchess insisted on the restoration of Bourbon dynasty. Her rebellion failed and she was arrested and imprisoned in 1832. Bugeaud was rough, arrogant and stringently firm in ensuring that the Duchess had no access to the outside world. He put in place strict conditions while allowing a doctor's visit to confirm if the Duchess was pregnant. Similarly, at the time of delivery of the child, the attending doctor was asked to record the mother's moans of labour pain and cries of the new born child. His action smacked of the same ruthlessness when he suppressed the 1834 popular uprising in Paris. Yet it was for the people of Algeria to suffer his barbarity when France established its rule in that country.

Bugeaud took part in overseas military campaigns in the aftermath of French invasion of Algeria. In 1830, King Charles ordered the invasion of Algiers over an alleged insult to the French consul. In essence France owed money for wheat it had purchased from two merchants of Algiers. Governor of Algiers, Hussein Dey, confronted the French consul over the issue and playfully gave few slaps of fly whisk on his cheek. An enraged King Charles ordered the invasion of Algiers. On 12th June 1830, French soldiers landed at the coastal town of Sidi Ferruch and after a 3-week-long brutal military campaign, captured Algiers. Bertrand Clauzel, a soldier politician who became governor of the occupied territory, began settling European farmers on confiscated fertile lands of the Arab natives to raise cotton for the French textile industry. French moves enraged the natives who started insurrection against French occupation. In 1832, a religious leader of aggressive disposition, Emir Abdel Kader started a guerrilla war from the Atlas Mountains. In 1836 Bertrand Clauzel, who moved against him, was defeated. French humiliation at the hands of Abdel Kader catapulted Thomas Bugeaud, a lieutenant general of the French army to the scene. He moved against Abdul Kader but, after failed ruthless counter insurgency operations, negotiated a peace deal with him. The 1837 treaty granted the Emir a sort of autonomy over areas outside French control. It was an expedient French measure to avoid an inevitable conflict.

Algerians wanted to get rid of foreign intruders from their motherland. Bugeaud was determined to destroy Abdel Kader, break the back of Algerian resistance, and firmly establish French rule over that country. The French decided to promote state-sponsored colonisation of Algeria even if that involved ruthless repression of the natives.[8] French resolve strengthened with Bugeaud taking over as governor-general of French-controlled territories in Algeria. In his speech of 15th January 1840 in the French Chamber of Deputies, Bugeaud asserted that the only things dear to him were French interests and in this aspect, he will never display any act of philanthropy towards the Algerians. In 1841 he returned to Algeria to pacify the country. As a governor-general, he had about 100,000 troops at his command. Bugeaud took on Berber Arabs or Algerian Kabyles[9] who were supporting insurgency. These people lived in the Kabylia region of northern Algeria. He decided to either force them out of their lands or eliminate them altogether and seize their properties, cattle and food stock. For this purpose, he opted for an aggressive method of the form used by Bedouins against their adversaries in the desert wars i.e., Ghaziya/Razzia/plundering raids.

Bugeaud executed Razzia through mobile military columns to take on unsuspecting villagers by surprise, causing wanton destruction, killing all men they could entrap, seize all livestock, food stock, violate women, and take them along with their children as hostages. The hostages were subsequently bartered away for horses or auctioned in the open market. Bugeaud's motive was to deprive the natives of any sustenance. He burnt their crops and orchards. His actions smacked thinking of Alexis de Tocqueville, a respected French political thinker of the time, who believed that the ravaging of a country and its populace was justified for the colonisation of Algeria. Tocqueville's penchant for colonising Algeria was fuelled by his desire to invigorate France politically and economically. During his 1841 visit to Algeria, he applauded the practice of Razzia started by Bugeaud as a means to that end. It meant that he condoned mass massacres of Arabs, violation of their women, and the taking of hostages. But in his 1846 visit Tocqueville disproved of destruction and the atrocities visited by the Arab society at the hands of Bugeaud. He bemoaned that the French way of waging war against Algerians was more barbaric than that of the Arabs whom they considered barbarians. He admitted that Arabs represented civilization, French did not.

By May 1844, France had captured Algerian territory from Tunis and Morocco in the west to the seashore to Sahara in the south but had failed to capture the Arab spirit. Abdel Kader was still in the field and banking on Moroccan support. France permitted Bugeaud to attack Morocco. On 14th August 1844, he defeated the forces of Mulai Abd al Rahman on the bank of the River Isly. This victory earned him the title of Duke of Isly. The defeated Sultan outlawed Abdel Kader. Bugeaud loathed prospect of his force running into war fatigue and become uncivil in such a frame of mind. He ordered his commanders to curb insurgency at any cost. Thus, 1845 witnessed the horrible massacre of the Algerians. The atrocities of these years surfaced in 1857 when the International Red Cross discovered that the French army and police inflicted indiscriminate torture on Algerians in the form of electric current applied to sensitive parts of human body, hanging people upside down, drowning in water, and inserting foreign objects in body cavities. Thousands of Algerians were massacred in a short period of time. Bugeaud, who was only interested in the end result, condoned these atrocities. In fact, he participated in "Razzia" expeditions and patted his most cruel generals.

One "Razzia" expedition became notorious for its viciousness. It was executed by Colonel Aimable Pelissier, a trusted lieutenant of General Bugeaud. The general wanted to punish the tribes of the coastal mountain range who supported the activities of insurgent leaders. Bugeaud deployed flying columns for this purpose. French forces heaped the cruellest possible atrocities on the Arabs. They would behead a fellow Arab in front of his companions. On 19th June 1845 Colonel Pelissier raided the tribe of Ouled Riah of Orleansville, alleged to be shielding insurgent leader Bou Maza whose actual name was Mohammad bin Abdullah. The tribesmen were hounded out of their homes on 18th June. They took shelter in mountain caves near Chlef. Pelissier blocked all accesses in to the caves except one. Arabs had taken refuge there along with their animals. He ordered his troops to pile up wood, grass, and other incendiary material to block the opening. The purpose was to smoke out the tribesmen. There were around 500 to 1500 men, women and children, besides their animals in the cave. Pelissier ordered the Arabs to come out but no one heard the order. Piled up incendiary material was lit. Troops heard the agonizing cries of suffocating men, women and children and the bellowing of cattle. Fire was kept alive the next day with added fuel. When it was all quiet, the troops entered the caves with lanterns. They found contorted corpses, asphyxiated babes clinging to their dead mothers, and the dead remains of cattle among human bodies. Only a few people survived the ordeal. An elated Pelissier sent report of his expedition to the then French war minister Nicolas Soult, who was an adversary of General Bugeaud. The latter being in Paris at the time, could not stop dispatch of the said report. Soult took no time to report this episode to the Chamber of Deputies. He told Bugeaud that he was not expected to order his commanders for such callous liquidation of the foe for whatever reason. An unapologetic Bugeaud defended Pelissier and declared that such actions might be repeated and exhorted other commanders to act strongly against those Arabs who supported insurgent leaders. A month later, he ordered the Sbeah tribe of the area to abandon the caves lest they were incinerated alive.

Weeks after the massacre of Ouled Riah, another Razzia was executed on 19th August 1845 a few kilometres away in the Dahra region. The perpetrator was another of Bugeaud's ferocious commanders, Colonel Armand de Saint-Arnaud and the victims were another faction of the Sbeah tribe. On 8th August 1845, some 500 to 1500 members of this tribe fleeing from another Razzia attack by Saint-Arnaud, took refuge in mountain caves and refused to surrender. The colonel ordered all exit routes to be sealed with solid rocks thereby entombing the hapless tribesmen alive. He ordered that no one should talk about the operation but boasted of his achievement in a private message to Bugeaud. He assured his boss that no one except him went into the cave to confirm the death of the tribesmen. Hence his actions remained a secret with the French public but not with the Arabs who were incensed. Emir Abdel Kader vowed to seek revenge. On 23rd September Lieutenant Colonel Lucien de Montagnac, another fierce commander of Bugeaud, commanding 400 troops of light infantry and Hussars of the Second Regiment, waylaid Arab fighters who were themselves eager to confront the French. In a three-hour fight in the mountains, Colonel Montagnac was killed and Abdel Kader himself was injured in the face. The French retreated to regroup and attack Abdel Kader fighters at Sidi Brahim. Algerian Berbers overwhelmed French troops and decimated them. Only fifteen men of the Infantry and one cavalry man survived and returned to the base camp.

The French could not live with the humiliation of Sidi Brahim. Bugeaud deployed eighteen flying columns to capture Emir Abdel Kader. The Emir fled to Morocco. Bugeaud retaliated by perpetrating atrocities on Berbers. Algerian resistance leader Boumaza was still holding on. French forces slaughtered villagers, and destroyed their crops and orchards to lay hands on Boumaza who finally gave in. Abdel Kader was also captured in 1847 with help of the Sultan of Morocco. Algerians could not resist the atrocious tactics of Bugeaud, who butchered thousands of their kin, and gave in. Algeria became a French colony in 1848.

Raymond Pierre Paul-Westerling: Raymond Pierre Paul-Westerling was a captain in the Dutch East Indies Armed Forces (KNIL). He was born to a Greek mother and Dutch father in August 1919 in Istanbul, Turkey. His birthplace earned him the nickname of "The Turk". Westerling was sent to Scotland in July 1942 for special commando training preparatory to his deployment with the Dutch forces in Indonesia. His training bestowed him with cold-blooded toughness along with all the mean traits needed to either subdue or eliminate the adversary. His atrocious manners in Indonesia revealed the kind of brute he had become. In a way he betrayed the genre of earlier Dutchmen who butchered innocent Indonesians during the early years in that country. Houtman, a French navigator massacred hundreds of natives because their Sultan failed to broker a business deal for him in the face of local disturbances. An uncompromising Houtman took scores of locals as prisoners and massacred them. At another halting station he sank a flotilla of native boats approaching his ships for the customary welcome. After landing, Houtman killed natives with a barrage of canon fire. Another Dutchman Jan Pieterszoon Coen, governor-general of East Indies, earned the ignominy of "butcher of Banda" an island famous for trade in nutmeg. In 1621 he slaughtered, starved to death or expelled entire population of the islands to monopolize the production and trade in nutmeg.

In the 1940's the Japanese overran Dutch-held Indonesia during the Second World War. But after their surrender in the Second World War

Japan tried to pre-empt occupation of the country by the West and hand it over to the Indonesians. The Indonesians declared their independence on 17th August 1945 much to the discomfort of the western powers. Dutch and British forces landed there to run local administration. Indonesian fighters confronted these forces but were defeated. Nevertheless, Indonesians decided to wage guerrilla warfare against the new intruders. Dutch dominated major cities, but their authority did not run in the country side. In September 1945, the then Lieutenant Westerling, who was a member of the Dutch East Indies Armed Forces (KNIL), was parachuted into Sumatra. He was tasked to pacify the area. On 9th November 1946, the KNIL headquarters in Batavia decided to control national insurgency in the countryside. The insurgents were labelled rebels who needed to be punished. Westerling was promoted captain and asked to apply his commando training of Scotland to put together a unit, expert in counter-insurgency warfare and interrogation of the suspects. He picked out hardened Dutch and native soldiers for commando training and produced a Special Forces Unit (DST) consisting of 130 ruthless combatants. His first task was to prepare a list of suspected guerrillas operating in South Sulawesi (Celebes Island) in preparation for military action against them.

Westerling and his DST unit landed in South Sulawesi which had been infiltrated by insurgency leaders from Java. These leaders were allegedly inciting villagers against the Dutch colonialists. Westerling was on a mission of pacification but his campaign ended up in ruthless shedding of blood. On 5th December 1946 Westerling and his men arrived in Makassar (present Ujung Pandang) the capital of South Sulawesi. A list of guerrilla suspects with them was checked out through Dutch military intelligence. Action began on the evening of 11th December, when his forces surrounded Batua village along with small villages to the east of Makassar. Early next morning all village folks were ordered to assemble in an open compound outside Batua. Men were separated from women and children. Westerling spoke about his mission and then handed over a prepared list of wanted men to the village headman. The latter was asked to identify men on the list. Suspecting trouble, nine men tried to flee. They were shot dead before they could get away. Westerling was able to pick 35 men on his list. He had them shot on the spot. The same day, i.e., the evening of 12th December, the DST unit moved from Batua to the periphery of the village Tanjung Bunga for an overnight operation. Altogether 61 persons were summarily executed. On 14th December, Westerling raided the village Kalikuang on the outskirts of Makassar. He carried out his usual drill and shot dead 23 villagers. On 16th December 1946 he targeted Jongaya village where 33 persons were summarily executed.

After combing through Makassar and its immediate neighbourhood Westerling moved to the outlying villages. On 19th December 1946, his special teams raided Polobangkeng village and area to the south of Makassar in the Taklar residency where 33 villagers were massacred. Between 26th December 1946 and 3rd January 1947 Westerling forces conducted combing operations in the villages of the Gowa residency. In all 257 people were butchered by them. In the month of January 1947, Westerling and his troops raided several places like Parepare city and the villages of Barru, Enrekanng, Pinrang, Sidrap, and surrounding villages of the Majene and Mandar regencies of West Sulawesi. They slaughtered hundreds of innocent villagers. Most abominable slaughter took place in the village Galung Lombok on 2nd February 1947. Terrified villagers were ordered to assemble in a field before they were executed with gunfire. Around 650 villagers including women and children lay dead. Between February 7th and 17th Westerling's forces moved on to villages in the coastal area where he massacred 364 people. Death toll in villages then named Kulo, Amprita and Maroangin was 171. Tale of Dutch brutality did not end with Westerling. The incident that was noted by the United Nations belonged to the Javanese village of Rawagade. The Dutch were chasing an insurgent leader Lucas Kustario. On 9th December 1947 Dutch army major Alphons Wijnen and his 300 soldiers encircled this village. The residents were made to sit in a row with their hands tied at their backs. The Dutch suspected them to be accomplices of the wanted man. Alphons questioned them about the whereabouts of Kustario. No sooner had the villagers displayed ignorance about the man. Dutch soldiers showered them with bullets. Hapless villagers slumped to death at the spot. Those who tried to escape were mowed down in their tracks. The death toll which ran into hundreds did not go unnoticed. The International Court of Justice, the Hague, ordered payment of compensation to immediate relations of 431 victims many of whom had witnessed the crime. The Dutch government, however, claimed only 150 deaths. It tried to cover up the brutalities of Raymond Westerling. The British press, however, broke the news of extra-judicial killings of Westerling in South Sulawesi. There was international condemnation of the Westerling method. The Dutch government was obliged to recall Westerling to Batavia in March 1947. While military administration treated him as a hero, he did not escape an enquiry. Strangely no charges were brought out, but he was dismissed from service in 1948. The Indonesian delegation to the United Nations claimed that as many as 40,000 people were killed by Westerling and his associates. The Dutch conceded only 3000 deaths, but Westerling himself claimed that no more than 800 people were killed, of whom a majority were criminals.

General Adrian Dietrich Lothar von Trotha: Lothar von Trotha joined the Prussian army at the age of 17. In 1894 he became commander of the colonial force. The colony of German East Africa acquired by Carl Peters in 1885 had been in turmoil due to agitations of Africans living in coastal settlements. German Chancellor Otto Bismarck and the new Kaiser Wilhelm II sent Major Hermann von Wissmann to control the situation. Wissmann recruited decommissioned Sudanese of the Anglo-Egyptian army and Zulus from South Africa as mercenaries. Later these mercenaries became part of the Schutztruppe or protectorate force. Between 1894 and 1896 this force was used by von Trotha when he took over as commander of the colonial force to suppress African resistance to German rule. German forces attacked and overran positions of Wahehe resistance leader Mkwawa and captured hundreds of women and children along with their cattle and other livestock. By 1900, von Trotha became a major-general and saw temporary posting to China as brigade commander of the East Asian Expedition Corps. China had been financially ruined and politically humiliated by the British and other foreign powers. The state of despondency gave rise to a movement against the foreigners, Christian missionaries, and Chinese converts to Christianity. The movement was spearheaded by members of a secret society which believed in a mysterious boxing art. These people, named boxers, killed 18000 native Christians, dozens of missionaries and foreigners including the German Consul in Peking (Beijing). The situation created by the Boxers prompted the U.S. to depute her warships to suppress the Boxers. The Daily Express, London of 30th May 1900, feared that Boxers may have the sympathy of the entire Manchu army. European allies were not satisfied even after Chinese government had issued an edict against the Boxers. They decided to assemble an international combative force under the overall command of German Field Marshal Count von Waldersee.

Before German contingent departed on 27th July 1900, Kaiser Wilhelm II commanded his forces to make the name of Germans unforgettable in China for a thousand years so that no Chinese will ever again dare even to squint at a German. That was enough of an indication to Lothar von Trotha to crush the Chinese insurrection by all possible means. He unleashed ruthless brutality upon the Boxers, their sympathizers and even the innocent Chinese. A German naval battalion, supported by the Bengal Lancers, stormed the town of Liang, southwest of Peking, and burnt it. Battle losses were, 500 Boxers killed; of the Germans, one killed and five wounded.[10] The exhortation of Kaiser caused similar carnage in scores of villages unconnected with the Boxer movement.

Tacit radicalization rendered that the German forces behaved despicably when dealing with defiant African natives. With few exceptions, all major African tribes wanted an end to the colonial rule. But the German government supported German settlers, who were evicting natives from their pastures and seizing their cattle which were the sole wealth of the Herero and Nama native tribes. In 1897 Herero, a major tribe of South West Africa (now Namibia) had lost half of their cattle to rinderpest. Panicked, and under debt, they sold their remaining stock and pasture lands to the settlers. The situation was perfect for the German government because it matched its official policy of reducing natives to a state of serfdom. Germans equated African natives with baboons, but natives like the Herero, were not imbecile. They blamed only white man for their misery. Gradually, Herero frustration exploded. Their leader Samuel Maharero reacted against the injustices his tribe faced and in 1904, took direct action against the settlers. He asked his followers not to harm German women, children, missionaries, Englishmen, Boers, and other tribes. Hereros were humane in their conduct of war. They guided the entrapped German women and children to safety. But they were pitted in their war of survival against boorish German forces under Captain von Francois. Germans however, failed to subdue Herero resistance. Governor Theodor von Leutwein, who took charge, resisted Herero advance with superior weapons. But another Herero raid obliged him to order his men to retreat at nightfall and postpone counterinsurgency operations for another day. His decision dismayed German Kaiser Wilhelm II. The latter goaded by public opinion, decided to dispatch Lothar von Trotha, known for his ruthlessness in suppressing Wahehe in East Africa and Boxer insurgency in China, to SWA. He was designated commander-in-chief of German forces in SWA. Von Trotha assembled a heavily armed force which comprised a large number of German mercenaries who had fought under him against the Boxers in China. Herero holding traditional arms were backed by their womenfolk chanting. 'Herero land is our land'. Unluckily in their struggle for existence, they found themselves battling against the well-armed German settlers and German troops equipped with modern weapons.

On 11th August 1904 General von Trotha assaulted the Herero with 30 pieces of artillery and 12 machine guns.[11] He had planned to push Herero into the Omaheke desert. Herero, valiant fighters as they were withered against thrust of artillery and guns. In desperation they attempted to slip through German lines at the weakest point unaware that it was a trap laid by von Trotha. The wily general had deliberately left Omaheke flank weak to coax Herero into the extremely hot and arid desert and then let wilderness annihilate them completely. Herero could not fend off German assault. They fled as fast as they could with enemy in hot pursuit. Haggard natives were slaughtered by the Germans. Von Trotha took care that Herero did not change direction of their flight and thus escape from the desert. He disclosed that Herero were not only prevented from taking a westerly direction but were also kept away from water wells.[12] Within one-week, hapless natives were driven to the edge of the Omaheke sandvelt and thereafter pushed further into sandy waste past the last water hole. Von Trotha poisoned water holes and put a cordon on the west and southwest of Omaheke desert to prevent hungry and thirsty Herero from escaping the sandy death trap. Some German soldiers described how cattle and men lay dead or dying and surviving babies lying amidst flies swarming their faces. Water bodies were full of corpses. Thirsty for water, Hereros met an agonizing death. Von Trotha in an attempt to gloss over the tragedy claimed that the sandy wastes where action took place were by no means devoid of pastures and Germans had discovered newly formed water holes.[13] That was a complete travesty of facts. Germans shot to death those women and children who were too exhausted to flee for their life. Germans raped young girls and women before they were bayoneted to death.[14] Large groups of disarmed Hereros were herded into an enclosure and slaughtered. Another group lured into negotiations was instead mowed down with canon fire.

Von Trotha's policy of 'no prisoner and no mercy' was intended to destroy the Herero nation. He minced no words about it while addressing his letter of 2nd October 1904 to the Herero people. He proclaimed himself as great general of the German people and declared that the Herero were no longer considered German subjects. He further announced "Whoever turns over one of the kapteins to one of my garrisons as a prisoner, will receive 100 marks and he who hands over Samuel Maharero will be rewarded with 500 marks. Within the German boundaries, every Herero, whether found armed or unarmed, with or without cattle will be shot."[15] Eerie and blunt words harbingered his extermination drive. Ignominious readings of "civilized" white man's intent revolted against an order of "uncivilized" Herero chief who commanded his people that no harm should come to white women, children, missionaries, Boers, and the English during the insurgency. Surprisingly, no Imperial power took notice of the brutalities of von Trotha. Apparently, Europe was too preoccupied with the Russo-Japanese war.

After the Herero, von Trotha turned to the Nama tribes. Hendrick Witbooi chief of a Nama tribe was an ardent anti-colonialist. In October 1894, he took note of Samuel Maharero's call "Let us die fighting". General von Trotha signed a proclamation on 22nd April 1905 asking the Nama tribes to surrender. "A Nama who chooses not to surrender and lets himself to be seen in a German area will be shot, until all are terminated". Germans were reluctant to face Nama in guerrilla warfare. But von

Trotha was prepared to unleash the might of his weaponry and money. He offered a reward of 5000 marks for "dead or alive" Hendrik Witbooi; 3000 marks each for Nama leaders like the Witbooi prophet Skippers Sturmann, and Cornelius Fredricks; and 1000 marks for the remaining insurgent leaders. Witbooi was finally killed. In December 1905, an imperial decree declared all Herero land as Crown territory. The population census showed that von Trotha had almost wiped out the native tribes. In 1911, there were only 15,130 Herero people out of their previous population of 80,000. Similarly, out of 20,000 Nama of the tribe of SWA, only 9781 souls survived the genocide. Unwittingly, General von Trotha had culled the large work force of the territory. Labour became scarce in the colony. Surviving natives were incapacitated by ravages of war and harshness of the desert. Over 10,000 Nama had been killed and others confined in concentration camps. The much-maligned German government repealed the extermination order and called back von Trotha in 1905.

General Herbert H. Kitchener: Horatio Herbert Kitchener was born in 1850 in Ireland. He was commissioned in the Royal engineers in 1871. His first stint abroad was in Palestine where he surveyed the country between 1874 and 1877 to prepare maps of the area now falling between Israel and Palestine. Kitchener was appointed second-in-command of the Egyptian cavalry after Britain seized Egypt in 1883. In 1884, British General Charles Gordon, who had gone to Khartoum in Sudan, to evacuate the Egyptian army, was himself besieged by the Mahdi fighters. A relief expedition was dispatched under General Garnet Wolseley with Kitchener as aide-de-camp. But it could neither save Khartoum nor General Gordon from the Mahdi onslaught. Kitchener used this opportunity to grasp the outlay of Sudanese terrain. In 1892, Kitchener was appointed commander-in-chief (Sirdar) of the Egyptian army. In this capacity he trained and prepared his army to avenge Gordon's annihilation. British at the time apprehended growing French influence in Sudan. Kitchener was, therefore, asked to lead an expedition to Sudan under the banner of Egypt. His expedition advanced through both the River Nile and by railroad. On 28th August 1898, Kitchener's force of 8200 British and 17600 Egyptian soldiers assembled on the left bank of the river at Royan. Meanwhile Mahdi Khalifa Abdulla had mustered thousands of his followers (Dervishes) outside Omdurmn where Kitchener's army and the Mahdis clashed in September 1898. The Islamic fundamentalists/Mahdis/Dervishes numbered around 50,000. They were armed with traditional weapons like swords and spears against the well-drilled British, Egyptians and Sudanese troops armed with superior weaponry. Kitchener's flotilla of boats was holding on the River Nile. Poorly armed desert tribesmen (Dervishes) were mowed down by Maxim gun and artillery. Within hours, close to 12000 Dervishes lay dead all around. Those alive were badly injured. Kitchener boasted that his forces gave the enemy a good dusting. Winston Churchill, then correspondent for the Morning Post witnessed the slaughter. On 2nd September 1898 he wrote about Kitchener's brutal conduct of war. He was also scandalized by Kitchener's desecration of the Mahdi tombs and barbarous way in which he had carried Mahdi's skull in a kerosene can as a trophy. Press versions in England contrasted British war technology with the barbarous ways of the opponent. Invasion was called a crusade for civilization and an act of vengeance for Gordon's blood. Ardently autocrat Kitchener, coming from a protestant Ulster stock, was a dedicated imperialist. He fought the Sudan war in the name of civilization and accordingly treated Mahdis with extreme ruthlessness.[16]

Mahdi corpses counted in the field numbered 10,563. Kitchener left wounded Mahdi on the field to die and moved on for the city of Khartoum to engage in plunder. Five thousand Mahdis were taken prisoners and many of them summarily shot. Thereafter, he entrusted Major William Gordon, a nephew of General Gordon, with the task of razing Khalifa's tomb to the ground. Remains of the Mahdi were exhumed to insult his followers for whom the tomb was a place of pilgrimage. Kitchener justified his action as politically advisable telling Prime Minister Lord Salisbury that the tomb, being centre of pilgrimage and fanatical feelings, needed to be destroyed. Mahdi's skull, unusually large, was kept as a trophy and skeleton bones were thrown into the Nile. Majority of British public disapproved of the sacrilegious actions of Kitchener. Churchill criticized Kitchener for his callousness toward the Mahdis on the field and for his desecration of the Mahdi tomb and his remains.[17] Several members of the British Parliament, provoked by outrageous accounts of Omdurman and Khartoum, opposed the consideration of an award of 30,000 pounds sterling to Kitchener for his services in Sudan. Instead, he was accused of executing his military campaign against the rules of civilized conduct. Parliamentarians were annoyed over the exhumation of Mahdi remains and the making cup of his skull. Kitchener offered the skull to the Royal College of Surgeons with a request for its exhibition along with the guts of Napoleon.[18] One Tory member supported Kitchener bringing civilization to a dark continent but an Irish M.P. wondered if murder, rapine, whisky and bible were ingredients of this civilization.[19] In spite of strong opposition, Kitchener got his reward, a part of which he donated to the Gordon Memorial at Khartoum. Skull of the Mahdi was taken back to Egypt and secretly buried.

Kitchener's execution of the Second Boer war (1899 to 1902) a year after his Sudan campaign, was similarly highly unethical. Boers, descendants of early Dutch settlers, were farmers and cow herders. They disliked the British way of governing the Cape Colony. The 1885 discovery of gold in the Transvaal had escalated British ambitions. Johannesburg attracted large amounts of British capital, English migrants, and Uitlanders (Afrikaans: foreigners). Britain pressurized Boer administration to enfranchise Uitlanders and protect their mining interests. In 1895, a partner of Cecil Rhodes sponsored the abortive and ill-timed Jameson Raid designed to provoke a revolt in Johannesburg. Boers loathed the British haughtiness. On 12th October 1899, Boers with covert arms assistance from the Germans flexed their military muscle. On their part, the English reinforced their army under Lord Roberts (Frederick Roberts) with Kitchener as his chief of staff and seized the initiative from the Boers. Lord Roberts began to burn Boer farms[20] in the Orange Free State, but sickness compelled him to return to England in November 1900. Kitchener took over command of the British forces which comprised 118,000 white and 43000 coloured personnel. Boers who had 50,000 part-time soldiers could not face the formidable British onslaught. They started guerrilla warfare. Kitchener reacted by resorting to "scorched earth" policy extending Lord Robert's policy of denying the Boers living resources. About 30,000 Boer farms were burnt down, livestock was slaughtered, and all necessities of life were either taken away or destroyed. Since the Boer men had joined guerrilla force,

Kitchener rounded up women, old persons and children. He erected 8000 block houses for the troops and constructed 3700 miles (5900 km) of wire fence. The latter was a trap into which the Boer commanders were driven before being slaughtered. Women children and civilians were herded into 18 unhygienic concentration camps. By 1901, 77,000 Boers and 21,000 coloured persons were interned. In the next six months the figure rose to 118,000 Boers and 43,000 coloured persons. In one instance beautiful white horses of a Boer farmer were put in the stable before torching his house and stable. Of Boer internees, 28,000 inmates, mainly children and women, died of disease and neglect. Thousands of African natives died in separate camps. A Quaker spinster, Emily Hobhouse, who visited some camps, highlighted the pitiable conditions of concentration camps built for Boer women and children. Kitchener remorselessly commented that her zeal outran her sense of propriety. Intellectuals from several countries condemned the barbarism displayed in the war and challenged the Christianity of the British rulers. St. John Broderick, secretary of state for war, who faced a tough time in the Parliament complained to Kitchener about the appalling conditions in the camps. Indomitable Kitchener called it clamour of defeatist propaganda. He rather threatened to charge Boer women of manslaughter calling them ladies from the wild who neglected the safety of their children. Eventually Kitchener had to relent and give up placing women and children in the concentration camps.

Kitchener hired black tribesmen to hunt Boer guerrillas. This was his way of insulting superiority conscious Boers who were desperate to find a place of refuge. He started another controversial campaign against Boer commandos who never donned any regular uniform. After their own clothes were in shreds during the struggle, they shifted to wearing uniforms of captured British soldiers. Kitchener considered the change in attire as an attempt to disguise themselves. He ordered Boers wearing British uniforms to be tried at the spot and shot by the commander. Although Kitchener denied passing such an order, the oblique hint led to the much-argued "Breaker Morant case". Celebrated Australian horseman and bush poet Lt. Harry "Breaker" Morant was arrested and court-martialled for summarily executing Boer prisoners as well as for the murder of a German missionary. Morant and another Australian Lt.

Peter Handcock were found guilty and sentenced to death. On 27th February 1902 they were shot by a firing squad at Pietersburg. Death warrants were signed by Kitchener. The trial and executions were challenged in Australia. Australians called the court-martial a sham meant to secure pre-determined conviction. The convicts could not appeal in time because Kitchener purposely left on tour immediately after signing the death warrants. Morant and Handcock seemed to be scapegoats, who unfairly took the blame for the killings to cover up Kitchener's 'no prisoner's policy'. Records pertaining to this episode were made to disappear in an effort to conceal British involvement.

Kitchener passionately believed in racial superiority of the Europeans. He considered non-Europeans inferior and dispensable as revealed by his brutal military campaigns. Kitchener claimed that a native however clever, highly educated, brave, cultured, and whatever rank he held, would never match a British officer of the same status. Kitchener returned from South Africa in 1902. Lord Rosebery (Archibald Primrose), a liberal imperialist and supporter of the Boer war wanted Kitchener to reorganize the British military. St. John Broderick, the then secretary of state for war, disliked the idea and sent him to India. Lord Curzon, the viceroy of India, knew that Kitchener's methods were detested by the Egyptian army when he was their Sirdar. Moreover St. St. John Broderick, secretary of state for foreign affairs and a friend of Curzon cautioned the latter that Kitchener's methods had produced a serious state of feeling in the Egyptian army.[21] Lord Roberts, with whom he had been in the Boer war, intervened and Kitchener got a posting to India. Between 1902 and 1909 he commanded imperial forces in India from his headquarters in Calcutta (Kolkata). In Calcutta he ruled the roost and considered himself above any rule book.[22] He frightened city inhabitants out of their wits by thundering through the town on the wrong side of the road in a mail-phaeton drawn by a magnificent pair of black horses. Kitchener would hold the reins only in one hand, which also held his cigar and a glove. The sentries on the bridge to Fort William fled for their life at the approach of the commander-in-chief. Kitchener crossed swords with Curzon over control of the army. The viceroy did not condone military excesses when sufferers were the hapless natives. But it was the viceroy who had to resign such was the backing which

Kitchener enjoyed back home. In 1916, Kitchener died on a mission to Russia when his ship was sunk by the Germans.

Acting Brigadier General Reginald Dyer: (Substantive rank Colonel) Dyer became the most hated military officer of British India. By end of the nineteenth century people of India had become politically conscious and begun to oppose the policies of the colonial government. The British were equally determined to hold on to India. Dyer's action illustrates that determination. His horrible deed of firing upon a peaceful gathering of people at Amritsar on 13th April 1919 left indelible scars on the Indian psyche even after more than 100 years. The action of Dyer was so barbarous that a recent book on him is entitled 'The Butcher of Amritsar, General Reginald Dyer.'[23] Amritsar tragedy climaxed draconian measures set up by the British government of the day to suppress the resentment of Indians against her harsh Acts. Cause of immediate provocation was the infamous Rowlatt Act, a replacement for Defense of India Act and the retrograde Press Act meant to severely curtail civil liberties. Even after the First World War, the colonial government was anxious to continue restrictions on the liberties of the Indian people. Immediate cause of unrest was the increase in land revenue, continuation of tax burden imposed during the War, and several unpopular administrative measures. Rowlatt Bills provided for arrest and in-camera trial of any person by a tribunal without even a preliminary hearing or the presence of a jury. No appeal was allowed against judgment of the tribunals. The Bill became Act after it was signed by the viceroy of India. The secretary of state for India never made a case in its favour. There was a public outcry against the government action.[24] Popular English newspaper of Lahore, The Tribune of 21st March 1919 questioned the draconian action it called a fatal plunge. The writing was dubbed seditious, and its editor Kalinath Ray was arrested, and publication of the paper was suspended.

The Indian public, reeling under heavy taxes witnessed wide-spread famine caused by the failure of the monsoon rains. The government employed the Rowlatt Act as an instrument to crush public opinion against its apathy. On 29th March, a prominent Punjab leader Dr. Satya Pal, a votary of non-violent civil disobedience, was prohibited from public speaking. On 4th April four more leaders, including Saif-ud-din

Kichlew, were prohibited from speaking in public. Mahatma Gandhi's call for observing 6th April as a day of humiliation and prayer received public support in all towns of the Punjab. This infuriated Michael O'Dwyer, the Lt. Governor of Punjab. On 8th and 9th April, he ordered the deputy commissioner of Amritsar to banish Dr. Satya Pal and Dr. Kichlew from Amritsar. Both were secretly bundled off to Dalhousie in the Punjab hills. Both were thorough gentlemen and supporters of non-violence. Dr. Satya Pal, a medical practitioner, had served in the British medical service and Dr. Kichlew was an advocate and an alumnus of Cambridge. Mahatma Gandhi, on his way to Punjab, was taken off the train and sent over to Bombay (Mumbai). These actions of the colonial government provoked the public. Amritsar market was closed on 10th April. A crowd marched towards the bungalow of the deputy commissioner to enquire about the whereabouts of Satya Pal and Kichlew. People were stopped by a military picket at the Hall Gate railway crossing. The police fired two volleys on the crowd causing several casualties. People carried the dead and injured in a procession inciting public anger against the colonial rulers. Angry crowds targeted Europeans, two banks were looted, and several government buildings and a church were torched. An English lady, Marcella Sherwood, a missionary of the Church of England, was caught in the mob. She was injured, but some shopkeepers of the area rescued her and took her to the safety of British protection.

The government clamped restrictions on all demonstrations. On 11th April funeral of the Hall Gate firing victims was conducted peacefully. The same day deputy commissioner of Amritsar notified the public at large that military has been ordered to restore normalcy in Amritsar by all means necessary. Public gatherings were prohibited and groups of four or more risked being fired upon. An eerie peace now descended on the city.[25] The same evening Dyer arrived from Jullundur with a force of one thousand men to take charge of the situation. Resentment against government crackdown in Amritsar spread to other towns of the Punjab. On 12th April crowds damaged railway lines, post offices, telegraph wires, and a train carrying some Europeans was attacked at Kasur. Michael O'Dwyer was determined that if troops had to fire, they should make an example. He also informed the government of India at Simla about the gravity of the situation. Dyer took a round of Amritsar city on the morning of 12th April in a show of force. He warned inhabitants of the city that offenders of government orders will be punished according to military law. All meetings and gatherings were prohibited. The lieutenant governor recommended the governor-general to suspend functions of ordinary criminal courts in Amritsar and Lahore districts and declare martial law. He received sanction of his proposal on 14th April, under the State Offences Regulation of 1804.[26]

Evidently, Amritsar was not officially under martial law on 13th April. In spite of that Dyer along with deputy commissioner of Amritsar and the troops, marched through a part of the city proclaiming that no resident will leave the city. He, who leaves his house after 8 o' clock, will be shot. No procession of any kind was to be permitted and force will be used against all gatherings. Above proclamation was made when no martial law had been clamped. Dyer did not ensure that proclamation was conveyed to all residents in the city and notices to that effect were posted at all prominent places including the Jallianwala Bagh, an open compound used for local gatherings. The day of proclamation, i.e., 13th April was a holiday when Sikhs visit the Golden Temple situated near the Jallianwala Bagh. Unaware of the proclamation people from the peripheral villages thronged to the Golden Temple for religious discourse. A protest meeting was being held at Jallianwala Bagh. Many of the devotees joined the protest meeting. Dyer heard of the protest. He marched to the site with a posse of fifty soldiers, 25 Baluchis and 25 Gurkhas armed with 303 Lee Enfield rifles (composition of the contingent is not independently confirmed). There were 40 Gurkhas bearing khukhries (curved knives) and two armed cars bearing machine guns. Barely thirty seconds after entering the Bagh Dyer ordered his men to open fire. Dyer deposed before the enquiry committee that he entered the Jallianwala Bagh by a very narrow lane which necessitated leaving his armoured cars behind. On entering, he saw a crowd of about 5000 listening to a speaker. (Those present in the gathering put the figure at 15000 to 20,000 because of visitors from nearby villages). Dyer trained his guns on jammed exits and ordered rapid fire. Some retired Sikh soldiers who were in the crowd advised people to lie down to escape bullets but to little avail. Dyer's men fired 1650 rounds in ten minutes.

No one had a chance to escape. In the melee many fell into an open well in the compound and drowned. A callous Dyer marched his men back to the barracks leaving the dead and wounded where they lay. They were left to suffer the whole night without water and medical attention. Of about twelve hundred casualties, three hundred and seventy-nine were killed (Indians claim a larger number of deaths). Wheeler termed it a stark massacre and for the Indians it put a blot on the escutcheon of British military that has never been wiped away.[27] Nationalist English newspaper of northern India *The Tribune* thus described the agony of Indians on first anniversary of the Jallianwala Bagh massacre. "The deeds of agony, wanton cruelty and outrage serves to indicate how unspeakably wicked, how utterly depraved humanity can be in spite of tons of paint and glitter and gloss it loves to put on itself to advertise its vaunted civilisation and culture".[28]

The news of Amritsar massacre spread rather slowly due to complete black out of news from the city. Official organ, The *Civil and Military Gazette* headlined the news 'Illegal Meeting Dispersed.' Benjamin Horniman, editor of the *Bombay Chronicle*, defied British censorship and reported what occurred. He went to Britain where he showed pictures of the massacre to bring the truth to the notice of British people. The All India Congress Committee learnt something about it in the month of July. On 19th April 1919 *Times* published a distorted version "The troops came into collision with the mob, and there were 200 casualties among the rioters".[29] It was a fallacy. Dyer had fired upon a peaceful assembly of persons gathered in a walled compound with just one escape route and that too occupied by his men. Inaccurate accounts were reaching London because actual news of the massacre got hushed up for eight months through strict censorship and surveillance of communication with Punjab and other provinces.[30] Dyer was not finished after the above horrible action. He announced at the church, that the spot where Miss Sherwood was attacked was sacred. He, therefore, deployed pickets on both sides of the 150 yards street called Kucha Kaurianwala and ordered that every Indian passing through the street must crawl through it on all fours. The order was enforced by 18 British troops who ensured that belly of the crawler touched the ground. Anyone with a raised torso was kicked on the back. Those who failed to crawl properly had to repeat the act.

Electricity and water supply to the city was cut off. All fans, radios and electric installations in private homes were ripped off and given over to the troops for their own use. No one was aware of what was happening in the town. A night curfew was clamped between 8 p.m. and 6 a.m. The crawling order made certain that no vegetable seller, milkman, sweeper or even a doctor could enter the street. There being no flush latrines in the city at the time, night soil and rubbish piled up in homes. Sick remained unattended. People failed to buy foodstuff because they could not crawl back with the merchandise. Only 50 residents crawled through the street. Even those shopkeepers who had rescued Miss Sherwood suffered the ignominy of the crawling order. Collett has narrated instances of humiliation heaped on residents of the street.[31]

The crawling order was so servile that Dyer was asked to rescind it. Thereafter he turned to those accused of attacking Miss Sherwood. Having no inkling of the actual culprits, Dyer picked up six teenage boys out of detainees from the street. They had to receive punishment whether guilty or not. A triangle was erected on the street to flog the boys. Each of them was given 30 lashes with a stripe. All of them fainted after a few lashes. They were revived with water and lashed again. Dyer claimed that 30 lashes were not excessive because in old days it used to be several hundred lashes. Indians were ordered to salute every British. They were required to dismount their mode of conveyance and salute each white man they came across. Those with open umbrellas were to close the same and respectfully salute the white man with their right hand. Many in the public and British Parliament were horrified when news of the Amritsar massacre and the actions of Dyer surfaced in England. Yet there were diehards who supported Dyer's action. In the Parliament, secretary of state for India, E.S. Montague, angrily questioned his defenders if they were going to keep British hold over India by terrorism, racial humiliation, subordination and frightfulness. Churchill denounced the massacre as monstrous, without precedent or parallel in the modern history of the British Empire.[32] Enquiry into his conduct was ordered but it was acted upon after seven months. A Scotch judge Justice Rankin of the Calcutta High Court headed the enquiry. When the judge confronted Dyer if his action was a form of frightfulness, Dyer replied in the negative and added that it was a horrible duty he had to perform. He thought it was a merciful thing. His aim was to shoot well and shoot strong, so that he or anybody else should not have to shoot again. Dyer admitted that if passage to the place had been wide enough for the armoured car, he would have fired with the machine guns and casualties would have been higher. He even agreed that the crowd could disperse without firing any shot, but he did not want to make a fool of himself if they returned. About the crawling order he explained to the committee, it meant the street should be regarded as a holy ground. In short, Dyer was unrepentant for his actions. Pandit Nehru overheard his conversation with fellow British officers while travelling between Amritsar and Delhi. Dyer boasted how he had the whole town at his mercy, and he had felt like reducing the rebellious city to heap of ashes, but he took pity and refrained.[33]

Majority report of the Rankin Committee signed by the British members tried to whitewash Amritsar happenings. Disciplinary action against Dyer came several months later. Belated act of justice was mocked at in Britain. A majority of members in the House of Lords and many in the House of Commons supported Dyer's actions and even opposed his arraignment. It was argued that formal punishment would provoke a white backlash. "It was the story of Governor Eyre again; the same sudden tragedy, the same arguments and the same inconclusive ending. But it made an ominous prologue for diarchy."[34] The right-wing *Morning Post* opened a General Dyer Fund under the heading 'The man who saved India' and collected 26,000 pounds. Even Rudyard Kipling discharged his part of 'white man's burden' by donating ten pounds to the fund. British justice or lack of it enraged many Indians. Indian nationalist leaders were indignant that so many voted in favour of Dyer in the House of Lords. Sir Rabindranath Tagore, the Noble Laureate, condemned it. Jawaharlal Nehru educated at Harrow and Cambridge, who was to become first Prime Minister of independent India, called British reaction a cold-blooded approval of the deed. Sane voices in Britain stood muted against imperial arrogance. Dyer, designated Defender of the Empire, was dined, wined, and presented a gilt sword with inscription "Saviour of Punjab".

Minority report submitted by Indian members of the committee criticized Dyer severely for (1) suggesting that he would have used machine guns if those could have been brought into action; (2) opening fire without warning and continuing after the crowd had begun to disperse until the ammunition had been spent; (3) firing not merely to disperse the crowd but to punish it and produce a moral effect on Punjab; and (4) assuming that the crowd before him consisted of persons guilty of outrages of 10th April.[35] The majority report of the inquiry committee and supremacist response of most British parliamentarians smacked of undiluted racism.

Chapter 12
Company Clerks to Society Nabobs

European mercantile companies, their employees, and enterprising individuals who sailed to distant lands, lost no opportunity to amass wealth by fair means or foul. Once on foreign soil they realized that besides trade, there were other means of acquiring resources and wealth of those countries. To start with, companies managed to obtain some land on the coast to set up a fort/bastion/factory which they garrisoned. In practice, the so-called factory was operational quarters as well as a safe house for merchandise and arms. Conspiracies against native rulers and plans to intercede in their internecine conflicts were made behind walls of these factories. In time, using coercion, armed might, or sheer perfidy, they prevailed over the host country. In the early years, company officials ruled the roost being unguarded from close scrutiny of the home country. These companies recruited all kinds of young people. Some were jobless at home while others dreamed of making a quick buck abroad. Even less qualified persons landed highly authoritative positions they would never have dreamt of at home. They misused these positions, did very much what they liked, and terrorized the natives. Thomas Macaulay, speaking in the House of Commons on 10th July 1833 said that it was natural for men who had risen by so rapid an ascent to so dizzy an eminence to become profuse and rapacious, imperious, and corrupt.[1] Such men made dishonourable gains without compunction or remorse and accumulated riches through numerous ways. Besides trade, their avenues of making money were the mines and plantations in Africa, the Caribbean, and other European colonies. Hobson called them the South African brand whose methods of making money were brazen, their character formed in despotic Empire, and incomes maintained by furtherance of despotic rule.[2] Cecil Rhodes of the De Beers Company was most successful miner in South Africa. He was highly unscrupulous when it came to making money, acquiring resources, or appropriating native lands. He made millions out of the diamond trade and helped his country in expanding the British Empire in Africa. Upon his death he left about 3.5 million pounds to the Rhodes Trust. A lesser rival to Rhodes in South Africa was Barney Barnato. Penniless, the latter landed in Africa when the Kimberly diamond mines were discovered. His diamond mining company made him a millionaire within ten years. Rhodes tried to bribe him. Barnato refused his offer. Like Rhodes, he entered the Cape Parliament but in 1897, on his way back to England, committed suicide.

Joseph Mylchreest became a large planter of the West Indies. He left England at a very young age as ship's carpenter. He travelled to several countries in the Americas and Australia as prospector of precious metals and minerals until he ended up at Kimberley. Mylchreest was fabulously rich when he returned home. Roland "Tiny" Rowland was born in a detention camp during the First World War. He moved to Rhodesia in 1948 to set up a tobacco farm in the Mashonaland. He rose to be chief executive of the Rhodesian Mining and Land Company. Plantation economy of the Caribbean produced a number of millionaires. One of them was Sir Thomas Modyford. In 1647, he went to Barbados as a young man interested in plantation economy. His connections promoted him to the post of governor of Barbados. He became governor of Jamaica in February 1664 but was called back to England in 1670 for a trial. He was imprisoned for two years in the Tower of London. Although Modyford had placed the sugar industry of Barbados and Jamaica on a sound footing, his dishonesty let him down. He surreptitiously pocketed a lot of money from this industry. As a rich man he had developed right connections in England which saved him from long term behind bars.

The Persian word 'Nawab'[3] was the title used in India for governors of provinces and conferred on opulent dignitaries during the Moghul rule. The British adopted the Bengali pronunciation of this title, *Nabob*. In England, this title came to be associated with those employees of the EIC who had made fortunes in India. They returned in style to England and flaunted heir opulence in different ways. These people had shared the wealth that befell company's way in Bengal, but back to their country, they looked socially segregated. They were despised for their ill-gotten wealth and cynically called *Nabobs*. Elton described their situation. These employees shared "the shower of gold which had descended the company's servants in Bengal and was already producing its curious consequences at home."[4] Such men were objects of envy and derision. They were rich, their ways were vulgar, and they were misfit in the society they came from and were shamed by the aristocracy they wanted to be part of. Many of them had joined the EIC at a very young age and risen to hold important positions while in their twenties. Edward Stephenson and Robert Clive were eighteen when they arrived in India. Richard Benyon, orphaned at birth in 1698, entered the company service as a pre-teenager and in 1735 became governor of Fort St. George at Madras. He returned to England with 75000 pounds in his pocket and an exquisite collection of furniture, chests, porcelain and other valuables. There was a scramble for riches in a regime of corruption as notable as anything seen since the days of Rome.[5] Strachey candidly stated that the British, for a short period of fifteen years in Bengal, established a robber state where, without reference to rights of others, they freely plundered and looted under cover of their rights.[6] Young men with lesser or no opportunities in England eagerly awaited a chance to go to India, make a fast buck, and return home to display their riches. The EIC, itself steeped in bribery never objected to her employees finding ways to easy and quick enrichment.

About one hundred years after the EIC arrived at the authorized trading post of Surat, it secured a concessional custom permit from Moghul ruler Farrukh Siyar that catapulted her fortunes. Moghul rulers, who succeeded Aurangzeb, were weak and inconsequential monarchs who ceded control of large areas outside northern India to princes, Nawabs and regional powers. Their decrees carried weight only on the whims of the local governors. In 1715, the company deputed Sir John Surmon, Edward Stephenson and a Physician William Hamilton for seeking special trade rights from the Moghul ruler Farrukh Siyar. They carried with them gifts worth thirty thousand pounds. In the beginning, they presented 1001 gold *mohars* to the Emperor and then other gifts one by one. Still the Englishmen failed to achieve their mission for months together even after bribing court officials. Fortuitously for them, the emperor was inflicted by a mysterious disease. Dr. Hamilton was able to cure him. The gratified ruler came around and issued an imperial 'Farman' in 1717 granting a trade permit which exempted the company from paying prevalent custom duty for an annual payment of rupees three thousand only. The EIC lost no time in abusing this permit at custom duty check posts. Then started the "shower of gold" on company's servants.[7] The EIC issued a certificate or '*dastak*' to certify that the goods belonged to her. Company employees freely misused '*dastak*' for their private trade and obliged European traders and even native merchants by issuing certificates against large recompense. Bengal province generated considerable revenue. Consequently, abuse of '*dastak*' became a sore point between the EIC and Siraj-ud-Daula, the Moghul governor of Bengal. The latter claimed that in forty years beginning 1717, the EIC had defrauded Bengal government of more than 1.8 million pounds in custom duties.

The EIC permitted her employees to engage in private trade. This concession nurtured misuse of '*dastak*' whereby employees of the company collected money far exceeding their emoluments. In the beginning of the eighteenth century, the EIC paid just five pounds a year to a clerk. The salary was so meagre that a writer (clerk) could not afford to buy a candle and he slept early without dinner.[8] Several *Nabobs* including Robert Clive began their career as clerks in the company. A factor was paid fifteen pounds, while a junior merchant received 30 pounds per annum.[9] Emoluments increased in time as the company expanded her business. Company men freely received gifts and bribes in exchange for favours they granted to foreign and native merchants. In 1779, (just 15 years after Plassey) a select committee of the House of Commons listed that presents worth 2,169,665 pounds were received by the company employees.[10] Factors made small fortunes in a short period of time through private trade. They did whatever they fancied and accumulated immoral wealth without compunction. These men who had joined a company of traders were transformed from money makers to money takers. Money annually remitted from India to England ranged from 50,000 to 120,000 pounds between 1731 and 1756 though it was perhaps a fraction of the actual money transferred.[11]

Clive accredited with establishing the British Empire in India himself took bribes.[12] Edward Stephenson joined EIC in 1709 as a clerk and rose to be sub-accountant in 1713. Within a year he became factor at Hugli, a place highly suitable for private trade. He was a member of the mission to the Moghul court which secured the royal permit for duty-free trade, in the 'rich' province of Bengal.[13] Annual payment for the permit was only a fraction of what the company and her employees pocketed. In 1727, Stephenson was appointed company factor at Kassim Bazar, famous for its silk trade. Mysteriously though, he made lot of money at this place. Besides trade, he was apt in giving as well as seeking bribes and extorting money from the native traders. In 1728, he became governor of the Bengal establishment for a day. Stephenson returned to England in 1730 and bought lot of property in Bloomsbury. He was the first Bengal returnee to enter the House of Commons in 1734. He died in 1768 leaving some 500,000 pounds to his brother.

Robert Clive, during his term as governor of the EIC establishment in Bengal, tried to curb the extortion of money. He institutionalized pillage in his effort to cleanse the Augean stables. Clive established a private exclusive company consisting of 61 senior company employees including administrators, military officers, doctors and clergymen. This company was granted the monopoly to deal in the salt and betel nut trade and in the production and trade of tobacco. Indian masses consumed all three commodities. No one else could produce or deal in them. The company doubled the tax on salt which severely hurt the poor of Bengal. In fact, the Bengal famine of 1770 which killed almost one-third population of the province was a direct result of the heavy taxation levied by the EIC. Company officials continued to intimidate traders, officials, and peasants to extort money in the name of taxes and protection. They believed that to govern and extract wealth in India demanded maintaining sufficient social distance from the natives. They levied as much as 50 percent of the agricultural produce as annual revenue regardless of the state of agriculture because most crops were dependent on the rains. Revenue collection also became a source of illicit earnings by the company employees. Their plunder was shared by senior company officials. Ironically, all money was made through the ferocious pillage of the same country the company had come to trade with. Her employees merrily flaunted their Indian wealth after returning to their native England and styled themselves like actual *Nawabs*. Too wealthy and pretentious to associate with the classes they sprang from, these "vulgar *nouveaux rich"* were not accepted by the aristocracy they wanted to be part of.[14] Smitten by inferiority complex, some opted for ostentatious living and squandered away their ill-gotten wealth.

North American Review alluded to wealth gathered by the EIC and its officials through "oppressive and cruel" exactions. It wrote "but no fear of retribution could restrain the rapacious oligarchy, always sustained as they say by the English nobility, whose junior sons they enabled to accumulate fortunes in a few years, and whose ill-gotten treasure – the money wrung by fraud and torture from rich and poor — has continually been pouring into England."[15] Lamentably, the eighteenth-century British Empire was at best amoral.[16] England had become a sink of dishonestly acquired Indian wealth. British aristocracy and parliamentarians willy-nilly tolerated parading of such wealth by the company officials until the British Parliament was forced to intercede.

One of the celebrated cases deliberated by the British Parliament was that of Robert Clive credited as founder of the British Empire in India. Clive achieved this distinction by immoral and scandalous means. He was a born propagandist.[17] At an age of around eighteen Clive joined the EIC at Madras as a writer (clerk). Writers worked for lowly wages of five pounds to thirty pounds per annum. Clive joined the British navy thereafter and rose from the ranks to become deputy governor of the British establishment at Madras (Chennai). In 1756, he was dispatched to Calcutta along with Vice Admiral Charles Watson on an expedition against Siraj-ud-Daula, the Nawab of Bengal, who had seized properties of the EIC at Calcutta and Kassim Bazar. Clive recaptured Calcutta and entered a treaty with the Nawab who was anxious to normalize business with the company. Despite gaining huge concessions from the Nawab, Clive connived with Mir Jafar (Mir Jafar Ali Khan), the disgruntled former commander of Nawab's army and through him with the top brass of the Nawab's army. As part of the deal approved by the company, Mir Jafar offered cash rewards and jewels to Clive and other company officers. Clive was crafty and deceptive when dealing with Indian co-conspirators. Therefore, only the EIC, her employees, and English and Armenian merchants benefitted from the plunder of the Bengal treasury. In the nefarious deal, Mir Jafar agreed to disburse twelve lakh (1.2 million) rupees to the select committee of the EIC upon his installation as Nawab of Bengal. Subsequently this amount was doubled. Amount payable to the British forces was increased from four million rupees to five million rupees.[18] The EIC was richer by two and a half million pounds. Each member of the negotiating team received 27,000 pounds and each member of the Bengal Council around 12,000 pounds. Lion's share of plunder went to Clive who claimed the money as commander of the company forces, member of the negotiating team plus his share from the select committee money, all adding to 234,000 pounds. In 1758, the Court of Directors of the EIC appointed him governor of company's settlements in Bengal. Clive was penniless when he joined the company in 1743 but within 20 years he had become one of the richest men in England.[19] Clive returned to England in 1760, where he bought a seat in the British Parliament. Clive was only 34 when, between 1755 and 1760, he invested 220,000 pounds in business houses of England. His diamond collection was worth 25,000 pounds and his estate around Calcutta bequeathed to him by Mir Jafar brought in 27,000 pounds yearly. He ensured that the company let him draw that amount from the revenues of Bengal for life. The select committee of the House of Commons (1772–1773) was able to estimate that in 1757 presents worth 1,238,575 pounds were distributed out of the Bengal treasury. Clive himself received presents worth over 200,000 pounds besides his share in the other spoils.

Clive returned to England in 1767 in a style befitting an Indian Nawab. He took with him a slave boy, several dogs, birds, and a completely clothed monkey. He also carried gold jewellery and diamond-studded gifts for the British monarch.[20] Clive was knighted and acclaimed founder of the British Empire in India. In 1769 he claimed in the House of Commons that he transformed an inconsequential company to a great sovereign power presiding over revenues of more than four million pounds a year.[21] He used his Indian largess to buy several properties including the 45 Berkeley Square in Mayfair area of London. Despite the above honours and his wealth, Clive could not escape public scrutiny. There were whispers of his being the wealthiest but wickedest of the Nabobs.[22] He shamelessly defended his Indian gains and showed no remorse during the 1772 select committee hearings. Alluding to his entry into Nawab Siraj-ud-Daula's capital Murshidabad as a victor of Plassey, Clive boasted that a great prince (Mir Jafar) was dependent on his pleasure, an opulent city at his mercy, and its richest bankers longed for his smiles. He alluded to moving through vaults full of gold and jewels laid open for him. He carried on "Mr. Chairman, at this moment I stand astonished at my own moderation."[23] Much of the treasure he recounted lined the pockets of Clive, co-conspirators and officials of the EIC and produced several English *Nabobs*.

William Watts was another beneficiary of the munificence of Mir Jafar. Since the Alinagar Treaty, he was chief of the Kassim Bazar factory and the company's resident at the Moghul court of Murshidabad. He spoke languages like Bangla, Hindostani and Persian. Watts was, therefore, a point-man in the negotiations of 5th June 1757 with Mir Jafar and other intermediaries when the conspiracy against Siraj-ud-Daula was finalized. He received 114,000 pounds for his services in addition to his share of the amount meant for the pivotal Indian conspirator Omi Chand (Amin Chand) who had trade relations with the company. Watts was conferred governorship of Fort William in 1758 but he resigned four days later in favour of his benefactor Robert Clive. He returned to England and used his Indian plunder to build South Hall Park Mansion. He was contemplating purchasing another property in Buckinghamshire when he died in 1764.

The EIC created another opportunity to fleece Bengal when Fort William governor Henry Vansittart secretly arranged exit of Mir Jafar and installation of the latter's son-in-law Mir Qasim as Nawab of Bengal. The new Nawab was compelled to give away districts of Burdwan, Midnapore and Chittagong to the company and pay 58,333 pounds to Vansittart and large sums to other company officials.[24] Mir Jafar was weary of the company constantly fleecing him of money. Mir Qasim disliked the company's interference in his administration. For this reason, an independent-minded Mir Qasim was replaced with Mir Jafar to create another occasion to extort money. Vansittart, who had joined the EIC in 1745 as clerk at the age of just thirteen, was now in the position of a king maker. He made several opponents in the Bengal Council because, as a moderate and far-sighted person, he was disliked by corrupt employees. In desperation, he quit his position and returned to England. His actions were questioned by his critics in England. He wrote 'A Narrative of the Transactions in Bengal from 1760 to 1764' to absolve himself from the accusations. In 1765, he purchased manors in three townships of the

Parish of Fawley in the English county of West Berkshire and at Foxley. He also bought a house in Greenwich. Henry Vansittart bequeathed these manors to trustees for disposal and using proceeds for his wife and children. Vansittart lived in a lavish style like *Nabobs*. He had a huge collection of eastern curios, animals, and art objects. He lost a lot of money in his expensive living and in the stock market. In 1768, he won a seat in the parliament from the Borough of Reading, Berkshire. In 1769 he sailed for India along with two other supervisors to examine the working of the EIC. This was a chance for him to refurbish his financial position. Unfortunately, their vessel, the Aurora, which left Cape Town on 27th December was lost at sea.

Richard Barwell was another employee of the EIC who enriched himself through dubious means. He was the son of William Barwell former governor of Fort William in Bengal and a director of the company from 1758 to 1766. He used his father's clout to join the EIC in 1756 as clerk at the age of fifteen and landed in Calcutta. He rose to be member of the governing council of Bengal. He was a close associate of governor general of the company and like the latter had no qualms to extort money from the people. Barwell was notorious for his lust, dishonesty and injudicious behaviour. It is said that a part of his enormous wealth came from illegal trading in opium with Japan, China and possibly between India and Europe. He gathered his largest fortune while in Dacca.[25] As chief of the Dacca facility, he is rumoured to have exacted 44,225 Arcot rupees (the standard then used by the company in Bengal) from Dacca merchants on pain of lengthy imprisonment. Later the merchants were detained in a small room and released only after they promised to pay another 40,000 rupees. Barwell illicitly pocketed 20,000 rupees a year out of salt contracts besides his annual salary of 10,000 pounds as member of the Bengal council of the EIC. The company was very kind to him. It constructed the famous Writer's Building for his use. But he leased this facility to the company employees for their residence and earned hefty rents. The same year, he returned to England with a fortune of around half a million pounds, the largest ever amassed by a company *Nabob*. He bought his way to the House of Commons and remained a member of Parliament from St. Ives between 1781 to 1796 more as a necessity to ward off attacks against him about the sources of his wealth.

Barwell purchased Stansted Estate in Sussex at a bargain price of 90,000 pounds. He also acquired property in the area and a house in St. James Square in London, where he was reputed for loose living. He lost a part of his ill-gotten Indian wealth gambling in cards with Phillip Frances. Barwell never changed his lecherous behaviour, so he was disliked in his neighbourhood.

Sir Francis Sykes, son of a well-established farmer, was a menial employee before joining the EIC. Sykes came to be closely associated with Robert Clive and then Warren Hastings. Hence, he found himself holding important positions in the company like governor of factory at Kassim bazaar, member of Bengal council and resident at the court of the Nawab of Bengal at Murshidabad. Warren Hastings removed him from the last position, because he stole a lot of tax money for himself which otherwise would have gone to the company coffers. Sykes amassed his wealth out of tax-free trade at Kassim bazaar at a time when India was one of the wealthiest countries of the world generating considerable articles of trade for export to Europe. It is said that he kept for himself about five percent commission on taxes collected by the company. That would make tons of money. He made native merchants and peasants pay taxes through their noses. He lived in a large country house. During widespread famine of Bengal, the EIC hoarded all rice available for sale in the market and then sold it to the hungry natives at an exorbitant price. About one-third of the population of Bengal perished during the famine but company servants like Sykes made a neat 200,000 pounds from the above transaction. What could be a more disgusting example of immorality of someone from a professedly superior nation? But morality was not the point-not, at any rate, even to the later-day Victorians.[26] By 1770, now aged 40, he returned to England with 500,000-pound sterling in today's money. He had arrived in India with empty pockets but left the country when his pockets were bulging with ill-gotten wealth. In 1763, within two years of his first return to England he purchased Ackworth Park in Yorkshire. He also purchased Basildon Park in Berkshire from the heirs of Lord Fane. After his second time return to England, he purchased Gillingham estate in Dorset in 1774. He became a member of Parliament for Shaftsbury and then for Willingford. In 1781 he received title of Baronet of the United Kingdom from Basildon. Sykes was only next to Robert Clive in his Asiatic plunder. His source of wealth was private trade in association with a Bengali merchant Krishna Kanta Nandi (Canto baboo) and tax pilferage, but Clive had earned his fortune by plundering the treasury of the Nawab of Bengal.

Of the few Irishmen in the EIC service, James Alexander distinguished himself amongst her tribe of *Nabobs*. In 1752, at the age of 23, he joined the company at Madras as an understudy of the company's accountant. Within two years he became sub accountant as well as Sheriff of the Madras establishment. In 1757, he became junior merchant and in 1760 senior merchant at Masulipatnam (Machhlipatnam). Alexander moved to the EIC establishment in Bengal and held lucrative positions such as the revenue collector at Murshidabad and Patna. Both places offered plenty of illicit income because these were hubs of traders dealing in saltpetre, indigo, opium and textiles. Later he held the positions of member of the Bengal council at Fort William, Calcutta, warehouse keeper, custom master and mint master, all plum posts for skimming off money. Small wonder, that he possessed 150,000 pounds sterling when he left India in 1772. The above figure appears very modest to account for his acquisitions back home. In 1776, he purchased the Caledon estate in Tyron County for 96,000 pounds and built Caledon House in 1779. The estate comprised 9000 acres of land in Ulster, Northern Ireland. It was from here that he was subsequently created Viscount of Caledon in 1797. His unfinished concerns in India were worth more than 500,000 pounds, of these 298,000 pounds in Bengal itself. Much of his wealth came from revenue administration. Between 1775 and 1779, he was elected member of the Irish House of Commons for Londonderry. A great land owner of Ulster, he was created First Earl of Caledon in 1800, just two years before his death.

Employees of the EIC at Madras also earned illicit money but by different means from their Bengal compatriots. Company employees in Bengal milked the revenue system of Bengal, Bihar and Orissa and shared custom duty largesse afforded by the Moghuls. Madras-based employees invented other ways of collecting money. In the beginning the EIC was head quartered at Madras (Chennai). In 1684 its status was raised to Presidency of Madras. Elihu Yale was appointed its first President. Yale born in Boston, Massachusetts, joined the EIC where he rose to be President of her Madras establishment. Elihu Yale indulged in scandalous deals with Madras merchants and made large amounts of money. He also made money in the slave trade. He was dismissed as president after five years for illegal profiteering.[27] Yale was held back for another five years to pay back his fine. Yet, when he returned to England, he was a rich man. Unlike later-day Nabobs, Yale was a philanthropist. He received a request from his birth place for a donation to establish a college. Elihu Yale donated books, a portrait of King George I, and several boxes of Indian cottons. These items were auctioned for 800 pounds sterling. In recognition, the college carried his name. Subsequently Yale University was also named after him. The EIC had cultivated a rapport with regional rulers as well as rural artisans who made cloth from locally grown cotton. It was this product which Yale sent as gift.

While the company benefitted from subsidiary treaties executed with the bickering Nawabs of the South Indian States, its employees busied themselves in extorting money and jewels from them. One of the Moghul Nawabs they squeezed hard was Muhammad Ali Khan Wallajah. He was ever indebted to the British for their support in the succession battle with Hussain Dost who was supported by the French. He paid the EIC 160,000 pounds annually for the defence of his territory. The British also got money out of land grants of the Nawab. An Anglophile, he emulated British customs and socialized with the company officers. The Nawab patronized several portraitists through the company for drawing his portraits for presenting them to the British nobles as was custom of the day. One such portraitist was George Willison from Scotland who arrived in India in 1774. He made numerous portraits of the Nawab and charged him a price double of what he charged from his English clients. The Nawab owed him thousands of pounds by the time Willison decided to leave India. His outstanding bills totalling some fifteen to seventeen thousand pounds were finally settled by the company as part of Nawab's debts which the EIC always realized out of revenues of his land or by outright annexation of a part of his territory. Willison had got so much money that he was a rich person when he reached home via China. He became one of the affluent commoners settled in Edinburgh. Besides jewels, he carried home some 30,000 pounds in cash from India. No wonder people in Great Britain believed that it was only in the East where fortune was raised and not in any other direction.

One of the most derided *nabobs* of the EIC was Thomas Rumbold. Son of an employee of the company and once a waiter at the exclusive White's Club in London, he was inducted into the company's service as a writer at the age of sixteen. Later he was transferred to military service. He accompanied Robert Clive into the battle of Plassey as his aide de camp (ADC). In 1770 there was severe famine in Bengal. All available rice was bought by the company employees who refused to sell it to the hungry public at a reasonable price. They resold all important staple to the starving people at six-fold the price, thus earning huge profits within a short period. Rumbold amassed considerable wealth after 1763, when he was chief of the Patna revenue collection in Bihar known for its opium and indigo production. He was member of the Bengal council between 1766 and 1769 and is alleged to have swindled 600,000 pounds, as indicated by his remittances of money to England. This money was three times as large as his salary would permit. He returned to England in 1769 with his ill-gotten wealth. In 1770, he bribed his way into the British Parliament in a controversial election. Rumbold repeated the feat in 1774 election when he was accused of buying votes. He remained a director of the EIC for a better part of 1770's. In 1778, he succeeded Lord Pigot as governor of Fort St. George at Madras. Rumbold asked Zamindars (landlords) of Northern Sircar, a coastal strip under the company control, to meet him at Madras for finalizing their lease amount. Those who made the arduous journey to Madras were told to pay a bribe for having their lease fixed below the prevalent market rate. Similarly, Rumbold fleeced Nawab of Arcot of 75,000 pounds for watching his interest vis-à-vis the Raja of Thanjavur (Tanjore). During his two-year tenure as governor of Fort St. George Madras, Rumbold remitted 160,000 pounds to England although emoluments he earned from the company were around 13,335 pounds per annum and he had no other visible source of income. Rumbold had a stint of ten years as governor in Madras before he returned in 1780 with a fortune of 750,000 pounds, of which at least 180,000 pounds came as bribes from the Nawab of Arcot.[28] People quipped on his homecoming 'the East Indian fleet has brought Sir Thomas Rumbold on board whose value is estimated at a million.'

'Rumbold is the last waiter at White's whose babe will be rocked in a cradle of gems.'[29] Emulating fellow English *nabobs,* Rumbold bought an estate and a new house at Wood Hall Park, Hertfordshire. His ill-gotten wealth and acts of bribery came under scrutiny. Lord Advocate and President of the select committee of the House of Commons, Sir Henry Dundas, wanted to impeach him. He brought a bill of pains and penalties against Rumbold in dealing with affairs of Carnatic while he was governor of Fort St. George, Madras. Thomas Rumbold used his wealth and connections to stop this bill in the tracks. His daughter was married to nephew of Richard Rigby, an intimate associate of Henry Dundas. Rumbold had helped Rigby with money to save him from imminent impeachment. In 1783, Richard Rigby returned the favour and defended Rumbold from a bill of pains and penalties directed against him in the House of Commons. He was among the 30 notables who became "India's Members of Parliament."[30]

Paul Benfield was another unscrupulous EIC employee at Madras. He also fattened on largess of the anglophile Nawab of Arcot. Benfield joined the company as an Engineer but shifted to the lucrative construction business. He made fabulous amounts of money in this business to become a banker and financier. It was in the last vocation that in 1772, Benfield indulged in dubious loan deals with the Nawab who lived beyond his means. Alexander Wynch was governor of Fort St. George, Madras, when in August 1773 the Nawab of Arcot connived with the EIC to invade Tanjore. They captured Tanjore and imprisoned Raja of Tanjore, who had been installed as such on 1st January 1764, not long after George Pigot demitted his office of governor at Madras. Paul Benfield claimed that he had advanced loans of as much as two million rupees to the Nawab of Arcot against the revenues of Tanjore estate then possessed by the Nawab. The EIC also held stake in the revenues of Tanjore for her own claims of protection money and individual monetary favours from the Nawab. The court of directors of the company disapproved the whole affair. Tanjore revenue dispute showed that political morality among the employees of the EIC had reached its nadir. They recalled the governor and sent back George Pigot to restore the estate of the Raja of Tanjore. The Raja had offered a prized piece of land to the company to win its favour. The new governor restored the Raja, but his action annoyed the Nawab of Arcot and a majority of members of the council who were his protégés. Paul Benfield backed the Nawab for securing his own loan, which he alleged to have had extended to him against revenues of the Tanjore estate. The council members conspired with the military chief at Madras Robert Fletcher and had Lord Pigot taken into custody by Colonel James Stewart who was deputed to arrange for the restoration of Raja Tuljaji. The court of directors took strong notice of what transpired at Madras. Lord Pigot mysteriously died while in custody before any corrective steps could be taken. His death created furore in the British Parliament. Edmond Burke was unsparing in exposing dubious deals of Paul Benfield and the loans he claimed to have advanced to the Nawab of Arcot. Benfield, who was a junior employee of the company on a modest salary, lived in a lavish style. His claims of loans to the Nawab, said to range between 500,000 pounds to 800,000 pounds, were considered suspicious and were rejected. The Madras council negotiated peace with the Raja of Tanjore, but Benfield was unable to fully realize his claims linked to the estate of the Raja through the Nawab of Arcot. Yet, Benfield with a fortune of half a million pounds, bought the support of influential statesmen of the time and claimed a seat in the British Parliament. In this manner he enlisted himself among the English *Nabobs* who owned estates, political power and respectability all earned out of their ill-gotten wealth in India.

Some *Nabobs* joined the EIC as writers (junior clerks) but soon became contractors of the company and Royal Navy in the East Indies. They minted money on the side by exploiting the native suppliers of the merchandise. Basil Cochrane who had joined the company in 1769 at the age of sixteen became a wealthy businessman, inventor and writer. Between 1783 and 1785, he was revenue administrator of Nagapattinam where he earned the infamy of having two Indians beaten to death. He was arraigned for the death of one Vaidyananda but was acquitted by the Jury. At the time, textiles were an important export item from India. The EIC procured textiles from local weavers through contractors like Basil Cochrane. The latter colluded with influential landlords to entice native weavers into signing contracts for supplying cloth at prices which only favoured Cochrane. The uneducated artisans would discover the contract to their disadvantage and dither. Cochrane used coercion through visits of the company peons and native soldiers to force the weavers to honour their contracts until the Board of Trade in Madras intervened and forbade his use of company employees against the weavers. In 1792, his brother passed on his contract with the victualling board to him. The demand of provisions for the Royal Navy in the East Indies was so great that Cochrane installed his own flour mills and bakeries at Calcutta and Madras to honour his contract. Due to ill health, Cochrane decided to return to England in 1806. Meanwhile Cochrane was notified by the navy for a review of his accounts tallying 1,418,236 pounds (some 23.8 million pounds in today's money). Cochrane yielded the contract to Balfour and Baker and returned to England to pursue his case with the victualling office which lingered on until 1820. He built a house close to his family and participated in the election campaign of his brother for the British Parliament. Cochrane was rumoured to have connived with a naval officer and abused the system for his benefit. His brother Thomas Cochrane, an admiral, was often at odds with the navy and faced inquiries. John Jervis Earl of St. Vincent and First Lord of the Fleet, who investigated corruption in the Royal Navy, spoke of the untrustworthiness of Cochrane. Obviously, he had an unpleasant relationship with his compatriot. Basil Cochrane wrote pamphlets on his steam baths. In one pamphlet he criticized the victualling board and suggested a set of reforms which were finally introduced by the navy.

In 1795 James Balfour, a scion of a prosperous and influential family, joined as clerk in the EIC at Madras. In 1800, he became deputy commercial resident of the company at the Madras Presidency. He was however suspended from this position and dispatched home. Balfour returned to India in 1802 and became a merchant in partnership with Joseph Baker. In 1806 he took over the contract of the victualling board from Basil Cochrane. This contract gave him a breakthrough in his career. Both partners held the contract until 1815 when Baker quit the partnership. Thereafter, Balfour held it alone. At the time of his sailing back to England, he had accumulated a fortune of 300,000 pounds. Balfour bought exquisite real estate. He entered British Parliament in 1826.

John Graham joined the EIC at Calcutta in 1759. In 1765 he became secretary to the resident council at Midnapore. In 1772 he was appointed company chief at Patna. In the following year he became president of the Board of Customs thanks to his closeness to Warren Hastings. For the same reason he became a member of the supreme council at Calcutta. Graham made his fortune at Burdwan in Bengal. He remitted 70,000 pounds before leaving India. This was over and above the 25,000 pounds which he had remitted for buying an estate in Scotland.

Warren Hastings, the first governor-general, whose stint came under a cloud, was a typical *nabob.* He joined the EIC as a clerk, became resident at Murshidabad in 1758, and rose to be a member of the Bengal council. He, like other compatriots, made lot of money illicitly and returned to England in 1765. In 1769 he was assigned to the Madras council and in 1772 sent to Bengal as governor of the company's establishment. An all-pervading corruption in the EIC forced the hand of the British Parliament. Warren Hastings was appointed governor-general of the EIC establishment in India following the passage of the Lord North's Regulation Act of 1773. The above Act was meant to nail corruption and malpractices rampant in the functioning of the company. But Hastings not only failed to completely wipe out corruption in company administration, but he himself indulged in collecting money from Indians using questionable means. It was not entirely his fault. The court of directors of the company prodded their establishment in India to remit to them increasing amounts of money for paying fat dividends to the stock holders. Warren Hastings stooped to disgusting and immoral levels to extort money from different sources. He was always at loggerheads with most of his council and at one time fought a dual with his *bête noire* Philip Francis who had accused him of corruption. Francis held a letter given to him in 1775 by Nand Kumar (Nundocomar / Nuncomar) a prominent member of the Indian community of Calcutta. The latter had alleged that Hastings obtained a bribe of two hundred thousand rupees from Munni Begam, the widow of Mir Jafar, for appointing her the guardian of her minor stepson Nawab Mubark-ud-Daula instead of the latter's real mother. Members of the governor-general in council sought to discuss this issue. Hastings refused to preside over the meeting called for this purpose. A majority of the members elected a chairman, held the meeting as scheduled, and pronounced that the governor-general should deposit an amount upwards of 350,000 rupees into the company coffers. Without losing any time, a revengeful Hastings set up Nand Kumar in a case of forgery and had him condemned to death through his friend and chief justice, Sir Elijah Impey. The hapless Indian was entitled to protection but Impey had become the instrument of Hastings. He refused Nand Kumar to appeal. The proceedings were illegal.[31] Philip Francis was disgusted with the dishonest company administration. In 1780 he returned to England and joined hands with outspoken Member of Parliament Edmond Burke, in running down Warren Hastings. Burke addressed the bribery issue of Hastings in the Parliament. He claimed that Hastings gave and received bribes and was deeply mired into peculation and corruption. It came to light that Hastings, during his governorship of Bengal, dispatched home more than 220,000 pounds. This amount was nearly ten times his annual salary. Of a score of charges brought forward against him, the most serious charge was his disobeying 1773 Regulation Act prohibiting the acceptance of presents from the Indians. Other damaging charges included forced contributions from Raja Chait Singh of Benaras (Varanasi) over and above what he was obliged to pay the company, extortion of money from the Begam of Oudh under duress and other immoral actions, unjust execution of Nand Kumar, tyrannous exactions from peasants, and collecting huge amounts of money from Oudh for supplying English mercenaries against the Rohillas. Impeachment proceedings stretched over several years. In the end, Warren Hastings was let off, in view of his role in the extension of the British Empire in the East and because large sums of money he collected, regardless of the means, were expended in executing military campaigns not of his own making and in money dispatched to the company. Ironically, Hastings spent all the wealth he amassed through scandalous means, in defending himself in the British Parliament. He had remitted in all 218,000 pounds to England. Some of it was spent on gifts and defence of his case. He was left with only 75,000 pounds.[32] It was a division of spoils that rendered the trial of Hastings a solemn mockery. Important evidence against him, even his own letters and those of his agents and accomplices, were excluded by the Lords.[33]

The EIC came to trade with India but supplanted the crumbling Moghul rule. Her young employees, barely out of school rose to occupy important positions like governors of provinces with minimum accountability. They indulged in corruption among scramble for gathering as much money as they could and to return home in style. In India they behaved like lords and wanted the natives to address them like that (Latt sahib). Interestingly, the company had arrived at Surat on the west coast but found fertile ground for its ambitions only on the east coast of India.

Chapter 13
Colonies as Population Outlets

All non-European countries had native populations when Europeans barged in to establish their colonies. These countries were independent nations. They had their own codes of conduct howsoever primitive they might look to the Europeans. It was presumptuous to disturb the rhythm of their life by the foreigners. Columbus, during his voyages met natives of the Caribbean Islands, now known as Amerindian/Island Caribs/Taino or aborigines. They were friendly and one native chief helped salvage one of his ships that had run aground. Columbus established the first colony of the foreigners in the Americas. North America had its own indigenous population who traded with European explorers visiting their land. Columbus did not touch the North American continent but in 1513 Spanish explorer Don Juan Ponce de Leon caught sight of a land mass to the east of Gulf of Mexico. He named the new territory Florida, meaning land of flowers. The sixteenth century Spain was at the pinnacle of power in terms of naval strength and riches, thanks to its South American dominions. Spanish ships carrying gold and silver from the South and passing by the south eastern coast of North America were wary of the presence of French in the region. Spain tried to upstage French presence in the region, but its own colonizing efforts did not succeed. France had scaled down its ambitions in the East but was determined to expand its empire in the West. In 1562 Frenchman Jean Ribault explored the Port Royal region, presently in South Carolina, for settlement. This settlement was short-lived. But the 1564 French settlement effort on St. John's River, near the present-day Jacksonville succeeded. King Phillip II of Spain was alarmed at the French colonizing North America. He deputed Don Pedro Menendez de Aviles to sail to Florida, colonise the land, act as its governor and unsettle French colonizing efforts. Spanish action partly pursued the 1493 Bull of Pope Alexander IV granting Spain the right to colonise lands to the west of the Cape Verde Islands. Menendez landed on the Florida coast on 28th August 1565 along with 600 soldiers. He fortified Seloy, a native village, and named the settlement St. Augustine which became the first European colony on the North American soil. There was much bloodshed between the French and the Spaniards but the latter prevailed.

A debate erupted over the burgeoning population of England during the reign of Queen Elizabeth I. Thousands of small farmers fed up with the exploitation by big landlords sold their lands and moved to urban centres in search of employment. English clergy also shared concern over unemployment as a consequence of overcrowding. All evils like thievery, beggary, counterfeiting, lack of hygiene, vagrancy, etc., which had besieged the British society were linked in one way or the other to the population in excess of what the country could gainfully use. Mechanization of agriculture shrunk the demand for agricultural labour. Authorities concluded that the only way to reduce the number of vagabonds on the streets was to plant them elsewhere. Another explanation is clothed in the rising Spanish power. "The idea of Britain was the result of European contact with America, rooted in the search to create a policy that would prevent subjugation of the kingdoms in Britain and Ireland to the expanding power of a Spanish monarchy that could draw upon what seemed to be the inexhaustible riches of America."[1] In 1584 Queen Elizabeth I granted a charter to Sir Walter Raleigh to establish a colony in North America. Sir Raleigh sponsored a number of exploratory voyages to America for setting up a colony on the Chesapeake Bay. The captains of these expeditions named the territory Virginia in honour of the queen who was also known as the Virgin Queen. The 1587 expedition, comprising 117 persons, and led by John White, established a colony on the Roanoke Island. The first child born there in August 1587 was named Virginia Dare. No one is sure what happened in the intervening years but by 1590 this granddaughter of John White along with 80 men, 17 women and 11 children as also their colony had succumbed to the calamitous weather.

In 1603 the merchants of Bristol sponsored the voyage of Captain Martin Pring to explore the part of America earlier named Virginia. Pring arrived at the coast of present-day Maine and New Hampshire. At the time, the English treasury was almost empty from wars with Spain when

King James I ascended the English throne. The only way out was to explore the new world for gold and other riches and search the northwest passage to the Middle East and India. King James I granted charter to two branches of the Virginia Company. Hence British colonisation of foreign lands was meant to shift the surplus population and commercial use of the colonies. The Plymouth Company was permitted to establish a colony of one hundred miles square roughly between the Chesapeake Bay and the present-day Canada border. The other, the London Company, was permitted to settle people between the 34th and 41st parallels (from the mouth of the Potomac to present day New York). Both companies set sail in 1606. Plymouth Company ship which sailed in August was overpowered by the Spaniards near Florida. It never reached its destination. In the next attempt 200 colonists left Plymouth on 31st May 1607 in two ships. They set up Popham Colony, named after their leader in present-day Maine. The ships of the London Company, with 144 men and boys on board, left English shores in December 1606. Forty of the group died at sea. The survivors reached Chesapeake Bay and sailed on to the James Island. They established the settlement named James Town. Daily provisions needed for the settlement either came from home or were obtained through trade with the natives. In one of his sermons in 1609, Robert Gray supported emigration to North America as a solution to England's overpopulation. Another load of English Protestants, the Puritans, arrived in North America aboard the ship *Mayflower*. They settled at Plymouth colony in 1629. The colonies began to grow as more Britons poured into America to enjoy a better life. There were adherents to the more and merrier causes at home, but the bulk of influential public opinion saw, in the colonies, a welcome means for relieving England from demographic congestion.[2] Colonists brought in African captives to work for them. In 1700 one out of eleven Britons was an American colonist. Between 1700 and 1775, 120,700 emigrants moved from the British Isles to the American colonies.[3] By 1775, with other Europeans joining the influx, the colonies had 2.5 million whites besides a significant black population. In 1890, 9.25 million U.S. residents were foreign-born, Germany alone contributing 2.78 million emigrants.

At the time of the American Revolution one-third of American colonists claimed their ancestry to Ireland, the Netherlands and other

European countries. Altogether 250,000 African slaves had been shipped to North America to work on tobacco and the rice plantations in the South. After defeat of the English forces, about 50,000 loyalists to the British Crown left the country and settled in New Brunswick, Ontario, Nova Scotia and the Quebec provinces in Canada. Another 17000 sailed to sugarcane-growing British colonies in the Caribbean along with 75000 African slaves. Spain had to shift some of her black population to work on plantations and mining in her overseas colonies and thus overcome inhibition about slave trade. Yet Spain needed the additional backing of labour for her colonisation to succeed. Native labour was not up to the task. Moreover, during the subjugation of the Inca and Aztec empires, local population either perished defending their motherland or fled to the mountains. In Peru the natives were forced to work so hard that they no longer wanted to live. By end of the eighteenth century only one-tenth of the original native population survived.[4] Spain decided to settle virtuous and hard-working Catholics, especially retired soldiers, in these colonies in order to exploit their vast resources. The Portuguese, on the other hand, lacked resources to colonise even a small portion of the vast country of Brazil. It restricted itself to the coastal area. Changes in political fortunes of the Caribbean islands attracted English, Spanish and French nationals to settle in this part of the world and raise successful plantations of rice, sugarcane, tobacco, cocoa and coffee with the help of African labour. These commodities had a large export market in Europe and North America. British Colony of Barbados, established in 1627 and Jamaica, which was seized by Britain in 1855, supplied sugar to the world, thanks to the slave labour shipped from Africa. British colonies were established at St. Christopher in 1624, Nevis in 1628, and Montserrat and Antigua in 1632. These colonies had a mixed economy.[5]

The British used their colonies to cast aside prisoners convicted under certain provisions of the penal code. British prisons were so overcrowded that some prison population had to be interned in abandoned vessels. British public abhorred the conditions under which prisoners were housed. That is when British administration began transferring convicts to the American colonies. Between 1718 and 1783, about 50,000 British criminals landed in these colonies. British prisons again overflowed when the American War of Independence barred the shipment of British convicts to North America. Search ensued to find alternate place for convicts. After failed attempts with Newfound Land and other places, the British settled for the colony at New South Wales (Australia). In January 1788, the first fleet of 11 ships under the command of Captain Arthur Phillip arrived at Botany Bay in New South Wales. The fleet carried 1350 people comprising 780 convicts (male and female), 570 free men, women and children plus four companies of marines. One third of the convicts were of Irish origin. The second fleet arrived between 1791 and 1793. Free settlers also started arriving in 1793. Between 1788 and 1823 the colony of New South Wales was officially a penal settlement. Its population consisted of mainly convicts, marines and their wives. First batch of convicts arrived at Botany Bay, but convicts arriving subsequently, disembarked directly at destinations like Norfolk Island in 1788; Van Diemen's Island, named Tasmania, between 1803 and 1853; Moreton bay in Queensland in 1824; and Port Philip in Victoria in 1803. Van Diemen's Land had the largest convict population where some 70,000 convicts, or, about forty percent of the total convict population of Australia, were transported between 1812 and 1853. Convicts of Irish origin numbered 15,000. Women, comprising twenty percent among the first batches, were sent for employment in the fledgling textile industry. Male convicts were put to work on roads, bridges and as labourers on agricultural farms of free settlers. Economic depression of 1840's evoked opposition to the import of convicts because thousands of convicts and free settlers had already arrived in Australia in the previous eighty years. In 1896 the population of Australia excluding the natives had grown to 3,605,400. Free settler population of New Zealand was 703,360.

Migration to the African Colonies: Thickly populated Europe contended for the open and habitable lands of Africa abounding in natural resources for future settlements. Industrial Revolution had increased work avenues, but the African continent offered better prospects of rolling in agricultural and mineral wealth. In the late seventeenth century Portugal encouraged her entrepreneurs to settle on agricultural estates of Mozambique. By 1960 her colonies of Mozambique and Angola had 650,000 Portuguese settlers. The Dutch government also inspired her citizens to occupy lands in Africa and settle there. In 1707 settler population in the Cape area, they first settled in, was over fifteen hundred. By the beginning of the eighteenth century, European settlements had spread in South Africa. Their ethnic composition varied from Dutch Calvinists to French Huguenots. The Cape colony changed hands during the Napoleonic wars when it became the first permanent British settlement in Africa. Simultaneously Cecil Rhodes pioneered the white settlement of Rhodesia. He took upon himself the mission of usurping the best agricultural lands in Africa for creating white settlements. Cecil Rhodes reportedly said in 1895, "In order to save the forty million inhabitants of the United Kingdom from a bloody civil war, our colonial statesmen must acquire new lands for settling the surplus population of this country, to provide new markets for the goods produced in the factories and mines. The Empire, I have always said, is a bread-and-butter question. If you want to avoid civil war you must become imperialists."[6] Despite the ardent efforts of imperialists like Rhodes and his ilk, except for large plantation communities and mining business, Africa never became a favourite abode of the European immigrants. Largest concentration of whites was limited to the Cape Colony and there too, in 1875, whites were only 237,000 amongst a total population of 721,000.

Colonising frenzy also caught up with Germany. Enterprising Germans were eager to grab African wealth. German administration of the day and the military vacated the best agricultural lands in SWA (now Namibia) by evicting native Herero and Nama tribes who lived on those lands. German settlers established large farms to raise high-value export-oriented plantations. In 1981 there were 4000 commercial land owners, mostly white, who owned roughly 50 percent of the good arable land of the country. A hundred years after the establishment of the German protectorate hardly 20,000 ethnic Germans resided in Namibia due to the outflow that started after the First World War. The exodus of Germans was more than made up by expatriates from South Africa and later by the Afrikaners who resettled in Namibia following their disappointing attempt to settle in Angola in the Dorsland Trek. At its peak, the white population of Namibia was 14 percent of the total population. Presently 130,000 white population of Namibia is comprised of people with German, Afrikaners and Portuguese ancestry. In Algeria, France allotted the best lands of Arab Berbers free of cost to former French soldiers. French settlements sprang up in the mid-nineteenth century. By 1962 the European population had grown up to one million. Most of this population opted to quit the country during and after a prolonged War of Independence. Same story was repeated in other African colonies except Zimbabwe and South Africa where the Europeans wielded political power until 1980 and 1994, respectively. In South Africa only five percent of the white population initially left the country because the first post-independence President of South Africa, Nelson Mandela, adopted a policy of reconciliation. South Africa has a large mining industry. Its economy has gained strength, yet white population has nearly halved. Zimbabwe adopted a rigid policy towards the Europeans who controlled the economy of the country. About 40 percent of good farmland was held by about 50,000 white farmers who exported farm produce to Europe. President Robert Mugabe began a land redistribution plan resulting in confiscation of lands of the privileged white farmers. White settlers, who were early on pampered by Rhodes, were obliged to leave the country. Afrikaners moved into South Africa while English people either moved to England or to the colonies of Australia and New Zealand. Thus, peak populations of Europeans in Zimbabwe which was around 296,000 in 1975 dwindled to merely 30,000 in the first decade of the twenty-first century. Mass exit of French Pieds-Noirs, who numbered one million in 1962, occurred after Algeria won her independence following a fierce struggle. In Mozambique, the population of ethnic Portuguese, which was 200,000 in 1975, dropped to 45000. Portuguese left en masse in face of economic policies of the native government which militated against their wealth gathered in the colonial period. The Europeans stuck to their colonies as long as they enjoyed lordship over the natives and appropriated to themselves what was best to grab. They left when they lost those privileges. Their population on the African continent was less than five million by end of the twentieth century. Thus, Africa never became an important outlet for the European population. Those who went to that continent were hard-working entrepreneurs and businessmen, unlike some of the Europeans who voluntarily or involuntarily ended up in white colonies.

British Empire had number of colonies to accommodate people

leaving the British Isles. By 1871 Britain's population was twenty-one million. People had begun moving in to the colonies for greener pastures. By 1875 eight million people had left the British Isles[7]. Job-oriented people joined colonial civil and military service while the business class established mineral and agricultural enterprises in the colonies. In the British colonies except the settler colonies of Canada, Australia, and New Zealand, and to a large extent those of Spain and France, the Europeans migrated for commercial gains and for gainful employment. Writing on Imperialism as an outlet for population, English economist John A. Hobson admitted that it was in their national interest if surplus population settles in lands under the British flag. Britain should politically control those lands to provide homes as well as employment to such population.[8]

Christian missionaries often preceded the colonists. These emigrants formed a part of the floating population. Settler population in Australia started with the settlement of exiled outlaws. Colonial authorities induced the convicts to permanently settle in the colonies after expiry of their prison term. Some emigrants left their home country on their own looking for greener pastures abroad and settled in colonies like Australia and New Zealand ignoring colonial rules and regulations. In 1819 Great Britain opted for assisted emigration to release pressure of the impoverished population. In 1835, 5000 emigrants were assisted under the Poor Law Amendment Act. Assisted emigration through the Irish Poor Law Act of 1838 provided relief to the impoverished in Ireland who had been evicted by English landlords. Assisted emigration of Irish people to foreign lands was meant to decrease population pressure and misery in that country. At one time, the great famine of 1840s and attendant deaths and emigration, brought down the Irish population to one tenth of the expected numbers. A bulk of Irish emigrants ended up in the United States and Australia. From 1840 onwards, the Colonial Land and Emigration Commission monitored emigration from the British Isles to the British colonies and since 1848 to countries like the U.S.A. Between 1845 and 1856, some two million Irish people migrated abroad. Between 1830 and 1914 five million Irish went to the United States. Thus in 1890, two of every five Irish-born people lived abroad. The United Kingdom evicted Irish people under the Encumbered Estates Act of 1849. Many of them left for other countries with assisted emigration.

Several thousands of them even reached Argentina, where their number has grown to roughly one million. At present Irish people outside Ireland are fifteen times more than population of the mother country.

By the end of the nineteenth century about eight million Britons lived abroad. Of the twenty-eight million nationalities who sailed out of British ports between 1888 and 1933, the United States absorbed 51.6 percent while 38.8 percent ended up in the British dominions.[9] Thomas gave an interesting account of voluntary emigration of the Europeans.[10] Whereas only 100,000 Spaniards reached Americas in the sixteenth century, more French men immigrated to Spain during that period. Only 75000 Europeans left for the Americas in the seventeenth and eighteenth centuries against nine million Africans who were shipped to the region between 1490 and 1870. Between 1870 and 1890, people emigrated from the British Isles to the British colonies. Three million British subjects settled in the United States.[11] Out of the 17 million Britons who emigrated in the nineteenth and twentieth century 65 percent headed for the United States, and only five percent went to her African colonies. The remaining headed to the white colonies of Canada, Australia and New Zealand. Of the three million Italians who left Italy between 1880 and 1914 only 56,000 settled in overseas Italian colonies. The rest went to the Americas and other areas outside Italian control.[12]

Spain and Portugal pioneered searches for riches including diamonds, gold and silver in the non-European world. Since long, Portugal had traded with countries beyond her shores and even attempted to establish settlements in the early fourteenth century. But it was only in 1532 that it founded her first permanent settlement of Sao Vicente in Brazil which her explorer Pedro Alvares Cabral had discovered and claimed for Portugal in the year 1500. The Portuguese government did not encourage emigration to Brazil. It remained a trickle until the discovery of gold and diamond mines. Another boost came when Prince Regent of Portugal fled to Brazil in a fleet of 15 ships carrying a retinue of 15,000 of his family members and officials in the face of the invading armies of Napoleon. They arrived in Brazil in March 1808 and settled at Rio de Janeiro which became the headquarters of the Portuguese Empire and a port for the export of gold and other valuables. Portuguese began migrating to Brazil in large numbers after her independence. Between

1801 and 1841, ethnic Portuguese made up 15 percent of Brazil population. Between 1886 and 1966, 2.6 million people left Portugal for other countries. Of them, 30 percent settled in Brazil. Others went to the United States, Mozambique, Angola, Sao Tome and the Principe islands and other destinations. Hispaniola hosted the first Spanish settlement in 1493 when Christopher Columbus returned to the island along with 1300 settlers. Subsequent Spanish conquests were accompanied by expansion of the Spanish settlements in colonies of Latin America and the Caribbean. Mexico, Argentina, Chile, Colombia, South Brazil, Costa Rica, Cuba, Paraguay, Uruguay, Venezuela, Puerto Rico and the Philippines. Still, hardly 300,000 Spaniards migrated to the Spanish colonies during the three centuries of their rule which ended in the second decade of the nineteenth century. About 80 percent of Spanish immigrants were males. Hence, besides other whites and natives, the Mestizos (Parda, Castas, mixed race) comprised a significant portion of the population of Latin America. Mestizos who dominate the society in some Latin American nations are a product of war and occupation. Besides Portuguese and Spanish Argentina, Southern Brazil and Uruguay received a large number of French immigrants. There was a post-independence spurt in the immigration of the Europeans to Latin America. Between 1820 and 1932 more than six million Europeans settled in Argentina while Brazil hosted four million, mostly from Spain. Back and forth movement of Europeans between Europe and Latin America depended on economic opportunities. Presently 88 percent of the population of Uruguay, 85 percent of the population of Argentina and 54 percent of the population of Brazil is white. The natives of Cuba, who for the first time saw foreigners in the late fifteenth century, are a rare appearance now while Europeans constitute almost 65 percent population of that country. About 80 percent of the Taino population of the Antilles was lost within thirty years of the arrival of the Europeans. These high percentages are reminiscent of a tragedy which befell the native (Amerindian) population after the arrival of the white man. The natives were almost wiped out by diseases they contracted from the intruders, with physical annihilation by the conquistadors and deliberate destruction of sources of sustenance which had supported the natives since ages.

Chapter 14
Ruthless Supremacists or Crafty Freebooters

White supremacists of Europe believed it their divine right to subjugate non-white races of the world and impose upon them their own religions and culture. The notions of superiority were a psychological defence of their abominable acts against non-European nations. The white man's burden',[1] 'civilizing mission', 'the evolutionary destiny of the white race' were products of their being a self-professed superior race. It was engrained in the European mind that white skin, a stamp of hereditary aristocracy, was bound to lord over the servile non-whites. Kiernan poignantly wrote, "Colonizing countries did their best to cling to the conviction that they were spreading through the world not merely order, but civilization, which implied that other peoples were not civilized, but were capable of becoming so."[2] In India, inebriated white soldiers returning from a party would beat up their servants with impunity. On white-owned tea gardens, native labour had long learnt to take kicks and slaps as their daily routine.[3] "From perceived superiority of their civilization… they looked upon non-Europeans as half savage and half heathen."[4] Average German looked upon natives of their colonies as being on the same level as the higher primates. It is a fact that Nama and Herero natives were highly intelligent and brave people who dared to face German bullets to preserve their hereditary lands. Catholic Church reinforced belief of white superiority. In 1452 Pope Nicholas V authorized the king of Portugal to attack, conquer and enslave what he decreed non-believers. Europeans of the medieval period believed non-Roman nomadic tribes as saracens. This cultural animosity arose after the Turkish onslaughts into Western Europe. Papal bulletins betrayed an aggressive Christianity of the time that colonial Europe had embraced and carried to foreign lands. Europe's supremacism was not entirely 'white only' doctrine. Protestant White England considered Catholic Celtic whites of Ireland expendable. Their persecution was based on ethnicity and not on the colour of their skin. Britain followed a race-based policy to eliminate them during the potato-generated Irish famine of 1845.

Non-Christian natives of the white-ruled colonies were always treated with derision. Christopher Columbus was welcomed by natives of the Caribbean islands but he forced them to mine gold and silver day in, day out. Enslaved natives soon withered away. Many died of exhaustion and a good many from diseases they contracted from the Europeans. They escaped from misery by aborting foetuses and committing suicide by jumping off cliffs into the sea. Several Caribbean islands lost all the indigenous population to European diseases and due to the maltreatment of those who had come to evangelize them. Spaniards sailed to the outside world with the Book in one hand and a sword in the other hand. They were accompanied by friars. But as the events of the 1519–1521 expedition of Hernando Cortes unfolded, they wielded the sword only. Spaniards massacred all nobles and leaders of the temple city of Cholula after inviting them for talks. The moot question is who was culturally superior? Spaniards stripped bare Cholula temples of their gold and valuables. Cortes and his men repeated the mayhem in the magnificent capital city of Tenochtitlan. They displayed the worst form of racial arrogance, massacred all nobles and common citizens of the Aztec kingdom gathered for religious festivities. The death grip of the sword and the Book was revisited in 1531 when Francisco Pizarro raided the Inca Empire of the Andes. This well-developed thirteenth-century empire, though less known beyond its borders, matched historical empires elsewhere in the world, both in elegance and organization. Its ruler Atahualppa came forward for a customary welcome. A monk (friar) appeared with the Book and asked Atahualppa to accept Christianity and acknowledge the king of Spain as his sovereign. Atahualppa curtly refused the demand. Spaniards resorted to canon fire which killed Inca nobles and common citizens accompanying the king. A surprised Atahualppa earned short-lived reprieve by offering a room-full of gold as ransom. Altogether the gold was in tons. It was moulded into bricks and the share of the Spanish monarch was dispatched to him. In retrospect, the Spaniards did not prove culturally superior compared to the natives they annihilated. Their superiority only lay in their canon and horses that were alien to the South Americans. They carried the edict of the Pope but forgot compassion and righteousness when targeting the innocent natives.

Portugal led Europe in sailing to the old and non-European world for trade. In due course of time, the flag followed the trade not as an adjunct but as a catalyst. Portugal, then a premier naval power, was front runner in the ocean-based trade. The Portuguese sailor Vasco da Gama discovered the sea route to India rounding the Cape of Good Hope. He faced opposition of well-established Arab merchants trading with India. Expedition of Pedro Alvares Cabral to India lost several sailors. In 1502, an infuriated king of Portugal sent da Gama on a punitive expedition to India. Da Gama waylaid a ship carrying passengers on pilgrimage to Saudi Arabia. He set the ship on fire after confining its passengers to the hold and sunk it. Da Gama intercepted few commercial vessels on his way to the Indian coast. He dismembered limbs of his captives, chopped their ears and noses off to send a terse message to the Zamorin (governor) of Calicut (Kozhikode). The Zamorin disregarded his impertinence but refused him permission to establish a trade post. Actions of Da Gama did not behove those of an individual of a 'cultured' nation.

The Europeans who scrambled for a piece of African territory in the 1884 Berlin Conference, believed that the natives of Africa were imperfect beings and hence, irrelevant and unworthy of being part of their deliberations. They ignored the fact that these very people (Khoi Khoi) had helped marooned sailors of a Dutch vessel and hosted them for several months before they were rescued by another ship. Conversely, the Dutch, using their guns, evicted the cattle-rearing Khoi Khoi from their grazing grounds and shelters. They themselves occupied those lands and established the Cape Colony. King Leopold II who held control of the Congo Free State in the Berlin Conference unleashed a reign of terror to satiate his urge for gathering money. His people would fix a quota for individuals or communities to collect certain quantities of ivory and rubber. Those who failed to collect the designated quantity suffered punishment of having their hands chopped off. The natives were so sure of their fate that, should their collection appear to fall short of the designated quota, they would themselves prostrate on the ground to receive punishment. Leopold was responsible for the death of millions of Congolese in his pursuit of wealth. Such a demoniac behaviour was shameful for an emperor of a 'cultured' nation. In SWA, the Germans wanted to get rid of the native Herero and Nama tribes who lived on fertile lands rearing their cattle. They opposed the German occupation of their lands for raising plantations. General Lothar von Trotha took the task of evicting them. After the initial skirmishes, he herded them into the hot and dry Kalahari Desert where the only water holes were contaminated with dead animals. German soldiers bayonetted to death dehydrated men, women and children prostrating in the desert.[5]

Razzia[6] expeditions of the French army in Algeria were unnerving. Victims were the cattle rearing native Kabyles of the mountainous region of coastal Algeria. At one time France wanted her colonies to be an extension of the French empire through a policy of assimilation. Efforts to that end were fruitless because the Algerians despised French rule. The French military tried to suppress the rebellious Kabyles and evict them from their lands. It launched Razzia expeditions against them. In one episode few hundred fleeing Kabyles men, women, and children along with their cattle took refuge in a labyrinth of caves with only one opening. The French, who were in hot pursuit, lit a fire at the opening to the cave and kept it burning continuously for a couple of days. All the human beings and cattle in the cave were roasted alive leaving behind mangled carcasses. In another expedition, Kabyles hid in another system of tunnels again with a single opening for entry and exit. The French general ordered hermetically sealing the mouth of the tunnel. As a result, all the occupants, including animals, suffocated to death. These are classic cases of supremacists turned executioners. The French hunted the Kabyles as if they were wild animals.

The British acted craftily when seizing lands of the natives in their colonies. Cecil Rhodes, a diehard supremacist, established British colonies in South Africa by tricking chiefs of the native tribes. His agents, in complicity with the Christian missionaries, coaxed chiefs of the native tribes into signing ambiguous documents for a mere pittance as remuneration or for 'never to be honoured' defence pacts. Within a short time, it dawned upon the chiefs that they had lost the lands of their community to the white settlers. British settlers of African colonies, as elsewhere, were a law unto themselves. In Kenya, one Colonel Ewart Grogan, a prominent leader of white settlers, flogged two rickshaw pullers to death in front of a magistrate. All canons of judicial conduct fell when murder charges against Grogan were reduced to an assault and the white judge pronounced the sentence – internment of the defendant for two months at a place opposite a large hotel. Grogan was unruffled. He whipped three hand cart pullers, with their hands tied at their back, at a public place, on weird charge of showing disrespect to his sister. When a policeman asked him to stop the beatings, Grogan claimed his right to punish his servants. Whiteman's arrogance got the better of him simply because his victims were black. Similarly, a native, named Kitosh, was beaten to death merely for riding the mare of his master. Superiority complex blinded white colonists and plantation owners of Africa to justice and fairness.

The British military officers too did not cover themselves with glory. The 1890 campaign of Lord Kitchener against the Mahdi, a religious sect of Sudan, is an example of marked insensitivity toward religious feelings of others. Kitchener not only demolished the tomb of the Mahdi Khalifa (religious leader) but also desecrated his grave and remains. British General Charles Napier acted irrationally against amiable rulers of the Sind (Sindh), now in Pakistan. The rulers (Amir's of Talpur) signed a treaty with the British on the latter's terms leaving no room for provocation on part of the mighty British. But the latter were bent upon annexing Sind to clear their way to the river Indus and then on to the borders of Afghanistan. They provoked the Amirs in different ways but to no avail. Finding no feasible excuse, Napier attacked Sind, got the better of the Amirs, and annexed it to the British territory. Napier privately admitted that he had no right to seize Sind and his action was a humane piece of rascality. European approach toward the non-Europeans was to assert so much authority over them as to break their spirit to the point of complete submission. To that end they hanged 50 Africans a month to keep them subdued.[7]

The British harboured feelings of superiority and contempt against the Indians. They held the conviction that white skin and Christian faith made them superior in intellect and morals. Hence the Anglo-Saxon race had special attributes to govern the lesser people.[8] On 3rd September 1885 the Times wrote that the Indians were a "very small people" which a "very great people" had gone across the earth and taken possession of.[9]

In 1763, sometimes before the battle of Buxur, Major Hector Munroe who commanded EIC troops against the Moghuls, lined up twenty four *sepoys* (Indian soldiers of the EIC) and had them blown away with canon fire in front of their fellow soldiers.[10] The reason, '*sepoys*' looked rebellious and it was a lesson for the other *sepoys*. Indeed! It was a tragic way to instil the fear of the 'mighty white' among the poor natives. Indian *sepoys* had been part of the EIC's army for about one hundred years. They saw action not only in the wars within India but outside the borders as well. The last major battles they fought for the company were against the Sikhs. What went wrong that the *sepoys* lost confidence in their British officers? The missing link was failure of the British commanders to own their men. The British wanted obedience through despotism. All hell broke loose when one of the *sepoys* betrayed his emotions. Several British officers were killed. In a swift action, British officers marched *sepoys* from cantonments of the north and northwest India to the grounds where they were disarmed and then blown away with canon fire and guns or hanged there and then. A search ensued for those *sepoys* who had absconded from certain death. Recently, the remains of around one hundred *sepoys* who ran away from Lahore cantonment (now in Pakistan) were unearthed from an old well in Amritsar (India) where they had been executed.

British army and loyal Indian troops marched in hot pursuit of the *sepoys*. Any able-bodied person whether a *sepoy* or a common village folk, became the target of retribution. Trees along the roads carried the burden of thousands of Indians. One large banyan tree in a village had 150 corpses hanging from its branches.[11] Villages were burnt down, and women dishonoured. Tales of British action began reaching Kanpur through absconding *sepoys*. Hearsay stories provoked local *sepoys* into retaliation and the victims were the unfortunate British families of Kanpur. Women and children were moved to Bibighar (lady's home) where they were mercilessly butchered, no one knows by whom or under whose orders. News of the Bibighar killings stunned the British public. The Indian press had been shackled by the governor-general of India to hide British brutalities from Europe. Only distorted versions of events reached London through correspondents sitting in faraway Bombay (Mumbai). The England of 1857 shouted itself hoarse for bloody revenge forgetting it was a Christian country.[12] British officers ordered villages to be destroyed —— slaughter all men; take no prisoners —— there was altogether too much indiscriminate execution.[13] In a debate in the Oxford Union rhetoric was very wild. Speakers demanded that any talk of mercy should be considered only "when every gibbet in India is red with blood, when every bayonet creaks beneath its ghastly burden; when the ground in front of every canon is strewn with rags of flesh and shattered bone".[14] This is what their compatriots were doing in India. In Peshawar whole regiments of Indian soldiers were blown away by the guns. This dreadful news was read with delight in Britain.[15] Stray voices of reason were silenced in the face of stories and half-truths spread by biased reporters. Racism was at its worst. English public fed on self-proclaimed superiority was horrified that a lowly people take up arms against them. The *Times* (London) demanded that every tree and gable-end should have the burden in the shape of a mutineer's carcass.[16] An issue of the *Times* demanded the slaughter of Delhi to be punished with unsparing severity because Asiatics were not the people to whom rulers can safely grant impunity for crime.[17] An Englishman from India wrote to a newspaper that every 'nigger' we meet we either string up or shoot.[18] The truth is that Indians were not treated like men. Their women were flogged and violated in front of their husbands and tortured to emulate the inquisition in its worst days.[19] Indian correspondents in the EIC service and political functionaries were interested in concealing the dark side of the picture.[20]

Indians of every description were being butchered in Delhi where the British army searched homes to kill the inmates. Bloodletting in Delhi was worse than that perpetrated by the Persian ruler Nadir Shah in March 1739 in the same city. A young lad along with his old grandfather fell at the feet of a British officer and begged for mercy. The old man was shot dead immediately, but it took three bullets to kill the young boy because the 'gallant' officer's weapon misfired twice.[21] Sons of the Moghul ruler were publicly assassinated. Major Hudson presented their heads to the old emperor. Composed, the emperor said, "Praise be to God." Timur's descendants returning from an expedition presented themselves before their father with their faces invariably crimson either with flush of victory or with their life blood."[22] When asked why no tears for your sons. The father's response was that emperors do not cry. Delhi looked a deserted place with dead bodies strewn everywhere. In Oudh 150,000 were massacred of which 100,000 were civilians. Culprits behind the Bibighar killings of Europeans were not traced but all residents of Kanpur were held responsible for failing to prevent the incident. Brigadier-General (actual rank colonel in the British army) J.G.S. Neil began whipping the local population. On 25th July 1857, he ordered street sweepers to round up high-cast Brahmins along with others from the local market place. Each of them was asked to couch down in turn and lick clean one square foot of bloody Bibighar floor. They were forced to finish this abhorrent act amid whipping. This task was revolting for the Brahmins who do not touch meat. After this act, animal flesh was forced down their throats (another abhorrent act for them) before they were hanged to death.[23] The vengeance and above all contempt for religious sensitivities of the Indians continued for several weeks until it was stopped by the visiting British army chief Sir Collin Campbell.

Europeans holding even ordinary positions had a haughty disdain for the natives regardless of their educational or social ranking in the society. They suffered from megalomania and regarded themselves as tin gods.[24] Joseph Chamberlain, British secretary of state, claimed that the British race was greatest governing race the world has ever seen. Emphasizing British superiority over Indians, Huttenback averred that British superiority could not be defined in terms of education, climate, or the imperatives of economics or geography, it was due rather to the unique attributes of the British race. The self-professed attributes probably emerged from the barrel of the Maxim gun. No Indian, however eminent, was supposed to appear in a meeting presided over by a British official with his shoes on. The British magistrates or judges insisted that Indian lawyers and subordinate employees take off their footwear in deference to the authority of the court. The Englishmen were supposed to shun Indian dress to preserve the prestige of the ruling nation.[25] In 1857 Captain John Nicholson then deputy commissioner of Peshawar was given the command of Irregular Horse with the rank of brigadier general. He was moving to Delhi through Jalandhar when the Raja of Kapurthala offered to garrison the place with his own troops. The commissioner, Major Edward Lake, invited Nicholson to a *Durbar* at his residence and asked officers of Kapurthala troops to join. At the close of the function, General Mehtab Singh of the Kapurthala army took leave of Major Lake. He was about to cross the door when John Nicholson imperiously stopped him. He curtly told him to remove his shoes there and then and to hold them in his hands for everyone to notice his 'impertinence'. He also reminded the general that in future, he would never dare to come in his presence with his shoes on. As providence would have it Mehtab Singh never had to come face to face with John Nicholson, because the latter died of injuries he suffered in the Delhi campaign.

In November 1788, rule of the EIC was scrutinized in the British Parliament. Charles James Fox, during his speech, cautioned the parliament about the tyrannical rule of the company. He said that the 1784 bill was meant to annihilate this tyranny. Fox reminded them that a handful of men execute the most base and abominable despotism over millions of their fellow creatures and thirty million men gifted by providence with ordinary endowments of humanity should groan under a system of despotism unmatched in all histories of the world.[26] The 1784 bill failed to change the company's functioning on the ground. Warren Hastings who retired as governor-general of India was impeached by the House of Commons. He was charged to be guilty of gross injustice, cruelty and treachery against the faith of nations, hiring British soldiers for extirpating the innocent and hapless people; impoverishing and depopulating the country of Oudh and rendering the country, which was once a garden, an uninhabited desert. Most Englishmen from the lower rungs of society, with nominal education, continued to behave like despotic masters. Apathy for Indians permeated each section of the British society. Lieutenant Colonel H.B. Henderson who lived in India for twenty years published his recollections in 1829. He discovered "breath-taking arrogance in the company employees. "No native, however high rank, ought to approach within a yard of an Englishman... he shakes our ascendency in this country."[27] Even as eminent a person as Sir Winston Churchill had no kind words for Mahatma Gandhi when, on 17th February 1931, the latter was invited for a meeting with Lord Irwin, the viceroy and governor-general of India. Churchill blurted, "He felt nauseated at the humiliating spectacle of this one-time Inner Temple lawyer, now seditious fakir... striding half-naked up the steps of the viceroy's palace there to negotiate and parley on equal terms with the representative of the King Emperor."[28] Churchill affronted both Mahatma Gandhi and Jawahar Lal Nehru with his remarks "to abandon India to the rule of Brahmins would be an act of wicked negligence he said in the House of Commons."[29] Churchill insinuated to their being from a cast which denied democratic rights of existence to their sixty million countrymen. What a justification to perpetuate despotic British rule! In response to the 1943 American draft declaration in favour of national independence of all countries Churchill retorted against 'forty or fifty nations thrusting interfering fingers into the life's existence of the British Empire.'[30]

Why Europeans acquired colonies: Since ancient times human beings have voluntarily moved to every nook and corner of the world. Indigenous people were present wherever colonialists established the colonies. It was, however, an organized event when Christopher Columbus shipped Europeans into Hispaniola. This event was the advent of colonisation because Hispaniola was already inhabited. Subsequently Portugal and then Spain captured countries of South America and the Caribbean. Spanish conquistadors sailed for plunder and targeted gold and silver of those lands. Between 1500 and 1569, Spain shipped about 450,000 pounds weight of gold and thirty-one-million-pounds weight of silver from the Americas. This plunder was stamped with blood and sweat of the natives of South America. Millions of Inca slaves died in the mining of silver. Potosi silver mines of the highlands of Bolivia which enriched Spain, killed thousands of Inca slaves. Spanish miners hired these slaves from their masters in Peru. These Inca destitute had seen better days when they were masters of their country. The English nation graduated from piracy to colonisation after the defeat of the Spanish Armada in 1588. On 31st December 1600, Queen Elizabeth I granted a charter to a company of merchants of London for trading in the East Indies. Six years later, King James I granted charter to the Virginia Company with rights to establish settlements in North America. At that time, the financial position of England was too fragile to undertake such ventures. Hence one charter was root of the English title to the East and the other root of English title to the West. Churchill surmised that the EIC was a trading organization. Its directors wanted dividends not wars and

278

grudged every penny spent on troops. They established an empire by accident. Of India it has been said that British Empire was acquired in a fit of absence of mind.[31] Yet Joseph Chamberlain, once colonial secretary in the British government had no qualms in admitting that British Empire was commerce and India by far the greatest and most valuable customer that ever shall have.[32] Chamberlain's admission was mirrored in what colonial government practiced. It exported Indian food grains while the natives were starving to death. During the second half of nineteenth century exports of food grains from India multiplied about eleven times, while deaths from famine in India approached the millions.

It was not the merchant oligarchy alone, British politicians were also involved for the sake of their wards, likely to benefit from a bounteous India. Constitution of the EIC began in commerce and ended in empire. But the British never deviated from the commercial route. Probably for that reason Britain was called a 'nation of shopkeepers.' British never lost sight of profit in her relations with American colonies established by their own kith and kin. The British wanted American colonists to share the cost of seven year's war with France and pay extra taxes. The London government also passed acts to assert its authority on the colonies. Settler's protests turned into boycott of British goods and finally to the event known as the 'Boston Tea Party.' The British reacted by acting against the self-governing Massachusetts, closed the port, and constituted a shadow government. All colonies mustered their resources and willpower to defeat Britain and gain independence. It became clear to the British that they would also lose against the combined will of the people elsewhere. So, they stuck to the panacea of divide and rule in their colonies.

Europeans who sailed to foreign lands were not venture philanthropists. The Portuguese and the Dutch sailed for trade and reaped huge profits from transatlantic slaving, Spanish conquistadors plundered South America, and France and Britain competed in colonisation of foreign lands and reaping accompanying benefits. Europeans intended to appropriate maximum land in their colonies for white farming syndicates and individual entrepreneurs to set up plantations for the export market. They were attracted by open fertile land and good climate to grow a variety of crops and orchards under conditions not available in their home country. Displacement of natives was never a concern for them. They did this in North America, Africa, Australia, and the Caribbean. Cecil Rhodes contended that "every acre added to British territory provided for the birth of more English race that otherwise would not be brought into existence... The more we inhabit, the better it is for the human race."[33] White settlers established large plantations employing the same native labour whose lands they had filched for those plantations. The same labour also mined gold, silver, copper, iron, etc. There were restrictions on what native peasants could grow. High value crops like tea, cotton, and coffee with secure export market were reserved for the white settlers.[34] Native peasants could grow crops for local market only. In India indigo was grown in Bihar, Bengal, and other states for dying cloth for the local cotton industry and for meeting growing demand overseas. The British growers entered into agreement with the natives, forced them to accept low prices and thus scooped up profits. In Africa, the hut tax which was a major source of government revenue also provided cheap labour to white planters, because natives had to earn cash and discharge their tax obligations. Natives unable to pay hut tax often abandoned their lands and disappeared. In Africa natives could not plant cash crops, like tea and coffee, and thus compete with English planters. In India farmers were asked to grow export-oriented crops like cotton, opium poppy, indigo and jute instead of crops they needed to feed their families. Europe monopolized the world market in these commodities which were either consumer goods or raw materials for domestic industry. Colonies were captive sources of minerals, raw materials and labour for profitable investment of their surplus capital generated by the industrial revolution. The United States produced cotton with the help of slave labour. At one time Brazil, then the Honduras, followed by the Caribbean islands, and lastly Cuba held monopoly over sugar supply, all on account of imported African slave labour.

In India, land revenue was a major source of income for the EIC. About two-thirds of Bengal revenue added to the British pillage so much so that this fleecing had impoverished the State. For example, in 1772, Governor General Warren Hastings wrote the court of directors of the company that even with the loss of at least one-third of the inhabitants (due to famine) of the province of Bengal and consequent decrease of cultivation, the net collections of the year 1771 exceeded even those of 1768. "It was natural that diminution of the revenue kept an equal pace with the other consequences of so great a calamity. That it did not was owing to its being violently kept up to its former standard."[35] EIC rule in the seventeen sixties and seventies extracted from the Bengali peasant everything that could conceivably be extracted from him.[36] In India, a very popular movie "Lagaan" (land revenue) was filmed, based on the tyranny of the white revenue collector. The once opulent and productive land of Bengal had been so ruined and transformed into a place of famine and misery that it is easy to understand why the "drain" took so much hold in debates over the economic consequences of the empire. Next to land revenue it was opium which filled the coffers of the company. The evil of opium was thrust on China against her will. It created a large army of opium eaters in that country only to destroy them and England had no answer for it.[37] Bengal's plunder from Nawab's treasury was so excessive that it fuelled Industrial Revolution from 1760 and changed the world's lifestyle forever. Drain over India's resources was such that by 1850 the country's per capita income dropped by almost two-thirds.[38] Her GDP which was twice that of Europe in the beginning of eighteenth century slumped to one-half of that. It bottomed to less than five percent by the time the British left India. From the beginning British rule was immune to the plight of Indians. Company minions forced peasants normally cultivating food crops for family needs, to switch over to growing poppy (source of opium). They were obliged to sell produce to the company at a fraction of what it would fetch in the open market.[39] Opium became the most valuable adjunct to the ordinary revenues. In 1849-50, the EIC earned 3.30 million pounds sterling from illicit opium trade. The earned amount was equivalent to one half of the cost of maintaining the then best British naval fleet of the world. Little wonder that the company was so flush with money from the opium trade that it paid China for imports of tea, silk, porcelain, met its obligations to India, paid dividends to shareholders and was still left with enough cash.

Annual exports from India exceeded annual imports of merchandise and treasures by 20 million pounds sterling. Some of the excess paid interest on the capital borrowed for the construction of roads and a one-third of the above was shown for the army. Jones empathized with India for this 'heavy burden' because Indians did not need protection from anyone. Indian army consisted of 150,000 native *sepoys* and 75,000 Britons. He questioned why the army of that size and weight should hang as a milestone around India's neck.[40] About two-thirds of Bengal revenue went to British plunder and this pattern prevailed in all European colonies. In 1890 there were 1200 French government officials who were paid 1.75 million dollars per annum as salaries. The amount devoted for public works was 80,000 dollars of which a lot again went to the salaries of officials. So virtually no money was allotted for public works.[41] European mercantile companies vied for profiting from their colonies. The Dutch EIC (VOC) was a successful shipping company charted in 1602. Being a great naval power at the time, the Dutch ousted the Portuguese and the British from the spice trade in the Indonesian archipelago. Operations of the Dutch company were so successful, that by 1723, shares of its stockholders rose by twenty-five folds. Reportedly, a shareholder left to his heirs eight tons of gold.[42] Portugal, who pioneered the spice trade, was notorious for its boorish behaviour toward native chiefs of the East Indies. Portuguese behaved more like tyrants than traders. Consequently, they failed to establish a permanent base neither in Java which produced pepper, nor in the Moluccas, home to nutmeg and cloves. They surreptitiously killed Sultan Hairun of Ternate Island with whom they had a treaty on the clove trade.[43] The incensed natives revolted and expelled them from the islands in 1574.

The British established large tea estates in the salubrious climate of the highlands of Brahmaputra valley in Assam which were run by the white managers. By turn of the nineteenth century Assam was a big producer of black tea. The plantations were a labour-intensive enterprise. British managers hired labour from neighbouring areas through their agents. These bonded labourers cursed their fate once they landed at the tea estate. Brutal and ruthless managers were interested only in extracting maximum work from the undernourished labour. Unknown number of these unfortunate men and women died of exhaustion, unbearable torture and diseases. Those who absconded from abysmal living conditions were recovered through police on the strength of the bond these people happened to sign. Once back at the plantation, the labourers had to endure still harsher treatment often leading to their incapacitation or even death.

Lord Curzon, the viceroy of India, was aware of the working hazards faced by tea labour but felt helpless in bringing succour to them. He knew that the white judiciary and his own executive would never let their compatriots be punished for crimes against the natives. The British also monopolized coffee plantations, salt, and indigo trades. Salt was the third largest source of revenue through salt tax and indigo dye had large demand in Europe. The British also controlled jute processing and trade. Whereas Britain earned millions of pounds sterling from the export of agricultural commodities, India shared only a fraction of the earnings. Annual profit of 20 million pounds sterling that accrued to Britain was used up in England to service interest on the loans and to a large extent pay off salary, pensions, and other expanses on civil and military employees either working or retired from Indian service. Much of this expense was questionable.[44]

The 1897 Welby Commission (Royal Commission) on expenditure studied how the drain of wealth and resources of India by the British were the root cause of India's poverty and misery. Sir Henry Brackenbury told the Commission that Britain's interest in holding India was enormous. India afforded employment to thousands of Britons. The country employed millions of British capital and India's commerce was of an immense value to Great Britain. The British should pay a share of the expenditure.[45]

Imperial interests of Europeans prevailed upon the interests of their dependencies. The biggest casualty of British imperial policy was the handloom cotton textile industry of India, employing thousands of workers. Britain suffocated India's textile industry quality of whose products were unmatched in the world. India manufactured the finest muslins in Bengal and dyed cloth in southern India. Actually, India was the unofficial clothier of the world. It introduced cotton and cotton cloth to the world. Even the army of Alexander the Great substituted their woollens for the Indian cottons. In 1750 India's share in global manufacturing was 25 percent compared to only 1.9 percent for Britain. The colonial government in India had subordinated interests of their adopted country to the government in London. British wool and silk industry was wary of exports of fine quality cloth from India which was in huge demand in the higher rungs of the English society. Britain ensured that fine quality Indian cloth did not enter the country. Kozhikode (Calicut) gave its name to fine quality calico prints popular in Europe. Dacca in Bengal (now in Bangladesh) produced the enviable very fine quality muslins. The woollen cloth manufacturers in Britain detested the import of these textiles. Moreover, Indian calicos were cheaper than British silk and more comfortable than woollen clothing available in England. The British government was pressurized to pass the 1701 Act prohibiting sale and wearing of coloured Indian calicos. The Act of 1721 banned the use of Indian coloured cloth even when printed in England. Lancashire industry managed to influence the government and stall imposition of protective tariffs meant to protect the handloom-based cotton industry of India. They had already managed to throttle India's cotton industry through the 1896 Cotton Duties Act which imposed excise duty of 3.5 percent on cottons made and sold in India simply for the benefit of the Lancashire mills. The British policy was to restrain manufacturing in the colonies. Industrially the British suffocated India whose textiles were of a quality unique in the world. As a result, Indian cotton industry which once dominated world market gasped for breath. Beauchamp regretted, "It was the British intruder who broke up the Indian handloom and destroyed the spinning wheel. England began with driving out Indian cotton from the European market; it then introduced a twist into 'Hindostan' (India), and in the end inundated the very mother country of cotton." The whole pattern of trade reversed where India became net importer of British manufactures.[46] In 1824 Great Britain hardly exported one million yards of muslin to India but in 1837 it surpassed 64 million yards. The population of Dacca, famous for its muslins, decreased from 150,000 inhabitants to 20,000. On the contrary, the government of India was obliged to supply good quality raw cotton to the Lancashire industry as well as reduce tariffs on cloth imported to India. Mahatma Gandhi sought to revive the village cotton industry as a means of self-employment and symbolically carried a spinning wheel on his journeys.

Defrauding poor peasants and weavers: Economic deprivation of India did not stop with strangulating her cotton textile industry. The British had an eye for crops like opium poppy and indigo to profit from. They monopolized the trade in both commodities. India cultivated indigo crop largely in the provinces of Bengal and Bihar not far from the seat of the EIC. English planters captured the market by signing contracts with peasants who were tenants of the landlords. The peasants had to reserve a parcel of land for cultivating indigo. British planters acquired indigo from the growers at an agreed price which was often too small compared with the money that peasants could earn from other crops. Peasants had to accept the agreed price or pay the penalty. Bengal peasants revolted against this exploitation. In the meantime, cheaper synthetic dye began replacing the organic dye. Still, indigo planters of Bihar insisted on realizing contracted Indigo from the peasants or receive penalty of one hundred rupees per contract. The peasant protests shaped into the famous Champaran (Bihar) agitation. Mahatma Gandhi, who had just returned from South Africa, participated in the peaceful agitation. Ultimately, the penalty clause was removed from the contracts. Employees of the EIC fleeced weavers of South India, who weaved colourful cloth. They would meet them through their agents and strike bargains at dirt-cheap rates through clauses in the agreement unintelligible to the artisans who were ignorant of the English language. The weavers though suffering unbearable losses were made to honour their contract with visits of company peons (big bosses to poor natives) and even the militia. The EIC forbade use of its *sepoys* after it realized that it had earned bad publicity.

Britain was accumulating a lot of capital thanks to the industrial revolution and generous largesse of the EIC. Investment of this capital at home offered meagre returns. Hence it was profitable to shift this capital to the colonies for infrastructure development. Colonies like India promised avenues of investment. The EIC which actually generated this capital guaranteed a minimum interest of five percent on money loaned to the company. It employed this money to create infrastructure and promote her business in India. Interior of this large country needed to be connected with the major sea ports by railways in order to transport raw materials from the countryside to England and create a supply line for the manufacturers of England to all corners of India. John Strachey was a senior administrator of the EIC. He candidly admitted that thousands of Englishmen, not only soldiers, but Englishmen of every class, poured into India. Ten thousand things were demanded which India didn't have, but which it felt must be provided. The country must be covered with railway and telegraphs and roads and bridges. Irrigation canals must be made to preserve the people from starvation.[47] Clearly the EIC created infrastructure, not for the sake of Indian masses but to enhance her business and to govern the vast land it had captured. Strachey's reference to irrigation canals as means of preserving people from starvation was misplaced. Tanks were the main source of irrigation in the undulating terrain of southern India. Previously native kings regularly repaired them. The EIC ignored this task; the tanks deteriorated and went out of commission. Visiting English engineers even criticized the company for this neglect. It was the 1840 famine of Godavari delta that prompted the company to seek services of an irrigation engineer Sir Arthur Cotton. Sir Arthur proposed to repair the older canals and the construction of new canals for irrigation as well as means of transport in the interior. Canals increased revenue assessment manifolds. Appearing before the select committee on the promotion of European colonisation and settlement of India on 29th June 1858, Colonel W.C. Onslow testified that irrigation works at Godavari were yielding a permanent surplus of one to two million rupees annually, even though less than a quarter of the land was fully watered.[48] The company wanted raw cotton produced through irrigation in the interior areas and the rails to transport the same to harbours for shipping onwards to Britain. Interest on money invested for irrigation and railway works was five percent per annum. Irrigation works like Yamuna Canal, Sirhind Canal and the irrigation works on Godavari River yielded 26.7 to 35 percent on the capital invested. Between 1867 and 1878 the colonial government of India invested more than 18.5 million and 10.5 million pounds on railways and canals respectively.[49] The 1886 Imperial gazetteer of India noted that the average assessment on land in the Madras presidency increased more than four folds under canal irrigation.[50] The EIC was in a win-win situation by constructing canals with borrowed capital. Colonial governments advertised themselves for this benevolence which was clearly an embellishment.

Indian rulers constructed canals as public welfare works. The EIC, true to its wont, saw profit in this venture. The Moghul King Akbar through a *sanad* of 1568 ordered the restoration of the defunct Feroze

Shah Tughlak canal that irrigated the Hansi and Hissar areas in the present state of Haryana. "My wisdom wishes that the hopes, like the fields of those thirsty people may, by the showers of liberty and kindness, be made green and flourishing, and that the canal may, in my time, be renewed and that conducting other waters into it, may endure for ages."[51]

The EIC viewed the renovation of the same canal from a different angle. More than one hundred years later, Governor General Lord Hastings, who toured the area, saw profit in restoring this canal. "I will only say that my own inspection has fully convinced me of the facility and policy of immediately restoring this noble work. Setting aside the consideration of its certain effects[52] in bringing in cultivation, vast tracts of country now deserted and thereby augmenting importantly the land revenue of the honourable company, due to be collected from the distribution of water from it, would make a most lucrative return."[53] Lord Hastings added that money laid for this purpose would be more profitable than it would in any other mode of application. He was on the mark about profitability of the project. By 1926–27, accumulated surplus revenue produced by the canal stood at 67 million Indian rupees (then about five million pounds sterling), the canal had paid back four times the expenditure on its works. In 1902–03, the Lower Chenab canal, another canal in Punjab, produced a net profit of 21.3 percent on the capital invested. In 1903, Lower Ganga, Western Yamuna (Feroze Shah Tughlak canal), and Upper Bari Doab canals of India returned a net revenue of over 38 percent on the capital outlay. Clearly, capital invested on irrigation canals was a highly profitable venture for the EIC from the revenue angle alone.

Prime consideration for constructing irrigation canals in northern India was to produce long-staple cottons for the Lancashire textile industry. Himalayan rivers carried lot of water which could be profitably used. The British could sell all that water for a price to the farmers primarily for producing cotton. English industry depended upon cotton imports from the United States. Between 1820 and 1840, 75 percent of high-quality cotton was supplied by the Georgia and Mississippi states. The British were wary of the lone source of cotton supply. Now Britain had a colony like India to produce cotton for the home textile industry after harnessing the river water to irrigate semi-arid areas of the country.

The British government sent Lieutenant Thomas Bayles to the United States to collect seeds of promising cotton varieties. His mission was vehemently opposed by American planters who feared that India with its cheap labour would undersell its cotton. Nevertheless, Bayles collected cotton seeds and hired few experts for growing cotton in North-western India. British efforts fructified because by 1863, Britain was able to make up the shortfall in the cotton supply caused by blockade of southern ports by the Federal navy during the American Civil War. One effect of disruption in raw cotton supplies to Lancashire industry was the inflated prices which hurt world economy. India, once a supplier of textiles to the world was transformed by British policies into a supplier of raw cotton to the very country it used to clothe. Lord Ellenborough who was governor-general of India 1842–44 envisioned India as one great empire bound closely with Great Britain. He analysed that India will grow cotton for his country and Britain will sell cloth to India because cotton would enhance the buying capacity of the Indians.[54] It was not only India, but also the British colonies of Australia and the Caribbean which produced raw cotton for the British industry. Australia was the main source of wool for the British manufacturers. Retired army and naval officers had moved in there and captured lands of the natives to raise herds of sheep. The whites also captured lands of the natives along the rivers. When the natives protested, they were treated like wild dogs and shot.

Surplus British capital also found outlets in the construction of railroads across the colonies. Western financiers found that higher rate of return could be earned financing main line colonial railways than suburban lines in Europe. This was a very costly undertaking financed by borrowed capital which was to be repaid by India in foreign exchange. Lancashire cotton mills impressed upon the British government to connect Calcutta (Kolkata), Bombay (Mumbai), and Madras (Chennai) harbours with raw cotton supplying centres of India. Importance of railways as a fast mode of troop movement was realised in the 1857 sepoy uprising in India. It was a convenient mode of long-distance travel when British officers and officials moved to hill stations during the hot summer months. Development of rail transport for the sake of the natives was the least concern of the colonial government. Normally Indians could not board higher class coaches meant only for white passengers. In case they had a ticket for a particular coach they were asked to change the coach, regardless of empty berths, should a white passenger happen to board the same coach from a wayside station. In short Europeans travelled in style at the cost of poor Indian tax payers. Mahatma Gandhi, then a young lawyer in South Africa, booked a first-class seat for travel to Pretoria to appear for his client in a court of law. He was seated in the compartment when a white passenger boarded the same coach on the way. The white man protested to the railway guard for the presence of a non-white person in the compartment and insisted on shifting Gandhi to a third-class compartment. Gandhi refused to oblige the guard insisting that he held a booking for the first-class coach. Upon this the guard threw Gandhi along with his baggage on the railway platform where he spent the whole cold night in the open. This narrative has produced sceptics. Yet it is a fact that colonial governments constructed railway lines to meet their own needs. The British invested 10.57 million pounds sterling of borrowed capital on canal construction in India in the intervening years of 1867–68 and 1877–78.[55] During the same period 18.64 million pounds sterling of borrowed capital was spent on Indian railways. Most shareholders of Indian railways resided in London and collected their profits in pound sterling. The companies who invested their money received guaranteed interest come rain or shine in India.

Austin analysed advantages that accrued to the colonial powers from their colonies. Great Britain was the most successful coloniser followed by France.[56] Spain's experiment with colonies could not crystallise because Great Britain and America opposed its presence in areas they considered their domain. Moreover, Spanish colonies in South America and the Caribbean were captured by conquistadors, in the first place for plunder and then for harvesting their natural and mineral resources in the shortest possible time. Other Europeans scrambled for colonies to expand their empires, enlarge markets for their industrial products, secure supply of raw materials for their industries, plunder natural resources and minerals, and create job opportunities for the burgeoning unemployed at home. Great Britain created a large market for her industrial products especially textiles in India by strangulating the flourishing native textile industry. While Great Britain flourished in 1850, India's debt had grown to 53 million pounds. From 1850–1900, its per capita income had dropped by almost two-thirds.[57] It was only in the 1930s that the British government in India ignored opposition of home cotton industry to safeguard India's development. Africa was a great market for her textiles. In 1897, British colonies absorbed 41 percent of their imports from Great Britain, while the non-British world got just 14 percent of total imports from the same source.[58] Colonies provided Britain a market for her products worth 250 million dollars more than what she could expect from the non-British world. Expanded market for British manufacturers benefitted home labour. It is incorrect to ignore the time factor while evaluating the contributions of the Europeans to their colonies. Analysts are tempted to count roads, railways, post-offices, telegraph lines, and other infrastructure development forgetting that these were created for administration and with the march of time for the convenience of Europeans who were either employed in the colonial service, military, private business, or managed plantations and industries. India, for example paid for thousands of Europeans employed not only in India but also in England in the account of the government of India service. Europeans held all plum posts. As a matter of policy, no natives, howsoever deserving, were ever posted to a position of responsibility as head of a district or head of a department or institution. Lord Curzon found it strange that there were no Indian natives in the Government of India. Among all the 300 million people of the subcontinent there was not a single person capable of a job in the senior government positions.[59] British officers enjoyed, as prerequisites of their positions, large furnished and guarded bungalows with lawns maintained at government expense, all other living amenities for comfort, a retinue of native servants for cooking, cleaning, polishing shoes, ironing clothes, errand running and pulling fans in days when there were no electric fans. India supported thousands of such men each in civil service, foreign, police and military services and in departments of central and provincial governments. The Indian civil service, the backbone of the government, was white only in its covenanted category. It manned all strategic positions in the government providing the so-called 'steel-frame'. Indians entered the civil service through unconventional category meant for the lower rungs of administration. It was rare for a European to be subordinate to a native officer. Only five to 15 percent Indians entered this service; that too in the twentieth century. Europeans including former civil and military personnel received pensions and salaries and enjoyed all post-retirement benefits while resting in their own country. India Office in London was manned by staff paid by the government of India. The British maintained a large Indian army to match that of Germany and France. Many military campaigns and even expenses of the World Wars were a charge on India. The cost of maintaining the British army in India was paid by the Indians to the tune of 200 million dollars a year. Wars in which Indian troops fought for the British were paid by taxes on Indians to the tune of 1.2 billion dollars in the late 1800s. All of these charges had reduced India from once being the second largest world economy to a basket case by 1947.[60] Indians had begun questioning the drain of India's resources in the last decades of British rule. A resolution during the 1929 session of the All India Congress Committee referred to the British ruining India economically through revenue collection disproportionately to the income of the peasants, manipulation of customs and currency to heap burden on the peasantry and partiality in imposing custom duty on the import of British manufactures.[61]

The viceroys of India enjoyed opulent living in plains as well as in the hills during summer. They rarely visited the countryside to find out the living conditions of the natives. They held *Durbars* (imperial assembly) in honour of king/queen on their coronation as emperor/empress of the Indian empire. Lord (Edward Robert) Lytton held a *Durbar* in 1877 to proclaim Queen Victoria as empress of India. He invited 84,000 guests for the festivities at a time when India had not recovered from the 1876 famine of South India which claimed millions of lives. The 1903 *Durbar*, arranged by Lord Curzon, celebrated the succession of King Edward VII and Queen Alexandra as emperor and empress of India. It had hundreds of rajas and Nawabs in attendance felicitating honoured guests with marvellous presents. World press covered this magnificent event. Lord Harding held an opulent *Durbar* of 1911 in honour of King George V. A city of 40,000 tents was created near Delhi to house 300,000 guests. The pecuniary obligation for the poor Indians was close to one and a half million dollars (about one billion dollars in today's money).[62] A distinct feature of these *Durbars* was the protocol of salutations by the native rulers of India to the dignitary. It did not mean a token respect, but a complete submission expressed in the humblest way to acknowledge the superiority of the exalted ruler. Native princes (rulers) all bedecked with pearls and jewels would come forward, place their presents a few steps below the platform where the dignitary was seated, lay their sword and then bow reverently up to waist three times before the emperor/empress. According to the protocol they would withdraw a few steps backwards before stepping back laterally to the flanks without ever turning their back to the monarch. The only native ruler, who broke away from the protocol during the 1911 *Durbar*, was the Maharaja (Gaekwad) of Baroda, who presented himself before King George V without donning full regalia. He bowed only once and walked away turning his back to the monarch in, what was perceived, a disrespectful manner. That was how he despised the foreign rule. On their part the British always kept the Maharaja at bay.

The institution of native rulers was a system of indirect rule practiced in parts of British and French colonies. Native rulers were not entirely independent but at the mercy of foreign office or colonial office back home. In practice they were minions of the colonial government, overseen by a resident commissioner and in some cases a section of the army, all paid by the native state. The colonial government expected absolute obedience from them. Europeans were averse to let go their dominions and native rulers who were their eyes and ears helped them in this effort. Curzon had declared in no uncertain terms, "As long as we rule India, we are the greatest power in the world. If we lose it, we shall drop straight way to third-rate power."[63] Half the structure of British Empire was merely scaffolding for the possession of India. Churchill, a strong votary of imperialism, admitted that "shrinkage in foreign trade and shipping brings the surplus population of Britain within measurable distance of utter ruin... It is unsound logic therefore to suppose that England alone among the nations will be willing to part with her control over a great dependency like India."[64] The issue of *Times* (London) of 11th November 1942, carried his refrain that he had not become King's First Minister in order to preside over the liquidation of British Empire.[65] It was indeed only his war-time deputy prime minister Clement Attlee, who as Labour party prime minister, let go of India. The scaffolding of British Empire had begun to unravel and natives of other European

292

colonies intensified their struggle for independence from the colonial rule.

Of all European powers, Britain left marked footprints in her colonies. In India it was the remnants of the colonial civil service and subordinate services which avoided chaos during the transfer of power when India and Pakistan became independent countries. An important legacy of British colonial rule was the unification of the country which at the time of occupation existed as several warring ethnic and regional fiefdoms. The British enacted legislative measures to hold on to the country whose fringe benefit was bringing order out of disorder in the fractured Indian society. They introduced English to run the colony, but it became their single most important contribution to polity of the subcontinent. Economic growth of a nation is determined by the education level of its masses. Indians became keen to learn English after the supreme court was established in Calcutta (Kolkata) in 1773. The natives rose to the occasion and established the Hindu College in 1817. It was taken over by the British in 1855 and converted to Presidency College which produced scholars of eminence. Presidency College in Madras (Chennai) was established in 1857 and the University of Bombay also came up the same year. In South Africa, Afrikaners were only interested in biblical education imparted through the church and they opposed education in the English medium which began with the first such school in 1827. A multicultural South African college which came up in 1829 became the University of Cape Town in 1918. In Kenya, a school was opened in 1846 in Mombasa and one in Nairobi in 1903 which indicates low priority to education in Africa. The Africans were taxed but tax revenue was largely spent on providing services and economic benefits largely for the Europeans. In 1920–23 the Africans contributed 70 percent to the tax revenue of Kenya but almost nothing was spent on developing the native reserves. Racialist writers added to the course against the Africans. It was asserted that black Africans were genetically incapable of engaging in higher intellectual activity. In fact, non-British colonial powers had no interest in educating the natives. In the large French colony of Algeria, which was considered another province of France, only French settlers had the facility of education. Majority of the natives had no access to schools. The case of Portugal was worst. The natives of Angola and Mozambique, with few exceptions, were illiterate. In fact, until the first quarter of the twentieth century a majority of Portugal's own population was illiterate.

British *literati* especially scientists, geographers, and surveyors held passion for documenting natural resources of the colonies. In Africa, their occupation was to discover and evaluate groundwater and mineral resources of the colonies. In India, they established great scientific bodies in mineral, plant, animal, fisheries, and every conceivable subject demanding inquiry. Lord Curzon, the then viceroy of India, received a large sum of money for promoting science in India. A farsighted Curzon realized the importance of agriculture in India. He opened agricultural colleges in the agriculturally important provinces of India and an agricultural research institute at Pusa in Bihar. These colleges turned into agricultural universities in the independent India and helped the food grain-deficient land to become a surplus in food. The British created public health facilities which later became the model for the subcontinent. It is to their credit that they collected scattered religious literature and conserved it in the India Office Library. Good governance demands that people have no occasion for grievance. That goal requires great amount of sacrifice which most colonial governments were not ready for. They had to quit their colonies after obstinate resistance.

Notes

Introduction

1. Alan Moorhead, *The Fatal Impact: The Invasion of the South Pacific 1767-1840* (New York: Harper and Row Publishers, 1966), 230.

2. Thomas Keneally, *A Commonwealth of Thieves. The Improbable birth of Australia* (Australia: Random House, 2005), 365.

3. Horst Drechsler, *Let Us Die Fighting: The Struggle of Herero and Nama against German Imperialism 1884-1915 (*London: Zed Press, Caledonian Road, 1966), pp. 278.

4. Norman Leys, *Kenya* (London: Frank Cass, 1973), 425.

5. Caroline Elkins, *Imperial Reckoning. The untold story of Britain's Gulag in Kenya* (New York: Henry Holt and Co., 2010), 496.

6. *Another secret weapon inadvertently wielded by Europeans against the natives was the contagious diseases they carried in their bodies. Majority of natives with no resistance against diseases like smallpox and tuberculosis were wiped out.*

7. Why *Terra Nullius*? People had lived there since the last ice age and their ancestors had been in the hinterland for millennia longer (Keneally 2005, 60). Christian writes about the rich intellectual and mental world of Palaeolithic ancestors who produced cave art in many parts of Australia. See, David Christian, *Origin Story-A Big History of Everything* (New York: Little, Brown and Company, 2018).

Chapter 1: Europe's Eastern Trade and Colonisation

1. Richard S. Hall, *Empires of the Monsoon: A History of the Indian Ocean and its Invaders* (London: Harper Collins, 1996), 397.

2. *Portugal's naval prowess had declined due to her dwindling resources of wood for ship building and growing strength of the European rivals.*

3. Andre Maurois, *History of England* (New York: Farrar, Strauss & Co., 1937), 465.

4. Vyjayanti Raghvan and R. Mahalakshmi Eds. *A Comparative Study of India and Korea* (New Delhi: Academic Foundation, 2015), 261.

5. *The then British Monarchs wielded far more authority than being mere constitutional heads of the government.*

6. *The word factory is derived from factor — a person who acts for others in business or other transactions. The factory is therefore a business establishment.*

7. John Keay, *India: A History*, (New York: Atlantic Monthly Press, 2000), 390.

8. R. C. Majumdar, M. C. Raychaudhury and Kalikinkar Datta, *An Advanced History of India* (London: Macmillan & Co. Ltd. 1946).

9. Winston S. Churchill, *A History of English-Speaking Peoples #3. The Age of Revolution* (New York: Dodd; Mead & Company, 1957), 223.

10. Kumar Goshal, *People in the Colonies* (New York: Sheridan House Publishers, 1948), 124.

11. Nial Ferguson, *Empire: The Rise and Demise of the British World Order and the Lessons for Global Power* (New York: Basic Books, 2002), 44.

12. Brooks Adams, *The Law of Civilization and Decay. An Essay on History* (New York: The Macmillan Co.1896), 259.

13. Ramesh Dutt, *The Economic History of India Under Early British Rule* (New York: Augustus Kelley Publishers, 1969), 39.

14. John Strachey, *The End of Empire* (New York: Random House, 1960), 36.

15. Keay, 397. A part reason was that France wished to abandon India ambitions.

16. *Talpur Amirs of Sind were descendants of Mir Tala Khan Baloch. They were a Balochi-speaking tribe from Dera Gazi Khan who conquered Sind in 1783.*

17. Percival J. Griffiths, *Empire into Commonwealth* (London: Earnest Benn Ltd., 1969), 161.

18. *The agreement signed on April 5, 1849 with the young Maharaja of Punjab envisaged his resigning for himself and heirs all titles and claims to the sovereignty of the Punjab, confiscation of state property to pay expenses of war. The Maharaja was supposed to surrender the Koh-i-Noor diamond to the Queen of England.*

Chapter 2: Discovery and Colonisation of the Americas

1. V. G. Kiernan, *The Lords of Human Kind: Black Man, Yellow Man, and White Man in an Age of Empire* (Boston: Little Brown and Co., 1969), 9.

2. Poulten Bigelow, *The Children of the Nations: A Study of Colonisation and its Problems* (New York: Mclure, Philips and Co., 1901), 4.

3. Percival Griffths, *Empire into Commonwealth* (London: Earnest Benn Ltd., 1969), 5.

4. Herman Merivale, *Lectures on Colonisation and Colonies* (New York: A. M. Kelley, 1967), 4.

5. Mark Crocker, *Rivers of Blood, Rivers of Gold: Europe's Conflict with Tribal Peoples* (London: Jonathan Cape, 1998), 66.

6. Cottie Burland, *Aztecs, Gods, and Fate in Ancient Mexico*, (New York: Galahad, 1980), 119–120.

7. New Spain meant conquered Spanish possessions in the Caribbean and the Aztec Empire. Later it included all of Mexico and parts of south-western North America.

8. Bigelow, 26.

9. Ibid.

10. Merivale, *Lectures on Colonisation*, 5.

11. Bigelow, 34.

12. Virginia was an unnamed part of north-eastern America when Sir Walter Raleigh went there on a commission of Queen Elizabeth I. He named this part of the country Virginia in honour of the queen who fancied to be called Virgin Queen of England.

13. W. Alleyne Ireland, Growth of British Colonial Conception, *Atlantic Monthly*, Vol. 83.2, (April 1899): 489.

14. George B. Adams, "A Century of Anglo-Saxon Expansion", *Atlantic Monthly* 79 (April 1897): 531.

15. Thomas M. Anderson, "Our Rule in the Philippines — 1898–1912," The *North American Review* 170 (1900): 280.

16. Mark Twain, "To the person sitting in darkness." *The North American Review* 81(1901):171.

17. James A. Blount, *The American Occupation of the Philippines*

1898-1912 (New York: G. P. Putnam's Sons, 1912), 202.

18. Paul A. Kramer, *The Blood of Government, Race, Empire, the United States & the Philippines* (Chapel Hill: University North Carolina Press, 2006), 144.

19. Ibid. 143.

20. Blount, 91–92.

Chapter 3: Australasian Natives, the Innocent Victims

1. Alan Moorehead, *The Fatal Impact: The Invasion of the South Pacific* (New York: Harper and Row Publishers, 1966), 8.

2. Ibid, 106.

3. *Port Jackson was named after judge advocate of the Admiralty.*

4. *The illusion is to British losing her American colonies as a land for exiling the British convicts.*

5. The *Bloody Code was a list of offences which could attract death penalty. In 1776 the list included 220 offences. In 1823 judgment of Death Penalty Act made death penalty discretionary. By 1861 the list shrank to five offences.*

6. Thomas Keneally, *A Commonwealth of Thieves: The Improbable Birth of Australia* (Australia: Random House, 2005), 9.

7. Ibid, 163.

8. Ibid, 164.

9. David Christian, *Origin Story: A Big History of Everything* (New York: Little, Brown and Company, 2018), 218.

10. A. Grenfell Price, *White Settlers and Native Peoples: An Historical Study of Racial contacts between English-speaking whites and aboriginal peoples in the United States, Canada, Australia and New Zealand* (Melbourne: Georgian House, 1949), 106.

11. Keneally, 78.

12. Lyndall Ryan, *The Aboriginal Tasmanians* (Vancouver: University of British Columbia Press, 1981), 4.

13. Frank W. Nicholas and Jan M. Nicholas, *Charles Darwin in Australia* (Cambridge: Cambridge University Press, 1949), 30.

14. Keneally, 238.

15. Ibid, 328. Blumenbach inspector of the museum of natural history in Gottingen, Germany researched in comparative anatomy.

Blumenbach studied human skulls and on this basis he divided the human species into five races.

16. Moorehead, 169.

17. Price, 105.

18. Ibid, 113.

19. Albert Holt, *Forcibly Removed* (Broom, West Australia: Magabala Books, 2001), 20.

20. Price, 111.

21. Mark Crocker, *Rivers of Blood, Rivers of Gold. Europe conflict with Tribal Peoples* (New York: Grove Press, 1998), 125.

22. Nial Ferguson, *Empire: The Rise and Demise of British World Order and the Lessons for the Global Power* (New York: Basic Books, 2000), 109.

23. Price, 158.

24. George B. Adams, "A Century of Anglo-Saxon Expansion," *Atlantic Monthly* 79 (1897): 531.

25. Price, 117.

26. *Ngai in Bantu language is high God of the Kikuyu tribe of Kenya. It is also a Chinese family name. Several Kenyan tribes use this name which means creator. The origin of this name in Maori Society is either fortuitous or a subject of study.*

27. *Philippa Mein Smith, A Case History of New Zealand* (Cambridge, U.K.: Cambridge University Press, 2005), 36.

28. *Percival J. Griffths, Empire into Common Wealth* (London: Earnest Benn Ltd., 1969), 127.

29. Robert A. Huttenback, *Racism and Empire: White Settlers and Colored Immigrants in the British Self-Governing Colonies 1830-1910* (Ithaca: Cornell University Press, 1976), 52.

30. Ian H. Kawharu ed., *Waitangi: Māori and Pākehā Perspectives of the Treaty of Waitangi* (Auckland and New York: oxford University Press, 1989), 73.

31. Ibid, 73.

32. Colin MacInnes, *Australia and New Zealand*, (New York: Time Incorporated 1964), 28.

Chapter 4: Europe's Trespass to Plunder China

1. Anthony Esler, *The Western World: A Narrative History-Pre-History to Present* (Upper Saddle River, New Jersey: Prentice Hall, 1997), 345.

2. Easton Stewart, *The Rise and Fall of Western Colonialism* (New York: Fredrick A. Praeger, 1965), 11.

3. *Queen Catherine of Braganza, married to King Charles II of England was from Portugal, the importer of Chinese tea. She is said to have popularized tea as a drink and introduced England to cottons and porcelain which Portugal imported from India and China.*

4. Glen Melancon, *Britain's China Policy and Opium Crisis: Balancing Drugs, Violence, and National Honor, 1833–1840* (Aldershot, England: Ashgate Publishing, 2003), 18.

5. Spanish silver was the same silver which Spain hauled from South America in the sixteenth and seventeenth century.

6. Quoted by Melancon, 18.

7. John W. Kaye, *The Administration of East India Company: A History of Indian progress.* Reprinted (Allahabad: Kitab Mahal Pvt. Ltd.1966), 683.

8. Stephan L. Baldwin, *Mrs. "China-A Missionary's View"* (New York: Out Look, September 1900), 106.

9. John Strachey, *India its Administration and Progress* (London; Macmillan Company Ltd.1911), 153.

10. Melancon, 18. *While China was the only available source of tea, the EIC had the advantage of the trade monopoly for all tea imported in to Britain. In 1834 the Assam area was found to have some naturally growing tea plants but those were of poor quality.*

11. Strachey, 142. *The EIC was able to earn so much revenue because it had forced peasants to grow opium crops in place of food crops even at the cost of starving their families.*

12. Ibid, 153.

13. Melancon, 35. Napier was so confident of subduing the Chinese that he recorded in his diary that Empire was his own.

14. Baldwin Mrs.108. *Mention of "Opium Tea Party" symbolized "Boston Tea Party" Which was a precursor to the American Revolution.*

15. Bernard Porter, *Empire Ways. Aspects of British Imperialism* (London: I. B. Tauris, 2016), 59.

16. Baldwin Mrs., 110. *Being an American herself she was pained to point out that except one honorable exception all merchants of America fell for concessions like the other Europeans. The one trade item she had strong objection to was opium.*

17. David A Wells, The Truth about the Opium War (New York: *Atlantic Monthly*, 1896), 757–760.

18. Alexander Joseph, The Truth about the Opium War (The University of Northern Iowa: *The North American Review* 163, 1896), 381–83.

19. John Strachey, *The End of Empire* (New York: Random house, 1960), 71.

20. Paul S. Reinsch, *World Politics at the End of the Nineteenth Century as Influenced by the Oriental Situation* (New York: The Macmillan Co., 1900), 70.

21. Matt Schiavenza, How Humiliation Drove Modern Chinese History (New York: *The Atlantic October* 2013).

22. Baldwin Mrs. 110. *As a missionary she was appalled that European allies forced the Imperial government of China to decree that Catholic bishops will enjoy same ranks, powers and privileges as her own viceroys and governors.*

23. Bingham Woodbridge, Hillary Conroy, and Frank W. Ikle, *The History of Asia Vol. II; Old Empires. Western Penetration and the Rise of United Nations Since 1600* (Boston: Allyn and Bacon Inc., 1965), 336.

24. Strachey, 127.

25. Mark Twain, To the Person sitting in the Darkness (New York; *The North American Review*, February 1901), 161-76.

Chapter 5: Pan-European Slicing of Africa

1. C. Sehloane Keto, "The Africans and the Dutch in the Seventeenth and Eighteenth centuries. The failure of peaceful coexistence," *J. African Affairs*, Vol. III, 2, (1978): 197.

2. *The Times* , 3 September 1900.

3. Griqua land. The area occupied by Griquas who were a progeny of Boer males and Khoi Khoi females.

4. Uitlanders – *Afrikaner term for British and non-Afrikaner persons who migrated to the Boer Republics as prospectors of diamonds and*

gold. The British covertly encouraged migration of their compatriots to the Boer Republics.

5. Burgers were Boer volunteers who responded to call of duty from their compatriots.

6. James Morris, *Farewell Trumpets: An Imperial Retreat* (New York: Harcourt Brace Jovanovich, 1978), 66.

7. Denis Judd and Keith Surridge, *The Boer War* (London: John Murray, 2002), 191.

8. *The Times* 17 September 1900.

9. Niall Ferguson, *Empire: The Rise and Demise of British World order and Lessons for the British Global Power* (New York: Basic Books, 2002), 228.

10. Calvinists, Followers of the religious doctrine of John Calvin.

11. Andre Maurois, *History of England* (New York: Farrar, Strauss, & Co., 1937), 465.

12. Keith Irvine, "British Hanging 50 Africans a Month," *Africa Today. Bulletin of American Committee on Africa* (March-April 1955), 4.

13. To hang a person for possessing a couple of bullets speaks of the kind of highhandedness endured by the natives.

14. Alleyne Ireland W., "European Experience with Tropical Colonies," *Atlantic Monthly* 83 No.2 (1898): 528–39.

15. Barry Munslow, *Mozambique: The revolution and its origins*, (London: Longmans, 183).

16. Jean Stenger, *Britain and Germany in Africa. Imperial Rivalry and Colonial Rule,* In. Eds. Prosser Gifford, William Roger Louis, and Allison Smith. Yale University Concilium on International Studies (New Haven: Yale University Press, 1967), 340.

17. A. J. Temu, *Tanzanian Societies and Colonial Invasion 1875–1907. In Tanzania under Colonial Rule.* Ed. M.H.Y. Kaniki (London: Longman, 1980), 119.

18. Rhenish Missionary Society was the largest missionary society in Germany. Established in 1828 it sent her missionaries to South Africa. It was assisted in her mission by the well-established London Missionary Society. After South Africa, it expanded the operations to China, Sumatra, and New Guinea. It brokered peace deals between the tribes of South Africa.

19. Mark Crocker, *Rivers of Blood Rivers of Gold, Europe's Conquest of Indigenous Peoples* (London: Jonathan Cape, 1998), 326.

20. M. Semakula Kiwanuka, "Colonial Policies and Administration in Africa: The Myth of Contrasts," *African Historical Studies* III, 2 (1970): 295–315.

Chapter 6: Perfidious Treaties that Helped Colonisation

1. Kenneth O. Hall, Humanitarianism and Racial Subordination. John Mackenzie and the Transformation of Tswana Society. *The Inter. J. Hist. Studies* (Stockholm: 1966): 97–107.

2. M. Semakula Kiwanuka, "Colonial Policies and Administration in Africa: The Myth of Contrasts," *African Historical Studies* III, 2 (1970): 296.

3. Ronald Hyam and Ged Martin, *Reappraisals in British Imperial History* (London: Macmillan Press Ltd., 1975), 152.

4. John Mackenzie, *The Partition of Africa and European Imperialism 1800-1900 (Lancaster Pamphlets)* (London: Routledge, 1989), 152.

5. Niall Ferguson, *Empire: The Rise and Fall of the British World Order and Lessons for the Global Power* (New York: Basic Books, 2000), 225.

6. Eric Exelson, *Portugal and the Scramble for Africa 1870-1891* (Johannesburg: Witwatersrand, 1967), 149. The 1884 Berlin Conference, where Africa was partitioned, was in part an initiative of Portugal. The latter gave in when Britain refused to yield any land area between Portuguese colonies of Mozambique and Angola. Portugal's Pink map dream did not materialize against the British fortitude and Cecil Rhodes Cape to Cairo link plan which though stood thwarted by German East Africa (present Tanzania) and Belgian Congo.

7. Philemon T. Makonese, "Zapu and the Liberation of Zimbabwe," *Africa Quarterly*, 10(1): 41.

8. Ferguson, 225. Rudd Concession was obtained through malicious falsehood. The participants in this subterfuge were Rhodes men, and Helm who witnessed the deal, all members of a 'civilized white race'. The Concession was Rhodes first step to annex the Matabele Kingdom.

9. Lochner Concession was an epitome of duplicity and fraud very

cleverly played upon unsuspecting King Lewanika by Rhodes emissary Frank Lochner, one from a 'civilized white race.' The latter wove such a web of disinformation that an unsuspecting Lewanika was caught in it.

10. A foreign trading company arrogating itself to deal in thrones and install a governor of her liking shows that East India Company fortunes brightened because writ of the titular rulers of the time did not run beyond the palace walls. Grearson opined that had Moghul Empire been as in Jahangir's time the East India Company would still have been confined to its trading posts around rim of the subcontinent; See Edward Grearson, *The Imperial Dream. The British Commonwealth and Empire 1775–1969* (London: Collins, 1972), 41.

11. Charles Wilson, *Englishmen of Action. Lord Clive* (London: Macmillan and Co., 1899), 107.The author argues that Amin Chand (Omi Chand) deserved his share of spoils as promised because he had risked his life and put his future on the line had the plans failed.

12. Percival Spears, *Master of Bengal; Clive and His India* (London: Thames and Hudson, 1975), 85.

13. Mark Bence-Jones, *Clive of India* (London: Constable, 1974), 128.

14. Ibid, 147.

15. Ibid, 148.

16. There are various versions of the episode. Amin Chand must have been shocked by the trickery played on him by Clive and his associates. He held his head and sat down. It is unlikely that he fell down in shock.

17. Horst Drechsler, *Let Us Die Fighting: The Struggle of Herero and Nama People against German Imperialism 1884–1915* (57 Caledonian Road, London: Zed Press, 1966), 23.

18. Ibid, 24.

19. Ibid, 25.

Chapter 7: Natives Lose Their Lands in the Americas, Africa and Australasia

1. Collin Samson and Carlos Gioux, *Indigenous Peoples and Colonialism. Global Perspectives* (Cambridge U.K.: Polity Press, 2017), 146.

2. David A. Wells, "The Truth about the Opium War," *The North American Review* Vol. 102 No. 475 (June 1896), 759-60.

3. Stewart Easton, *The Rise and Fall of Western Colonialism* (New York: Fredrick A. Praeger Inc.1994), 122.

4. Stuart Banner, *How the Indians Lost Their Land: Law and Power of the Frontier* (Cambridge: The Bulknap Press of Harvard University Press, 2005).

5. Olufemi Osmosini, "The Gold Coast Land Question, 1894–1900: Some Issues Raised on West Africa's Economic Development," *International Journal of African Historical Studies* Vol. 3(1972): 455.

6. Elain A. Friedland, "The Political Economy of Colonialism in South Africa and Mozambique," *J. African Affairs* Vol. II No 1, (January 1997): 63.

7. Friedland, 63.

8. Ibid. 64.

9. Ibid. 62–63.

10. Gorden H. Mungeam, *British Rule in Kenya 1895–1912. The establishment of administration in the East Africa protectorate* (Oxford: Clarendon Press, 1966), 112.

11. Ibid. 112–13.

12. Ibid. 113.

13. Bethwell A. Ogot, "British administration in Central Nayanza district of Kenya 1900–60," *The J. African Hist.* IV, 2 (1963): 260.

14. Ibid. 258.

15. M. Semakula Kiwanuka, "Colonial Policies and Administration in Africa: The Myth of Contrasts," *African Historical Studies* III, 2 (1970): 296.

16. Ibid. 298.

17. Owen J. M. Kalinga, "European Settlers, African Apprehensions and Colonial Economic Policy. The North Nyasa Reserves Commission of 1929," *Intern. J. African His. Studies* 17, 4 (1984): 644.

18. Ibid. 645.

19. Kumar Goshal, *People in Colonies* (New York: Seridon House Publishers, 1948), 135.

20. Horst Drechsler, *"Let Us Die Fighting" The Struggle of Herero and Nama Against German Imperialism (1884–1915),* (London: Zed

Press Clarendon Road, 1966), 150.

21. Mark Crocker, *Rivers of Blood, Rivers of Gold. Europe's Conquest of Indigenous Peoples* (London: Jonathan Cape, 1998), 322.

22. Ibid. 333.

23. Azzedine Haddour, *Colonial Myths: History of Narrative* (Manchester: Manchester University Press, 2000), 113.

24. Ibid. 113.

Chapter 8: Slavery and Colonisation: The Connection

1. Giles Martin, *White Gold: The Extraordinary Story of Thomas Pellow and Islam's One Million Slaves* (New York: Ferrar, Straus and Giroux, 2005), 271.

2. Bernard Porter, *Critics of Empire: British Radical Attitudes to Colonialism in Africa 1895–1914* (London: MacMillan, 1968), 67.

3. William H. Woodward, *A Short History of the Expansion of the British Empire* (Cambridge: At the University Press, 1941), 308.

4. Eric R. Wolfe, *Europe and the People without History* (Berkeley, Los Angeles, London: University of California Press, 1982), 110.

5. Cesare Lombroso, Was Columbus Morally Irresponsible? *The Forum 27* (March 1899), 543.

6. George Orwell, *British Pamphleteers* (London: A Wingate, 1948), 243.

7. James Duffy, *Africa Speaks:* in James Duffy and Robert A. Manners eds. (Princeton: D. Van Nostrand, 1961), 134.

8. Eastern Stewart, *The Rise and Fall of Western Colonialism. A Historical Survey from the Nineteenth Century to the Present* (New York: Fredrick A. Praeger, 1964), 122.

9. Frank W. Pitman, *Development of the British West Indies 1700-1763* (New Haven: Yale University Press, 1917), 70.

Chapter 9: Instruments of Stranglehold: Muzzled Press

1. Nadiga Krishnamurti, *Indian Journalism: Origin, growth and development of Indian journalism from Asoka to Nehru* (Mysore: Mysore university Press, 1966), 52.

2. George D. Bearce, *British Attitudes towards India* (London: Oxford University Press, 1961), 97.

3. Arthur Hobhouse Sir, *The Vernacular Press*, Minutes by A. Hobhouse (Calcutta: Government Legislative Department, 1876), 260.

4. Margarita Barns, *The Indian Press* (London: George Allen & Unwin Ltd., 1940), 280–81.

5. John Strachey, *India, It's Administration & Progress* (London MacMillan and Co. Ltd., 1911), 310–11.

6. *The Tribune Lahore*, February 14, 1920.

7. Henry Wood Nevinson, *New Spirit in India* (London: Harper and Brothers 1908), 18.

8. Fred I. A. Omu, "The Dilemma of Press Freedom in Colonial Africa: The West Indian Example", *J. African History* IX 2 (1968): 279–298.

9. Ibid. 286.

10. *A number of native rulers and chiefs who were considered inconvenient were exiled by the British in order to stifle their voices. Political leaders who were imprisoned by them became head of free colonies. A celebrated example is of native leader Nelson Mandela who suffered long prison terms and later became President of South Africa.*

Chapter 10: Instruments of Stranglehold — Despotic Laws and Flawed Justice

1. Strachey John, *The End of Empire* (New York: Random House, 1960), 45.

2. Nuncomer is a corrupt pronunciation of Nand Kumar, a common North Indian name.

(Raja Nand Kumar is often referred to as Raja Nun Comar or simply Nuncomer by writers unfamiliar with pronunciation in spoken language of the Bengal, the state to which Nand Kumar then belonged to).

3. James F. Stephen, *The Story of Nun Comer and the Impeachment of Sir Elijah Impey. Vol. II* (London: MacMillan and Company, 1885), 4–9.

4. Mofussil is of Persian origin which was court language of the Moghuls. It means outside or in the countryside away from Presidency towns of the EIC.

5. United Kingdom. *Hansard's Parliamentary Debates*, 3rd ser. 18 (1829), Cols 730.

6. *The Times,* 27 June 1857.

7. John Strachey, *India, Its Administration, and Progress* (New York: Macmillan & Co., 1911), 117.

8. Ma Bap legislation – *a derogatory symbolism; literal meaning being father-mother legislation.*

9. Charles Allen, *Kipling Sahib, India and Making of Rudyard Kipling* (New York: 1st Pegasus Books, 2009), 130.

10. Nayana Goradia, *Lord Curzon: The Last of British Moghuls* (Oxford University Press, 1993), 165.

11. George N. Curzon, *British Government in India: The Story of Viceroys and Government Houses* (London; Cassel and Company Ltd, 1925), 243.

12. This derisive appellation was coined by the British to slight the natives of Bengal working for the company as well for the general public.

13. Niall Ferguson, *Empire: The Rise and Fall of the British World Order and Lessons for the Global Power* (New York: Basic Books, 2000), 197.

14. *The Times*, 26 February 1883.

15. S.M. Burke and S. Quraishi, *British Raj in India — A Historical Review* (Karachi: Oxford University Press, 1995), 58.

16. Goradia, 167.

17. Goradia, 103.

18. Burke and Quraishi, 58.

19. George Nathanial Curzon, *Lord Curzon in India, being a selection from his speeches as viceroy and governor general of India, 1898 – 1905* (New York: Macmillan and Co., Ltd., 1906), 44.

20. Henry J. May, *South African Constitution* (Cape Town: Juta and Company, 1949), 319–21.

21. Claire Palley, *"The Constitutional History and Law of Southern Rhodesia 1858–1965: With* S*pecial Reference to Imperial Control* (Oxford: Clarendon, 1966).

22. Kathyrine Tidrick, *Empire and the English Character* (London: I.B. Tauris and Co. Ltd., 1990), 140.

23. Norman Leys, *Kenya. With a New Introduction by George Shipperson* (London: Frank Cass, 1973), 176.

24. Ibid, 173.

25. Ibid, 182.

26. Jackey. Jackey was name given by English settlers to a native person Galamahra.

27. Evolue. *The term came up in French colonies when France turned to influence her Muslim subjects through French language and culture. Her subjects undergoing cultural change under French influence were called Evolues.*

28. Code de Indegenant was *a set of French laws meant to suppress the non-French through inferior legislative status for natives of French colonies like Algeria.*

29. Mark Crocker, *Rivers of Blood Rivers of Gold: Europe's Conflict with Tribal Peoples* (London: J. Cape, 1998), 317–318.

30. Helmuth Stoecker ed. *German Imperialism in Africa from beginning until the Second World War*, translated from German by Bernd Zollner, (London: C. Hurst, 1986).

31. D.E.K. Amenumey, "German administration in Southern Togo," *J. African History X*, 4(1969) 623–661.

32. Crocker, 317-18.

Chapter 11: The Embodied Terror for the Natives

1.   Mulatto probably originated from the Spanish word Mulo (mule) and refers to persons of mixed white and black parentage. This word is used for a person of white and black mixed race in Latin America, Spain and the Caribbean.

2.   Bernard Sammel, *Jamaican Blood and Victorian Conscience: The Governor Eyre Controversy* (London; MacGibbon and Kee, 1962), 17.

3.   John B. Priestley, *Victoria's Hey-day* (New York: Harper and Row Publishers, 1972), 361.

4.   *New York Harald*, 5 May 1900, Quoted by Sammel, 22.

5.   Sammel, 18.

6.   Ibid., 18.

7.   *Of these gentlemen Carlyle and Kingsley were Staunch Anglo-Saxsonists and Charles Dickens a Professor at Cambridge had Streaks of Racism. Their reaction to Eyre versus Jamaican Blacks can be visualized in this context.*

8. *Donald C. Holsinger,* "Muslim Responses to French Imperialism: An Algerian Saharan Case Study," *The International Journal of African Historical Studies*, 19, 1, 1986, 6.

9. Kabayles were Berber Arabs who lived in coastal mountainous region. They reared cattle and some of their members pirated on merchant's vessels sailing in the Mediterranean Sea along the North African coast.

10. *The Times* 18 September 1900.

11. Helmuth Stoecker, *German Imperialism in Africa: From the beginning until the Second World War, translated from German by Bernd and Zollner* (London: C. Hurst, 1986), 57.

12. *The Times,* 13 September 1904.

13. Ibid, 7 October 1904.

14. Mark Crocker, *Rivers of Blood, Rivers of Gold: Europe's Conflict with Tribal Peoples* (London: Jonathan Cape, 1998), 331.

15. Horst Drechsler, *Let Us Die Fighting: The Struggle of Herero and Nama against German Imperialism (1884–1915),* (London: Zed Press Clarendon Road, 1966), 155.

16. Lawrence James, *The Rise and Fall of British Empire* (London: Little Brown and Co., 1994), 282.

17. Roy Jenkins, *Churchill, A Biography* (New York: Farrar, Straus, and Grioux, 2001), 41.

18. Philip Magnus, *Kitchener — Portrait of an Imperialist* (New York: E. P. Dutton & Co. Inc 1959), 133.

19. James, 284.

20. Denis Judd and Keith Surridge, *The Boer War* (London: John Murray, 2002), 191.

21. David Dilks, *Curzon in India 1. Achievements* (New York: Taplinger Publishing Company, 1969), 203.

22. Nayana Goradia, *Lord Curzon: The Last of British Moghuls* (Delhi: Oxford University Press, 1993), 209.

23. Nigel Collett, *The Butcher of Amritsar: General Reginald Dyer* (New York: Palgrave Macmillan, 2005).

24. *The Times,* 2 April 1919.

25. Robert A. Huttenback, *Racism and Empire: White Settlers and Colored Immigrants in the British Self-Governing Colonies 1830–1910*

(Ithaca: Cornell University Press, 1976), 180.

26. *The Times,* 16 April 1919.

27. Post Wheeler, *India Against the Storm* (New York: E. P. Dutton, 1944), 159.

28. *The Tribune*, Lahore 14 April 1920.

29. *The Times,* 19 April 1919.

30. Joan Beauchamp, *British Imperialism in India* (London: Martin Lawrence Ltd, 1934), 174.

31. Collett, *The Butcher of Amritsar.*

32. Naill Ferguson, *Empire: The Rise and Fall of the British World Order and Lessons for the Global Power* (New York: Basic Books, 2000), *278.*

33. Huttenback, 182.

34. Ferguson, 326–327.

35. Disorders Enquiry Committee 1919–1920 *Reports* (Calcutta: Superintendent Government Printing, 1920), 275.

Chapter 12: Company Clerks to Society Nabobs

1. Keith Berridale ed., *Speeches and Documents on Indian Policy1750-1921 Vol. I* (London; Oxford University Press, *1922), 244. Thomas Macaulay a distinguished jurist who spent more than three years as head of Law Commission in India appreciated virtues of Indians but criticized East India company rule. In his essay on Lord Clive, he mentioned enormous fortunes that accumulated in Calcutta while* thirty million human beings were reduced to the last extremity of wretchedness.

2. John A. Hobson, *Imperialism* (New York: James Pott and Co., 1902), 151.

3. *Nawab is a word from Persian which was the court language of Moghul rulers of India. This tile was used for governors of provinces or conferred upon high-ranking dignitaries. In Bengali dialect it was pronounced as Nobob. The East India Company which began her territorial gains from Bengal picked up Bengali pronunciation of the word Nawab.*

4. Godfrey Elton, *Imperial Commonwealth* (London: Collins, 1945), 222.

5. Edward Grierson, *The Imperial Dream: The British*

Commonwealth and Empire 1775–1969 (London: Collins, 1972), 41.

6. John Strachey, *The End of Empire* (New York: Random House,1960), 31.

7. Elton, 222.

8. John W. Kaye, *The Administration of the East India Company. A History of Indian Progress* (London: R. Bentley, 1853).

9. Peter J. Marshall, *East India Fortunes: The British in Bengal in the Eighteenth Century* (Oxford; Clarendon Press, 1976), 159.

10. Ibid., 159.

11. Nicholas B. Dirks, *The Scandal of Empire: India and the Creation of Imperial Britain* (Cambridge: The Belknap Press of Harvard University Press, 2006), 39.

12. Grierson, 41.

13. *That Bengal was a rich Provence does not imply her populace was opulent. Bengal generated lot of revenue which was mopped up by the East India Company. Money was extracted and company revenues increased even during Bengal famine when one–third population from peasants to small professionals under duress perished.*

14. Elton, 222.

15. Huge Murray, The Rebellion in India *The North American Review*, Vol. 86, No. 179, 1858, 488.

16. Niall Ferguson, *Empire: The Rise and Demise of the World Order and the lessons for Global Power* (New York: Basic Books, 2002), 16.

17. Mark Bence Jones, *Clive of India* (London: Constable, 1974), 126.

18. Ibid., 126.

19. James Holzman, *The Nobobs in England. A study of the returned Anglo Indian, 1760–1785* (New York: Publisher not known, 1926), 10.

20. Mark Bence Jones, 243.

21. Nicholas B. Dirks, *Colonisation and Culture* (Ann Arbor: The University of Michigan Press, 1992), 15.

22. Elton, 223.

23. Dirks, 17.

24. Holzman, 11.

25. Marshal, 244.

26. Bence-Jones, 128.

27. Will Durant, *The Case for India* (New York: Simon and Schuster, 1930), 22.

28. Dirks, 75.

29. Grierson, 42.

30. Tillman W. Nechtman, *Empire and Identity in Eighteenth Century Britain* (New York: Cambridge University Press, 2010), 13.

31. James F. Stephan, *The Story of Nuncomar and Impeachment of Elijah Impey. Vol.2* (London: Macmillan and Co., 1885), 9.

32. Marshal, 245.

33. Huge Murray, 488.

Chapter 13: Colonies as Population Outlets

1. Alexander Murdoch, *British Emigration 1603–1914* (New York: Palgrave Macmillan, 2004), 1.

2. Kalaus E. Knorr, *British Colonial Theories 1570–1850* (Toronto: The University of Toronto Press, 1968), 68.

3. Murdoch, 27.

4. Poultney Bigelow, *The Children of the Nations: A Study of Colonisation and its Problems,* (W. Heinemann, 1901), *36.*

5. Oscar P. Austin, *Does Colonisation Pay?* (New York: The Forum Vol. 28, September 1889 - February 1900), 623.

6. Quoted in John Strachey, *End of the Empire* (New York: Random House1960), 146.

7. Winston S. Churchill, *A History of English-Speaking People: The Great Democracies,* (New York: Dodd, Mead & Co.,1958), 98.

8. John A. Hobson, *Imperialism* (New York: James Pott and Co., 1902), 57.

9. Grover Clark, *The Balance Sheet of Imperialism* (New York: Columbia University Press, 1936), 10.

10. Huge Thomas, *A History of the World* (New York: Harper Collins, 1979).

11. Alleyne W. Ireland, Growth of the British Colonial Conception (New York: *Atlantic Monthly* Vol., 83, 1899), 492.

12. Anthony Esler, *The Western World. A Narrative History to the Present* (Upper Saddle River, New Jersey: Prentice Hall, 1997), 585.

Chapter 14: Europeans, Tyrannical Supremacists or Crafty Freebooters

1. White man's burden: This was a poem published in 1899 by English author and votary of imperialism Rudyard Kipling. That was the period when the United States embarked on the road to imperialism after subjugating Spanish possessions of the Philippines, Puerto Rico and Cuba. Kipling wanted to justify euphemism for imperialism with this phrase under whose guise the white man denigrated natives of subjugated nations.

2. V.G. Kiernen, *The Lords of Humankind: Black Man, Yellow Man and White Man in an Age of Empire* (Boston: Little Brown Company 1901), 311.

3. Nayana Goradia, *Lord Curzon: The Last of British Moghuls* (Delhi: Oxford University Press, 1993), 116.

4. William Cunningham, "English Imperialism", *Atlantic Monthly* 78: 1–7 (July 1895), 553.

5. Mark Crocker, *Rivers of Blood, Rivers of Gold. Europe's Conflict with Tribal Peoples* (London: Jonathan Cape, 1998), 318.

6. Razzia expeditions were headlong raids of Bedouines against their adversaries. The French took a leaf from the Arabs.

7. Keith Irvine, British hanging 50 Africans a month (*Africa Today*, March-April 1955, Bloomington: Indiana University Press), 4.

8. Robert Huttonback, *Racism and Empire. White Settlers and Colored Immigrants in the British Self-governing Colonies 1830–1910* (Ithaca: Cornell University Press, 1976), 61.

9. George D. Bearce, *British Attitudes Towards India 1784–1858* (London: Oxford University Press, 1961), 211.

10. Huge Murray, The Rebellion in India. (Boston: *The North American Review* Vol. 86, Issue 179, 1858), 493.

11. Nial Ferguson, *Empire: The Rise and Demise of the British World and the Lessons for Global Power* (New York: Basic Books, 2002), 152.

12. John B. Priestley, *Victoria's Heyday* (New York: Harper and Row Publishers, 1972), 219.

13. Ibid., 219.

14. Edward Grearson, *The Death of Imperial Dream. The British*

Commonwealth Empire 1775–1969 (London: Collins, 1972), 85.

15. Ferguson, 152.

16. Ibid., 151.

17. *The Times*, Monday June 30, 1857.

18. Dalip Hiro, *Black British, White British. A History of Race Relations in Britain* (London: Grafton Books, 1991).

19. Huge Murray, 492.

20. Ibid., 487.

21. Ferguson, 152.

22. Pandit Sunder Lal, *British Rule in India* (New Delhi: Sagar Publications India Pvt. Ltd., 2018), 404.

23. Julia Spilsbury, *The Indian Mutiny* (London: Weidenfield and Nicolson, 2007), 84.

24. Bethwell Ogot, "British Administration in the Central Nynza district of Kenya 1900-60," *J. African History*, IV, 2 (1963), 249–73.

25. Radhika Singha, *A Despotism of Law: Crime and Justice in Early Colonial India* (Delhi: Oxford University Press, 1988), 290.

26. William J. Bryan ed., *The Worlds Famous Orations Vol. IV* (New York: Funk and Wagnalls, 1906).[1]

27. Lawrence James, *The Rise and Fall of British Empire* (London: Little Brown and Co., 1994), 335.

28. Robert Berneys, *Naked Faquir* (New York: Holt and Company, 1932), 125.

29. Robert Lewis Taylor, *The Amazing Mr. Churchill* (New York: McGraw-Hill Book Company Inc. 1952), 335.

30. Ferguson, 344.

31. Winston Churchill, *A History of English — Speaking Peoples: The Age of Revolution* (New York: Dodd, Mead and Company, 1934).

32. Mukhtar A. Ansari, *Presidential Address* Forty-Second Congress, Second Ser. 1911–1934 (Madras: G.A. Neteson and Company, 1934).

33. John B. Priestley, *Victoria's Heyday* (New York: Harper and Row Publishers, 1972), 417.

34. John Keay, India — A History (New York: *Atlantic Monthly*, Harper Collins Press, 2000), 236.

1

35. Joan Beauchamp, *British Imperialism in India* (London: Martin Lawrence Ltd., 1934), 23.

36. John Strachey, *The End of Empire* (New York: Random House, 1960), 43.

37. J.P. Jones, "British Rule in India," Madras: *North American Review*, Vol. 168, (March 1899), 465.

38. John William Kaye, *The Administration of the East India Company: A History of Indian Progress* (London: R. Bentley 1853).

39. John Strachey, *India: Its Administration and Progress* (New York: Macmillan and Co., 1911), 143.

40. Jones, 465.

41. Alleyne Ireland, "European experience with Tropical colonies," Riverside Press Cambridge: *Atlantic Monthly* Vol. 82, (1898): 729.

42. Keay, 163.

43. Ibid., 162.

44. Henry Wood Nevinson, *The New Spirit in India* (London: Harper R. Brothers, 1908).

45. Quoted in Jones, 465.

46. Beauchamp, 23.

47. Strachey, 10.

48. W.C. Onslow, Statement before the select committee on promotion of European colonisation and settlement of India — 29th June 1858. Quoted in Nirmal T. Singh, *Irrigation and Soil Salinity in the Indian Subcontinent: Past and Present* (Bethlehem: Lehigh University Press, 2005), 74.

49. R.B. Buckley, *The Irrigation Works in India Financial Results*. Quoted in Nirmal T. Singh, *Irrigation and Soil Salinity in the Indian Subcontinent: Past and Present* (Bethlehem: Lehigh University Press, 2005), 99.

50. Imperial Gazetteer of India (Provisional Series) "*Gazetteer of Madras Presidency*" (Calcutta: Government Central Press, 1886), 536.

51. G.U. Yule, Canal Act of the Emperor Akbar with some notes on the History of Western Yamuna Canal (Calcutta: *J. Asiatic Society Bengal*, 1846), 214.

52. *Possible effects of waterlogging and salinity on soils.*

53. John W. Kaye, 279.

54. George D. Bearce, *British Attitude toward India 1784–1888*

(London: Oxford University Press, 1961), 188.

55. Buckley, 1880, quoted in Nirmal T. Singh, *Irrigation and Soils Salinity in the Indian Subcontinent: Past and Present* (Bethlehem: Lehigh University Press, 2005), 89.

56. Oscar P. Austin, Does Colonisation Pay? (New York: *The Forum* Vol. 28, September 1899–February 1900), 631.

57. Michael Parenti, *Against Empire* (San Francisco: City Light Books, 1995), 57.

58. Austin, 625.

59. Jan Morris, *Farewell the Trumpets an Imperial Retreat* (New York: Harcourt Brace Jovanovich, 1978).

60. Will Durant, *The Case for India* (New Delhi: Gyan Publishing House, 2017).

61. Ibid.

62. Morris, 495.

63. George N. Curzon, *Lord Curzon in India: being a selection of his speeches as viceroy and governor-general of India 1898–1905* (London: Macmillan and Co Ltd., 1906).

64. Roy Jenkins, *Churchill — A Biography* (New York: Farrar, Straus and Giroux, 2001), 457.

65. Godfrey Elton, *Imperial Commonwealth* (London: Collins, 1945), 421.

Index

322

340